GETTYSBURG'S CONFEDERATE DEAD

AN HONOR ROLL FROM AMERICA'S GREATEST BATTLE

Robert K. Krick & Chris L. Ferguson

Angle Valley Press
VIRGINIA

For information contact:
Angle Valley Press, P. O. Box 4098, Winchester, VA 22604
www.AngleValleyPress.com

Designed and printed in the United States of America.

First Edition, First Printing

Illustrations: cover photo of Stonewall Confederate Cemetery at Winchester, Virginia with marker for Colonel Waller Tazewell Patton, 7th Virginia Infantry Regiment. Patton was KIA on July 3, 1863 and he shares a grave with his brother Colonel George S. Patton who was KIA on September 19, 1864 at Winchester. Back cover photo of Lieutenant Colonel David Read Evans Winn, 4th Georgia Infantry Regiment, who was KIA and initially buried on field at Gettysburg. For more on Winn see preface. Photo from *History of Doles-Cook Brigade* by Henry W. Thomas, 1903.

Publisher's Cataloging-in-Publication Data

Krick, Robert K.
    Gettysburg's Confederate dead : an honor roll from America's greatest battle /
Robert K. Krick & Chris L. Ferguson.
        pages cm
    ISBN: 978-0-9711950-8-0 (pbk.)
    1. Gettysburg, Battle of, Gettysburg, Pa., 1863. 2. United States—History—Civil
War, 1861–1865—Registers of dead. 3. Soldiers—Southern States—Registers.
4. Confederate States of America. Army. I. Ferguson, Chris, 1955– II. Title.
E475.53 .K76 2014
973.7'349—dc23
                                2014939987

In memory of all soldiers who lost their lives
from fighting at Gettysburg, Pennsylvania in 1863.

**Private Samuel J. G. Brewer, Co. I, 8th Georgia.
Mortally wounded at Gettysburg.**

Hollywood Cemetery collection

TABLE of CONTENTS

PREFACE

THE THREE DAYS OF SAVAGE COMBAT that exploded across Gettysburg's woods and fields and hills in July 1863 left perhaps as many as 10,000 American men and boys dead or mortally hurt. Keeping track of the victims in that era of haphazard recordkeeping focused *far* less attention on the individual dead than would be expected by modern standards.

This book endeavors to identify as many as possible of the Confederates who died as a result of the battle, supplying full names and even dates of birth where they could be found.

The official Compiled Service Records (CSR) themselves of course afford the best contemporary evidence. Even those invaluable documents, though, often suffer from gaps. The hard-used company clerks who executed the bimonthly musters produced them expressly to balance pay ledgers, not as documents of lasting historical portent. Those 19th-century scribblers had not even a faint notion that, decades and centuries later, the product of their pens would often be the only evidence available to eager students of the great events of the 1860s. A soldier killed at Gettysburg fell into the same status as one merely captured, for payroll purposes, leaving no imperative to clean up the record subsequently.

Postwar rosters of companies and regiments tend to deteriorate in reliability the later the date of publication (or at least of compilation). Those of early imprimatur often report war deaths omitted, or obscured, in CSRs. For instance, *"Roll of Honor" of Company D, 14th Regiment, S.C. Volunteers*, published in 1866, reports the fates of that company's men throughout the war. One of the Gettysburg dead from Company D has no mention of the battle in his CSR.

Impoverished, war-ravaged Southerners managed, at considerable effort and cost, to return many of their dead fathers and husbands and brothers to native soil for burial reasonably soon after the war. They rarely, though, endeavored to list the names of their dead in any detail.

In a gratifying exception to that unhappy tendency, South Carolinian dead moved from Gettysburg to Magnolia Cemetery in Charleston appear by name and unit as part of an 1871 pamphlet recording the program of *Confederate Memorial Day at Charleston, S.C. Re-interment of the Confederate Dead from Gettysburg*. General Richard H. Anderson introduced the ceremony, the Rev. Ellison Capers read a prayer, and then another preacher delivered an address that runs to

17 pages of fine print and says absolutely nothing at all interesting for historical purposes. Three turgid poems fill ten more pages. Then, atypically, the names and units and home origins for 78 Carolinians re-interred from Gettysburg appear as an appendix. Would that more such ceremonial publications contained equivalent rosters.

More typical than the 1871 Charleston pamphlet is *Pickett's Division Association. Address at the Unveiling of the Monument in Hollywood Cemetery,...by Major R. Taylor Scott, Warrenton, Va.* The emotional speech by a member of Pickett's staff invoked Thebes, Nineveh, and Babylon; Lodi, Waterloo, and Balaklava. The oration no doubt delighted the vast audience, and makes an alluring collectible today—but it mentioned the name of not a single one of the legion of dead Virginians whose graves immediately surrounded Scott's podium. Parents and wives and children of those dead men listened to Scott, but none of them ever systematically recorded the names of Gettysburg's victims.

The Introduction that follows explains the methodology that produced this roll of the dead, across four decades of research. It also establishes the protocols applied to identify men deemed eligible for admission to this listing. Those killed in action or mortally wounded and died on the field need no qualification. Issues of death after languishing at length require some definition; for instance, how long after a Gettysburg wound should it be attributable for death in a Federal prisoner-of-war hellhole?

The degree of thoroughness in individual listings reflects broadly the strength of the documentary resources available for the various Southern states. The H. E. Howard, Inc., regimental-history series, for example, covers every unit from Virginia. Some of the authors who wrote in the Howard series diligently winnowed local records of every kind and generated a gratifying volume of personal details—full names, birth, death, &c. Others in the same series, it must be sorrowfully admitted, do not deserve so much credit, or even any at all. The net result for this register, uneven though the volumes be, is a bit more detail about Virginians than others.

We have undertaken this roll with goals in mind that involve historical and genealogical utility. Beyond those quotidian benchmarks, the undertaking accrued a memorial aspect as it progressed. Gettysburg's Confederate dead were denied the general collection into a central burial location that was afforded many of the Federal dead—albeit imperfectly recorded in their case also.

Frances Mary Dean Winn belongs in the painfully large category of "other" victims of Gettysburg. Her husband, Dr. David Read Evans Winn, practiced medicine in Macon in the 1850s. He went to war as a lieutenant in the 4th Georgia Infantry, one of four regiments in what became the sturdy Doles-Cook Brigade, and by late 1862 had advanced to the rank of lieutenant-colonel. A staff officer fervently referred to Winn, in a private forum, as a "gallant...true patriot...perfect gentleman." A surviving uniformed photo resonates across a century and a half with a look of distinction and determination.

Lieutenant Colonel Winn led the 4th into action at Gettysburg, through the Blocher Farm, from a vantage point "several yards in front of the regiment." A bullet killed him instantly, four days short of his 32nd birthday. After the war a venal (to launch a thunderous redundancy) Yankee demanded $10 to allow the removal of Winn's body from his property. A gold plate in the corpse's mouth obviously required ransom. On October 6, 1871, V. O. Blocher signed a receipt for the demanded payment, and released the morbid souvenir to Winn's widow and orphans. Frances died less than three years later. Her well-documented plight can stand as exemplar for untold second-hand suffering that stretched well beyond July 1863.

Robert K. Krick
Fredericksburg, Virginia
March 2014

INTRODUCTION

W ILLIAM N. WOOD writes in his classic memoir, *Reminiscences of Big I,* about the beheading of the 19th Virginia's lieutenant colonel John T. Ellis on July 3 at Gettyburg: "The shells, bursting over and behind us, sent missiles upon anyone who might be lurking in the rear. Again the enemy was overshooting the mark and doing very little damage to the infantry. From Roundtop, two miles to our right, came those miserable enfilading solid shots which frequently struck the ground on our right, ricocheting along the line to the death and injury of many. Lt. Colonel Ellis was lying in a small wash on a hillside as one of these balls came bounding from the right. Some one hollered—'look out' and he raised his head just in time to receive the ball in the face." Ellis was killed instantly and buried in an orchard on the Alexander Curren's Farm located on the southern end of the battlefield thus beginning a 140 year search by the family to locate his remains. He now rests in Hollywood Cemetery in Richmond, Virginia.

Ellis is one of some 4000+ names appearing on index cards kept and maintained by Robert K. Krick until around 2002. At that time, Bob provided me the files and I have served as the caretaker of the records for the last twelve years. During this span of time, the ledger cards, as we now call them, have grown to a total of 5001 names—all appearing in the register now being published.

Over the years, names were gradually added because of on-line resources such as Fold3.com that provides complete access to the Confederate Compiled Service Records—thus making it easier to confirm death at Gettysburg. Other sources, not available to us prior to 2002, include numerous regimental histories and magazine articles detailing the Confederate dead. While our register is the most comprehensive list of the Confederate dead from the Battle of Gettysburg—it is by no means complete. There are probably more soldiers that should be included that have not been identified. The register remains a work in progress!

Numerous individuals helped to move this project forward, however special thanks go out to Keith Bohannon, Robert E. L. Krick and the staff at Richmond's Hollywood Cemetery for helping to clarify numerous names and assorted information listed on these pages.

The death register was compiled using the following criteria: A soldier had to be killed in action or mortally wounded in the fighting of July 1–4 and death had to occur prior to January 1, 1864, from wounds received during this four day period. Deaths occurring in the time period September–December 1863 most likely had an accompanying reason—such as typhoid fever, gangrene, and erysipelas. Soldiers who were not wounded, but were captured and later died in Union hands are not part of the register.

In researching the names and regiments of the soldiers, every effort was made to account for the identified dead reinterred in Richmond's Hollywood Cemetery and other Southern cemeteries in the early 1870s. About 3320 soldiers were removed to Southern soil by the various Ladies Memorial Associations of Charleston, SC (71 remains), Raleigh, NC (137 remains), Richmond, Va. (2,935 remains) and Savannah, Ga. (101 remains) and another 76 were removed by families or other interested parties. The identified dead are noted by the entry designating the place of removal. In addition, soldiers mortally wounded and who later died in the various Union prisoner of war camps are noted the same way—"Died as POW at Chester, Pennsylvania; David's Island, New York; Ft. Delaware, Delaware; Finn's Point, New Jersey; Point Lookout, Maryland." In all, the authors have uncovered the final resting place of 1544 soldiers or a little more than 30%. The rest of the dead are either still on the battlefield or part of the massive interment to Richmond's Hollywood Cemetery in the 1870s.

The toll in losses to the Army of Northern Virginia cannot be underestimated with 5 general officers, 55 senior field grade officers and 464 junior grade officers giving their lives for Southern Independence. Colonel Lewis Burwell Williams summed it up in his final moments on July 3rd as he clasped hands with his cousin, Colonel Waller Tazewell Patton, at the stone wall of the Union center line and shouted, "It's Our turn next, Tazewell!"—and the two men crossed the wall and fell in a bloody heap. More than 5000 other Southern soldiers who met a similar fate are listed in this book.

Chris Ferguson
Winchester, Virginia
April 2014

ABBREVIATIONS

Note that all units are infantry regiments unless so indicated

AAG	Assistant Adjutant General
ADC	Aide-de-camp
Adj.	Adjutant
AIG	Assistant Inspector General
Arty.	Artillery
Capt.	Captain
Col.	Colonel
Cpl.	Corporal
Lt.	Lieutenant
Lt. Col.	Lieutenant Colonel
Maj.	Major
Sgt.	Sergeant
SS	sharpshooters

Three dead Confederate soldiers buried on the Rose Farm—Known But to God.
Possibly 2nd South Carolina soldiers.

Library of Congress

NAME	REGIMENT	BIRTH	DEATH	COMMENT	BURIAL
Aaron, Edward S.	Co. G, 3rd Georgia		7/2/1863	Laurel Grove Cemetery, Savannah, Ga., reburial list	Savannah, GA
Aaron, George	Co. I, 8th Georgia		7/3/1863	Killed in action	Unknown
Abercrombie, James A.A.	Co. H, 10th Alabama		7/3/1863	Killed in action	Unknown
Abernathy, [Richard] Williamson	Co. A, 47th North Carolina	1833	7/1/1863	Killed in action	Unknown
Abernathy, David A.	Co. G, 52nd North Carolina	1828	7/3/1863	Killed in action	Unknown
Abernathy, John N.	Lt., Co. G, 34th North Carolina	1842	7/1/1863	Killed in action	Unknown
Ables, Obediah A.	Sgt., Co. H, 2nd Georgia		7/2/1863	Killed in action	Unknown
Acker, Samuel M.	Co. H, 11th Alabama	1838	7/3/1863	Killed in action	Unknown
Ackis, Richard William	Cpl., Brooks Arty. (S.C.) Rhett's	1838	7/3/1863	Killed in action per the Richmond Sentinel, July 27, 1863	Unknown
Acord, William H.	Co. E, 5th Virginia	1830	1863	Died of wounds on unknown date in Maryland	Maryland
Adair, Alexander	Co. I, 4th Virginia		7/25/1863	Mortally wounded and died at Camp Letterman	Unknown
Adair, William H.	Co. C, 1st Virginia Cavalry	12/2/1844	7/3/1863	Killed in action	Unknown
Adair, William Madison	Co. C, 3rd Georgia Sharpshooter Battalion	1829	7/4/1863	Mortally wounded-died at unknown place in Gettysburg	Unknown
Adams, A.B.	Co. K, 14th South Carolina	1824	8/5/1863	Died as POW at David's Island, NY	Cypress Hills, NY
Adams, Duncan L.F.	Co. A, 55th North Carolina		9/20/1863	Mortally wounded and died at Chester, PA	Phil. National Cem.
Adams, Edwin Thomas	Lt., Co. B, 8th Virginia		7/18/1863	Hollywood Cemetery, Richmond, Va., reburial lists	Richmond, VA
Adams, Elijah	Sgt., Co. G, 8th South Carolina	1839	7/17/1863	Mortally wounded per the Charleston Mercury, Aug. 28, 1863	Charleston, SC
Adams, Harris R.	Lt., Co. G, 8th South Carolina	1842	7/2/1863	Hollywood Cemetery, Richmond, Va., reburial lists	Richmond, VA
Adams, J.C.	Co. H, 23rd North Carolina		7/1/1863	Killed in action	Unknown
Adams, J.F.	Co. B, 14th Louisiana	1829	10/2/1863	Mortally wounded and died at Camp Letterman	Richmond, VA
Adams, James	Co. A, 13th Mississippi		7/3/1863	Hollywood Cemetery, Richmond, Va., reburial lists	Richmond, VA
Adams, John H.	Troup Artillery (Ga.)		7/3/1863	Killed in action; known as "Hop"	Unknown
Adams, John J.	Co. I, 2nd Mississippi	1834	7/1/1863	Killed in action	Unknown
Adams, John L.	Co. F, 44th Alabama	1829	Jul. 1863	Missing in action and presumed dead	Unknown
Adams, Robert J.	Co. H, 22nd Virginia Battalion		7/3/1863	Killed in action	Unknown
Adams, Robert L.	Co. E, 12th North Carolina	9/22/1828	7/1/1863	Killed in action	Unknown
Adcock, Dixon L.	Co. C, 13th Alabama		7/3/1863	Killed in action	Unknown
Aderholt, Jacob E.	Co. D, 55th North Carolina	1828	7/30/1863	Mortally wounded and died at Camp Letterman	Raleigh, NC
Adkins, John O.	Co. E, 38th Virginia		Jul. 1863	Hollywood Cemetery, Richmond, Va., reburial lists	Richmond, VA
Adkins, Joshua Martin	Sgt., Co. D, 42nd Mississippi	1837	7/1/1863	Killed in action	Unknown
Adkins, Peter H.	Co. C, 57th Virginia		7/8/1863	Mortally wounded-died at unknown place in Gettysburg	Unknown

NAME	REGIMENT	BIRTH	DEATH	COMMENT	BURIAL
Adkins, Richard	Co. B, 38th Virginia		1863	Mortally wounded, July 3, and died at Pt. Lookout on unknown date	Pt. Lookout, MD
Adkins, Sydenham Peter	Lt., Co. D, 14th Virginia		7/3/1863	Killed in action	Unknown
Adkins, William H.	Sgt., Co. E, 53rd North Carolina	1827	7/2/1863	Killed in action	Raleigh, NC
Adkins, Wilson J.	Co. B, 18th Virginia		10/25/1863	Died of wounds at Ft. Delaware, DE	Finn's Point, NJ
Adkinson, Benjamin	Co. B, 8th South Carolina		7/1/1863	Hollywood Cemetery, Richmond, Va., reburial lists	Richmond, VA
Adrian, John German	Lt., Co. E, 47th Alabama	10/30/1827	7/2/1863	Killed in action	Unknown
Agee, Alexander	Co. D, 37th Virginia		7/13/1863	Hollywood Cemetery, Richmond, Va., reburial lists	Richmond, VA
Agnew, William H.	Co. G, 11th Virginia	1831	8/8/1863	Mortally wounded per the Charleston Mercury, Aug. 28, 1863	Unknown
Aiton, Thomas L.	Cpl., Co. G, 7th South Carolina	11/6/1841	7/2/1863	Killed in action; obit Edgefield Advertiser, Oct. 14th, 21 yrs, 8 mo's, 26 days at death	Unknown
Akers, Columbus	Co. E, 42nd Mississippi	12/24/1835	7/3/1863	Killed in action	Unknown
Akers, David Clarence	Co. D, 7th Virginia	1834	7/3/1863	Killed in action	Unknown
Akers, James Lafayette	Co. K, 2nd Mississippi	10/23/1845	7/3/1863	Killed in action	Unknown
Alban, J. [John] W.	Capt. Shira's Co., 12th VA Cavalry		7/3/1863	Killed in action	Mercersburg, PA
Albert, Thomas M.	Sgt., Co. K, 22nd Georgia		7/2/1863	Killed in action	Unknown
Albright, George M.G.	Capt., Co. F, 53rd North Carolina	1837	7/16/1863	Mortally wounded and died at Frederick, MD; interred in Mt. Olivet Cemetery	Frederick, MD
Albright, John S.	Co. F, 6th North Carolina	1837	Aug. 1863	Mortally wounded and in Lynchburg Hospital, Aug. 21, 1863, No further record	Lynchburg, VA
Alcorn, Andrew J.	Co. E, 45th North Carolina	1840	7/1/1863	Killed in action	Unknown
Alderman, Chesley	Co. I, 9th Georgia	4/13/1840	7/19/1863	Mortally wounded-died at unknown place in Gettysburg	Unknown
Alderman, James M.	Cpl., Co. K, 50th Georgia	1840	7/2/1863	Killed in action	Unknown
Aldridge, George L.	Cpl., Co. G, 15th Louisiana	1841	Jul. 1863	Hollywood Cemetery, Richmond, Va., reburial lists	Richmond, VA
Alexander, Dionysius E.	Co. H, 7th North Carolina	1842	7/3/1863	Killed in action	Unknown
Alexander, Henry Lee	Cpl., Co. A, 7th North Carolina	1839	7/3/1863	Missing in action and presumed dead	Unknown
Alexander, Hezekiah C.	Co. B, 13th North Carolina	1840	7/1/1863	Killed in action	Unknown
Alexander, Julius J.	Lt., Co. B, 43rd North Carolina	1843	7/18/1863	Hollywood Cemetery, Richmond, Va., reburial lists	Richmond, VA
Alexander, Marshall E.	Lt., Co. B, 53rd North Carolina		7/13/1863	Mortally wounded-died at unknown place in Gettysburg	Unknown
Alexander, William Horace	Co. B, 53rd North Carolina	1822	7/3/1863	Killed in action; buried Poplar Tent Presbyterian Church	Cabarrus Co., NC
Alford, John W.	Cpl., Co. D, 59th Georgia		7/20/1863	Mortally wounded-died at unknown place in Gettysburg	Unknown
Allan, John	Adj., 6th Virginia Cavalry	8/23/1831	7/3/1863	Killed in action	Baltimore, MD
Allen, Albert L.	Co. A, 16th Georgia		7/13/1863	Hollywood Cemetery, Richmond, Va., reburial lists	Richmond, VA
Allen, Andrew J.B.	Co. K, 57th Virginia		7/3/1863	Killed in action	Unknown

NAME	REGIMENT	BIRTH	DEATH	COMMENT	BURIAL
Allen, Benjamin A.	Co. A, 17th Georgia		7/2/1863	Killed in action	Unknown
Allen, Daniel	Co. F, 12th North Carolina	1841	7/16/1863	Mortally wounded-died at unknown place in Gettysburg	Unknown
Allen, E.M.	Co. K, 6th North Carolina	1843	Jul. 1863	Missing in action and presumed dead	Unknown
Allen, Ferdinand R.	Co. B, 38th Virginia	1840	7/3/1863	Missing in action and presumed dead	Unknown
Allen, Francis Marion	Lt., Co. D, 48th Georgia	1829	7/2/1863	Killed in action	Unknown
Allen, George	Co. A, 3rd North Carolina		10/2/1863	Mortally wounded-died at unknown place in Gettysburg	Unknown
Allen, Gideon, Jr.	Co. D, 9th Louisiana	1844	7/6/1863	Killed near Williamsport, PA	Unknown
Allen, Henry Hartwell	Co. K, 23rd North Carolina	1838	7/26/1863	Mortally wounded-died at unknown place in Gettysburg	Unknown
Allen, Jasper	Co. K, 5th North Carolina	1843	7/1/1863	Killed in action; KIA on Oak Ridge (Iverson's Brigade)	Richmond, VA
Allen, John	Co. B, 48th Georgia	1825	7/14/1863	Died of wounds received on July 2nd	Unknown
Allen, Lafayette J.	Capt., Co. H, 3rd Arkansas	1832	7/2/1863	Killed in action	Unknown
Allen, Lorenzo D.	Co. G, 12th Virginia		7/3/1863	Killed in action per the Richmond Sentinel, July 15, 1863	Unknown
Allen, Robert Clotworthy	Col., 28th Virginia	6/22/1834	7/3/1863	Killed in action	Unknown
Allen, Rufus T.	Lt., Co. C, 38th North Carolina	1829	9/19/1863	Died as POW at David's Island, NY	Cypress Hills, NY
Allen, Titus G.	Co. G, 16th Georgia	1834	7/3/1863	Killed in action	Unknown
Allen, W. Riley	Co. E, 2nd South Carolina		7/2/1863	Killed in action	Charleston, SC
Allen, William A.	Cpl., Co. E, 11th Mississippi	1824	7/3/1863	Killed in action	Unknown
Allen, William Frasier	Lt., Co. C, 14th Virginia Cavalry	2/13/1842	7/2/1863	Killed in action; reinterred by father in Augusta Co., VA	Augusta Co., VA
Alley, Daniel Stuart	Co. F, 11th Virginia	10/5/1844	7/27/1863	Mortally wounded and died at Camp Letterman	Richmond, VA
Alley, Isaiah V.	Co. F, 47th North Carolina	1841	8/14/1863	Oakwood Cemetery, Raleigh, NC, reburial list	Raleigh, NC
Allison, Joseph P.	Co. H, 1st Tennessee	1841	9/20/1863	Mortally wounded-died at unknown place in Gettysburg	Unknown
Allridge, William	Co. G, 26th North Carolina	1826	7/1/1863	Killed in action	Unknown
Almand, John C.	Lt., Cobb's Legion (Ga.)	1836	7/2/1863	Hollywood Cemetery, Richmond, Va., reburial lists	Richmond, VA
Almand, Reuben T.	Cobb's Legion (Ga.)	1837	7/13/1863	Mortally wounded-died at unknown place in Gettysburg	Unknown
Almand, William F.	Cobb's Legion (Ga.)	1841	7/2/1863	Killed in action	Unknown
Alspaugh, Albert	Lt., Co. D, 21st North Carolina	1843	7/2/1863	Killed in action	Unknown
Amason, James H.	Co. E, 3rd Arkansas	1839	7/2/1863	Killed in action	Unknown
Ambrose, Joseph H.	Co. A, 32nd North Carolina	1843	7/2/1863	Killed in action	Unknown
Ambroselle, John J.	Co. I, 7th Virginia	1837	7/3/1863	Killed in action	Unknown
Ames, Benjamin Franklin	Cpl., Co. F, 3rd Virginia	5/23/1836	7/3/1863	Hollywood Cemetery, Richmond, Va., reburial lists	Richmond, VA
Amick, Drayton J.	Co. I, 15th South Carolina	1846	7/22/1863	Mortally wounded, July 3rd, and died at Hagerstown, MD	Hagerstown, MD
Amick, Elijah R.	Co. C, 15th South Carolina	1843	9/6/1863	Mortally wounded and died at Camp Letterman	Charleston, SC

NAME	REGIMENT	BIRTH	DEATH	COMMENT	BURIAL
Amick, Henry Luther	Sgt., Co. I, 15th South Carolina	1835	7/2/1863	Killed in action	Unknown
Ammons, George W.	Co. K, 53rd Virginia	1843	7/3/1863	Killed in action	Unknown
Amos, Charles D.	Co. D, 24th Virginia		Jul. 1863	Mortally wounded-died at unknown place in Gettysburg	Unknown
Amos, James M.	Cpl., Co. L, 21st North Carolina		7/27/1863	Mortally wounded-died at U.S. Seminary Hospital, Hagerstown, Md.	Hagerstown, MD
Anderson, James W.	Co. H, 47th Virginia	1834	10/3/1863	Hollywood Cemetery, Richmond, Va., reburial lists	Richmond, VA
Anderson, Jesse A.	Co. B, 14th North Carolina	1838	7/10/1863	Mortally wounded-died on unknown date in Gettysburg	Unknown
Anderson, John D.G.	Co. D, 61st Georgia		7/1/1863	Laurel Grove Cemetery, Savannah, Ga., reburial list	Savannah, GA
Anderson, Mitchell A.	Lt., Co. K, 7th Tennessee		7/3/1863	Killed in action	Unknown
Anderson, Samuel Woodward	Co. C, 1st Maryland Battalion		9/17/1863	Hollywood Cemetery, Richmond, Va., reburial lists	Richmond, VA
Anderson, Thomas J.	Co. G, 42nd Mississippi		8/8/1863	Hollywood Cemetery, Richmond, Va., reburial lists	Richmond, VA
Anderson, Uriah R.	Co. F, 48th Georgia	1840	7/2/1863	Killed in action	Unknown
Anderson, William C.	Co. G, 13th Georgia		7/1/1863	Killed in action	Unknown
Anderson, William D.	Co. E, 56th Virginia	1843	Jul. 1863	Killed in action	Unknown
Anderson, William Pinkney	Co. G, 5th Texas	1838	7/2/1863	Killed in action	Unknown
Anderson, William W.	Sgt., Co. K, 11th North Carolina	1840	7/1/1863	Killed in action	Unknown
Anderton, Joseph A.	Co. G, 5th North Carolina	1827	7/11/1863	Hollywood Cemetery, Richmond, Va., reburial lists	Richmond, VA
Andress, William Potts	Co. C, 5th Alabama	9/18/1837	7/31/1863	Mortally wounded-died at unknown place in Gettysburg	Unknown
Andrews, Henry H.	Co. E, 13th Mississippi		Jul. 1863	Hollywood Cemetery, Richmond, Va., reburial lists	Richmond, VA
Andrews, Hezekiah L.	Lt. Col., 2nd North Carolina Battalion	1840	7/1/1863	Killed in action	Unknown
Andrews, J.D.	Co. G, 10th Alabama		7/2/1863	Killed in action	Unknown
Andrews, James T.	Sgt., Co. H, 47th North Carolina	1843	7/3/1863	Killed in action	Unknown
Andrews, Robin	Co. G, 48th Georgia	1839	7/2/1863	Killed in action	Unknown
Andrews, Thomas Colquitt	Sgt., Co. A, 53d Georgia	1830	9/20/1863	Mortally wounded-died at unknown place in Gettysburg; reinterred in GA after the war	Griffin, GA
Andrews, Wesley	Co. G, 11th North Carolina	1833	7/10/1863	Mortally wounded-died at unknown place in Gettysburg	Unknown
Andrews, William Potts	Co. C, 5th Alabama	9/18/1837	8/2/1863	Mortally wounded-died at unknown place in Gettysburg	Unknown
Anglin, J.H. "Henry"	Co. D, 38th Virginia		10/8/1863	Died of wounds at Ft. Delaware, DE.	Finn's Point, NJ
Anthony, George	Co. M, 16th North Carolina	1838	7/1/1863	Killed in action	Unknown
Anthony, P.B.	Co. B, 11th North Carolina	1834	7/18/1863	Died of wounds at Harrisonburg, VA	Harrisonburg, VA
Apple, Lewis C.	Co. A, 56th Virginia		Jul. 1863	Mortally wounded per the Richmond Sentinel, July 29, 1863;	Unknown
Apraan, James	Co. K, 7th Virginia		Jul. 1863	Missing in action and presumed dead	Unknown
Ard, William F.	Co. G, 48th Georgia	1839	7/19/1863	Mortally wounded-died at unknown place in Gettysburg	Unknown

NAME	REGIMENT	BIRTH	DEATH	COMMENT	BURIAL
Arent, William R.	Lt., Co. H, 52nd North Carolina	1840	8/6/1863	Mortally wounded and died at Camp Letterman	Raleigh, NC
Armantrout, John	Cpl., Co. E, 5th Virginia	6/24/1832	8/5/1863	Died as POW at David's Island, NY	Cypress Hills, NY
Armes, Benjamin F.	Sgt., Co. F, 3rd Virginia		Jul. 1863	Died of wounds received at Gettysburg on unknown date	Unknown
Armistead, Lewis Addison	Brigadier General	2/18/1817	7/5/1863	Mortally wounded, July 3rd, and died two days later	Baltimore, MD
Arnold, David C.	Co. B, 8th Alabama		7/3/1863	Hollywood Cemetery, Richmond, Va., reburial lists	Richmond, VA
Arnold, Dawson W.	Co. G, 5th Florida	1845	9/15/1863	Hollywood Cemetery, Richmond, Va., reburial lists	Richmond, VA
Arnold, Henry	Co. K, 8th Georgia		Jul. 1863	Mortally wounded-died on unknown date in Gettysburg	Unknown
Arnold, John H.	Co. H, 11th Georgia	4/5/1843	7/3/1863	Killed in action	Unknown
Arnold, Patrick, E.	Co. G, 19th Mississippi		7/2/1863	Killed in action	Unknown
Arrendale, Willis	Co. E, 24th Georgia		7/2/1863	Killed in action	Unknown
Arrington, Charles	Co. H, Cobb's Legion Cav. (Ga.)		7/2/1863	Killed in action	Unknown
Arthur, John Calvin	Lt., Co. F, 3rd Virginia	1838	7/3/1863	Mortally wounded and died the same day	Unknown
Artz, William P.	Co. B, 20th North Carolina	1839	7/1/1863	Killed in action	Unknown
Arwood, Gilbert	Co. F, 38th North Carolina	1835	7/1/1863	Killed in action	Unknown
Asbury, Smith Manassas	Co. C, 16th Virginia Cavalry	1831	Jul. 1863	Mortally wounded-died on unknown date in Gettysburg	Unknown
Ash, John Rutherford	Co. A, 2nd Georgia	9/28/1837	7/3/1863	Killed in action; Hebron Pres. Ch., Franklin, GA	Franklin, GA
Ashburn, James T.	Co. G, 40th Virginia	1840	7/1/1863	Killed in action	Unknown
Ashburn, John W.	Sgt., Co. B, 2nd North Carolina Battalion	1843	7/1/1863	Killed in action	Unknown
Ashby, James Samuel	Co. B, 8th Virginia	1843	7/3/1863	Killed in action	Unknown
Ashley, Charles Harrison	Co. H, 20th Georgia		7/2/1863	Killed in action	Unknown
Ashley, Robert	Co. B, 6th North Carolina	1840	7/1/1863	Killed in action	Unknown
Ashley, W.N.	Co. B, 7th South Carolina	1839	7/16/1863	Mortally wounded-died at unknown place in Gettysburg	Unknown
Ashton, Burditt Washington	Co. C, 9th Virginia Cavalry	2/27/1840	7/3/1863	Killed in action	Unknown
Askew, Joseph Wesley	Lt., Co. H, 2nd North Carolina Battalion	1840	7/15/1863	Hollywood Cemetery, Richmond, Va., reburial lists	Richmond, VA
Askew, Thomas William	Co. H, 2nd North Carolina Battalion	4/23/1827	7/1/1863	Hollywood Cemetery, Richmond, Va., reburial lists	Richmond, VA
Aston, Thomas Carrell	Co. C, 37th Virginia	9/30/1844	7/22/1863	Died of wounds in enemy hands; Interred North Street Church Cem., Lebanon, Va.	Lebanon, VA
Atha, Thomas F.	Co. H, 11th Georgia	Oct. 1842	7/2/1863	Killed in action	Unknown
Atkins, Edgar S.	Co. M, 55th Virginia		7/3/1863	Hollywood Cemetery, Richmond, Va., reburial lists	Richmond, VA
Atkins, Thomas Washington	Capt., Co. A, 53rd Georgia	11/6/1835	7/4/1863	Hollywood Cemetery, Richmond, Va., reburial lists	Richmond, VA
Atkinson, Claiborne T.	Taylor's Battery (Va.)		1863	Mortally wounded-died on unknown date in Gettysburg	Unknown

NAME	REGIMENT	BIRTH	DEATH	COMMENT	BURIAL
Atkinson, Thomas L.B.	Co. C, 9th Georgia	10/2/1828	7/2/1863	Killed in action	Unknown
Atkinson, William Ruffin "Rufus"	Lt., Co. G, 13th North Carolina	8/12/1843	8/2/1863	Mortally wounded-died at unknown place in Gettysburg	Unknown
Attaway, J. Simon	Co. G, 1st South Carolina	1847	8/8/1863	Mortally wounded and died at Camp Letterman	Raleigh, NC
Austin, E. Coleman	Lt., Co. C, 28th North Carolina		7/3/1863	Killed in action	Unknown
Austin, Marion G.	Co. D, 21st Virginia	1839	12/2/1863	Mortally wounded and died at Baltimore, MD-buried there	Baltimore, MD
Austin, Nathaniel	Lt., Co. E, 14th South Carolina	1839	8/22/1863	Magnolia Cemetery, Charleston, SC, reburial list	Charleston, SC
Austin, William Cornelius	Lt., Co. E, 18th Virginia	1840	7/8/1863	Hollywood Cemetery, Richmond, Va., reburial lists	Richmond, VA
Autaway, Abraham J.	Cpl., Co. H, 55th North Carolina	1835	Jul. 1863	Mortally wounded-died at unknown place in Gettysburg	Unknown
Auten, P.S.	Co. A, 11th North Carolina	1836	8/1/1863	Hollywood Cemetery, Richmond, Va., reburial lists	Richmond, VA
Autery, Robert A.	Co. E, 6th Alabama	1842	7/2/1863	Killed in action	Unknown
Avery, Issac Erwin	Col., 6th North Carolina	12/20/1828	7/3/1863	Mortally wounded July 2nd, died the next day	Hagerstown, MD
Awalt, William	Co. I, 11th Mississippi		7/3/1863	Killed in action	Unknown
Aycock, Joel J.	Co. A, 8th Georgia	1840	7/2/1863	Killed in action	Unknown
Aycock, Madison	Co. B, 17th Georgia		1863	Mortally wounded per the Augusta Chronicle & Sentinel, July 30, 1863	Unknown
Ayers, David S.	Co. H, 5th Florida	1840	7/2/1863	Mortally wounded, July 2nd, and died the same day	Unknown
Ayers, Thomas	Co. E, 17th Georgia		Jul. 1863	Mortally wounded per the Augusta Chronicle & Sentinel, July 30, 1863	Unknown
Ayre, William Thomas	Lt., Co. F, 8th Virginia	8/22/1842	7/25/1863	Mortally wounded per the Richmond Sentinel, August 11, 1863; died at Chester, PA	Fauquier Co., VA
Bachman, Joseph Binnelker	Co. A, 42nd Mississippi	1/7/1845	Jul. 1863	Killed in action	Unknown
Backhurst, George T.	Co. K, 53rd Virginia	1830	7/3/1863	Killed in action	Unknown
Bagley, James Madison	Cpl., Co. C, 10th Georgia	6/16/1842	7/21863	Mortally wounded per the Augusta Chronicle & Sentinel, July 30, 1863	Unknown
Bagwell, Charles	Co. F, 42nd Mississippi		7/6/1863	Mortally wounded and died on Samuel Lohr's Farm	Unknown
Bagwell, James A.J.	Co. G, 15th Alabama	1842	7/3/1863	Killed in action	Unknown
Bagwell, James W.	Co. I, 13th South Carolina	1831	7/3/1863	Killed in action	Unknown
Bailess, William R.	Co. A, 18th Virginia		7/3/1863	Killed in action per the Richmond Sentinel, July 30, 1863	Unknown
Bailey, C.A.	Co. G, 2nd Georgia		7/2/1863	Laurel Grove Cemetery, Savannah, Ga., reburial list	Savannah, GA
Bailey, C.A.	Lt., Co. A, 10th Georgia		8/12/1863	Mortally wounded per the Augusta Chronicle & Sentinel, July 25, 1863, d. at Camp Letterman	Unknown
Bailey, Edwin S.	Co. D 8th Virginia		Jul.1863	Mortally wounded-died at unknown place in Gettysburg	Unknown
Bailey, George H.	Co. D, 3rd Virginia	1835	7/3/1863	Killed in action	Unknown

NAME	REGIMENT	BIRTH	DEATH	COMMENT	BURIAL
Bailey, James W.	Co. H, 60th Georgia		9/14/1863	Laurel Grove Cemetery, Savannah, Ga., reburial list	Savannah, GA
Bailey, Robert Watkins	Lt., Co. H, 44th Virginia	3/13/1840	Jul. 1863	Hollywood Cemetery, Richmond, Va., reburial lists	Richmond, VA
Bailey, Walter Warren	Co. D, 1st Virginia Cavalry	7/17/1839	7/8/1863	Mortally wounded-died at unknown place in Gettysburg	Unknown
Bailiff, Joab	Co. A, 7th Tennessee	4/6/1836	7/16/1863	Mortally wounded-died at unknown place in Gettysburg	Unknown
Bailiss, William R.	Co. A, 18th Virginia		7/3/1863	Killed in action	Unknown
Baines, Robert G.	Sgt., Co. K, 52nd North Carolina	1842	7/13/1863	Hollywood Cemetery, Richmond, Va., reburial lists	Richmond, VA
Bains, Henderson	Co. E, 7th North Carolina	1840	7/26/1863	Mortally wounded-died at unknown place in Gettysburg	Unknown
Baird, John A.	Co. E, 37th North Carolina	1843	7/3/1863	Missing in action and presumed dead	Unknown
Baird, William T.	Sgt., Co. G, 7th Tennessee		7/3/1863	Killed in action	Unknown
Baker, Andrew J.	Co. B, 47th Alabama		Jul. 1863	Missing in action, July 2nd, and presumed dead	Unknown
Baker, Edgar Gideon	Co. E, 21st Mississippi	11/24/1832	7/14/1863	Hollywood Cemetery, Richmond, Va., reburial lists	Richmond, VA
Baker, Elijah W.	Co. I, 56th Virginia		8/7/1863	Hollywood Cemetery, Richmond, Va., reburial lists	Richmond, VA
Baker, Evan F.	Co. A, 14th South Carolina	1840	7/3/1863	Killed in action	Unknown
Baker, Henry Hyer	Lt., Co. A, 33rd North Carolina	1839	7/3/1863	Killed in action	Unknown
Baker, Henry Simpson H.	Co. E, 37th North Carolina	1839	8/1/1863	Mortally wounded and died at Chester, PA	Phil. National Cem.
Baker, Jacob Calton	Co. A, 26th North Carolina	4/25/1829	7/29/1863	Mortally wounded and died in Richmond, VA	Richmond, VA
Baker, Jacob Martin	Co. F, 38th North Carolina	1832	7/14/1863	Mortally wounded-died at unknown place in Gettysburg	Unknown
Baker, James	Co. A, 26th North Carolina	1841	7/1/1863	Killed in action	Unknown
Baker, James H.	Cpl., Co. B, 2nd North Carolina Battalion	7/5/1839	7/1/1863	Killed in action	Unknown
Baker, James M.	Co. I, 3rd Georgia		7/2/1863	Killed in action	Unknown
Baker, Jesse Johnson	Co. E, 20th North Carolina	6/21/1844	7/3/1863	Oakwood Cemetery, Raleigh, NC, reburial list	Raleigh, NC
Baker, Joseph	Co. F, 5th North Carolina	1841	7/1/1863	Killed in action	Unknown
Baker, Thomas W.	Lt., Co. D, 43rd North Carolina	1840	7/26/1863	Hollywood Cemetery, Richmond, Va., reburial lists	Richmond, VA
Baldwin, Absalom J.	Cpl., Co. A, 14th Georgia		7/2/1863	Killed in action	Unknown
Baldwin, Thomas H.	Co. C, 14th Tennessee		Jul. 1863	Missing in action, July 3rd, and presumed dead	Unknown
Ball, Franklin	Co. I, 2nd Mississippi	1842	7/1/1863	Killed in action	Unknown
Ball, James E.	Cpl., Co. K, 38th Georgia	1844	7/10/1863	Mortally wounded-died at unknown place in Gettysburg	Unknown
Ball, John W.	Cpl., Co. E, 11th Mississippi	1838	7/3/1863	Killed in action	Unknown
Ballard, C.M.	Capt., Co. C, 8th Georgia	1837	7/2/1863	Laurel Grove Cemetery, Savannah, Ga., reburial list	Savannah, GA

NAME	REGIMENT	BIRTH	DEATH	COMMENT	BURIAL
Ballard, James E.	Co. A, 11th Mississippi		7/3/1863	Killed in action	Unknown
Ballard, James Hamby	Co. E, 28th North Carolina	11/26/1835	9/20/1863	Mortally wounded and died at Chester, PA	Phil. National Cem.
Ballard, Thomas A.	Lt., Co. F, 50th Georgia		7/5/1863	Hollywood Cemetery, Richmond, Va., reburial lists	Richmond, VA
Ballard, William G.	Co. H, 56th Virginia	1840	Jul. 1863	Missing in action and presumed dead	Unknown
Ballard, William R.	Co. D, 2nd South Carolina		7/2/1863	Killed in action	Charleston, SC
Ballou, Hugh	Co. A, 26th North Carolina	1832	7/1/1863	Killed in action	Unknown
Bamberg, Josephus L.	Co. A, 42nd Mississippi	1844	7/15/1863	Mortally wounded-died at unknown place in Gettysburg	Unknown
Bankston, Thomas M.	Co. C, 16th Mississippi	1843	7/3/1863	Killed in action	Unknown
Barber, James A.	Co. D, 38th Virginia		7/3/1863	Killed in action per the Richmond Sentinel, August 1, 1863	Unknown
Barber, Joseph Wyatt	Lt., Co. C, 1st Maryland Battalion	11/8/1837	7/20/1863	Mortally wounded-died at unknown place in Gettysburg	Unknown
Bare, Leander "Lee"	Co. A, 26th North Carolina	1842	7/1/1863	Killed in action	Unknown
Barker, Edward	Co. A, 26th North Carolina	1842	8/13/1863	Mortally wounded and died at Camp Letterman	Raleigh, NC
Barker, Leroy H.	Co. F, 13th Alabama		7/1/1863	Killed in action	Unknown
Barker, Nathan David	Co. M, 22nd North Carolina	1834	8/4/1863	Mortally wounded and died at Chester, PA	Phil. National Cem.
Barksdale, William	Brigadier General	8/21/1821	7/2/1863	Killed in action	Jackson, MS
Barlow, William	Cpl., Co. G, 10th Georgia		Jul. 1863	Mortally wounded per the Augusta Chronicle & Sentinel, July 25, 1863	Unknown
Barmore, William Calvin	Co. B, 7th South Carolina	1841	7/2/1863	Hollywood Cemetery, Richmond, Va., reburial lists	Richmond, VA
Barnard, L.B.	Co. A, 9th Louisiana		7/1/1863	Killed in action	Unknown
Barnes, George	Sgt., Co. G, 37th North Carolina	1838	7/3/1863	Killed in action	Unknown
Barnes, Larry	Co. A, 55th North Carolina		7/1/1863	Killed in action	Unknown
Barnes, Robert	Co. G, 59th Georgia		Jul. 1863	Mortally wounded-died at unknown place in Gettysburg	Unknown
Barnes, Robert R.	Sgt., Co. B, 5th Florida	1842	7/2/1863	Killed in action	Unknown
Barnes, Rufus	Co. G, 26th North Carolina	1827	8/9/1863	Mortally wounded and died in Richmond, VA	Richmond, VA
Barnes, Smith F.	Co. G, 37th North Carolina	1831	7/20/1863	Hollywood Cemetery, Richmond, Va., reburial lists	Richmond, VA
Barnes, W.F.	Co. B, 59th Georgia		1863	Mortally wounded-died at unknown place in Gettysburg	Unknown
Barnett, L.B.	Co. I, 26th North Carolina	1829	7/3/1863	Killed in action	Unknown
Barnett, Thomas Charles	Co. I, 53rd Georgia	11/27/1842	7/5/1863	Laurel Grove Cemetery, Savannah, Ga., reburial list	Savannah, GA
Barnette, John Lafayette	Co. A, 11th North Carolina	11/8/1834	7/5/1863	Mortally wounded-died at unknown place in Gettysburg	Unknown
Barnette, William Azmon	Co. B, 53rd North Carolina	8/1/1834	7/3/1863	Killed in action	Unknown
Barnow, Elias	Co. C, 5th Florida	1845	7/2/1863	Killed in action	Unknown
Barrett, James	Co. D, 17th Mississippi	1837	7/2/1863	Killed in action	Unknown

NAME	REGIMENT	BIRTH	DEATH	COMMENT	BURIAL
Barrett, Jesse	Co. D, 7th Virginia		7/3/1863	Killed in action	Unknown
Barrett, John R.	Louisiana Guard Artillery		Jul. 1863	Hollywood Cemetery, Richmond, Va., reburial lists	Richmond, VA
Barrett, Lewis W.	Co. H, Cobb's Legion Cav. (Ga.)		1863	Mortally wounded-died at unknown place in Gettysburg	Unknown
Barrett, Thomas Riley	Co. H, Cobb's Legion Cav. (Ga.)		7/2/1863	Laurel Grove Cemetery, Savannah, Ga., reburial list	Savannah, GA
Barringer, Henry H.	Co. I, 52nd North Carolina	1840	7/3/1863	Mortally wounded and died the same day	Unknown
Barrons, Robert	Co. H, 8th Florida	1837	7/2/1863	Killed in action	Unknown
Barry, Michael	Co. E, 1st Maryland Battalion		Jul. 1863	Hollywood Cemetery, Richmond, Va., reburial lists	Richmond, VA
Barry, William H.	Co. C, 11th Alabama		Jul. 1863	Buried on Michael Fiscel's Farm as 14th Ala., body not recovered	Unknown
Bartley, Charles	Co. H, 8th South Carolina		7/2/1863	Hollywood Cemetery, Richmond, Va., reburial lists	Richmond, VA
Bartley, Nathan L.	Co. D, 14th South Carolina	1830	7/1/1863	Killed in action	Unknown
Bartley, William J.	2nd Rockbridge Arty. (Va.)	1828	7/3/1863	Killed in action	Unknown
Barton, John	Co. D, Phillips Legion (Ga.)		7/2/1863	Killed in action	Unknown
Barton, William Alexander	Co. H, 11th Mississippi	1843	7/3/1863	Killed in action	Unknown
Barton, William M.	Cpl., Co. I, 12th South Carolina	1837	7/1/1863	Killed in action	Unknown
Barwick, R.S.	Co. G, 14th South Carolina	1838	7/1/1863	Killed in action	Unknown
Baskervill, George Thomas	Capt., Co. I, 23rd North Carolina	11/1/1830	7/2/1863	Killed in action	Granville Co., NC
Baskin, William Holmes	Lt., Co. K, 11th Georgia	1842	7/21/1863	Died of wounds at Macon, GA	Macon, GA
Bass, George W.	Co. B, 3rd North Carolina		7/2/1863	Killed in action	Unknown
Bass, James H.	Co. K, 43rd North Carolina	1830	7/6/1863	Mortally wounded-died at unknown place in Gettysburg	Unknown
Bate, T.B.	Co. C, 9th Louisiana		7/21/1863	Mortally wounded-died at unknown place in Gettysburg	Unknown
Bates, Julius Erwin	Lt., Co. K, 12th Alabama	1841	Jul. 1863	Died of wounds on either July 3rd or 4th	Unknown
Bates, Thomas	Co. I, 5th Texas		7/2/1863	Killed in action	Unknown
Batman, Peter F.	Co. K, 3rd Arkansas	1832	7/2/1863	Killed in action	Unknown
Batten, Archer J.	Co. I, 3rd Virginia	1840	7/3/1863	Killed in action	Unknown
Battle, Wesley Lewis	Lt., Co. D, 37th North Carolina	10/13/1843	8/23/1863	Oakwood Cemetery, Raleigh, NC, reburial list	Raleigh, NC
Battley, William H.	Sgt. Maj., 18th Mississippi	1840	7/2/1863	Killed in action	Unknown
Baucum, William O.	Co. I, 17th Mississippi	1837	7/2/1863	Killed in action	Unknown
Baudwin, Albert	Co. F, 5th Texas		7/2/1863	Killed in action	Unknown
Baugh, John C.	Co. G, 5th Florida		7/2/1863	Killed in action	Unknown
Baughan, David M.	Co. D, 21st Virginia	1827	7/2/1863	Killed in action	Unknown
Baxter, Frank	Co. D, 1st Maryland Battalion		1863	Mortally wounded and died at Camp Letterman	Unknown
Bazemore, William D.	Co. C, 2nd Mississippi	1838	7/1/1863	Killed in action	Unknown
Beacham, T.P.	Co. B, 13th South Carolina		Jul. 1863	Mortally wounded and left on the field	Unknown

NAME	REGIMENT	BIRTH	DEATH	COMMENT	BURIAL
Beadles, James Cornelius	King William Artillery (Va.)	4/9/1838	7/1/1863	Killed in action	Unknown
Beal, Benjamin M.	Co. E, 26th North Carolina	1839	7/1/1863	Killed in action	Unknown
Beale, Nathaniel L.	Co. B, 9th Virginia		Jul. 1863	Mortally wounded-died at unknown place in Gettysburg	Unknown
Beall, James A.	Co. G, 12th Georgia		7/1/1863	Killed in action	Unknown
Beall, James E.	Co. E, 44th Georgia		7/1/1863	Killed in action	Unknown
Beam, Andrew J.	Co. D, 2nd North Carolina Battalion		7/2/1863	Killed in action	Unknown
Bearden, William	Lt., Co. K, 3rd South Carolina	12/27/1829	7/5/1863	Mortally wounded-died at unknown place in Gettysburg	Unknown
Beasley, Nelson	Co. C, 6th Alabama	1844	Jul. 1863	Mortally wounded-died at unknown place in Gettysburg	Unknown
Beason, Jonathan	Co. F, 3rd Arkansas	1842	7/2/1863	Killed in action	Unknown
Beaty, J.L.	Co. A, 2nd Mississippi	1843	11/25/1863	Mortally wounded-died at unknown place in Gettysburg	Unknown
Beauchamp, Henry P.	Cpl., Co. E, 18th Mississippi	1839	7/20/1863	Hollywood Cemetery, Richmond, Va., reburial lists	Richmond, VA
Beauchamp, John	Co. K, 5th Virginia		Jul. 1863	Mortally wounded-died at unknown place in Gettysburg	Unknown
Bebber, John G.	Co. B, 37th North Carolina	1835	7/3/1863	Mortally wounded and died the same day	Unknown
Beck, Jasper Newton, Jr.	Co. E, 3rd Battalion Georgia SS	5/10/1832	7/3/1863	Killed in action	Unknown
Beck, William Lylleton Johnson	Co. A 42nd Mississippi	1835	7/1/1863	Killed in action	Unknown
Beckett, William F.	Co. K, 53rd Virginia		7/3/1863	Killed in action	Unknown
Beckham, -	Co. G, 3rd Alabama		7/9/1863	Mortally wounded-died at unknown place in Gettysburg	Unknown
Beckworth, James A.	Co. D, 49th Georgia	1842	7/2/1863	Killed in action	Unknown
Beddingfield, Robert R.	Cpl., Co. C, 47th North Carolina	1836	7/3/1863	Mortally wounded and died the same day	Unknown
Bedinger, George Rust	Capt., Co. E, 33rd Virginia	7/10/1840	7/3/1863	Killed in action	Unknown
Beecher, Rudolph A.	Sgt., Co. G, 4th Texas		7/2/1863	Killed in action	Unknown
Beeler, James H.	Carpenter's Battery (Va.)		7/2/1863	Killed in action	Unknown
Beeman, Christopher Columbus	Co. G, 3rd Arkansas	1840	7/10/1863	Hollywood Cemetery, Richmond, Va., reburial lists	Richmond, VA
Beeson, Richard M.	Co. K, 13th Mississippi	1842	7/2/1863	Killed in action	Unknown
Belcher, Samuel P.	Lt., Co. I, 11th Georgia	1831	7/12/1863	Hollywood Cemetery, Richmond, Va., reburial lists	Richmond, VA
Belcher, Thomas-delete	Co. E, 13th South Carolina		7/1/1863	Killed in action	Unknown
Belk, Jehu W.	Co. B, 43rd North Carolina	1837	8/14/1863	Died in Virginia; Interred Bethlehem United Methodist Church, Waxhaw, NC (Union Co.)	Union County, NC
Bell, Augustus L.	Co. F, 43rd North Carolina	1/26/1842	7/1/1863	Killed in action	Unknown
Bell, Charles W.	Co. K, 2nd South Carolina	1829	8/14/1863	Mortally wounded per the Charleston Mercury, August 28, 1863	Unknown
Bell, Christopher C.	Co. A, 14th Virginia	1834	7/3/1863	Killed in action	Unknown
Bell, Henry	Co. F, 44th Virginia	1840	7/3/1863	Killed in action	Unknown
Bell, Isaac G.	Co. I, 11th Mississippi	1837	7/3/1863	Killed in action	Unknown

NAME	REGIMENT	BIRTH	DEATH	COMMENT	BURIAL
Bell, James A.	Co. K, 11th North Carolina	1845	7/10/1863	Mortally wounded–died at unknown place in Gettysburg	Unknown
Bell, Lewis Leavel	Co. F, 7th Virginia		7/3/1863	Killed in action	Unknown
Bell, Samuel E.	Co. A, 14th Virginia	1830	7/3/1863	Killed in action	Unknown
Bellomy, George W.	Co. H, 57th Virginia	1836	7/10/1863	Hollywood Cemetery, Richmond, Va., reburial lists	Richmond, VA
Bendall, Benjamin Franklin	Co. F, 53rd Virginia		8/6/1863	Hollywood Cemetery, Richmond, Va., reburial lists	Richmond, VA
Bender, Griffin M., Jr.	Co. H, 2nd Louisiana	1839	7/6/1863	Hollywood Cemetery, Richmond, Va., reburial lists	Richmond, VA
Bennett, Charles Henry	Sgt., Co. I, 24th Virginia		7/3/1863	Killed in action	Unknown
Bennett, Isaac	Co. A, 43rd North Carolina	1829	7/3/1863	Killed in action	Unknown
Bennett, James H.	Co. H, 53rd North Carolina	1837	7/10/1863	Died of Wounds at Williamsport, MD	Williamsport, MD
Bennett, Jerry Washington	Co. F, 21st North Carolina	1840	7/2/1863	Killed in action	Unknown
Bennett, R.E.	Co. K, 8th Alabama		8/5/1863	Hollywood Cemetery, Richmond, Va., reburial lists	Richmond, VA
Bennett, Richard T.	Cpl., Co. E, 20th North Carolina	1842	7/1/1863	Killed in action	Unknown
Bennett, William B.	Co. G, 9th Virginia	1843	7/3/1863	Killed in action	Unknown
Benns, Charles	Co. B, 2nd Georgia Battalion		7/2/1863	Killed in action	Unknown
Benshoof, Benjamin	Co. K, 5th Virginia	1829	7/8/1863	Mortally wounded and died at Winchester, VA	Winchester, VA
Benson, Archibald T.	Cpl., Co. H, 3rd North Carolina	1841	7/2/1863	Killed in action	Unknown
Benson, Charles Haywood	Co. G, 55th North Carolina	1841	7/1/1863	Killed in action	Unknown
Benson, Jesse W.	Co. B, 45th North Carolina		7/25/1863	Mortally wounded–died at unknown place in Gettysburg	Unknown
Benton, B.P.	Co. B, 8th Alabama		7/2/1863	Killed in action	Unknown
Benton, James M.	Lt., Co. H, 45th North Carolina	1846	7/3/1863	Killed in action	Unknown
Berry, William George	Co. I, 7th South Carolina	1830	7/25/1863	Mortally wounded per the Richmond Sentinel, August 11, 1863	Phil. National Cem.
Berthancourt, Alexandra	Co. F, 10th Louisiana		7/9/1863	Mortally wounded–died at unknown place in Gettysburg	Unknown
Betterton, Nathan J.	Co. B, 18th Virginia	1838	Jul. 1863	Missing in action and presumed dead	Unknown
Bettis, Thomas J.	Co. G, 49th Virginia		7/3/1863	Killed in action	Unknown
Betts, William S.	Co. B, 8th Alabama	1843	7/2/1863	Killed in action	Unknown
Beverage, Jacob Elim, Jr.	Lt., Co. E, 31st Virginia	1836	7/3/1863	Hollywood Cemetery, Richmond, Va., reburial lists	Richmond, VA
Bibby, Bailey L.	Co. C, 15th Alabama	1828	7/2/1863	Killed in action	Unknown
Bierly, Andrew J.	Co. K, 57th Virginia		7/3/1863	Killed in action	Unknown
Biggers, William E.	Troup Artillery (Ga.)	1836	8/20/1863	Mortally wounded and died in Richmond, VA	Richmond, VA
Billings, Peter	Co. I, 32nd North Carolina	1842	7/3/1863	Killed in action	Unknown
Binford, James L.	Co. E, 14th Virginia	1839	7/3/1863	Killed in action	Unknown
Binns, Charles D.	Co. K, 53rd Virginia	1/3/1843	10/3/1863	Hollywood Cemetery, Richmond, Va., reburial lists	Richmond, VA
Binns, Major E.	Co. K, 53rd Virginia	1838	7/23/1863	Hollywood Cemetery, Richmond, Va., reburial lists	Richmond, VA

NAME	REGIMENT	BIRTH	DEATH	COMMENT	BURIAL
Bird, Alfred	Sgt., Co. F, 50th Georgia	1831	7/2/1863	Laurel Grove Cemetery, Savannah, Ga., reburial list	Savannah, GA
Bird, George W.	Capt., Co. K, 11th Mississippi	1836	7/3/1863	Killed in action	Unknown
Bird, Henry B.	Co. F, 48th Georgia	1838	7/2/1863	Killed in action	Unknown
Bird, Samuel W.	Co. C, 57th Virginia		7/3/1863	Killed in action	Unknown
Bird, W.L.	Co. G, 2nd South Carolina		8/29/1863	Died as POW at David's Island, NY	Cypress Hills, NY
Bird, William W.	Co. E, 2nd Georgia	8/30/1832	11/15/1863	Mortally wounded and died at Staunton, VA-buried there	Staunton, VA
Bird, Wilson T.	Co. G, 57th Virginia	1842	7/3/1863	Killed in action	Unknown
Birge, James W.	Co. C, 17th Mississippi	1835	7/15/1863	Hollywood Cemetery, Richmond, Va., reburial lists	Richmond, VA
Birmingham, John	Co. D, 11th Mississippi	ca. 1823	7/27/1863	Died as POW at David's Island, NY	Cypress Hills, NY
Bish, Daniel	Cpl., Co. D, 7th Virginia		7/3/1863	Killed in action	Unknown
Bishop, Aaron A. "Dock"	Co. H, 12th Alabama	1841	7/1/1863	Killed in action	Unknown
Bishop, George W.	Co. G, 44th Georgia		7/3/1863	Killed in action	Unknown
Bissell, William Rombough	Capt., Co. A, 8th Virginia	1811	7/13/1863	Hollywood Cemetery, Richmond, Va., reburial lists	Richmond, VA
Bivens, D. Cullen	Co. K, 31st Georgia		7/2/1863	Killed in action	Unknown
Black, Duncan	Co. K, 38th North Carolina	1845	7/19/1863	Mortally wounded-died at unknown place in Gettysburg	Unknown
Black, Ephraim	Co. M, 16th North Carolina	6/17/1839	7/1/1863	Killed in action	Unknown
Black, John	Co. B, 5th Alabama Battalion	1825	7/1/1863	Killed in action	Unknown
Black, John C.	Co. I, 33rd Virginia		7/15/1863	Hollywood Cemetery, Richmond, Va., reburial lists	Richmond, VA
Black, John L.	Co. C, 48th Virginia	1838	8/11/1863	Hollywood Cemetery, Richmond, Va., reburial lists	Richmond, VA
Black, William Clendinin	Co. I, 13th Mississippi	5/26/1842	7/2/1863	Killed in action	Unknown
Blackburn, Aurelius C.	Capt., Co. K, 52nd North Carolina	1840	7/1/1863	Hollywood Cemetery, Richmond, Va., reburial lists	Richmond, VA
Blackburn, Leander C.	Color Sgt., 53rd Virginia		7/4/1863	Mortally wounded-died at unknown place in Gettysburg	Unknown
Blackhan, L.C.	Sgt., Co. E, 50th Virginia		12/2/1863	Mortally wounded-died at unknown place in Gettysburg	Unknown
Blackistone, William J.	Sgt., Co. A, 1st Maryland Battalion		8/1/1863	Mortally wounded and died at Hagerstown, MD-buried there	Hagerstown, MD
Blackman, M.W.	Co. G, 5th Texas		7/2/1863	Killed in action	Unknown
Blackmon, Stephen	Co. G, 20th Georgia		7/2/1863	Killed in action	Unknown
Blackwelder, Charles M.	Co. A, 52nd North Carolina	1833	9/21/1863	Mortally wounded and died at Chester, PA	Phil. National Cem.
Blackwell, Michael Andrew	Co. B, 2nd Mississippi	1839	7/1/1863	Killed in action	Unknown
Blackwell, Robert	Co. I, 23rd North Carolina	1836	7/1/1863	Killed in action	Unknown
Blackwell, William	Co. B, 2nd Mississippi		7/1/1863	Killed in action	Unknown
Blair, George H.	Co. L, 3rd Georgia	11/7/1833	7/2/1863	Killed in action	Unknown
Blair, Sutter F.	Co. B, 38th Virginia	3/20/1843	7/15/1863	Mortally wounded-died at unknown place in Gettysburg	Unknown

NAME	REGIMENT	BIRTH	DEATH	COMMENT	BURIAL
Blake, Council W.	Co. E, 18th North Carolina	1842	7/27/1863	Mortally wounded and died at Winchester, VA	Winchester, VA
Blake, Enoch P.	Carpenter's Battery (Va.)		8/18/1863	Mortally wounded–died at unknown place in Gettysburg	Unknown
Blake, Joel Clifton	Lt., Co. K, 5th Florida	2/3/1831	7/2/1863	Killed in action	Unknown
Blakeley, John L.	Co. M, 21st North Carolina	1823	Jul. 1863	Missing in action and presumed dead	Unknown
Blakely, W.R.	Co. F, 14th South Carolina		7/2/1863	Mortally wounded and died the same day	Unknown
Blankenship, Elijah P.	Co. E, 57th Virginia		7/23/1863	Mortally wounded–died at unknown place in Gettysburg	Unknown
Blevins, Isham	Co. K, 37th North Carolina	4/16/1830	7/3/1863	Killed in action	Unknown
Blevins, Stephen	Co. A, 26th North Carolina	1835	Jul. 1863	Killed in action	Unknown
Blick, William A.	Lt., Co. E, 56th Virginia	1839	7/3/1863	Killed in action per the Richmond Sentinel, July 29, 1863	Unknown
Bligh, John	Co. D, 2nd South Carolina		7/2/1863	Magnolia Cemetery, Charleston, SC, reburial list	Charleston, SC
Bliss, Frederick	Lt., Co. B, 8th Georgia	9/10/1839	7/4/1863	Laurel Grove Cemetery, Savannah, Ga., reburial list	Savannah, GA
Block, Moses	Co. A, 3rd Georgia		7/2/1863	Killed in action	Unknown
Blocker, Cornelius	Co. B, 61st Georgia		7/3/1863	Died of wounds received July 1	Unknown
Blount, L. William	Co. G, 13th North Carolina	1844	8/13/1863	Died as POW at David's Island, NY	Cypress Hills, NY
Blount, Richard Henry Jasper	Co. B, 5th North Carolina	1843	7/1/1863	Hollywood Cemetery, Richmond, Va., reburial lists	Richmond, VA
Bluffkin, William H.	Co. F, 1st South Carolina		7/1/1863	Killed in action	Unknown
Bly, James P.	Co. K, 6th Alabama		7/3/1863	Killed in action	Unknown
Blythe, Lewis J.	Co. F, 2nd Mississippi	1838	Jul. 1863	Killed in action either July 1st or July 3rd	Unknown
Boatwright, Joseph E.	Co. K, 11th Mississippi	1835	7/3/1863	Killed in action	Marshall Co., MS
Bobbitt, P.S.	Co. G, 47th North Carolina	7/27/1843	8/20/1863	Mortally wounded and died at Camp Letterman	Creedmoor, NC
Bodenhamer, Christian Louis	Co. G, 33rd North Carolina	1832	7/1/1863	Killed in action	Unknown
Boggan, William Wellington	Lt., Co. H, 43rd North Carolina	11/15/1841	7/2/1863	Killed in action	Raleigh, NC
Boggs, John R.	Co. H, 50th Virginia	1835	8/4/1863	Mortally wounded–died at unknown place in Gettysburg	Unknown
Boggs, Richard H.H.	Co. E, 38th Georgia		7/20/1863	Mortally wounded–died at unknown place in Gettysburg	Unknown
Boggs, William B.	Co. E, 13th North Carolina	1843	Jul. 1863	Mortally wounded–died at unknown place in Gettysburg	Unknown
Bolch [Bolick], Anthony	Co. F, 23rd North Carolina	1840	7/1/1863	Killed in action	Unknown
Bolch, Logan	Co. C, 28th North Carolina	1824	9/30/1863	Mortally wounded and died at Chester, PA	Phil. National Cem.
Bomar, Irwin	Co. A, 21st Georgia		7/2/1863	Killed in action	Unknown
Bond Jr., John Mitchell Dooly	Capt., Co. I, 53rd Georgia	1837	7/2/1863	Laurel Grove Cemetery, Savannah, Ga., reburial list	Savannah, GA
Bond, W.	Co. A, 2nd Florida		7/2/1863	Killed in action	Unknown
Bonds, James Wright	Co. A, 2nd Mississippi	8/30/1838	7/1/1863	Killed in action	Unknown

NAME	REGIMENT	BIRTH	DEATH	COMMENT	BURIAL
Bonds, Robert	Co. H, 15th South Carolina		7/1/1863	Killed in action	Unknown
Bonham, Oscar Love	Co. D, 48th Virginia	1/5/1832	7/2/1863	Killed in action	Unknown
Bonnell, Henry	Co. C, 2nd Florida	1841	Jul. 1863	Mortally wounded, July 2nd, believed to have died later in month	Unknown
Bonnell, John	Co. C, 2nd Florida	1844	7/30/1863	Mortally wounded-died at unknown place in Gettysburg	Unknown
Book, Henry Loving	Co. B, 28th Virginia	9/26/1839	7/3/1863	Killed in action	Unknown
Boon, Daniel H.	Co. F, 2nd North Carolina Battalion	1816	7/10/1863	Mortally wounded-died at unknown place in Gettysburg	Unknown
Boothe, John	Co. E, 5th Texas		7/2/1863	Hollywood Cemetery, Richmond, Va., reburial lists	Richmond, VA
Boothe, William H.	Sgt., Co. D, 26th North Carolina	1833	8/20/1863	Mortally wounded-died at unknown place in Gettysburg	Unknown
Booton, William Sinclair	Co. A, 8th Georgia	11/9/1838	7/2/1863	Killed in action	Unknown
Booze, William G.	Sgt., Co. G, 19th Virginia		Jul. 1863	Mortally wounded, July 3rd, believed to have died later in month	Unknown
Boozer, Burr A.	Co. G, 13th South Carolina	1843	7/3/1863	Mortally wounded, July 1st, and died two days later	Unknown
Boozer, William	Musician, Co. G, 57th North Carolina	1845	Jul. 1863	Missing in action and presumed dead	Unknown
Boring, Robert McBride	Co. K, 4th Georgia	11/3/1842	7/23/1863	Laurel Grove Cemetery, Savannah, Ga., reburial list	Savannah, GA
Borland, W.E.	Co. C, 31st Georgia		7/1/1863	Killed in action	Unknown
Born, Charles W.	Cpl., Co. B, 35th Georgia		7/3/1863	Killed in action	Unknown
Boss, James P.	Co. H, 8th Virginia	1842	7/19/1863	Mortally wounded, July 3rd, and died at Winchester, VA; interred Union Cemetery, Leesburg, Va.	Leesburg, VA
Bost, Jacob W.	Sgt., Co. F, 57th North Carolina		8/16/1863	Mortally wounded and died in Petersburg, VA after POW exchange	Petersburg, VA
Bost, Jethro Calvin	Co. E, 57th North Carolina	1836	7/2/1863	Killed in action	Unknown
Bost, William H.	Co. A, 20th North Carolina	1839	7/1/1863	Killed in action	Unknown
Bostian, Aaron A.	Cpl., Co. K, 5th North Carolina	1834	11/14/1863	Mortally wounded, Juyl 1st, and died at Washington, DC	Washington, DC
Bostick, Andrew Jackson	Co. H, 11th Alabama	1838	7/2/1863	Hollywood Cemetery, Richmond, Va., reburial lists	Richmond, VA
Bostick, John C.	Co. B, 3rd North Carolina	1838	8/2/1863	Mortally wounded-died at unknown place in Gettysburg	Unknown
Boswell, Doctor Franklin	Co. A, 13th Mississippi	1845	10/7/1863	Hollywood Cemetery, Richmond, Va., reburial lists	Richmond, VA
Boswell, John L.C.	Sgt., Co. E, 57th Virginia		7/14/1863	Hollywood Cemetery, Richmond, Va., reburial lists	Richmond, VA
Bouknight, Daniel Reuben	Sgt., Co. H, 13th South Carolina	1839	7/1/1863	Killed in action	Unknown
Bowden, William	Co. G, 47th North Carolina	1835	7/1/1863	Killed in action	Unknown
Bowdoin, Colin M.	Co. G, 26th North Carolina	1838	7/1/1863	Killed in action	Unknown
Bowen, A. Cornelius	Co. G, 1st SC Rifles		7/8/1863	Magnolia Cemetery, Charleston, SC, reburial list	Charleston, SC
Bowen, Berry A.	Co. K, 14th Virginia	1842	7/3/1863	Missing in action and presumed dead	Unknown
Bowen, Elisha W.	Lt., Co. I, 9th Georgia	6/17/1844	7/2/1863	Killed in action	Unknown

NAME	REGIMENT	BIRTH	DEATH	COMMENT	BURIAL
Bowen, Hamilton Newton	Co. K, 61st Georgia	1840	7/8/1863	Mortally wounded and died at Williamsport, MD-buried there	Williamsport, MD
Bowen, John	Co. B, 7th Virginia	2/5/1826	8/15/1863	Mortally wounded-died at unknown place in Gettysburg	Unknown
Bowen, John A.	Co. A, 19th Virginia		Jul. 1863	Missing in action and presumed dead	Unknown
Bowen, John H.	Co. H, 53rd North Carolina	1843	7/3/1863	Killed in action	Unknown
Bowers, Frank	Co. A, 23rd North Carolina	1843	7/14/1863	Mortally wounded-died at unknown place in Gettysburg	Unknown
Bowers, John	Co. I, 48th Georgia	1834	10/30/1863	Died as POW at Pt. Lookout, MD	Pt. Lookout, MD
Bowers, William H.	Co. A, 33rd North Carolina	1837	7/10/1863	Mortally wounded-died at unknown place in Gettysburg	Unknown
Bowery, James H.	Co. K, 53rd Virginia	1835	7/3/1863	Killed in action	Unknown
Bowles, Gibson R.	Sgt., Co. F, 42nd Virginia	1840	7/13/1863	Died of wounds in US hospital at Frederick, MD	Frederick, MD
Bowley, William Hollins	Co. A, 1st Maryland Battalion		Jul. 1863	Mortally wounded and died on unknown date	Unknown
Bowlin, John P.	Co. C, 1st Virginia Cavalry	1845	Jul. 1863	Hollywood Cemetery, Richmond, Va., reburial lists	Richmond, VA
Bowling, B.L.	Co. B, 1st Texas		8/5/1863	Died as POW at Pt. Lookout, MD	Pt. Lookout, MD
Bowling, Jermon S.	Cpl., Co. C, 3rd Georgia		7/2/1863	Killed in action	Unknown
Bowman, Abel Jackson	Co. E, 32nd North Carolina	1832	7/15/1863	Hollywood Cemetery, Richmond, Va., reburial lists	Richmond, VA
Bowman, Bethel H	Sgt., Co. G, 59th Georgia		7/3/1863	Killed in action	Unknown
Bowman, Crockett	Co. K, 50th Virginia	1838	Jul. 1863	Killed in action on July 1st or 2nd	Unknown
Bowman, Gilbert E.	Co. F, 49th Virginia		7/4/1863	Died as POW at Pt. Lookout, MD	Pt. Lookout, MD
Bowman, John T.	Co. I, 16th North Carolina	1841	9/22/1863	Died of wounds in U.S. General Hospital, Harrisburg, PA	Harrisburg, PA
Bowman, Lanson	Co. A, 12th North Carolina	1838	7/1/1863	Killed in action	Unknown
Bowman, William	Co. K, 26th North Carolina	1834	7/1/1863	Killed in action	Unknown
Bowman, William H.	Co. F, 49th Virginia		7/3/1863	Killed in action	Unknown
Bowyer, Leonidas R.	Sgt., Co. B, 19th Virginia		Jul. 1863	Mortally wounded per the Richmond Sentinel, August 11, 1863	Unknown
Box, George T.	Co. A, 17th Mississippi	1834	8/21/1863	Hollywood Cemetery, Richmond, Va., reburial lists	Richmond, VA
Boyans, James	Co. C, 4th Virginia		Jul. 1863	Mortally wounded and died on unknown date	Unknown
Boyd, Benjamin H.	Co. C, 38th Georgia	1831	7/28/1863	Died of wounds in US Hospital at Frederick, MD	Frederick, MD
Boyd, David Caswell	Co. B, 1st South Carolina	1842	7/3/1863	Killed in action	Unknown
Boyd, George Fulton	Lt., Co. A, 45th North Carolina	12/30/1838	7/1/1863	Killed in action	Unknown
Boyd, James A.	Co. D, 13th South Carolina	1840	7/20/1863	Mortally wounded and died at Baltimore, MD-buried there	Baltimore, MD
Boyd, Nathaniel	Co. B, 2nd Mississippi	1845	7/1/1863	Killed in action	Unknown
Boyd, Robert T.	Co. C, 23rd North Carolina		7/1/1863	Killed in action	Unknown
Boydston, Samuel Y.	Co. D, 11th Mississippi	1842	7/3/1863	Killed in action	Unknown

NAME	REGIMENT	BIRTH	DEATH	COMMENT	BURIAL
Boyles, John	Co. I, 11th North Carolina		8/10/1863	Mortally wounded-died at unknown place in Gettysburg	Unknown
Boyles, John W.	Cpl., Co. H, 53rd North Carolina	1842	7/1/1863	Killed in action	Unknown
Boyles, William Riley	Co. D, 53rd North Carolina	1839	7/25/1863	Mortally wounded-died at unknown place in Gettysburg	Unknown
Boylin, William C.	Co. K, 26th North Carolina	1845	7/1/1863	Killed in action	Unknown
Bracewell, Wiley Kinchen	Co. G, 49th Georgia	1839	8/27/1863	Laurel Grove Cemetery, Savannah, Ga., reburial list	Savannah, GA
Brackett, Williamson F.	Co. F, 55th North Carolina	1843	7/1/1863	Killed in action	Unknown
Bradberry, W.J.	Cpl., Co. G, 59th Georgia		7/3/1863	Killed in action	Unknown
Bradford, Robert C.	Sgt., Co. B, 20th North Carolina	11/25/1840	7/1/1863	Killed in action	Unknown
Bradley, George W.	Lt., Co. A, 13th Mississippi	1819	7/11/1863	Hollywood Cemetery, Richmond, Va., reburial lists	Richmond, VA
Bradley, John M.	Maj., 13th Mississippi	1827	7/28/1863	Mortally wounded and died at US Hospital, Williamsport, MD	Williamsport, MD
Bradley, Thomas J.	Co. B, 16th Georgia	11/8/1839	7/1/1863	Killed in action	Unknown
Bradner, Thomas H.	Co. B, 38th Virginia	1844	Jul. 1863	Mortally wounded and died on unknown date	Unknown
Bradshaw, Hartwell H.	Co. G, 7th Tennessee		7/15/1863	Hollywood Cemetery, Richmond, Va., reburial lists	Richmond, VA
Bradshaw, James P.	Sgt., Co. E, 13th North Carolina	1836	8/9/1863	Died as POW at David's Island, NY	Cypress Hills, NY
Brady, Calvin B.	Co. H, 48th Georgia	1843	7/2/1863	Killed in action	Unknown
Brady, William	Co. E, 38th Virginia		7/3/1863	Killed in action per the Richmond Sentinel, August1, 1863	Unknown
Bragg, James P.	Co. F, 47th North Carolina	1843	7/3/1863	Killed in action	Unknown
Brainard, Henry C.	Lt., Co. G, 15th Alabama	1840	7/2/1863	Killed in action	Unknown
Bramham, A.N.	Co. B, 40th Virginia		7/1/1863	Killed in action	Unknown
Branagan, C.P.B.	Capt., Co. I, 8th Alabama	1838	7/3/1863	Killed in action	Unknown
Branch, Jesse B.	Cpl., Co. A, 61st Georgia	4/4/1842	7/1/1863	Laurel Grove Cemetery, Savannah, Ga., reburial list	Savannah, GA
Branch, John H.	Co. D, 3rd Virginia	1837	7/3/1863	Killed in action	Unknown
Branch, William S.	Sgt., Co. E, 6th North Carolina	1829	7/2/1863	Killed in action	Unknown
Brandon, George W.	Cpl., Co. C, 13th North Carolina	1/3/1843	8/26/1863	Mortally wounded and died at Chester, PA	Phil. National Cem.
Brandon, Robert M.	Capt., Co. D, 2nd Mississippi	1839	7/15/1863	Mortally wounded-died at unknown place in Gettysburg	Unknown
Brandon, William T.	Lt., Co. C, 13th North Carolina	1839	7/9/1863	Mortally wounded-died at unknown place in Gettysburg	Unknown
Branham, Nathaniel	Co. C, 56th Virginia		Jul. 1863	Missing in action and presumed dead	Unknown
Brannock, Thomas J.	Co. K, 47th North Carolina	1834	7/1/1863	Killed in action	Unknown
Brantley, Thomas H.	Co. G, 2nd Florida		7/3/1863	Killed in action	Unknown
Branum, Nathaniel	Co. C, 56th Virginia		Jul. 1863	Mortally wounded and died on unknown date	Unknown
Branyon, William L.	Lt., Co. K, 26th Alabama	1/2/1833	7/1/1863	Killed in action	Unknown
Brashear, Charles Duvall, Jr.	Co. F, 5th Texas	3/22/1840	7/2/1863	Killed in action	Unknown

NAME	REGIMENT	BIRTH	DEATH	COMMENT	BURIAL
Brasington, George Cauthen	Lt., Co. H, 2nd South Carolina	3/21/1836	7/6/1863	Magnolia Cemetery, Charleston, SC, reburial list	Charleston, SC
Brassfield, Reuben	Co. C, 6th North Carolina	1842	7/1/1863	Killed in action	Unknown
Braswell, Robert M.	Co. F, 26th North Carolina	1835	7/1/1863	Killed in action	Unknown
Bratton, George B.	Co. F, 42nd Mississippi	1845	7/1/1863	Killed in action	Unknown
Braus, Justinien F.	Co. K, 8th Louisiana		7/2/1863	Killed in action	Unknown
Brawley, Robert Mossman	Co. A, 4th North Carolina	1829	7/1/1863	Killed in action	Unknown
Brawner, William T.	Co. B, 15th Georgia		7/28/1863	Laurel Grove Cemetery, Savannah, Ga., reburial list	Savannah, GA
Bray, William Alexander	Lt., Co. B, 2nd North Carolina Battalion	11/28/1834	7/1/1863	Mortally wounded, July 1st, and died the same day	Raleigh, NC
Bray, William Harvie	Capt., Co. B, 53rd Virginia	1839	7/14/1863	Hollywood Cemetery, Richmond, Va., reburial lists	Richmond, VA
Brazelton, Elijah W.	Co. G, 16th Georgia		7/3/1863	Killed in action	Unknown
Brazelton, Martin Van Buren	Co. F, 1st Tennessee		7/1/1863	Missing in action and presumed dead	Unknown
Breedlove, Henry	Co. I, 22nd North Carolina	1842	7/3/1863	Killed in action	Unknown
Brenan, Peter	Maj., 61st Georgia	1811	7/1/1863	Laurel Grove Cemetery, Savannah, Ga., reburial list	Savannah, GA
Breslin, Edward W.	Co. G, 1st Maryland Battalion		Jul. 1863	Mortally wounded and died on unknown date	Unknown
Bresnahan, W. Mathew	Co. H, 1st Virginia	1837	8/1/1863	Hollywood Cemetery, Richmond, Va., reburial lists	Richmond, VA
Brewer, Samuel J.G.	Co. I, 8th Georgia		7/5/1863	Hollywood Cemetery, Richmond, Va., reburial lists	Richmond, VA
Brewer, Samuel M. [Coleman]	Co. A, 11th Mississippi	1838	7/3/1863	Killed in action	Unknown
Brewer, Thomas J.	Co. I, 47th Virginia		8/30/1863	Mortally wounded-died at unknown place in Gettysburg	Unknown
Brewer, William Domas	Co. H, 26th North Carolina	1835	7/1/1863	Killed in action	Unknown
Brewer, William J.	Co. C, 47th Virginia	1844	8/30/1863	Hollywood Cemetery, Richmond, Va., reburial lists	Richmond, VA
Brewer, William L.	Co. K, 51st Georgia	1824	8/10/1863	Laurel Grove Cemetery, Savannah, Ga., reburial list	Savannah, GA
Brewerton, Frederick	Co. L, 21st Mississippi		7/24/1863	Hollywood Cemetery, Richmond, Va., reburial lists	Richmond, VA
Brian, Doctor Jack	Chesapeake Artillery (Md.)		7/2/1863	Killed in action	Baltimore, MD
Brice, William W.	Co. A, 6th Alabama		10/4/1863	Mortally wounded and died atHarrisburg, PA	Harrisburg, PA
Bridges, Jefferson	Lt., Co. B, 12th Alabama		7/15/1863	Mortally wounded-died at unknown place in Gettysburg	Unknown
Bridges, John H.	Co. I, 17th Mississippi	1841	Jul. 1863	Killed in action on July 1st or 2nd	Unknown
Bridges, Newit D.	Co. C, 5th North Carolina	1840	7/1/1863	Killed in action	Richmond, VA
Bridwell, John	Co. D, 14th South Carolina	1841	7/1/1863	Killed in action	Unknown
Briggs, Henry L.	Co. C, 24th Virginia		Jul. 1863	Hollywood Cemetery, Richmond, Va., reburial lists	Richmond, VA
Briggs, Jackson	Co. F, 53rd North Carolina	1843	7/1/1863	Killed in action	Unknown
Bright, Josiah F.	Co. C, 52nd Virginia	1/8/1830	7/3/1863	Hollywood Cemetery, Richmond, Va., reburial lists	Richmond, VA

NAME	REGIMENT	BIRTH	DEATH	COMMENT	BURIAL
Brigman, Isaac J.	Co. G, 3rd Georgia		7/2/1863	Killed in action	Unknown
Brigman, James B.	Co. B, 12th South Carolina	1836	7/1/1863	Killed in action	Unknown
Briley, James	Cpl., Co. I, 43rd North Carolina	1832	7/1/1863	Killed in action	Unknown
Briley, Tilman T.	Co. K, 26th North Carolina	1844	9/4/1863	Oakwood Cemetery, Raleigh, NC, reburial list	Raleigh, NC
Brimer, Alfred	Co. B, 13th North Carolina	1837	7/1/1863	Killed in action	Unknown
Brinkley, Granville	Co. I, 9th Virginia	1840	7/3/1863	Killed in action	Unknown
Brinkley, Mills	Co. I, 9th Virginia	1841	7/3/1863	Killed in action	Unknown
Briscoe, Robert	Cpl., Co. F, 11th North Carolina	1820	8/10/1863	Mortally wounded and died at Chester, PA	Phil. National Cem.
Brisentine, John M.	Co. B, 28th Virginia		7/5/1863	Mortally wounded-died at unknown place in Gettysburg	Unknown
Brison, G.W.	Co. G, 11th Alabama		Jul. 1863	Hollywood Cemetery, Richmond, Va., reburial lists	Richmond, VA
Brister, Hockaday	Co. I, 13th Mississippi	5/2/1840	7/13/1863	Hollywood Cemetery, Richmond, Va., reburial lists	Richmond, VA
Britt, Elijah B.	Co. F, 48th Georgia	1841	7/2/1863	Killed in action	Unknown
Britt, James	Co. A, 3rd North Carolina	1844	7/2/1863	Killed in action	Unknown
Britt, John	Co. A, 2nd North Carolina	1842	7/2/1863	Killed in action	Unknown
Brittain, Washington	Co. B, 45th North Carolina	1843	7/1/1863	Killed in action	Unknown
Britton, William A.	Woolfolk's Battery (Va.)		7/3/1863	Killed in action per the Richmond Sentinel, July 15, 1863	Unknown
Broach, J.R.	Co. A, 8th South Carolina		7/2/1863	Hollywood Cemetery, Richmond, Va., reburial lists	Richmond, VA
Broadfoot, William J.	Lt., Co. E, 1st Maryland Battalion	1838	8/4/1863	Mortally wounded and died at Martinsburg, VA, interred in Loudoun Park Cemetery	Baltimore, MD
Broadway, William	Co. F, 3rd Arkansas	1844	7/2/1863	Killed in action	Unknown
Broadwell, J.A.	Co. A, 22nd Georgia		Jul. 1863	Mortally wounded, July 2nd, and died on unknown date	Unknown
Brock, J.L.	Co. B, 11th Georgia		7/2/1863	Killed in action	Unknown
Brock, John A.J.	Co. D, 59th Georgia	1839	7/20/1863	Mortally wounded-died at unknown place in Gettysburg	Unknown
Brock, Tarlton Fleming	Cpl., Co. F, 57th Virginia		7/3/1863	Killed in action	Unknown
Brockenbrough, Austin, Jr.	Capt., Co. D, 55th Virginia	1/18/1842	7/2/1863	Mortally wounded and died at 7pm on 7/2; reinterred at Essex Co., VA	Essex Co., VA
Brogan, Frank	Cpl., Co. H, 10th Louisiana	1831	7/13/1863	Mortally wounded-died at unknown place in Gettysburg	Unknown
Brooks, Cicero C.	Co. H, Cobb's Legion Cav. (Ga.)	1828	7/2/1863	Laurel Grove Cemetery, Savannah, Ga., reburial list	Savannah, GA
Brooks, Eli W.	Co. H, 12th Georgia		7/1/1863	Mortally wounded and died the same day	Unknown
Brooks, Isaac N. [M]	Co. B, 47th Alabama	1833	9/18/1863	Hollywood Cemetery, Richmond, Va., reburial lists	Richmond, VA
Brooks, James G.	Co. H, 14th Virginia	1840	Jul. 1863	Mortally wounded, July 3rd, and died on unknown date	Unknown

NAME	REGIMENT	BIRTH	DEATH	COMMENT	BURIAL
Brooks, Moses P.	Sgt., Co. H, 16th North Carolina	1835	7/18/1863	Hollywood Cemetery, Richmond, Va., reburial lists	Richmond, VA
Brooks, Robert D.	Co. I, 32nd North Carolina	1843	7/3/1863	Killed in action	Unknown
Brooks, William	Raines' Battery (Va.)		7/19/1863	Mortally wounded and died at Dranesville, VA	Dranesville, VA
Broom, John G.W.	Co. C, 12th South Carolina	7/22/1842	7/2/1863	Killed in action	Unknown
Broughton, Benjamin	Co. I, 47 North Carolina	1834	8/13/1863	Hollywood Cemetery, Richmond, Va., reburial lists	Richmond, VA
Broussard, Stanislas	Co. C, 8th Louisiana	1843	Jul. 1863	Mortally wounded and died on unknown date	Unknown
Brown, Alexander	Co. B, 45th North Carolina	1844	7/1/1863	Killed in action	Unknown
Brown, Arthur A.	Co. D, 5th Florida	1846	7/14/1863	Mortally wounded-died at unknown place in Gettysburg	Unknown
Brown, D.A.	Cpl., Co. I, 7th Georgia		7/2/1863	Killed in action	Unknown
Brown, Francis	Co. I, 59th Georgia		7/16/1863	Mortally wounded-died at unknown place in Gettysburg	Unknown
Brown, Harrington E.	Co. B, 13th South Carolina		10/12/1863	Died as POW at David's Island, NY	Cypress Hills, NY
Brown, J.A.J.	Co. G, 2nd North Carolina Battalion	1826	7/5/1863	Mortally wounded-died at unknown place in Gettysburg	Unknown
Brown, J.T.	Co. B, 12th South Carolna		8/15/1863	Mortally wounded and died at Chester, PA	Phil. National Cem.
Brown, James A.	Co. D, 1st Maryland Battalion		7/2/1863	Killed in action	Front Royal, VA
Brown, James M.	Co. K, 15th Alabama	1840	7/2/1863	Killed in action	Unknown
Brown, Jason J.	Sgt., Co. H, 2nd North Carolina Battalion	1842	7/1/1863	Oakwood Cemetery, Raleigh, NC, reburial list	Raleigh, NC
Brown, Jesse S.	Co. H, 26th North Carolina		Jul. 1863	Mortally wounded and died on unknown date	Unknown
Brown, John	Co. B, 14th South Carolina	1837	7/2/1863	Killed in action	Unknown
Brown, John	Sgt., Co. E, 59th Georgia		7/2/1863	Killed in action	Unknown
Brown, John	Co. A, 12th Georgia		7/10/1863	Laurel Grove Cemetery, Savannah, Ga., reburial list	Savannah, GA
Brown, John Daniel	Co. B, 3rd North Carolina	1840	7/18/1863	Mortally wounded-died at unknown place in Gettysburg	Unknown
Brown, John W.	Co. L, 1st Texas	1839	7/10/1863	Hollywood Cemetery, Richmond, Va., reburial lists	Richmond, VA
Brown, Kader	Co. C, 5th North Carolina	1839	7/1/1863	Killed in action; KIA on Oak Ridge (Iverson's Brigade)	Richmond, VA
Brown, Marshall	Co. G, 26th North Carolina	11/30/1837	7/1/1863	Killed in action per the Fayetteville Observer, August 15, 1864	Unknown
Brown, Moore	Co. G, 13th South Carolina		Jul. 1863	Killed in action per the Charleston Mercury, July 1863	Unknown
Brown, Nathaniel	Co. E, 56th Virginia		7/11/1863	Hollywood Cemetery, Richmond, Va., reburial lists	Richmond, VA
Brown, Owen Neil	Maj., 37th North Carolina	1836	7/24/1863	Mortally wounded-died at unknown place in Gettysburg	Unknown
Brown, William	Co. F, 15th South Carolina	1843	7/2/1863	Killed in action	Unknown
Brown, William	Co. A, 13th South Carolina		7/1/1863	Killed in action	Unknown

NAME	REGIMENT	BIRTH	DEATH	COMMENT	BURIAL
Brown, William Dawson	Capt., Chesapeake Artillery (Md.)		7/11/1863	Mortally wounded and reinterred at Green Mount Cemetery	Baltimore, MD
Brown, William S.	Co. C, 17th Georgia		7/2/1863	Killed in action	Unknown
Browning, John	Co. D, 5th Florida		7/4/1863	Killed in action	Unknown
Browning, John C.	Page's Artillery (Va.)	1830	7/1/1863	Killed in action	Unknown
Brownlee, William Alexander	Lt., Co. H, 10th Alabama	1840	7/12/1863	Hollywood Cemetery, Richmond, Va., reburial lists	Richmond, VA
Brownlee, William H.	Co. F, 48th Virginia	7/10/1834	7/25/1863	Mortally wounded; obit. Abingdon Virginian, November 13th, 29yrs, 15d	Unknown
Broy, Charles William	Co. G, 49th Virginia	1841	Jul. 1863	Missing in action and presumed dead	Unknown
Broyles, William Yancy	Co. K, 49th Virginia	1825	Jul. 1863	Missing in action and presumed dead	Unknown
Bruce, E. Mack	Co. K, 44th Georgia		7/1/1863	Killed in action	Unknown
Bruce, William	Co. A, 1st Maryland Battalion		7/3/1853	Killed in action	Unknown
Bryan, N.F.	Co. D, 26th North Carolina	1838	7/3/1863	Killed in action	Unknown
Bryan, W.C.	Co. A, 2nd Florida	1834	7/2/1863	Killed in action	Unknown
Bryant, Charles W.	Co. A, 38th Virginia		7/3/1863	Killed in action per the Richmond Sentinel, August 1, 1863	Unknown
Bryant, Dempsey H.	Co. E, 2nd Florida	1834	10/23/1863	Died of wounds at Ft. Delaware, DE	Finn's Point, NJ
Bryant, Felix M.	Sgt., Co. F, 8th Florida	1837	7/2/1863	Hollywood Cemetery, Richmond, Va., reburial lists	Richmond, VA
Bryant, George Andrew	Co. C, 43rd North Carolina	1826	7/28/1863	Oakwood Cemetery, Raleigh, NC, reburial list	Raleigh, NC
Bryant, Peter	Co. I, 57th Virginia		Jul. 1863	Killed in action, July 1-3	Unknown
Bryant, Rowland [Roland]	Co. E, 13th South Carolina	6/17/1841	7/3/1863	Killed in action	Unknown
Bryant, Stephen Nichols	Co. K, 1st North Carolina	1832	7/17/1863	Oakwood Cemetery, Raleigh, NC, reburial list	Raleigh, NC
Bryant, Thomas H.	Co. F, 18th Virginia	1832	7/3/1863	Killed in action	Unknown
Bryant, William O.	Co. B, 55th North Carolina		7/1/1863	Killed in action	Unknown
Bryens, George H.	3rd Co., Washington Arty. (La.)	1845	7/3/1863	Killed in action per the Richmond Sentinel, July 17, 1863	Unknown
Bryson, Henry J.	Co. F, 3rd South Carolina	1843	7/2/1863	Killed in action	Unknown
Buchan, Joseph D.	Co. G, 8th Florida	1831	7/31/1863	Hollywood Cemetery, Richmond, Va., reburial lists	Richmond, VA
Buchanan, Benson F.	Co. D, 5th Virginia		7/3/1863	Killed in action	Unknown
Buchanan, Henry	Co. G, 26th North Carolina		7/1/1863	Killed in action	Unknown
Buchanan, James M.	Co. K, 48th Alabama		Jul. 1863	Killed in action, July 1-3	Unknown
Buchanan, Samuel	Co. H, 37th Virginia	1/4/1842	7/3/1863	Hollywood Cemetery, Richmond, Va., reburial lists	Richmond, VA
Buckner, Mike W.	Co. B, 8th Alabama	1837	7/2/1863	Killed in action	Unknown
Budd, Augustus W.	Co. G, 8th Georgia		7/3/1863	Killed in action	Unknown
Buffkin, William H.	Co. F, 1st South Carolina		7/1/1863	Killed in action	Unknown
Buford, Parham Morgan	Co. G, 11th Mississippi	1843	8/15/1863	Hollywood Cemetery, Richmond, Va., reburial lists	Richmond, VA
Bugg, Lucius Tandy	Co. C, 14th Virginia	7/23/1843	7/3/1863	Killed in action	Unknown
Bulger, L.P.	Co. B, 8th Alabama	1844	7/2/1863	Killed in action	Unknown

NAME	REGIMENT	BIRTH	DEATH	COMMENT	BURIAL
Bull, William A.	Co. A, 3rd Arkansas	11/20/1843	7/12/1863	Mortally wounded–died at unknown place in Gettysburg	Unknown
Bull, William H.	Co. G, 52nd Virginia	1842	7/2/1863	Killed in action	Unknown
Bullard, Emory	Co. C, 20th North Carolina	1843	7/1/1863	Killed in action	Unknown
Bullard, N.D.	Co. E, 51st Georgia		7/2/1863	Killed in action	Unknown
Bullen, Jesse	Co. H, 21st North Carolina	1837	7/2/1863	Killed in action	Unknown
Bullis, Simeon	Co. C, 26th South Carolina		9/2/1863	Died as POW at David's Island, NY	Cypress Hills, NY
Bullman, H. Spencer	Co. C, 13th South Carolina	1844	7/2/1863	Killed in action	Unknown
Bumgarner, A.	Co. C, 26th North Carolina	1833	7/1/1863	Killed in action	Unknown
Burch, Charles	Co. I, 48th Georgia	1827	7/2/1863	Killed in action	Unknown
Burch, James Raney	Co. A, 18th Virginia		7/3/1863	Killed in action	Unknown
Burch, Joel S.	Co. I, 9th Georgia	1843	7/2/1863	Killed in action	Unknown
Burganer, Isaac	Lt., Co. F, 3rd Arkansas	1839	7/9/1863	Mortally wounded–died at unknown place in Gettysburg	Unknown
Burge, James Edward	Co. E, 18th Virginia	10/18/1829	7/3/1863	Killed in action	Unknown
Burgess, Franklin M.	Co. H, 15th South Carolina		7/16/1863	Magnolia Cemetery, Charleston, SC, reburial list	Charleston, SC
Burgess, William Alvin	Co. F, 22nd Georgia	10/7/1836	7/2/1863	Killed in action	Unknown
Burgin, John A.	Lt., Co. K, 11th North Carolina	1839	7/3/1863	Oakwood Cemetery, Raleigh, NC, reburial list	Raleigh, NC
Burgin, John W.	Lt., Co. E, 1st North Carolina	1839	7/3/1863	Killed in action	Unknown
Burgwyn, Henry King	Col., 26th North Carolina	10/3/1841	7/1/1863	Killed in action	Raleigh, NC
Burke, Martin V.	Co. A, 22nd Georgia		7/11/1863	Hollywood Cemetery, Richmond, Va., reburial lists	Richmond, VA
Burkett, John	Co. D, 13th Georgia		7/6/1863	Mortally wounded–died at unknown place in Gettysburg	Unknown
Burkhalter, Isaac	Capt., Co. G, 50th Georgia	10/29/1830	7/2/1863	Laurel Grove Cemetery, Savannah, Ga., reburial list	Savannah, GA
Burkhalter, Joseph Clinton	Co. E, 61st Georgia	1842	7/1/1863	Laurel Grove Cemetery, Savannah, Ga., reburial list	Savannah, GA
Burly, James Calvin	Co. I, 12th Mississippi	1/25/1836	7/30/1863	Hollywood Cemetery, Richmond, Va., reburial lists	Richmond, VA
Burnette, Luceillus S.	Cpl., Co. I, 11th Mississippi	1841	7/26/1863	Mortally wounded and died at Chester, PA	Phil. National Cem.
Burney, James	Co. D, 5th Florida		7/3/1863	Killed in action	Unknown
Burns, James Hall	Capt., Co. E, 6th North Carolina	1840	7/1/1863	Killed in action; reinterred in NC on 10/4/1866	North Carolina
Burns, James J.	Co. G, 42nd Mississippi		8/6/1863	Mortally wounded and died at Chester, PA	Phil. National Cem.
Burns, John W.	Co. C, 18th Virginia		7/3/1863	Killed in action per the Richmond Sentinel, July 30, 1863	Unknown
Burnside, James Pierson	Co. K, 48th Georgia	2/1/1834	7/2/1863	Killed in action	Unknown
Burnside, John Mitchell Dooley	Lt., Co. K, 48th Georgia	5/5/1835	7/7/1863	Hollywood Cemetery, Richmond, Va., reburial lists	Richmond, VA
Burrell, Butler	Co. F, 1st South Carolina Cavalry	11/30/1826	7/3/1863	Killed in action	Unknown

NAME	REGIMENT	BIRTH	DEATH	COMMENT	BURIAL
Burress, Charles W.	Co. G, 24th Virginia	1835	8/3/1863	Hollywood Cemetery, Richmond, Va., reburial lists	Richmond, VA
Burroughs, Cornelius T.	Cpl., Co. H, 8th Florida	1838	7/16/1863	Mortally wounded, July 2nd, and buried on the Jacob Schwartz Farm	Unknown
Burrow, Charles Wesley	Co. A, 6th North Carolina	1840	7/2/1863	Missing in action and presumed dead	Unknown
Burruss, William H.	Lt., Co. H, 53rd Virginia		8/15/1863	Mortally wounded per the Richmond Sentinel, August 8, 1863	Unknown
Burt, Joseph H.	Co. D, 26th North Carolina	1837	7/1/1863	Killed in action	Unknown
Burton, John T.	Lt., Co. E, 56th Virginia	1839	Jul. 1863	Mortally wounded-died at unknown place in Gettysburg	Unknown
Butler, Charles W.	Sgt., Co. B, 1st Texas	1837	7/1/1863	Killed in action	Unknown
Butler, George H.	Co. G, 49th Virginia		7/3/1863	Hollywood Cemetery, Richmond, Va., reburial lists	Richmond, VA
Butler, Lucien	Co. F, 50th Georgia	1840	8/7/1863	Hollywood Cemetery, Richmond, Va., reburial lists	Richmond, VA
Butler, Thomas Osborne Loundes	Sgt., Co. I, 2nd South Carolina Cavalry	4/29/1841	7/3/1863	Killed in action	Greenville, SC
Butler, William C.	Sgt., Co. F, 2nd Florida	1837	8/15/1863	Hollywood Cemetery, Richmond, Va., reburial lists	Richmond, VA
Butler, William Calvin	Co. E, 3rd South Carolina	1840	7/2/1863	Killed in action	Unknown
Butler, William R.	Cpl., Co. H, 4th Georgia		7/1/1863	Killed in action	Unknown
Butler, William R.	Cpl., Co. G, 3rd Georgia		7/2/1863	Killed in action	Unknown
Butts, Frank	Co. K, 61st Georgia		7/1/1863	Laurel Grove Cemetery, Savannah, Ga., reburial list	Savannah, GA
Butts, Walter	Lt., Co. F, 9th Virginia	1841	7/11/1863	Hollywood Cemetery, Richmond, Va., reburial lists	Richmond, VA
Buzbee, John	Co. I, 17th Mississippi	1842	7/2/1863	Killed in action	Unknown
Buzhardt, Milton P.	Lt., Co. B, 3rd South Carolina	1837	7/2/1863	Magnolia Cemetery, Charleston, SC, reburial list	Charleston, SC
Byers, J.B.	Co. E, 5th Alabama		7/24/1863	Mortally wounded-died at unknown place in Gettysburg	Unknown
Bynum, James Franklin	Co. H, 52nd North Carolina	1841	7/3/1863	Missing in action and presumed dead	Unknown
Byrd, Ed	Co. G, 15th Alabama	1841	Jul. 1863	Killed in action	Unknown
Byrnes, F.M.	Co. A, 2nd Florida		7/2/1863	Killed in action	Unknown
Cabiness, Marion C.	Co. D, 2nd Georgia Battalion		7/7/1863	Mortally wounded-died at unknown place in Gettysburg	Unknown
Cadle, James	Co. F, 7th South Carolina		7/2/1863	Killed in action	Unknown
Caffey, Hooper Patrick	Co. H, 3rd Alabama	3/26/1837	9/13/1863	Hollywood Cemetery, Richmond, Va., reburial lists	Richmond, VA
Caho, William A.	Lt., Co. I, 1st Virginia	1836	7/31/1863	Mortally wounded and died at Chester, PA	Phil. National Cem.
Cain, James R.	Co. A, 17th Mississippi	1839	7/2/1863	Killed in action	Unknown
Caldwell, Benjamin	Co. E, 2nd North Carolina Battalion	10/20/1830	7/2/1863	Killed in action	Unknown
Caldwell, C. Frank	Co. F, 57th North Carolina	1831	7/1/1863	Missing in action and presumed dead	Unknown
Caldwell, Henry C.	Co. H, 10th Alabama		7/3/1863	Killed in action	Unknown
Caldwell, John	Lt., Co. E, 33rd North Carolina	5/24/1845	7/2/1863	Killed in action	Unknown
Caldwell, R.W.	Co. F, 57th North Carolina		10/12/1863	Died of wounds at Ft. Delaware, DE	Finn's Point, NJ

NAME	REGIMENT	BIRTH	DEATH	COMMENT	BURIAL
Calfee, Henderson French	Co. G, 24th Virginia	1841	7/7/1863	Mortally wounded–died at unknown place in Gettysburg	Unknown
Calhoun, John C.	Co. I, 9th Louisiana	1835	7/2/1863	Killed in action	Unknown
Calhoun, Levi Harris	Co. E, 5th Florida	1837	7/3/1863	Killed in action	Unknown
Calhoun, Nahi B.	Co. C, 45th North Carolina		7/1/1863	Killed in action	Unknown
Califor, George W.	Co. E, 23rd North Carolina		7/1/1863	Killed in action	Unknown
Callahan, Sherrod Washington	Lt., Co. B, 7th South Carolina	6/3/1831	7/18/1863	Mortally wounded–died at unknown place in Gettysburg	Unknown
Callais, Josiah	Co. E, 28th North Carolina		7/25/1863	Hollywood Cemetery, Richmond, Va., reburial lists	Richmond, VA
Callaway, Isaac W.	Capt., Co. K, 22nd Georgia	4/30/1825	7/18/1863	Mortally wounded–died at unknown place in Gettysburg	Unknown
Callcote, Alexander Daniel	Lt. Col., 3rd Virginia	Jun. 1830	7/3/1863	Killed in action	Unknown
Calvert, Robert H.	Co. E, 4th Virginia		7/3/1863	Killed in action	Unknown
Camack, Samuel	Co. E, 15th South Carolina	1821	7/2/1863	Killed in action	Unknown
Camak, Thomas	Maj., Cobb's Legion (Ga.)	9/13/1829	7/2/1863	Killed in action	Columbus, GA
Camden, Joseph S.	Co. H, 27th Virginia	1844	8/31/1863	Died as POW at David's Island, NY	Cypress Hills, NY
Cameron, James F.	Co. C, 11th Alabama		7/2/1863	Killed in action	Unknown
Cameron, John	Co. E, 44th Alabama	1825	7/2/1863	Killed in action	Unknown
Campbell, Adolphus L.	Co. C, 28th North Carolina	1836	7/18/1863	Oakwood Cemetery, Raleigh, NC, reburial list	Raleigh, NC
Campbell, Benjamin A.	Lt., Co. G, 1st Texas		7/2/1863	Killed in action	Unknown
Campbell, Burgess A.	Co. H, 4th North Carolina	1844	7/3/1863	Killed in action	Unknown
Campbell, D.P.	Co. F, 28th Virginia		Jul. 1863	Killed in action per the Richmond Sentinel, July 30, 1863	Unknown
Campbell, Elcanah M.	Blount's Battery (Va.)		7/3/1863	Killed in action	Unknown
Campbell, Harmon	Co. B, 23rd North Carolina	1838	7/13/1863	Mortally wounded–died at unknown place in Gettysburg	Unknown
Campbell, John	Co. G, 18th Virginia	1825	7/3/1863	Killed in action	Unknown
Campbell, Joseph A.	Co. K, 7th North Carolina	1838	8/15/1863	Mortally wounded and died at Chester, PA	Phil. National Cem.
Campbell, Malcolm M.	Co. D, 47th Alabama		8/2/1863	Mortally wounded and died at Chester, PA	Phil. National Cem.
Campbell, Martin R.	Adjutant, 48th Mississippi	1841	7/3/1863	Hollywood Cemetery, Richmond, Va., reburial lists	Richmond, VA
Campbell, N.G.	Co. H, 38th North Carolina	1844	Jul. 1863	Missing in action and presumed dead	Unknown
Campbell, Thomas J.	Cpl., Co. H, 11th North Carolina	1840	7/1/1863	Killed in action	Unknown
Campbell, Thomas K.	Lt., Co. B, 2nd Georgia Battalion		7/2/1863	Killed in action	Unknown
Canaday, John D.	Cpl., Co. E, 7th Virginia	1834	7/3/1863	Killed in action	Unknown
Canady, J.Wesley	Co. I, 3rd South Carolina		7/23/1863	Mortally wounded per the Charleston Mercury, August 28, 1863	Unknown
Cannady, James	Sgt., Co. F, 1st South Carolina	1832	7/2/1863	Killed in action	Unknown
Cannon, William Henry	Co. B, 42nd Mississippi	1829	Jul. 1863	Died of wounds at Ft. Delaware, DE	Finn's Point, NJ
Capel, Lemuel W.	Co. H, 43rd North Carolina	1844	7/17/1863	Mortally wounded–died at unknown place in Gettysburg	Unknown

NAME	REGIMENT	BIRTH	DEATH	COMMENT	BURIAL
Capps, Doctor	Co. C, 45th North Carolina	1830	7/1/1863	Killed in action	Unknown
Card, Julius J.	Cpl., Co. B, 12th Georgia		7/2/1863	Killed in action	Unknown
Cardin, William B.	Co. E, 19th Virginia	1841	7/3/1863	Killed in action	Unknown
Caricofe, John H. Jr.	Co. I, 5th Virginia		7/10/1863	Hollywood Cemetery, Richmond, Va., reburial lists	Richmond, VA
Carlisle, William R.	Co. D, 43rd North Carolina	1837	7/1/1863	Killed in action	Unknown
Carlton, Cornelius M.	Co. B, 37th North Carolina	1844	7/6/1863	Mortally wounded-died at unknown place in Gettysburg	Unknown
Carlton, Elias	Co. C, 9th Louisiana	1844	Jul. 1863	Missing in action and presumed dead	Unknown
Carlton, John	Co. D, 6th North Carolina	1829	7/1/1863	Killed in action on either July 1st or 2nd	Unknown
Carlton, Walton C.	Co. C, 22nd Georgia	1843	7/2/1863	Mortally wounded, July 2nd, and died the same day	Unknown
Carmichael, Peter H.	Sgt., Co. H, 17th Georgia		7/2/1863	Killed in action	Unknown
Carneal, Henry	Co. D, 53rd Virginia		7/3/1863	Killed in action	Unknown
Carnes, James Canada	Co. H, 8th Georgia	1841	8/31/1863	Laurel Grove Cemetery, Savannah, GA., reburial list	Savannah, GA
Carpenter, Churchwell	Co. D, 28th North Carolina	1844	7/3/1863	Killed in action	Unknown
Carpenter, F.T.	Co. B, 28th North Carolina	1841	7/18/1863	Mortally wounded-died at unknown place in Gettysburg	Unknown
Carpenter, Henry	Co. I, 11th North Carolina	1823	7/31/1863	Mortally wounded and died at Baltimore, MD-buried there	Baltimore, MD
Carpenter, Jacob John	Co. I, 11th North Carolina	1/7/1838	7/21/1863	Mortally wounded-died at unknown place in Gettysburg	Unknown
Carpenter, John F.	Co. E, 19th Virginia		Jul. 1863	Mortally wounded and died on unknown date	Unknown
Carpenter, Joseph	Co. G, 34th North Carolina	9/17/1824	7/3/1863	Killed in action; reinterred at Zion Methodist Church Cemetery, Lincolnton, NC	Lincoln Co., NC
Carpenter, Michael	Co. K, 53rd North Carolina	1836	7/1/1863	Killed in action	Unknown
Carpenter, Owen Francis	Co. L, 2nd Mississippi	6/23/1837	7/1/1863	Killed in action	Unknown
Carpenter, Pinkney D.	Co. G, 16th North Carolina	1842	7/4/1863	Mortally wounded, July 3rd, and died the next day	Unknown
Carpenter, William D.	Sgt., Co. B, 23rd North Carolina	11/11/1831	7/1/1863	Killed in action; reinterred at St. Matthew's United Church of Christ, Lincolnton, NC	Lincoln Co., NC
Carr, Thomas	Sgt., Co. E, 11th Mississippi	1837	7/3/1863	Killed in action	Unknown
Carr, Thomas W.	Co. G, 47th North Carolina	1836	7/3/1863	Killed in action	Unknown
Carr, William A.	Lt., Co. E, 5th North Carolina	1841	7/1/1863	Oakwood Cemetery, Raleigh, NC, reburial list	Raleigh, NC
Carr, William G.	Co. F, 48th Georgia		7/2/1863	Killed in action	Unknown
Carrell, Rawley B.	Co. E, 45th North Carolina	1839	7/3/1863	Killed in action	Unknown
Carroll, George L.	Co. H, 48th Virginia	1825	7/18/1863	Hollywood Cemetery, Richmond, Va., reburial lists	Richmond, VA
Carroll, John	Co. F, 6th Louisiana	1821	7/2/1863	Killed in action	Unknown
Carroll, Stephen S.	Sgt., Co. B, 3rd North Carolina		7/2/1863	Killed in action	Unknown
Carroll, William A.	Co. K, 22nd Georgia		7/2/1863	Killed in action	Unknown

NAME	REGIMENT	BIRTH	DEATH	COMMENT	BURIAL
Carter, Benjamin	Co. C, 11th North Carolina	1840	Jul. 1863	Killed in action	Unknown
Carter, Benjamin Franklin	Lt. Col., 4th Texas	1831	7/21/1863	Mortally wounded, July 2nd, and died at Chambersburg, PA, interred at Cedar Grove Cemetery	Chambersburg, PA
Carter, Benjamin T.	Co. K, 13th North Carolina	1828	8/29/1863	Mortally wounded and died at Chester, PA	Phil. National Cem.
Carter, Daniel M.	Co. E, 26th North Carolina	1839	7/20/1863	Mortally wounded and died at Jordan Springs Hospital, Winchester, VA	Winchester, VA
Carter, Elias M.	Co. B, 20th North Carolina	1833	7/1/1863	Killed in action	Unknown
Carter, James B.	Co. H, 45th North Carolina	1836	7/3/1863	Killed in action	Unknown
Carter, James L.	Co. C, 53rd Virginia		7/3/1863	Killed in action	Unknown
Carter, James T.	Sgt., Co. B, 5th Texas		7/31/1863	Hollywood Cemetery, Richmond, Va., reburial lists	Richmond, VA
Carter, James William	Col., 13th Mississippi	1831	7/2/1863	Hollywood Cemetery, Richmond, Va., reburial lists	Richmond, VA
Carter, Jesse J.	Co. F, 34th North Carolina	1843	7/1/1863	Killed in action	Unknown
Carter, John M.	Co. F, 45th North Carolina	1841	7/1/1863	Killed in action	Unknown
Carter, Josiah	Cpl., Co. D, 13th Georgia		7/22/1863	Mortally wounded-died at unknown place in Gettysburg	Unknown
Carter, Lewis W.	Co. C, 52nd North Carolina	1836	7/27/1863	Hollywood Cemetery, Richmond, Va., reburial lists	Richmond, VA
Carter, S.J.N.	Cpl., Co. E, 8th South Carolina		7/2/1863	Killed in action	Unknown
Carter, Sidney	Lt., Co. A, 14th South Carolina	1832	7/8/1863	Died of wounds received July 1	Unknown
Carter, Thomas B.	Co. F, 45th North Carolina		7/1/1863	Killed in action	Unknown
Carter, William F.	Co. D, 10th Alabama		7/2/1863	Killed in action	Unknown
Cary, George Edward	Sgt., Co. G, 49th Virginia	3/10/1842	7/3/1863	Killed in action	Unknown
Casey, Brian	Letcher Artillery (Va.)		7/2/1863	Killed in action	Unknown
Casey, Thomas	Sgt., Co. B, 6th Louisiana	1838	7/30/1863	Hollywood Cemetery, Richmond, Va., reburial lists	Richmond, VA
Casey, William Parker	Brooks Arty. (S.C) Rhett's	1843	7/2/1863	Killed in action per the Richmond Sentinel, July 27, 1863	Unknown
Cash, Richard E.	Co. E, 5th Florida		7/3/1863	Killed in action	Unknown
Cashin, John	Co. I, 8th Alabama		7/3/1863	Killed in action	Unknown
Caskey, J.P.	Co. I, 12th South Carolina		7/1/1863	Killed in action	Unknown
Cason, William G.	Co. H, 57th Virginia	1825	7/17/1863	Hollywood Cemetery, Richmond, Va., reburial lists	Richmond, VA
Casper, Joseph W.	Co. C, 11th North Carolina	1842	7/1/1863	Killed in action	Unknown
Cassell, Benjamin Franklin	Capt., Co. C, 18th Mississippi	11/20/1836	7/2/1863	Killed in action	Unknown
Casson, James Hampton	Co. A, 2nd South Carolina	1840	7/7/1863	Magnolia Cemetery, Charleston, SC, reburial list	Charleston, SC
Castlebury, Judson C.	Cpl., Co. I, 6th North Carolina	1839	7/2/1863	Killed in action	Unknown
Castleman, James W.	Sgt., Co. H, 3rd Arkansas	1843	Jul. 1863	Hollywood Cemetery, Richmond, Va., reburial lists	Richmond, VA
Caswell, Robert N.	Co. F, 26th North Carolina	1828	7/1/1863	Killed in action	Unknown
Cates, John R.	Co. E, 1st Tennessee	1838	9/21/1863	Mortally wounded and died at Chester, PA	Phil. National Cem.

NAME	REGIMENT	BIRTH	DEATH	COMMENT	BURIAL
Cathey, Robert A.	Cpl., Co. I, 11th North Carolina	1837	7/3/1863	Killed in action	Unknown
Cato, Cullen	Co. B, 59th Georgia		7/2/1863	Killed in action	Unknown
Cator, William B.	Co. G, 1st Maryland Battalion		7/1/1863	Killed in action	Unknown
Causey, Robertson [Robinson] C.	Sgt., Co. C, 45th North Carolina	1836	7/20/1863	Oakwood Cemetery, Raleigh, NC, reburial list	Raleigh, NC
Cauthen, John H.	Co. H, 44th Georgia	1838	11/30/1863	Mortally wounded, July 1, and died as POW	Unknown
Center, James W.	Co. D, 20th Georgia		7/2/1863	Killed in action	Unknown
Center, Wilson	Co. A, 28th North Carolina	1837	Jul. 1863	Killed in action, Jul 1-3; surname appears as Senter in some records	Unknown
Certain, F.M.	Co. H, 47th North Carolina	1841	Jul. 1863	Mortally wounded, July 3rd, and died on unknown date	Unknown
Chadick, Richard	Cpl., Co. H, 1st Virginia	1834	7/3/1863	Killed in action	Unknown
Chalfinch, John H.	Fraser's Battery (Ga.)		7/3/1863	Killed in action	Unknown
Chalker, William H.	Co. A, 48th Georgia	1842	7/16/1863	Hollywood Cemetery, Richmond, Va., reburial lists	Richmond, VA
Chambers, Daniel Gibbes	Co. B, 1st South Carolina	1845	7/1/1863	Killed in action	Unknown
Chambers, James T.	Co. A, 24th Georgia		Jul. 1863	Killed in action per the Augusta Chronicle & Sentinel, August 13, 1863	Unknown
Chambers, Thomas J.	Lt., Co. D, 13th North Carolina	1839	7/1/1863	Killed in action	Unknown
Champion, Charles William	Lt., Co. G, 23rd North Carolina	1837	7/1/1863	Oakwood Cemetery, Raleigh, NC, reburial list	Raleigh, NC
Chandler, Andrew J.	Co. A, 28th North Carolina		7/3/1863	Killed in action	Unknown
Chandler, Jackson A.	Co. B, 5th Alabama Battalion		Jul. 1863	Missing in action and presumed dead	Unknown
Chandler, William S.J.	Co. A, 1st Maryland Battalion		7/9/1863	Hollywood Cemetery, Richmond, Va., reburial lists	Richmond, VA
Chaney, Jacob H.	Co. K, 13th South Carolina	1841	8/9/1863	Magnolia Cemetery, Charleston, SC, reburial list	Charleston, SC
Chapman, G.W.	Co. G, 3rd Georgia		7/2/1863	Laurel Grove Cemetery, Savannah, Ga., reburial list	Savannah, GA
Chapman, J.C.	21st North Carolina		7/6/1863	Mortally wounded-died at unknown place in Gettysburg	Unknown
Chapman, Joshua	Co. A, 6th North Carolina		9/19/1863	Mortally wounded, July 1st, died at Staunton, VA	Staunton, VA
Chapman, Richard Franklin	Lt., Co. E, 9th Virginia		7/15/1863	Obituary Richmond Dispatch, November 7, 1863	Unknown
Chappel, Franklin T.	Sgt., Co. C, 26th North Carolina	1841	8/29/1863	Oakwood Cemetery, Raleigh, NC, reburial list	Raleigh, NC
Chappell, Jesse A.	Co. F, 53rd Virginia		7/3/1863	Missing in action and presumed dead	Unknown
Chappell, Joel	Co. F, 12th South Carolina	1835	7/17/1863	Mortally wounded-died at unknown place in Gettysburg	Unknown
Chappell, Rolin	Co. E, 52nd North Carolina	1817	7/22/1863	Mortally wounded per the Richmond Sentinel, August 11, 1863	Phil. National Cem.
Chatten, William B.	Co. A, 38th Virginia	1840	8/24/1863	Died of wounds at Ft. Delaware, DE	Finn's Point, NJ
Cheatham, Samuel O.	Co. D, 14th Virginia		7/17/1863	Hollywood Cemetery, Richmond, Va., reburial lists	Richmond, VA
Cheaves, Thomas Worrel	Co. B, 47th North Carolina	2/19/1841	7/3/1863	Killed in action	Unknown

NAME	REGIMENT	BIRTH	DEATH	COMMENT	BURIAL
Cheek, Allen Jasper	Lt., Co. C, 6th North Carolina	1836	7/1/1863	Killed in action	Unknown
Cheek, Jesse H.	Co. G, 28th North Carolina	1844	7/16/1863	Mortally wounded-died at unknown place in Gettysburg	Unknown
Cheek, John D.	Co. E, 26th North Carolina	1838	7/24/1863	Mortally wounded-died at unknown place in Gettysburg	Unknown
Cheek, John P.	Co. E, 3rd South Carolina Battalion	1828	7/2/1863	Killed in action per the Charleston Mercury, August 28, 1863	Unknown
Cheesborough, John Weaver	Lt., Co. A, Cobb's Legion Infantry	12/19/1837	7/5/1863	Laurel Grove Cemetery, Savannah, Ga., reburial list	Savannah, GA
Childress, William Y.	Co. D, 14th Virginia		7/3/1863	Missing in action and presumed dead	Unknown
Childs, John C.	Co. C, 14th Virginia	1844	8/9/1863	Mortally wounded and died at Chester, PA	Phil. National Cem.
Chipley, William Marshall	Co. C, 4th North Carolina	6/17/1843	7/3/1863	Killed in action	Unknown
Choate, Jasper E.	Co. E, 13th Mississippi	1840	7/2/1863	Killed in action	Unknown
Choate, Sowell J.	Co. F, 22nd North Carolina	1841	7/2/1863	Mortally wounded and died the same day	Unknown
Choplin, Sidney	Co. F, 28th North Carolina	10/2/1836	7/3/1863	Killed in action	Unknown
Chrisenbery, Thomas Cope	Co. D, 11th North Carolina	1833	7/1/1863	Killed in action; surname may be Christenbury	Unknown
Christian, William T.	Co. H, 1st Tennessee	1842	7/3/1863	Killed in action	Unknown
Christie, Daniel Harvey	Col., 23rd North Carolina	3/28/1833	7/17/1863	Mortally wounded, July 1st, and died at Winchester, VA	Winchester, VA
Christin, L.R.	Co. A, 2nd Florida		7/2/1863	Killed in action	Unknown
Christy, James F.	Co. E, 11th North Carolina	1837	9/4/1863	Mortally wounded, July 1, and died at home in Raleigh, North Carolina	Raleigh, NC
Churchill, Jordon G.	Co. K, 8th Florida	1833	Jul. 1863	Missing in action, July 3rd, and presumed dead	Unknown
Clanton, John Beatty	Lt., Co. E, 11th North Carolina	6/20/1831	7/27/1863	Mortally wounded-died at unknown place in Gettysburg	Unknown
Clark, Albert Henry	Co. F, 42nd Mississippi	2/9/1844	7/17/1863	Mortally wounded-died at unknown place at Gettysburg; son of Thomas Goode Clark	Unknown
Clark, Archibald A.	Co. H, 26th North Carolina		7/1/1863	Killed in action	Unknown
Clark, D.P.	Co. A, 22nd North Carolina	1844	7/22/1863	Mortally wounded per the Richmond Sentinel, August 11, 1863	Phil. National Cem.
Clark, Ellis A.	Co. K, 14th Virginia	1835	7/3/1863	Killed in action	Unknown
Clark, G.W.	Co. G, 53rd Virginia		7/3/1863	Killed in action	Unknown
Clark, George McIntosh	Maj., 34th North Carolina	1838	Jul. 1863	Killed in action; buried in front of Gettysburg College-remains not located after war	Unknown
Clark, James A.	Co. E, 11th North Carolina	1825	7/1/1863	Killed in action	Unknown
Clark, James D.	Co.C, 1st Virginia		7/22/1863	Died of wounds at Ft. Delaware, DE	Finn's Point, NJ
Clark, Jonathan	Co. F, 42nd Mississippi	1/28/1842	7/1/1863	Killed in action; son of Thomas Goode Clark	Unknown
Clark, Joseph	3rd Co., Washington Arty. (La.)		7/3/1863	Killed in action per the Richmond Sentinel, July 17, 1863	Unknown
Clark, Nathaniel Alexander	Co. K, 11th Mississippi	1843	7/3/1863	Killed in action	Unknown

NAME	REGIMENT	BIRTH	DEATH	COMMENT	BURIAL
Clark, Samuel C.	Co. D, 10th Alabama	1838	7/8/1863	Hollywood Cemetery, Richmond, Va., reburial lists	Richmond, VA
Clark, Thomas Goode	Capt., Co. F, 42nd Mississippi	10/4/1815	7/1/163	Killed in action	Unknown
Clarke, John D.	Co. D, 53rd Virginia		7/3/1863	Killed in action	Unknown
Clarke, M.T	Co. A, 4th North Carolina	1835	Jul. 1863	Mortally wounded-died at unknown place in Gettysburg	Unknown
Clarke, Reuben W.L.	Co. D, 3rd Georgia		7/2/1863	Killed in action	Unknown
Clay, Henry E.	Co. F, 34th North Carolina	1842	8/17/1863	Mortally wounded-died at unknown place in Gettysburg	Unknown
Claybrook, Samuel	Co. H, 22nd North Carolina	1840	7/27/1863	Mortally wounded and died at Chester, PA	Phil. National Cem.
Clayton, John Kerr	Co. E, 56th Virginia	1836	7/3/1863	Killed in action	Unknown
Clayton, Julian T.	Co. D, 3rd Virginia	1843	7/3/1863	Killed in action	Unknown
Clegg, Thomas D.	Co. I, 32nd North Carolina	1838	7/3/1863	Killed in action	Unknown
Clem, Michael	Carpenter's Battery (Va.)	9/2/1833	7/2/1863	Hollywood Cemetery, Richmond, Va., reburial lists	Richmond, VA
Clement, A.M.	Cpl., Co. E, 17th Mississippi	1832	7/2/1863	Killed in action	Unknown
Clements, Green W.	Cpl., Co. A, 38th Virginia	1832	7/3/1863	Killed in action per the Richmond Sentinel, August 1, 1863	Unknown
Clements, Mathew J.	Co. I, 7th Virginia	1838	7/3/1863	Killed in action	Unknown
Clements, Thomas William	Sgt., Co. D, 8th Georgia	8/11/1840	7/7/1863	Hollywood Cemetery, Richmond, Va., reburial lists	Richmond, VA
Clements, William J.	Co. C, 13th Georgia		7/1/1863	Killed in action	Unknown
Cliett, Elijah W.	Co. D, 20th Georgia		Jul. 1863	Hollywood Cemetery, Richmond, Va., reburial lists	Richmond, VA
Clifford, Joseph Calvin	Co. G, 5th North Carolina	11/20/1839	7/1/1863	Hollywood Cemetery, Richmond, Va., reburial lists	Richmond, VA
Cline, Julius Calvin	Co. F, 23rd North Carolina	7/15/1837	7/1/1863	Killed in action	Unknown
Cline, William H.	Co. B, 20th North Carolina	1842	7/1/1863	Killed in action	Unknown
Cline, William Pinkney	Co. E, 32nd North Carolina	2/28/1829	7/3/1863	Died of wounds on or about July 3rd	Unknown
Clink, Robert H.	Co. K, 5th Virginia		7/10/1863	Mortally wounded and died at Winchester, VA	Winchester, VA
Clonts, S. Mortimore	Co. F, 26th North Carolina	1841	11/8/863	Mortally wounded, July 1st, and died at Staunton, VA	Staunton, VA
Closs, Thomas Oliver	Co. G, 4th Texas	1833	7/2/1863	Killed in action	Unknown
Clyde, Charles E.	Sgt., Co. C, Phillips Legion (Ga.)		7/20/1863	Hollywood Cemetery, Richmond, Va., reburial lists	Richmond, VA
Coan, S.C.	Co. G, 2nd South Carolina		7/23/1863	Mortally wounded-died at unknown place in Gettysburg	Unknown
Cobb, James	Co. K, 11th Mississippi	1832	7/3/1863	Killed in action	Unknown
Cobb, Joseph	Co. G, 61st Virginia	1843	7/15/1863	Mortally wounded and died at Winchester, VA	Winchester, VA
Cobb, Livingston G.	Co. H, 45th North Carolina	1826	8/16/1863	Oakwood Cemetery, Raleigh, NC, reburial list	Raleigh, NC
Cobb, William D.	Co. I, 2nd Mississippi	1840	7/2/1863	Mortally wounded, July 1st, and died the next day	Unknown

NAME	REGIMENT	BIRTH	DEATH	COMMENT	BURIAL
Cochran, John Scot	Lt., Co. D, 5th Florida	1839	11/29/1863	Died of wounds received July 2nd at Batltimore, MD	Baltimore, MD
Cochran, William Hunter	Co. A, 11th Mississippi	1835	7/15/1863	Mortally wounded, July 3rd, and buried on Jacob Schwartz Farm	Unknown
Cochran, William Lee	Co. B, 43rd North Carolina	1844	7/3/1863	Killed in action	Unknown
Cocke, James H.	Co. G, 4th Alabama	1842	7/2/1863	Killed in action while carrying the colors	Unknown
Cocke, William Fauntleroy	Lt., Co. E, 18th Virginia	8/2/1836	7/3/1863	Killed in action	Charlotte Co., VA
Cockerham, Jesse Woodson	Sgt., Co. A, 28th North Carolina	7/31/1832	7/3/1863	Killed in action	Unknown
Cockerham, Samuel Bly	Sgt., Co. B, 18th Mississippi	3/16/1830	7/2/1863	Killed in action	Unknown
Cockfield, Joseph Cleland	Co. G, 15th South Carolina	1844	7/2/1863	Killed in action	Unknown
Cockrell, Jonathan	Co. A, 47th North Carolina	4/17/1844	8/12/1863	Mortally wounded-died at unknown place in Gettysburg	Unknown
Cody, Absalom	Co. I, 11th North Carolina	1846	7/1/1863	Killed in action	Unknown
Cody, Barnett Hardeman	Lt., Co. G, 15th Alabama	2/21/1845	7/23/1863	Hollywood Cemetery, Richmond, Va., reburial lists	Richmond, VA
Coe, Dudley	Co. B, 2nd North Carolina Battalion	1842	7/1/1863	Killed in action	Unknown
Coe, William Wood	Sgt., Co. M, 21st North Carolina	1838	9/17/1863	Oakwood Cemetery, Raleigh, NC, reburial list	Raleigh, NC
Coffee, Andrew Joseph	Co. D, 56th Virginia		Jul. 1863	Mortally wounded per the Richmond Sentinel, July 29, 1863	Unknown
Coffey, Cleveland	Co. F, 26th North Carolina	1837	7/3/1863	Died of Wounds received on July 1	Unknown
Coffey, Hezekiah	Co. F, 49th Virginia	1835	Jul. 1863	Killed in action, July 1-3	Unknown
Coffey, J.H.	Co. F, 26th North Carolina	1840	7/1/1863	Killed in action	Unknown
Coffey, James Grayson	Co. F, 26th North Carolina	1839	8/24/1863	Died as POW at David's Island, NY	Cypress Hills, NY
Coffey, Thomas Milton	Co. F, 26th North Carolina	1835	8/12/1863	Hollywood Cemetery, Richmond, Va., reburial lists	Richmond, VA
Coffey, William S.	Co. F, 26th North Carolina	1845	8/20/1863	Died of Wounds received on July 1	Unknown
Cogbill, Williamson Willis Tilghman	Capt., Co. D, 14th Virginia	9/12/1821	7/3/1863	Killed in action	Unknown
Cogdell, Lewis Marion	Sgt., Co. E, 20th North Carolina	1842	8/29/1863	Mortally wounded and died at Staunton, VA-buried there	Staunton, VA
Cogdell, Richard S.	Co. I, 38th North Carolina	1832	7/1/1863	Killed in action	Unknown
Cohen, S.	Co. A, 5th Texas		7/2/1863	Killed in action	Unknown
Coker, John E.	Cpl., Co. A, 59th Georgia		7/2/1863	Killed in action	Unknown
Colbert, Thomas W.	Co. B, 44th Alabama	Jan. 1844	7/2/1863	Killed in action	Unknown
Colbert, William C.	Co. K, 16th North Carolina	1843	7/1/1863	Killed in action	Unknown
Cole, Dudley	Co. D, 23rd North Carolina	1844	7/1/1863	Killed in action	Unknown
Cole, J.M.	Co. C, 22nd Georgia		7/2/1863	Killed in action	Unknown
Cole, Larkin	Co. C, 11th Mississippi	1814	9/30/1863	Died of wounds at Ft. Delaware, DE	Finn's Point, NJ
Cole, William J.	Co. E, 51st Georgia	1835	7/2/1863	Killed in action	Unknown
Coleman, B.G.	Sgt., Co. A, 19th Mississippi	1841	7/4/1863	Hollywood Cemetery, Richmond, Va., reburial lists	Richmond, VA
Coleman, Henry L.	Co. L, 2nd Mississippi	1833	7/1/1863	Killed in action	Unknown
Coleman, James Madison	Co. H, 24th Virginia	1830	7/3/1863	Killed in action	Unknown

NAME	REGIMENT	BIRTH	DEATH	COMMENT	BURIAL
Coleman, James T.	Sgt., Co. I, 53rd Virginia	1839	7/3/1863	Killed in action	Unknown
Coletrane, James Madison	Co. I, 22nd North Carolina	1836	7/1/1863	Killed in action	Unknown
Coley, Marcellus A.	Sgt., Co. E, 23rd North Carolina	1840	7/1/1863	Killed in action	Unknown
Collins, Peter H.	Co. D, 14th North Carolina	1839	7/8/1863	Mortally wounded-died at unknown place in Gettysburg	Unknown
Collins, Philip B.	Sgt., Co. E, 6th North Carolina	5/12/1831	7/2/1863	Killed in action	Unknown
Collins, William	Co. I, 26th North Carolina	1844	7/1/1863	Killed in action	Unknown
Colquitt, James Banks	Co. G, 6th Alabama	7/19/1829	7/1/1863	Hollywood Cemetery, Richmond, Va., reburial lists	Richmond, VA
Colum, William	Cpl., Co. G, 21st Mississippi		7/6/1863	Mortally wounded-died at unknown place in Gettysburg	Unknown
Comes, Charles L.	Co. K, 8th Louisiana	1841	7/1/1863	Killed in action	Unknown
Commander, Joseph G.	Co. A, 14th South Carolina	1840	7/1/1863	Killed in action	Unknown
Compton, James	Co. I, 8th Georgia		7/3/1863	Hollywood Cemetery, Richmond, Va., reburial lists	Richmond, VA
Conaway, Charles	Co. F, 48th Georgia	1818	7/2/1863	Killed in action	Unknown
Condrey, William J.	Co. K, 2nd Mississippi	1842	7/1/1863	Killed in action	Unknown
Cone, Neverson	Co. A, 47th North Carolina	1843	8/26/1863	Oakwood Cemetery, Raleigh, NC, reburial list	Raleigh, NC
Conley, Joseph T.	Capt., Co. B, 22nd North Carolina		7/29/1863	Died of wounds received July 3 at Winchester, VA	Winchester, VA
Conley, William Baird	Co. F, 17th Mississippi	4/1/1843	7/2/1863	Hollywood Cemetery, Richmond, Va., reburial lists	Richmond, VA
Connard, John H.	Co. I, 14th Virginia	1843	7/3/1863	Killed in action	Unknown
Connell, Ira T.	Lt., Co. G, 30th North Carolina	1844	7/3/1863	Killed in action	Unknown
Connell, William	Moody's Artillery (La.)		9/9/1863	Mortally wounded and died at Chester, PA	Phil. National Cem.
Connelly, James D.	Lt., Co. C, 11th Virginia	1836	7/3/1863	Killed in action	Unknown
Conner, Edwin	Cpl., Co. E, 10th Louisiana	1833	7/2/1863	Killed in action	Unknown
Conner, George Ashby	Co. K, 5th Virginia	1830	8/23/1863	Mortally wounded and died at Winchester, VA	Winchester, VA
Conner, John	Co. K, 5th Alabama		7/1/1863	Killed in action	Unknown
Conner, Miles S.	Co. F, 2nd North Carolina Battalion	1838	7/1/1863	Killed in action	Unknown
Conner, William Gustine	Maj., Jeff Davis Legion Cavalry	4/5/1826	7/3/1863	Killed in action	Unknown
Conrad, James Dallas	Co. F, 28th North Carolina	12/20/1844	9/16/1863	Mortally wounded and reinterred at Conrad Cemetery, Yadkin Co., NC	Yadkin Co., NC
Conway, Alexander F.	Co. A, 38th Virginia	1841	7/3/1863	Killed in action per the Richmond Sentinel, August 1, 1863	Unknown
Conway, Barney	Co. A, 10th Louisiana	1831	7/2/1863	Killed in action	Unknown
Cook, Columbus Martin	Co. D, 11th Mississippi	11/28/1840	7/3/1863	Killed in action	Unknown
Cook, James G.	Co. D, 17th Mississippi	1824	7/2/1863	Killed in action	Unknown
Cook, James M.	Co. B, 26th North Carolina	1835	7/23/1863	Mortally wounded-died at unknown place in Gettysburg	Unknown
Cook, John Henry	Co. D, 11th Mississippi	10/29/1843	7/2/1863	Killed in action; brother of Columbus M. Cook	Unknown
Cook, Joseph A.	Co. F, 27th Virginia	1837	7/3/1863	Killed in action	Unknown

NAME	REGIMENT	BIRTH	DEATH	COMMENT	BURIAL
Cook, Nathaniel L.	Co. E, 28th North Carolina	1838	9/1/1863	Mortally wounded–died at unknown place in Gettysburg	Unknown
Cooley, Joseph W.	Carpenter's Battery (Va.)	1836	Jul. 1863	Hollywood Cemetery, Richmond, Va., reburial lists	Richmond, VA
Cooley, Lemuel	Co. B, 47th North Carolina	1847	7/3/1863	Hollywood Cemetery, Richmond, Va., reburial lists	Richmond, VA
Coon, J.	Co. H, 8th Alabama		8/26/1863	Mortally wounded and died at Chester, PA	Phil. National Cem.
Cooper, C.E.	Co. A, 2nd Florida	1839	Jul. 1863	Killed in action, July 1-3	Unknown
Cooper, Giles H.	Lt., Co. D, 24th Virginia	1833	9/28/1863	Hollywood Cemetery, Richmond, Va., reburial lists	Richmond, VA
Cooper, Jacob O.	Co. I, 21st Virginia		7/2/1863	Killed in action	Unknown
Cooper, Joseph F.	Co. A, 17th Mississippi		7/2/1863	Mortally wounded, July 2nd, and died the same day	Unknown
Cooper, Tazwell Taliaferro	Co. D, 24th Virginia	1838	7/3/1863	Killed in action	Unknown
Cooper, Thomas J.	Cpl., Co. D, 11th Mississippi	1843	7/3/1863	Killed in action	Unknown
Cooper, Thomas Watson	Lt., Co. C, 11th North Carolina	1841	7/1/1863	Killed in action and reinterred at Green Mount Cemetery, Baltimore, MD	Baltimore, MD
Cooper, William H.	Co. H, 11th Georgia	2/3/1842	7/2/1863	Killed in action	Unknown
Cooper, William S.	Co. D, 24th Virginia		7/18/1863	Mortally wounded and died at Lynchburg, VA-buried there	Lynchburg, VA
Copelan, W.O.	Co. I, 8th Georgia		7/5/1863	Hollywood Cemetery, Richmond, Va., reburial lists	Richmond, VA
Copelan, William H.	Cpl., Co. K, 44th Georgia	1837	7/1/1863	Killed in action	Unknown
Copeland, James L.	Co. C, 2nd South Carolina		7/17/1863	Mortally wounded per the Charleston Mercury, August 28, 1863	Unknown
Copeland, Luther Josiah	Co. H, 9th Georgia	11/29/1838	7/2/1863	Killed in action	Unknown
Corbett, Julius Clement	Co. D, 15th South Carolina	5/26/1836	7/2/1863	Killed in action	Unknown
Corley, Abner P.	Cpl., Co. E, 51st Georgia	1822	7/3/1863	Killed in action	Unknown
Corley, Charles L.	Co. F, 44th Alabama	1832	7/31/1863	Mortally wounded-died at unknown place in Gettysburg	Unknown
Corley, Freeman H.	Co. D, 14th South Carolina	1841	7/6/1863	Mortally wounded-died at unknown place in Gettysburg	Unknown
Corley, Henry N.	Co. K, 13th South Carolina	1842	7/2/1863	Killed in action	Unknown
Corley, William L.	Co. F, 28th Virginia		7/3/1863	Missing in action, July 3rd, and presumed dead	Unknown
Cormier, Louis Adolphe	Capt., Co. C, 6th Louisiana	5/20/1841	7/3/1863	Hollywood Cemetery, Richmond, Va., reburial lists	Richmond, VA
Cornelison, Isaac	Co. A, 1st Tennessee	1842	7/1/1863	Killed in action	Unknown
Cornelius, H. Forrest	Co. I, 7th North Carolina	1832	7/3/1863	Mortally wounded, July 3rd, and died the same day	Unknown
Cornell, Charles A.	Letcher Artillery (Va.)		7/1/1863	Killed in action	Unknown
Cornwell, Joel A.	Co. C, 14th Georgia	1838	7/2/1863	Killed in action	Unknown
Cosby, James Rufus	Co. B, 16th Georgia	1829	7/2/1863	Laurel Grove Cemetery, Savannah, Ga., reburial list	Savannah, GA
Cosper, William Marion	Co. I, 44th Alabama	7/20/1832	7/2/1863	Killed in action	Unknown

NAME	REGIMENT	BIRTH	DEATH	COMMENT	BURIAL
Costello, Patrick	Raines' Battery (Va.)	1838	8/16/1863	Died as POW at David's Island, NY	Cypress Hills, NY
Coulter, George	Co. I, 3rd Virginia		7/3/1863	Killed in action	Unknown
Coulter, Russell Smith	Co. E, 12th Georgia	1834	7/7/1863	Laurel Grove Cemetery, Savannah, Ga., reburial list	Savannah, GA
Counts, George W.	Cpl., Co. E, 5th Texas		Jul. 1863	Mortally wounded, July 2nd, and died on unknown date	Unknown
Cousins, Masston C.	Co. G, 44th Virginia		7/2/1863	Hollywood Cemetery, Richmond, Va., reburial lists	Richmond, VA
Covin, Oscar Warren	Co. K, 15th South Carolina	1836	8/11/1863	Mortally wounded and died at Chester, PA; reinterred in Magnolia Cemetery after the war	Charleston, SC
Covington, David G.	Co. H, 14th Virginia		7/3/1863	Killed in action	Unknown
Cowan, George W.	Lt., Co. A, 7th Tennessee		7/3/1863	Killed in action	Unknown
Cowan, Thomas Allison	Lt., Co. A, 33rd North Carolina	8/15/1845	7/3/1863	Killed in action	Unknown
Cowand, Joseph John	Co. G, 32nd North Carolina	1838	7/3/1863	Killed in action	Unknown
Cowdrey, James E.	Co. A, 51st Georgia		7/2/1863	Killed in action	Unknown
Cox, Charles L.	Co. D, 8th Virginia		Jul. 1863	Mortally wounded and died on unknown date	Unknown
Cox, Chastain	Co. D, 42nd Virginia		7/3/1863	Killed in action	Unknown
Cox, Elijah H.	Co. G, 14th Virginia		7/3/1863	Killed in action	Unknown
Cox, Elisha	Co. K, 8th Florida		7/2/1863	Killed in action	Unknown
Cox, George H.	Sgt., Co. H, 3rd North Carolina	1842	7/25/1863	Mortally wounded-died at unknown place in Gettysburg	Unknown
Cox, Henry C.	Co. F, 2nd North Carolina Battalion	1843	7/1/1863	Oakwood Cemetery, Raleigh, NC, reburial list	Raleigh, NC
Cox, James C.	Co. I, 5th Florida	1829	7/3/1863	Killed in action	Unknown
Cox, Joseph Jasper	Co. D, 2nd Mississippi	12/23/1841	7/1/1863	Killed in action	Unknown
Cox, Samuel N.	Co. I, 10th Georgia	11/11/1813	8/24/1863	Hollywood Cemetery, Richmond, Va., reburial lists	Richmond, VA
Coxwell, William Gray	Co. F, 48th Georgia		7/2/1863	Hollywood Cemetery, Richmond, Va., reburial lists	Richmond, VA
Cozart, Thomas Jefferson	Co. F, 26th North Carolina	7/4/1841	7/3/1863	Killed in action	Unknown
Crabtree, Leonard	Co. I, 16th North Carolina	1825	1863	Mortally wounded and died on unknown date	Unknown
Crabtree, William E.	Co. G, 28th North Carolina	1838	7/3/1863	Killed in action	Unknown
Craig, Chester	Co. K, 24th Virginia		Jul. 1863	Missing in action and presumed dead	Unknown
Craig, James Porter	Co. H, 37th North Carolina	12/5/1838	7/3/1863	Killed in action	Unknown
Craig, William S.	Co. G, 42nd Virginia		7/13/1863	Hollywood Cemetery, Richmond, Va., reburial lists	Richmond, VA
Crain, Jesse	Co. A, 32nd North Carolina	1840	7/1/1863	Killed in action	Raleigh, NC
Crain, John T.	Co. G, 16th North Carolina	1825	7/3/1863	Killed in action	Unknown
Cranfield, John W.	Co. C, 26th North Carolina	1840	7/1/1863	Killed in action	Unknown
Cranford, Tyson	Co. H, 38th North Carolina	1843	7/3/1863	Killed in action	Unknown
Crawford, Prince A.	Co. K, 48th Georgia		7/2/1863	Killed in action	Unknown
Crawford, Richard T.	Adjutant, 9th Louisiana	1833	7/2/1863	Killed in action	Unknown

NAME	REGIMENT	BIRTH	DEATH	COMMENT	BURIAL
Crawford, Robert Newton	Co. B, 11th Alabama	3/9/1841	7/3/1863	Hollywood Cemetery, Richmond, Va., reburial lists	Richmond, VA
Crawford, W.M.	Co. K, 59th Georgia		7/2/1863	Killed in action	Unknown
Crawford, William C.	Lt., Co. G, 17th Mississippi	5/27/1837	7/2/1863	Killed in action	Unknown
Creasman, Joseph Henry	Co. K, 11th North Carolina	5/3/1823	7/1/1863	Killed in action	Unknown
Creecy, William Pryor	4th Co., Washington Arty (La.)	1842	7/3/1863	Killed in action	Unknown
Crenshaw, J.B.	Co. B, 28th North Carolina	1843	7/4/1863	Mortally wounded and died on the field	Unknown
Crenshaw, Joseph William	Co. I, 12th South Carolina		7/15/1863	Mortally wounded-died at unknown place in Gettysburg	Unknown
Crenshaw, Robert A.	Co. B, 11th Mississippi	1839	7/3/1863	Killed in action	Unknown
Crenshaw, William H.	Co. C, 1st Virginia		7/2/1863	Killed in action	Unknown
Cress, Edmund	Co. F, 57th North Carolina	1840	7/9/1863	Mortally wounded-died at unknown place in Gettysburg	Unknown
Crews, Armistead C.	Co. H, 38th Virginia		7/3/1863	Killed in action	Unknown
Crews, Asberry	Co. E, 2nd North Carolina Battalion		7/6/1863	Mortally wounded-died at unknown place in Gettysburg	Unknown
Crews, Joshua J.	Co. K, 8th Florida		7/25/1863	Mortally wounded-died at unknown place in Gettysburg	Unknown
Crews, Samuel	Co. I, 8th Florida		9/13/1863	Died of wounds at Ft. Delaware, DE	Finn's Point, NJ
Crickenberger, Benjamin F.	Co. I, 10th Virginia	1840	7/2/1863	Killed in action	Unknown
Crittenden, Addison Hall	Lt., Co. F, 47th Virginia		7/9/1863	Mortally wounded-died at unknown place in Gettysburg	Unknown
Crocker, Harvey D.	Lt., Co. D, 14th South Carolina	1834	7/2/1863	Killed in action	Unknown
Crocker, Thomas E.	Co. D, 2nd North Carolina Battalion		1863	Mortally wounded, July 3rd, died on unknown date in 1863	Unknown
Cromer, William Philander	Capt., Co. D, 13th South Carolina	9/5/1836	7/2/1863	Hollywood Cemetery, Richmond, Va., reburial lists	Richmond, VA
Cronin, Patrick	Co. D, 2nd Georgia Battalion.		7/2/1863	Killed in action	Unknown
Crosby [Cosby], James R.	Co. B, 16th Georgia		7/2/1863	Killed in action	Unknown
Crosby, Walter Scott	Co. D, 12th South Carolina	3/5/1845	7/15/1863	Mortally wounded-died at unknown place in Gettysburg	Unknown
Crouch, Thomas Wade	Co. C, 2nd Georgia	1825	7/2/1863	Killed in action	Unknown
Crow, Berry	Co. F, 6th Alabama	1831	9/12/1863	Hollywood Cemetery, Richmond, Va., reburial lists	Richmond, VA
Crow, Elisha Melton Pinckney	Co. C, 38th North Carolina	1827	Jul. 1863	Killed in action; surname may be Crowe	Unknown
Crowder, George W.	Co. F, 14th Virginia		7/22/1863	Mortally wounded-died at unknown place in Gettysburg	Unknown
Crowder, Henry Clay	Co.C, 14th Alabama	11/14/1843	7/3/1863	Hollywood Cemetery, Richmond, Va., reburial lists	Richmond, VA
Crowell, Alfred H.	Sgt., Co. B, 53rd Georgia		7/2/1863	Killed in action	Unknown
Crowley, John J.R.	Co. I, 50th Georgia		7/31/1863	Mortally wounded-died at unknown place in Gettysburg	Unknown
Croxton, John Quincy	Co. G, 2nd South Carolina	12/9/1836	7/21/1863	Mortally wounded-died at unknown place in Gettysburg	Unknown
Croy, Jack	Co. E, 9th Georgia		7/2/1863	Killed in action	Unknown

NAME	REGIMENT	BIRTH	DEATH	COMMENT	BURIAL
Crumbley, William A.	Co. A, 53rd Georgia	1829	7/12/1863	Mortally wounded per the Augusta Chronicle & Sentinel, August 13, 1863	Unknown
Crump, Thomas J.	Co. F, 26th North Carolina	1842	7/10/1863	Mortally wounded and died at Martinsburg, VA	Martinsburg, WV
Crump, Willis J.	Co. E, 13th Mississippi	1838	7/3/1863	Hollywood Cemetery, Richmond, Va., reburial lists	Richmond, VA
Crumpler, Benajah	Sgt., Co. F, 20th North Carolina	1839	7/1/1863	Killed in action	Unknown
Cruse, Tobias	Co. K, 5th North Carolina	3/14/1831	7/1/1863	Killed in action; KIA on Oak Ridge (Iverson's Brigade)	Richmond, VA
Crutchfield, Joseph R.	Cpl., Co. D, 2nd Georgia Battalion.		7/27/1863	Hollywood Cemetery, Richmond, Va., reburial lists	Richmond, VA
Cryer, Marselan Terrance	Co. F, 1st Texas	7/2/1836	7/4/1863	Mortally wounded, July 2nd, and died two days later	Unknown
Culbertson Jr., Young James	Sgt., Co. C, 3rd South Carolina Battalion	1835	7/2/1863	Magnolia Cemetery, Charleston, SC, reburial list	Charleston, SC
Culhane, Martin J.	Co. G, 12th Mississippi	1838	7/3/1863	Killed in action per the Richmond Enquirer, July 16, 1863	Unknown
Culler, Henry L.	Cpl., Co. E, 1st SC Cavalry	1840	7/6/1863	Mortally wounded July 2nd	Columbia, SC
Culp, John Wesley	Co. B, 2nd Virginia	1839	7/2/1863	Killed in action on family homestead known as Culp's Hill	Unknown
Culpepper, John	Co. C, 17th Georgia		7/2/1863	Killed in action	Unknown
Culver, Everard Hamilton	Co. K, 15th Georgia	9/27/1844	7/3/1863	Killed in action	Hancock Co., GA
Cumans, L.H.	Marmaduke Johnson's Battery (Va.)		7/4/1863	Mortally wounded July 2nd	Unknown
Cumbest, Thomas H.	Co. E, 17th Georgia		Jul. 1863	Killed in action per the Augusta Chronicle & Sentinel, July 30, 1863	Unknown
Cummings, Columbus C.	Co. K, 8th Alabama		7/10/1863	Hollywood Cemetery, Richmond, Va., reburial lists	Richmond, VA
Cundiff, Albert A.	Co. D, 24th Virginia	1840	7/3/1863	Killed in action	Unknown
Cundiff, Samuel C.	Co. D, 24th Virginia	1837	7/3/1863	Killed in action; brother of Albert Cundiff	Unknown
Cunningham, George H.	Co. G, 4th North Carolina	1839	Jul. 1863	Killed in action	Unknown
Cunningham, James	Co. D, 10th Louisiana	1822	7/3/1863	Mortally wounded, July 3rd, and died the same day	Unknown
Cunningham, John H.	Co. A, 13th South Carolina	1842	7/1/1863	Killed in action	Unknown
Cunningham, Joseph P.	Capt., Co. G, 2nd South Carolina	7/6/1834	7/2/1863	Killed in action	Charleston, SC
Cunningham, Patrick	Co. E, 5th North Carolina	1844	7/17/1863	Mortally wounded-died at unknown place in Gettysburg	Unknown
Curenton, Jasper	Co. E, 15th Alabama	1844	7/2/1863	Killed in action; surname may be Curenton	Unknown
Currie, Neill A.	Co. H, 26th North Carolina	1826	7/3/1863	Killed in action	Unknown
Currie, Thomas	Co. E, 61st Georgia	1832	7/2/1863	Killed in action	Unknown
Currin, George W.	Co. K, 55th North Carolina		7/1/1863	Killed in action	Unknown
Currin, Hugh	Co. K, 55th North Carolina		7/29/1863	Mortally wounded and died at Hagerstown, MD-buried there	Hagerstown, MD
Currin, James D.	Co. K, 55th North Carolina		7/1/1863	Killed in action	Unknown
Curtis, James	Co. C, 26th North Carolina	1840	7/3/1863	Killed in action	Unknown

NAME	REGIMENT	BIRTH	DEATH	COMMENT	BURIAL
Curtis, William R.	Sgt., Co. I, 43rd North Carolina	1833	7/6/1863	Mortally wounded-died at unknown place in Gettysburg	Unknown
Cushing, Robert Henry	Sgt., Co. C, 1st Maryland Battalion	9/24/1835	7/3/1863	Killed in action, body shipped to Winchester, VA after the battle	Winchester, VA
Cusick, Frederick	Chesapeake Artillery (Md.)		1863	Mortally wounded and died on unknown date at Baltimore, MD	Baltimore, MD
Custer, Alexander	Co. E, 57th Virginia		7/3/1863	Killed in action	Unknown
Custis, Revill W.	Co. I, 61st Virginia		7/2/1863	Killed in action	Unknown
Cutbirth, Daniel Boone	Co. F, 2nd Mississippi	1838	7/3/1863	Killed in action	Unknown
Cutts, Newton A.	Co. H, 13th Georgia	1840	7/1/1863	Killed in action	Unknown
Dabbs, David Sydney	Sgt., Co. K, 26th North Carolina	8/15/1838	7/1/1863	Killed in action	Unknown
Dail, Newson	Co. K, 33rd North Carolina	1840	7/3/1863	Killed in action	Unknown
Dailey, Franklin Oliver	Lt., Co. A, 2nd Mississippi	1831	7/3/1863	Killed in action	Unknown
Daley, John	Cpl., Co. G, 14th Louisiana		7/18/1863	Hollywood Cemetery, Richmond, Va., reburial lists	Richmond, VA
Dalton [Daulton], John A.	Co. A, 18th Virginia		7/3/1863	Hollywood Cemetery, Richmond, Va., reburial lists	Richmond, VA
Dalton, Robert	Cpl., Co. K, 16th North Carolina	1839	7/1/1863	Killed in action	Unknown
Dance, James A.	Co. B, 3rd Georgia		7/2/1863	Killed in action	Unknown
Daniel, George J.	Sgt., Co. D, 48th Georgia	1828	7/2/1863	Killed in action	Unknown
Daniel, James Madison	Lt., Co. E, 7th South Carolina	Feb.1836	7/3/1863	Hollywood Cemetery, Richmond, Va., reburial lists	Richmond, VA
Daniel, John P.	Cpl., Co. H, 11th Virginia	1837	7/30/1863	Hollywood Cemetery, Richmond, Va., reburial lists	Richmond, VA
Daniel, William J.	Co. H, 3rd North Carolina	1841	7/3/1863	Mortally wounded and POW, July 3, died in Baltimore, MD	Baltimore, MD
Daniel, William Lowndes	Lt., Co. I, 2nd South Carolina	1833	7/2/1863	Killed in action	Charleston, SC
Danley, Henry	Co. H, 47th North Carolina	1832	8/5/1863	Mortally wounded-died at unknown place in Gettysburg	Raleigh, NC
Dann, Horace L.	Co. G, 8th Florida	1841	12/22/1863	Killed in action	Unknown
Danner, Joshua G.	Co. I, 28th North Carolina	1842	7/4/1863	Mortally wounded-died at unknown place in Gettysburg	Unknown
Darrold, J.L.	Co. K, 11th North Carolina		7/26/1863	Died as POW at David's Island, NY	Cypress Hills, NY
Darwin, John Taylor	Sgt., Co. I, 4th Alabama		7/2/1863	Killed in action	Unknown
Daugherty, J.T.	Co. I, 5th Alabama		7/12/1863	Mortally wounded-died at unknown place in Gettysburg	Unknown
Daughtry, George L.	Lt., Co. C, 38th North Carolina	1842	7/1/1863	Killed in action	Unknown
Davenport, Henry	Capt., Co. E, 42nd Mississippi	1/6/1836	7/17/1863	Hollywood Cemetery, Richmond, Va., reburial lists	Richmond, VA
Davenport, R.W	Co. F, 3rd South Carolina		7/2/1863	Killed in action	Unknown
Davenport, Theophilus R.	Sgt., Co. C, 11th Mississippi	1843	7/10/1863	Mortally wounded-died at unknown place in Gettysburg	Unknown
Davers, Anthony	Co. E, 2nd North Carolina Battalion		7/7/1863	Hollywood Cemetery, Richmond, Va., reburial lists	Richmond, VA
Davidson, George	Co. F, 50th Virginia		7/19/1863	Mortally wounded-died at unknown place in Gettysburg	Unknown

NAME	REGIMENT	BIRTH	DEATH	COMMENT	BURIAL
Davidson, James	Co. H, 19th Virginia		Jul. 1863	Missing in action, July 3rd, and presumed dead	Unknown
Davidson, James T.	Co. A, 12th South Carolina	1836	7/4/1863	Mortally wounded-died at unknown place in Gettysburg	Unknown
Davidson, Lewis	Co. F, 11th North Carolina		7/27/1863	Died as POW at David's Island, NY	Cypress Hills, NY
Davidson, William Jasper	Co. G, 5th Alabama	8/20/1839	7/1/1863	Killed in action	Unknown
Davis Augustine H.	Cpl., Co. K, 38th Virginia		7/3/1863	Killed in action	Unknown
Davis, A.O.	Co. G, 40th Virginia		7/4/1863	Mortally wounded-died at unknown place in Gettysburg	Unknown
Davis, Anderson Barton Cook	Sgt., Co. K, 2nd Louisiana	3/15/1838	Jul. 1863	Missing in action, July 2nd, and presumed dead	Unknown
Davis, Archibald J.	Co. K, 32nd North Carolina	1839	7/3/1863	Oakwood Cemetery, Raleigh, NC, reburial list	Raleigh, NC
Davis, Arthur M.	Co. C, 43rd North Carolina	1835	7/3/1863	Killed in action	Unknown
Davis, Charles L.	Co. B, 16th Georgia		7/2/1863	Killed in action	Unknown
Davis, George W.	Sgt., Co. F, 48th Georgia	1838	7/2/1863	Killed in action	Unknown
Davis, Hamilton	Co. K, 52nd North Carolina	1831	7/11/1863	Hollywood Cemetery, Richmond, Va., reburial lists	Richmond, VA
Davis, Issac	Co. D, 52nd North Carolina	1842	7/3/1863	Missing in action, July 3rd, and presumed dead	Unknown
Davis, Issac Ramsey	Co. D, 5th North Carolina	8/24/1844	7/1/1863	Hollywood Cemetery, Richmond, Va., reburial lists	Richmond, VA
Davis, J.D.	Co. A, 2nd Georgia Battalion		7/2/1863	Killed in action	Unknown
Davis, Jackson	Co. I, 57th Virginia	10/1/1843	7/1/1863	Killed in action	Unknown
Davis, Jacob N.	Co. A, 1st Maryland Battalion		Jul. 1863	Removed from battlefield in 1874 to Baltimore, MD; interred in Loudon Park Cemetery	Baltimore, MD
Davis, James H.	Sgt., Co. H, 20th North Carolina	1840	7/1/1863	Killed in action	Unknown
Davis, James T.	Co. A, 2nd Georgia Battalion		7/2/1863	Killed in action	Unknown
Davis, James Thomas	Capt., Co. D, 12th Alabama	3/15/1829	7/1/1863	Killed in action	Unknown
Davis, John	Co. E, 47th North Carolina	1838	7/3/1863	Killed in action	Unknown
Davis, John F.	Sgt., Co. I, 11th Georgia		7/2/1863	Laurel Grove Cemetery, Savannah, Ga., reburial list	Savannah, GA
Davis, John M.	Co. I, 9th Louisiana	1816	7/2/1863	Killed in action	Unknown
Davis, John Samuel	Co. F, 18th Virginia	1840	7/7/1863	Mortally wounded per the Richmond Sentinel, July 30, 1863	Unknown
Davis, Joseph	Co. E, 8th Virginia		7/11/1863	Hollywood Cemetery, Richmond, Va., reburial lists	Richmond, VA
Davis, Joseph W.	Co. I, 13th Mississippi	1838	7/12/1863	Hollywood Cemetery, Richmond, Va., reburial lists	Richmond, VA
Davis, Michael	Co. C, 1st Maryland Battalion		1863	Mortally wounded-died on unknown date in Gettysburg	Unknown
Davis, Oren M.	Cpl., Co. F, 3rd Georgia		7/5/1863	Died of wounds received on July 2nd	Unknown
Davis, Peter	Co. B, 53rd Virginia	1838	7/3/1863	Killed in action	Unknown
Davis, Philip	Co. I, 14th Virginia	1838	7/24/1863	Mortally wounded and buried on Jacob Schwartz Farm	Unknown
Davis, Robert R.	Co. H, 48th Georgia	1842	7/2/1863	Killed in action	Unknown

NAME	REGIMENT	BIRTH	DEATH	COMMENT	BURIAL
Davis, Robert W.	Co. D, 52nd North Carolina	1841	7/3/1863	Missing in action, July 3rd, and presumed dead	Unknown
Davis, Thomas	Co. C, 7th Virginia		7/3/1863	Killed in action	Unknown
Davis, W.G.	Co. K, 59th Georgia		7/2/1863	Killed in action	Unknown
Davis, W.P.	Co. K, 2nd Louisiana		7/2/1863	Hollywood Cemetery, Richmond, Va., reburial lists	Richmond, VA
Davis, Wesley	Co. I, 3rd North Carolina	1826	7/3/1863	Hollywood Cemetery, Richmond, Va., reburial lists	Richmond, VA
Davis, William H.	Co. I, 10th Virginia		Jul. 1863	Missing in action, July 2nd, and presumed dead	Unknown
Davis, William J.	Co. E, 48th Georgia		7/2/1863	Laurel Grove Cemetery, Savannah, Ga., reburial list	Savannah, GA
Davis, William J.	Co. H, 8th Alabama		7/3/1863	Killed in action	Unknown
Davis, Winborn C.	Sgt., Co. F, 1st North Carolina	1841	Jul. 1863	Hollywood Cemetery, Richmond, Va., reburial lists	Richmond, VA
Dawson, Leroy T.	Co. H, 24th Virginia		7/21/1863	Hollywood Cemetery, Richmond, Va., reburial lists	Richmond, VA
Dawson, William P.	Sgt., Co. K, 52nd North Carolina	1835	7/1/1863	Hollywood Cemetery, Richmond, Va., reburial lists	Richmond, VA
Day, Allen B.	Co. B, 38th Georgia	1835	7/1/1863	Killed in action	Unknown
Deal, James	Co. F, 26th North Carolina	1833	Jul. 1863	Killed in action	Unknown
Deal, Lewis H., III	Co. H, 8th Alabama	4/17/1831	7/3/1863	Hollywood Cemetery, Richmond, Va., reburial lists	Richmond, VA
Dean, Charles N.	Co. K, 3rd Georgia		7/2/1863	Laurel Grove Cemetery, Savannah, Ga., reburial list	Savannah, GA
Dean, Levi	Co. D, 17th Georgia		7/4/1863	Died of wounds received on July 2nd	Unknown
Dear, Thomas A.	Cpl., Co. I, 8th Virginia		Jul. 1863	Missing in action, July 3rd, and presumed dead	Unknown
Dearman, William F.	Co. I, 16th North Carolina	1838	10/13/1863	Oakwood Cemetery, Raleigh, NC, reburial list	Raleigh, NC
Deaton, T.J.	Co. A, 2nd Georgia Battalion		7/2/1863	Killed in action	Unknown
Deboe, Joseph	Co. E, 57th Virginia		Jul. 1863	Missing in action, July 3rd, and presumed dead	Unknown
Dedman, William H.	Cpl., Co. A, 56th Virginia		Jul. 1863	Killed in action per the Richmond Sentinel, July 29, 1863	Unknown
Deems, Theodore DeSausure	Lt., Co. G, 5th North Carolina	5/27/1844	7/17/1863	Mortally wounded, July 1st, and died in Gettysburg hospital; reinterred after the war	Wilmington, NC
Dees, Clement Allen	Co. B, 43rd North Carolina	2/9/1834	9/1/1863	Oakwood Cemetery, Raleigh, NC, reburial list	Raleigh, NC
Deets, M.L.	Co. E, 32nd North Carolina	1845	7/2/1863	Mortally wounded in action, July 2nd, and died the same day	Unknown
Defnall, David	Co. G, 10th Georgia		9/16/1863	Mortally wounded-died at unknown place in Gettysburg	Unknown
Deggs, C.W.	Co. A, 5th Texas		7/2/1863	Killed in action	Unknown
Dehart, Jesse H.	Co. A, 24th Virginia	1830	Jul. 1863	Mortally wounded and died on unknown date	Unknown

NAME	REGIMENT	BIRTH	DEATH	COMMENT	BURIAL
Deisher, Jacob	Co. F, 26th Virginia Battalion	6/28/1823	7/4/1863	Mortally wounded-died at unknown place in Gettysburg	Unknown
DeLauney, Edward White	Sgt., Co. H, 4th Georgia	12/25/1841	7/2/1863	Killed in action	Unknown
Dellinger, George Shelton	Sgt., Co. K, 23rd North Carolina	1834	7/14/1863	Mortally wounded-died at unknown place in Gettysburg	Unknown
Dellinger, Peter Frank	Co. I, 11th North Carolina	10/23/1863	Jul. 1863	Killed in action	Unknown
DeLoach, Judson	Co. B, 20th Georgia		7/2/1863	Killed in action	Unknown
Dement, Albert L.	Sgt., Co. F, 47th North Carolina	1842	7/23/1863	Hollywood Cemetery, Richmond, Va., reburial lists	Richmond, VA
Dempsey, Elvin W.	Co. F, 5th Florida	1838	9/3/1863	Mortally wounded and died at Winchester, VA	Winchester, VA
Demptser, John	Co. E, 4th North Carolina Cav.		7/4/1863	Oakwood Cemetery, Raleigh, NC, reburial list	Raleigh, NC
Denham, Simeon	Co. D, 13th Georgia		8/24/1863	Mortally wounded, July 2nd, and died at Staunton, VA	Staunton, VA
Dennis, Samuel	Co. I, 49th Virginia	1832	7/3/1863	Hollywood Cemetery, Richmond, Va., reburial lists	Richmond, VA
Denton, John T.	Co. D, 56th Virginia	1833	8/2/1863	Hollywood Cemetery, Richmond, Va., reburial lists	Richmond, VA
Denton, William M.	Co. I, 10th Georgia		7/2/1863	Killed in action	Unknown
Derrick, E.P.	Co. A, 1st Texas		7/2/1863	Killed in action	Unknown
Derrick, Frederick Earl	Co. I, 15th South Carolina	1839	8/22/1863	Magnolia Cemetery, Charleston, SC, reburial list	Charleston, SC
Derrick, George Melvin	Co. H, 13th South Carolina	7/13/1845	7/24/1863	Magnolia Cemetery, Charleston, SC, reburial list	Charleston, SC
DeSaussure, William Davie	Col., 15th South Carolina	12/12/1819	7/2/1863	Killed in action; interred First Presbyterian Church, Columbia, SC	Columbia, SC
DeShazor, Abner Waddell	Co. G, 44th Virginia	6/6/1831	7/2/1863	Killed in action	Unknown
DeVane, George J.	Lt., Co. D, 5th Florida	11/20/1832	7/24/1863	Mortally wounded and died at Winchester, VA	Winchester, VA
Devine, James	Co. K, 5th Louisiana	1834	7/3/1863	Killed in action	Unknown
Dewberry, Seaborn H.	Co. C, 2nd Georgia		7/1/1863	Killed in action	Unknown
Dezell, Z.Y.	Sgt., Co. C, 5th Texas		7/2/1863	Killed in action	Unknown
Dicken, J.M.	Co. B, 59th Georgia		7/21/1863	Mortally wounded-died at unknown place in Gettysburg	Unknown
Dickerson, Nelson Lumpkin	Capt., Co. F, 2nd Georgia		7/3/1863	Killed in action	Unknown
Dickerson, William	Co. F, 47th North Carolina	1812	10/14/1863	Mortally wounded and died at Richmond, VA-interred in Hollywood Cemetery	Richmond, VA
Dickinson, Frederick W.	Co. C, 17th Georgia		7/2/1863	Killed in action	Unknown
Dickson, Joseph C.	Co. K, 15th Geogia		7/3/1863	Hollywood Cemetery, Richmond, Va., reburial lists	Richmond, VA
Dickson, Samuel W.G.	Co. C, 8th South Carolina	1841	7/1/1863	Hollywood Cemetery, Richmond, Va., reburial lists	Richmond, VA
Diemer, Milton H.	Co. G, 1st Tennessee	1842	Aug. 1863	Died of wounds at Ft. Delaware, DE	Finn's Point, NJ
Dillahunt, Alexander C.	Co. G, 2nd North Carolina	1843	7/1/1863	Killed in action	Unknown

NAME	REGIMENT	BIRTH	DEATH	COMMENT	BURIAL
Dinkle, Enos	Sgt., Co. H, 7th Virginia Cavalry		7/3/1863	Killed in action; body recovered and shipped to Winchester, VA	Winchester, VA
Dix, Tanda W.	Co. A, 38th Virginia		7/3/1863	Killed in action	Unknown
Dixon, Benjamin Franklin	Sgt., Co. B, 7th Louisiana	1839	10/6/1863	Mortally wounded and died at Camp Letterman	Unknown
Dixon, James M.	Co. K, 50th Georgia		7/2/1863	Killed in action	Unknown
Dixon, John E.	Co. K, 3rd Georgia		7/2/1863	Killed in action	Unknown
Dixon, Thomas W.	Co. I, 3rd Georgia		7/2/1863	Killed in action	Unknown
Dixon, William	Co. G, 5th North Carolina	1827	7/19/1863	Mortally wounded–died at unknown place at Gettysburg	Richmond, VA
Dixon, William W.	Co. E, 11th North Carolina	1820	9/1/1863	Mortally wounded, July 2nd, and died at unknown place before Sept. 1st	Unknown
Dobbs, Benjamin F.	Sgt., Co. D, 2nd Georgia Battalion.		7/2/1863	Killed in action	Unknown
Dobbs, William C.	Co. D, 1st Texas		7/2/1863	Killed in action	Unknown
Dobey, John L.	Co. K, 14th South Carolina	1844	7/1/1863	Killed in action	Unknown
Dobson, John O.	Co. A, 2nd North Carolina		9/3/1863	Oakwood Cemetery, Raleigh, NC, reburial list	Raleigh, NC
Dobson, John W,	Co. M, 2nd Florida		Jul. 1863	Missing in action and presumed dead	Unknown
Dodson, Josephus B.	Co. C, 38th Virginia		7/6/1863	Mortally wounded–died at unknown place in Gettysburg	Unknown
Doherty, William W.	Lt., Co. C, 37th North Carolina	1840	7/3/1863	Killed in action	Unknown
Dollar, Rayford M.	Co. D, 17th Georgia		8/23/1863	Mortally wounded and died at Staunton, VA–buried there	Staunton, VA
Dolman, Abram Hickman	Co. G, 5th Alabama	6/14/1827	7/1/1863	Killed in action	Unknown
Done, John	Co. C, 47th North Carolina	1841	11/22/1863	Mortally wounded in lungs and died at Pt. Lookout	Pt. Lookout, MD
Dorsey, Joel	Co. E, 53rd Georgia	1836	7/3/1863	Killed in action	Unknown
Dortic, Alfred Cumming	Sgt., Co. C, 48th Georgia	11/18/1839	12/15/1863	Mortally wounded and reinterred in Magnolia Cemetery, Augusta, GA	Augusta, GA
Doss, Gehn	Co. G, 1st Virginia		7/3/1863	Killed in action	Unknown
Doss, Robert L.	Co. F, 2nd Georgia		7/2/1863	Killed in action	Unknown
Doss, Thomas Henry	Co. I, 42nd Virginia	1830	7/2/1863	Killed in action	Unknown
Dougherty, Daniel	Cpl., Chesapeake Artillery (Md.)		7/2/1863	Killed in action	Baltimore, MD
Dougherty, Joseph	Co. E, 28th Virginia		1863	Missing in action and presumed dead	Unknown
Douglas, N.	Co. D, 5th Texas		7/2/1863	Killed in action	Unknown
Douglass, James	Lt., Co. G, 50th Georgia		7/2/1863	Killed in action	Unknown
Dove, Leslie Chambliss	Courier	12/24/1845	7/12/1863	Died of wounds at Hagerstown, MD [body taken home to Richmond]– Hollywood Cemetery	Richmond, VA
Dowdy, Aaron Wiley	Co. H, 61st Georgia	1838	7/1/1863	Killed in action	Unknown
Dowdy, James H.	Co. E, 18th Virginia		7/11/1863	Hollywood Cemetery, Richmond, Va., reburial lists	Richmond, VA
Dowdy, John A.	Co. B, 14th Virginia		7/3/1863	Killed in action	Unknown
Downer, David C.	Co. G, 61st Georgia		7/1/1863	Laurel Grove Cemetery, Savannah, Ga., reburial list	Savannah, GA
Downey, William Henry Clay	Co. F, 3rd Arkansas	1842	7/2/1863	Killed in action	Unknown

NAME	REGIMENT	BIRTH	DEATH	COMMENT	BURIAL
Doyle, William H.	Co. E, 9th Virginia		7/3/1863	Killed in action	Unknown
Dozier, Richard H.	Cpl., Co. A, 47th North Carolina	1819	7/3/1863	Killed in action	Unknown
Dozier, Woody	Lt., Co. D, 14th Alabama		7/3/1863	Killed in action	Unknown
Drake, Robert B.	Co. A, 57th Virginia	1844	7/8/1863	Mortally wounded-died on unknown date in Gettysburg	Unknown
Drakeford, William H.	Co. C, 3rd Alabama		Jul. 1863	Killed in action per the Montgomery Advertiser	Unknown
Draper, Lazarus	Co. B, 5th North Carolina	1833	7/6/1863	Mortally wounded-died at unknown place in Gettysburg	Unknown
Drean, John Thomas	Co. A, 53rd Virginia	1837	11/5/1863	Hollywood Cemetery, Richmond, Va., reburial lists	Richmond, VA
Drewry, Abraham Richard	Co. I, 5th Alabama	1834	7/5/1863	Mortally wounded-died at unknown place in Gettysburg	Unknown
Drewry, Carey B.	Co. G, 28th Virginia	1837	7/10/1863	Mortally wounded-died at unknown place in Gettysburg	Unknown
Driggers, Zachariah	Co. K, 61st Georgia		7/1/1863	Killed in action	Unknown
Driscoll [Driskill], Larkin R.	Co. I, 56th Virginia	1838	7/28/1863	Mortally wounded and died at Chester, PA	Phil. National Cem.
Driver, William J.	Co. B, 17th Georgia		7/3/1863	Killed in action per the Augusta Chronicle & Sentinel, July 30, 1863	Unknown
Drumheller, Benjamin H.	Co. D, 19th Virginia	1839	7/3/1863	Killed in action per the Richmond Sentinel, August 11, 1863	Unknown
Drummond, J.H.W.	Cpl., Co. G, 22nd Georgia		7/2/1863	Killed in action	Unknown
Dry, Christopher	Co. I, 52nd North Carolina	1831	7/3/1863	Killed in action	Unknown
DuBose, John E.	Sgt., Co. C, 5th Alabama		7/22/1863	Mortally wounded-died at unknown place in Gettysburg	Unknown
Duckett, Joseph N.	Lt., Co. H, 2nd North Carolina Battalion	1835	7/7/1863	Hollywood Cemetery, Richmond, Va., reburial lists	Richmond, VA
Duckworth, William	Co. B, 11th North Carolina	1838	7/1/1863	Killed in action	Unknown
Dudding, James O.	Co. C, 28th Virginia	1841	9/13/1863	Hollywood Cemetery, Richmond, Va., reburial lists	Richmond, VA
Dudley, George H.	Lt., Co. H, 59th Georgia		8/27/1863	Mortally wounded and died at Staunton, VA-buried there	Staunton, VA
Dudley, Ransom A.	Co. D, 48th Georgia	1839	7/2/1863	Killed in action	Unknown
Duff, James S.	Co. F, 4th Alabama	1833	7/2/1863	Killed in action	Unknown
Duffie, Thomas A.T.	Co. G, 20th Georgia		7/2/1863	Killed in action	Unknown
Duffus, George Eubank Leefe	Co. I, 1st South Carolina	1841	8/30/1863	Magnolia Cemetery, Charleston, SC, reburial list	Charleston, SC
Dugger, Casper Constable	Co. C, 8th Virginia	2/14/1838	Jul. 1863	Missing in action and presumed dead	Unknown
Duggins, J.R.	Co. M, 21st North Carolina		10/15/1863	Died as POW at David's Island, NY	Cypress Hills, NY
Duke, Archibald Y.	Co. C, 17th Mississippi	1844	7/30/1863	Hollywood Cemetery, Richmond, Va., reburial lists	Richmond, VA
Duke, David L.	Co. B, 5th Florida		7/3/1863	Killed in action	Unknown
Duke, James Monroe	Co. C, 59th Georgia	1836	7/3/1863	Killed in action	Unknown
Dulaney, Jeremiah	Co. C, 1st Maryland Battalion		7/2/1863	Killed in action	Unknown
Dulin, John	Co. B, 26th North Carolina		9/16/1863	Mortally wounded-died at unknown place in Gettysburg	Unknown

NAME	REGIMENT	BIRTH	DEATH	COMMENT	BURIAL
Dumas, John A.J.	Co. A, 14th Georgia		7/2/1863	Killed in action	Unknown
Duncan, John E.	Sgt., Co. C, 44th Virginia		7/23/1863	Mortally wounded–died at unknown place in Gettysburg	Unknown
Duncan, John F.	Co. D, 21st Virginia		7/2/1863	Killed in action	Unknown
Duncan, John M.	Co. C, 22nd Georgia		7/2/1863	Killed in action	Unknown
Duncan, Joseph D.	Cpl., Co. F, 6th Alabama		7/9/1863	Mortally wounded–died at unknown place in Gettysburg	Unknown
Duncan, Robert M.	Co. D, 9th Alabama	4/12/1834	7/3/1863	Killed in action	Unknown
Duncan, William Frank	Co. C, 13th Mississippi	1838	7/17/1863	Hollywood Cemetery, Richmond, Va., reburial lists	Richmond, VA
Duncan, William Jefferson	Co. F, 17th Mississippi	1840	7/12/1863	Mortally wounded–died at unknown place in Gettysburg	Unknown
Dunderdale, John A.F.	Co. K, 9th Virginia	1840	7/21/1863	Mortally wounded–died at unknown place in Gettysburg	Unknown
Dunford, Robert J.	Co. F, 3rd Virginia	1843	Jul. 1863	Missing in action and presumed dead	Unknown
Dungan, Thomas W.	C. D, 48th Virginia	1/2/1837	7/2/1863	Hollywood Cemetery, Richmond, Va., reburial lists	Richmond, VA
Dunklin, William Arnold	Capt., Co. G, 44th Alabama	11/6/1828	7/2/1863	Killed in action, body recovered and reinterred in Live Oak Cemetery, Selma, AL	Selma, AL
Dunkum, William B.	Co. A, 57th Virginia		10/26/1863	Died of wounds at Ft. Delaware, DE	Finn's Point, NJ
Dunlap, John McKee	Co. C, 1st Virginia Cavalry	7/17/1836	7/3/1863	Killed in action, body recovered and reinterred in McKee Cemetery, Rockbridge Co, VA	Rockbridge Co., VA
Dunn, David D.	Sgt., Co. C, 17th Georgia		Jul. 1863	Killed in action July 1-3	Richmond, VA
Dunn, John R.	Sgt., Co. G, 9th Virginia	1835	7/3/1863	Killed in action	Unknown
Dunn, Simeon	Co. K, 5th Texas	1828	7/2/1863	Killed in action	Unknown
Dunn, T.F.	Co. A, 1st South Carolina		7/2/1863	Killed in action	Unknown
Dunn, Thomas W.S.	Co. H, 56th Virginia	1/15/1838	7/3/1863	Killed in action per the Richmond Sentinel, July 29, 1863	Unknown
Dunston, James Henry	Co. D, 14th Virginia	1838	9/12/1863	Hollywood Cemetery, Richmond, Va., reburial lists	Richmond, VA
Dunwoody, Henry Macon	Maj., 51st Georgia	3/18/1826	7/2/1863	Killed in action and reinterred in Roswell, Georgia	Roswell, GA
Duren, Griffin F.	Sgt., Co. B, 7th Georgia		7/3/1863	Killed in action	Unknown
Durham, Alfred	Co. A, 18th Georgia		7/2/1863	Killed in action	Unknown
Durham, Charles J.	Co. E, 12th North Carolina	1838	7/13/1863	Mortally wounded–died at unknown place in Gettysburg	Unknown
Durham, Joseph W.	Co. K, 11th Mississippi	1837	7/3/1863	Killed in action	Unknown
Durham, William S.	Co. G, 11th North Carolina	1838	7/3/1863	Mortally wounded, July 1st, and died two days later	Unknown
Durisoe, Charles Laque	Co. D, 14th South Carolina	8/26/1838	7/23/1863	Died as POW at David's Island, NY	Cypress Hills, NY
Duty, George W.	Co. B, 12th North Carolina	1843	7/1/1863	Killed in action	Unknown
Duval, John M.	Sgt., Co. B, 11th North Carolina		Aug. 1863	Mortally wounded July 1, died at Hagerstown, MD	Hagerstown, MD
Duvall, William Anthony	Cpl., Co. G, 1st Texas	12/13/1833	7/2/1863	Killed in action	Unknown

NAME	REGIMENT	BIRTH	DEATH	COMMENT	BURIAL
Duvall, Samuel Coleman	Co. C, 1st Maryland Battalion	11/24/1841	7/2/1863	Killed in action, body recovered and reinterred in Duvall Family Cemetery, Crownsville, MD	Crownsville, MD
Dyer, Thomas S.	Sgt., Co. F, 57th Virginia		Jul. 1863	Killed in action, July 1-3	Unknown
Dyer, William H.	Co. G, 18th North Carolina		Jul. 1863	Missing in action, July 3rd, and presumed dead	Unknown
Dyess, Reuben M.	Co. A, Sumter Artillery Bn. (Ga.)	1843	7/3/1863	Laurel Grove Cemetery, Savannah, Ga., reburial list	Savannah, GA
Dyson, Benjamin	Sgt., Co. C, 9th Virginia	1834	7/3/1863	Obituary in Richmond Dispatch, July 30, 1863	Unknown
Eaddy, John Foster	Co. G, 15th South Carolina	1841	7/7/1863	Mortally wounded per the Charleston Mercury, August 28, 1863	Charleston, SC
Eady, Thomas Henry D.	Co. L, 6th Alabama		Jul. 1863	Obituary in Richmond Dispatch, August 24, 1863	Unknown
Eakin, Jonathan W.	Co. G, 11th Virginia	1840	7/3/1863	Killed in action	Unknown
Eanes, William T.	Co. D, 38th Virginia		7/3/1863	Killed in action per the Richmond Sentinel, August 1, 1863; known as Tap	Unknown
Early, H.F.	Co. D, 11th Georgia		7/23/1863	Died as POW at David's Island, NY	Cypress Hills, NY
Earnest [Ernest], Louis	Co. C, 12th Alabama		Jul. 1863	Killed in action	Unknown
Earnheardt, J.H.	Co. A, 11th North Carolina	1840	7/1/1863	Killed in action	Unknown
Earp, Calvin	Co. E, 7th North Carolina	1840	7/15/1863	Mortally wounded-died at unknown place in Gettysburg	Unknown
Easley, Frederick B.	Co. E, 14th Virginia	1836	7/3/1863	Killed in action	Unknown
Easley, James M.	Sgt., Co. D, 28th North Carolina	1842	7/3/1863	Killed in action	Unknown
Easley, Robert C.	Co. I, 53rd Virginia		7/3/1863	Killed in action	Unknown
Eason, Alfred	Cpl., Co. E, 33rd North Carolina	1827	8/1/1863	Mortally wounded and died at Seminary Hospital, Gettysburg, PA	Unknown
Eason, William	Brooks Arty. (S.C) Rhett's	1838	7/3/1863	Killed in action per the Richmond Sentinel, July 27, 1863	Unknown
Easterling, Josiah K.	Co. G, 8th South Carolina	1843	7/2/1863	Hollywood Cemetery, Richmond, Va., reburial lists	Richmond, VA
Eastham, George C.	Capt., Co. I, 33rd Virginia		7/3/1863	Killed in action	Unknown
Eastridge, John	Co. B, 48th Virginia		7/29/1863	Hollywood Cemetery, Richmond, Va., reburial lists	Richmond, VA
Eatherly, John W.	Co. I, 7th Tennessee		7/3/1863	Killed in action	Unknown
Ebbs, -	Co. B, 23rd North Carolina		7/4/1863	Mortally wounded-died at unknown place in Gettysburg	Unknown
Echols, J.H.	Lt., Co. H, 8th Georgia		7/2/1863	Killed in action	Unknown
Echols, Stoakley Marrell	Co. C, 17th Mississippi	1828	7/2/1863	Killed in action	Unknown
Eckford, William J.	Capt., Co. B, 13th Mississippi	1831	7/1/863	Killed in action	Unknown
Eckles, James W.	Co. G, 18th Virginia		7/3/1863	Killed in action	Unknown
Edgar, Thomas	Co. C, 1st Maryland Battalion		Jul. 1863	Killed in action, July 1-3	Unknown
Edgcomb, Edward	Cpl., Co. G, 10th Louisiana		7/3/1863	Killed in action on Culp's Hill	Unknown
Edge, Stephen Clinton	Co. D, 8th Georgia	8/20/1830	7/21/1863	Hollywood Cemetery, Richmond, Va., reburial lists	Richmond, VA

NAME	REGIMENT	BIRTH	DEATH	COMMENT	BURIAL
Edington, Robert B.	Lt., Co. E, 42nd Virginia	1841	7/4/1863	Mortally wounded, July 2nd, and died two days later	Unknown
Edmonds, Edward Claxton	Col., 38th Virginia	1/21/1835	7/3/1863	Killed in action	Unknown
Edwards, A.B.	Co. K, 26th North Carolina	1838	8/1/1863	Mortally wounded and died at Baltimore, MD-buried there	Baltimore, MD
Edwards, Abbie C.	Sgt., Richmond Fayette Arty. (Va.)		7/3/1863	Killed in action per the Richmond Dispatch, July 16, 1863	Unknown
Edwards, Allen R.	Co. K, 26th North Carolina	1840	8/1/1863	Mortally wounded and died at Baltimore, MD-buried there	Baltimore, MD
Edwards, Cephus M.	Co. C, 60th Georgia		7/1/1863	Killed in action	Unknown
Edwards, Charles W.	Co. F, 47th North Carolina	1837	7/3/1863	Killed in action	Unknown
Edwards, Cornelius	Co. G, 11th North Carolina	1836	7/6/1863	Mortally wounded and died at Williamsport, MD-buried there	Williamsport, MD
Edwards, David H.	Sgt., Co. G, 26th North Carolina	1840	7/1/1863	Killed in action	Unknown
Edwards, David S.	Co. D, 1st Virginia	1839	9/13/1863	Hollywood Cemetery, Richmond, Va., reburial lists	Richmond, VA
Edwards, DeSaussure	Lt., Co. K, 2nd South Carolina		7/2/1863	Killed in action	Unknown
Edwards, George Washington	Co. E, 11th Mississippi	1839	7/3/1863	Killed in action	Unknown
Edwards, Hinnant	Co. D, 18th North Carolina	1840	7/3/1863	Killed in action	Unknown
Edwards, J.J.	Co. E, 55th North Carolina	1843	8/9/1863	Mortally wounded and died at Hagerstown, MD-buried there	Hagerstown, MD
Edwards, James D.	Co. C, 57th Virginia		7/18/1863	Mortally wounded and died at Chester, PA	Phil. National Cem.
Edwards, John	Co. K, 26th North Carolina	1843	7/3/1863	Killed in action	Unknown
Edwards, John H.	Co. E, 13th Alabama		7/2/1863	Killed in action	Unknown
Edwards, John N.	Co. K, 9th Georgia		7/3/1863	Killed in action	Unknown
Edwards, John T.	Co. D, 32nd North Carolina	1843	7/2/1863	Killed in action	Unknown
Edwards, Joseph R.	Cpl., Co. D, 3rd Virginia		7/3/1863	Killed in action	Unknown
Edwards, Richard H.	Co. E, 9th Virginia	1822	7/3/1863	Killed in action	Unknown
Edwards, William H.	Cpl., Co. B, 3rd Georgia		7/2/1863	Killed in action	Unknown
Edwards, William H.	Co. K, 9th Georgia		7/3/1863	Killed in action	Unknown
Edwards, Wilson L.	Sgt., Co. K, 17th Mississippi	1838	7/2/1863	Killed in action	Unknown
Efird, Israel S.	Co. C, 1st North Carolina Cavalry	1843	Jul. 1863	Mortally wounded and died on unknown date	Unknown
Einstein, Harvey	Co. F, 11th Virginia	1843	Jul. 1863	Missing in action and presumed dead	Unknown
Elam, George W.	Sgt., Co. F, 18th Virginia	1839	7/3/1863	Killed in action	Unknown
Elam, Isaac	Co. F, 44th Alabama	1838	7/2/1863	Killed in action	Unknown
Elder, Abner Richard	Co. I, 42nd Virginia	1820	7/6/1863	Mortally wounded-died at unknown place in Gettysburg	Unknown
Elder, Joseph A.	Co. G, 18th Virginia	1841	7/3/1863	Killed in action	Unknown
Elington, William P.	Co. E, 26th North Carolina	1838	7/21/1863	Hollywood Cemetery, Richmond, Va., reburial lists	Richmond, VA
Ellett, Lemuel Overton	Cpl., Co. I, 1st Virginia		7/3/1863	Hollywood Cemetery, Richmond, Va., reburial lists	Richmond, VA
Elliott, James O.	Co. B, 7th Virginia	1842	circa Aug 1	Mortally wounded, July 3rd, died prior to Aug. 1st	Unknown

NAME	REGIMENT	BIRTH	DEATH	COMMENT	BURIAL
Elliott, Robert	Co. I, 56th Virginia	1/20/1836	7/3/1863	Killed in action	Unknown
Elliott, Titus M.	Co. K, 34th North Carolina	1836	7/1/1863	Killed in action	Unknown
Elliott, William Andrew	Co. A, 11th North Carolina	6/20/1843	7/1/1863	Killed in action	Unknown
Elliott, William E.	Co. F, 59th Georgia		7/2/1863	Killed in action	Unknown
Elliott, William N.	Co. G, 61st Georgia		7/3/1863	Mortally wounded, July 1st, and died two days later	Unknown
Ellis, Alexander	Co. C, 3rd Alabama		7/1/1863	Killed in action	Unknown
Ellis, Jack W.	Co. H, 4th Texas	1841	7/31/1863	Died as POW at David's Island, NY	Cypress Hills, NY
Ellis, James H.	Sgt., Co. F, 28th Virginia	1839	7/3/1863	Missing in action and presumed dead	Unknown
Ellis, John Thomas	Lt. Col., 19th Virginia	3/16/1827	7/3/1863	Hollywood Cemetery, Richmond, Va., reburial lists	Richmond, VA
Ellis, Robert Stapleton	Lt., Co. C, 56th Virginia		Jul. 1863	Mortally wounded per the Richmond Sentinel, July 29, 1863	Orange Co. VA
Ellison, James Henry	Capt., Co. C, 15th Alabama	1837	7/2/1863	Killed in action	Unknown
Ellison, James R.	Madison Light Artillery (La.)		Jul. 1863	Mortally wounded per the Richmond Sentinel, July 27, 1863	Unknown
Ellisor, Warren Preston	Co. D, 13th South Carolina	1843	7/1/1863	Killed in action	Unknown
Ellixson, James B.	Cpl., Co. A, 56th Virginia		Jul. 1863	Mortally wounded per the Richmond Sentinel, July 27, 1863	Unknown
Elmer, Ferdinand	Page's Artillery (Va.)		7/14/1863	Mortally wounded-died at unknown place in Gettysburg	Unknown
Elmore, James	Co. C, 28th Virginia	1828	7/3/1863	Killed in action per the Richmond Sentinel, July 30, 1863	Unknown
Elmore, Thomas Appleton	Co. A, 7th Georgia	3/12/1842	7/7/1863	Hollywood Cemetery, Richmond, Va., reburial lists	Richmond, VA
Elms, John P.	Lt., Co. I, 37th North Carolina	1838	7/3/1863	Killed in action	Unknown
Elrod, William Boyd	Co. G, 16th Georgia	1837	Jul. 1863	Laurel Grove Cemetery, Savannah, Ga., reburial list	Savannah, GA
Em[m]erson, Elisha W.	Co. D, 38th Virginia		7/3/1863	Killed in action per the Richmond Sentinel, August 1, 1863	Unknown
Emerson, John R.	Lt., Co. E, 26th North Carolina		8/11/1863	Died as POW at David's Island, NY	Cypress Hills, NY
Emory, John	Co. F, 33rd North Carolina	1842	1863	Mortally wounded, July 3rd, and died on unknown date in 1863	Unknown
Endy, Wilson	Co. F, 5th North Carolina	1835	7/1/1863	Killed in action	Richmond, VA
English, William H.	Sgt., Co. L, 6th Alabama	1841	7/1/1863	Killed in action	Unknown
Ennis, Benjamin Thomas Martin	Co. E, 14th Alabama	4/17/1844	7/26/1863	Mortally wounded and buried on Jacob Schwartz Farm	Unknown
Epps, William D.	Co. B, 53rd North Carolina	1832	7/4/1863	Oakwood Cemetery, Raleigh, NC, reburial list	Raleigh, NC
Erwin [Irwin], Thomas M.	Sgt., Co. H, 7th North Carolina	1/26/1826	7/3/1863	Killed in action	Unknown
Erwin, Rufus	Co. F, 26th North Carolina	1838	7/15/1863	Mortally wounded-died at unknown place in Gettysburg	Unknown
Eskridge, G.W.	Co. D, 5th Texas		7/2/1863	Killed in action	Unknown
Estep, Harden	Co. B, 26th North Carolina	2/21/1834	7/1/1863	Killed in action	Unknown
Estes, Richard B.	Co. H, 45th North Carolina	1831	7/23/1863	Oakwood Cemetery, Raleigh, NC, reburial list	Raleigh, NC

NAME	REGIMENT	BIRTH	DEATH	COMMENT	BURIAL
Estes, Robert G.	Co. H, 56th Virginia		Jul. 1863	Missing in action and presumed dead	Unknown
Estes, W.Joe	Co. H, 56th Virginia		Jul. 1863	Killed in action per the Richmond Sentinel, July 29,1863	Unknown
Estes, W.T.	Co. A, 11th Mississippi		7/10/1863	Mortally wounded-died at unknown place in Gettysburg	Unknown
Estis, Thomas B.	Sgt., Co. C, 56th Virginia		8/8/1863	Died of wounds in a Richmond, VA Hospital	Richmond, VA
Etheridge, Gilford [Guilford]	Co. B, 14th South Carolina	1838	7/3/1863	Killed in action	Unknown
Ethridge, Nathan	Co. G, 5th North Carolina	1843	7/1/1863	Hollywood Cemetery, Richmond, Va., reburial lists	Richmond, VA
Etter, Andrew James	Co. E, 28th Virginia	1841	7/3/1863	Killed in action per the Richmond Sentinel, July 29, 1863	Unknown
Eudailey, Moses	Co. E, 22nd Virginia Battalion	1825	Jul. 1863	Missing in action and presumed dead	Unknown
Eudailey, Samuel P.	Co. G, 56th Virginia	1843	Jul. 1863	Killed in action per the Richmond Sentinel, July 29, 1863	Unknown
Eudy, William R. [Wilson]	Co. K, 28th North Carolina	7/21/1834	7/1/1863	Killed in action	Unknown
Eure, James R.	Co. C, 52nd North Carolina	1839	9/20/1863	Mortally wounded and died at Chester, PA	Phil. National Cem.
Eustace, John Conway	Lt., Fredericksburg Artillery (Va.)	1840	7/3/1863	Killed in action	Unknown
Evans, Burwell	Co. H, 5th North Carolina	1837	7/1/1863	Hollywood Cemetery, Richmond, Va., reburial lists	Richmond, VA
Evans, David	Co. H, 32nd North Carolina	1838	7/3/1863	Killed in action	Unknown
Evans, John	Lt., Co. G, 13th Mississippi	1842	7/3/1863	Mortally wounded, July 3rd, and died the same day	Unknown
Evans, John A.S.	Co. C, 49th Virginia		Jul. 1863	Missing in action and presumed dead	Unknown
Evans, John W.	Co. D, 13th North Carolina	1842	7/1/1863	Killed in action	Unknown
Evans, Tandy Servis	Co. A, 7th Virginia		7/3/1863	Killed in action	Unknown
Evans, Thomas M.	Co. A, 45th North Carolina	1837	7/3/1863	Killed in action	Unknown
Evans, William	Sgt., Co. D, 17th Georgia		7/2/1863	Killed in action	Unknown
Evans, William M.	Co. H, 2nd North Carolina Battalion.	1842	7/1/1863	Killed in action	Unknown
Everett, James	Co. E, 33rd North Carolina		Jul. 1863	Mortally wounded and died on unknown date	Unknown
Everett, James L.	Co. E, 55th North Carolina	1841	7/1/1863	Killed in action	Unknown
Everett, John C.	Sgt., Co. D, 61st Georgia		7/1/1863	Killed in action	Unknown
Everett, Richard B.L.	Co. D, 3rd Virginia	1837	7/3/1863	Killed in action	Unknown
Everton, David	Co. I, 17th Mississippi	1837	7/2/1863	Killed in action	Richmond, VA
Ewing, Joseph Kent	Lt., Co. G, 4th Virginia	1/23/1838	7/4/1863	Mortally wounded, July 3rd, and died the next day	Unknown
Ezell, Zebeon [Zibeon]	Co. E, 13th South Carolina	2/27/1832	7/13/1863	Mortally wounded, July 3rd, and died at Williamsport, MD	Williamsport, MD
Fain, Newton Van Buren	Sgt., Co. F, 11th Georgia	1835	7/3/1863	Killed in action	Unknown
Fair, William H.	Co. C, 8th Virginia		7/3/1863	Killed in action per the Richmond Sentinel, July 28, 1863	Unknown
Fairbairn, John A.	Sgt., Co. G, 3rd South Carolina	1840	7/2/1863	Killed in action	Unknown
Faircloth, John C.	Co. G, 55th North Carolina		Jul. 1863	Killed in action	Unknown
Faircloth, Levi	Co. F, 20th North Carolina	1837	7/1/1863	Killed in action	Unknown

NAME	REGIMENT	BIRTH	DEATH	COMMENT	BURIAL
Fallon [Fallin], Thomas	Co. I, 8th Alabama	1836	Aug. 1863	Missing in action and presumed dead	Unknown
Fant, J.B.	Co. G, 17th Mississippi	1832	7/4/1863	Mortally wounded, July 3rd, and and died the next day	Unknown
Farmer, Absalom	Co. G, 57th North Carolina	1834	7/26/1863	Mortally wounded-died at unknown place in Gettysburg	Unknown
Farmer, Adoniram Judson	Co. F, 11th Mississippi	12/10/1844	7/5/1853	Hollywood Cemetery, Richmond, Va., reburial lists	Richmond, VA
Farmer, Chesley M.	Co. H, 14th Virginia	1840	7/3/1863	Killed in action	Unknown
Farmer, I.H.	Co. G, 10th Alabama		7/2/1863	Killed in action	Unknown
Farmer, W.	Co. G, 3rd South Carolina Battalion		8/14/1863	Mortally wounded, July 2nd, died in Union Hospital, Gettysburg, PA	Unknown
Farrar, Andrew W.	Lt., Co. H, 8th Georgia		7/21/1863	Mortally wounded and died at Chester, PA	Phil. National Cem.
Farson, Stephen	Co. H, 1st Virginia	1827	8/29/1863	Hollywood Cemetery, Richmond, Va., reburial lists	Richmond, VA
Faucett, William F.	Co. E, 13th North Carolina	1833	1863	Mortally wounded and died on unknown date	Unknown
Faucett, William H.	Co. D, 13th North Carolina	1825	7/3/1863	Killed in action	Unknown
Faulk, James L.	Co. L, 7th South Carolina		7/2/1863	Killed in action	Unknown
Faulkner, John H.	Fraser's Battery (Ga.)		7/2/1863	Killed in action	Unknown
Fears, Charles A.	Co. K, 21st Virginia	1837	7/15/1863	Mortally wounded-died on unknown date in Gettysburg	Unknown
Featherston, Daniel A.	Lt., Co. F, 11th Mississippi	1836	7/3/1863	Hollywood Cemetery, Richmond, Va., reburial lists	Richmond, VA
Felce, Alsey	Co. I, 55th North Carolina	1822	7/3/1863	Killed in action	Unknown
Felder, William E.	Co. D, 2nd South Carolina		7/2/1863	Magnolia Cemetery, Charleston, SC, reburial list	Charleston, SC
Felton, Shadrack	Co. H, 5th North Carolina	1838	7/1/1863	Hollywood Cemetery, Richmond, Va., reburial lists	Richmond, VA
Felts, Richard A.	Co. G, 3rd Virginia	1841	7/3/1863	Killed in action while carrying the colors	Unknown
Fendrich, Rudolph	Co. E, 44th Virginia	1845	7/3/1863	Killed in action	Unknown
Fentswait, J.R.	Co. G, 1st Maryland Battalion		1863	Mortally wounded and died on unknown date	Unknown
Fergurson, Thomas J.	Lt., Co. A, 31st Georgia		7/1/1863	Killed in action	Unknown
Ferguson, John P.	Co. A, 2nd Georgia Battalion		Jul. 1863	Mortally wounded, July 2nd, and died on unknown date	Unknown
Ferguson, Julius A.	Sgt., Co. H, 45th North Carolina	1836	7/1/1863	Killed in action	Unknown
Ferguson, Martin P.	Blount's Battery (Va.)		7/3/1863	Killed in action	Unknown
Ferrell, S. Dave	Co. G, 4th Texas		7/2/1863	Killed in action, body recovered and shipped to Holly Springs, MS	Holly Springs, MS
Fields, F.L.	Co. C, 4th Texas		7/2/1863	Hollywood Cemetery, Richmond, Va., reburial lists	Richmond, VA
Fields, John Calvin	Cpl., Co. C, 45th North Carolina	1842	7/1/1863	Killed in action	Unknown
Fields, P.C.	Co. A, 14th South Carolina	1842	7/11/1863	Mortally wounded-died at unknown place in Gettysburg	Unknown

NAME	REGIMENT	BIRTH	DEATH	COMMENT	BURIAL
Fields, William Henry Harrison	Co. K, 5th Texas	8/10/1843	7/16/1863	Mortally wounded–died at unknown place in Gettysburg	Unknown
Filger, Daniel	Co. D, 44th Virginia		7/4/1863	Hollywood Cemetery, Richmond, Va., reburial lists	Richmond, VA
Fincannon, John W.	Co. A, 7th North Carolina	1830	Jul. 1863	Mortally wounded and died on unknown date	Unknown
Finch, Charles Henry	Co. B, 11th Virginia	12/2/1833	7/3/1863	Killed in action	Unknown
Fincher, James A.	Co. B, 26th North Carolina	1840	Jul. 1863	Mortally wounded and died on unknown date	Unknown
Finger, Robert Pinckney	Co. I, 11th North Carolina	7/13/1841	7/3/1863	Killed in action	Unknown
Finnerty, Patrick	Sgt., Co. C, 7th Louisiana	1832	7/1/1863	Killed in action	Unknown
Finton, John W.	Cpl., Co. H, 8th Alabama		7/3/1863	Killed in action	Unknown
Fiser, James H.	Co. C, 14th Tennessee	6/10/1833	8/2/1863	Hollywood Cemetery, Richmond, Va., reburial lists	Richmond, VA
Fishel, Charles	Co. G, 2nd North Carolina Battalion.	1842	8/2/1863	Mortally wounded–died on unknown date in Gettysburg	Unknown
Fisher, Newton Jasper	Co. E, 2nd Mississippi	1842	7/1/1863	Killed in action	Unknown
Fisher, Phillip David	Co. B, 28th Virginia	1830	7/3/1863	Killed in action	Unknown
Fisher, Platt Buell	Lt., Co. B, Jeff Davis Legion Cavalry	5/20/1840	Jul. 1863	Mortally wounded and died on unknown date	Unknown
Fisher, Ulysses W.	Cpl., Co. C, 6th Louisiana		9/6/1863	Died as POW at David's Island, NY	Cypress Hills, NY
Fisher, William R.	Co. H, 4th Virginia	1841	7/3/1863	Killed in action	Unknown
Fitzgerald, Frank Marion	Co. H, 5th Texas	1842	7/2/1863	Killed in action	Unknown
Fitzgerald, Michael	Co. E, 8th Alabama		7/3/1863	Killed in action	Unknown
Flake, John	Co. K, 26th North Carolina	1843	7/1/1863	Killed in action	Unknown
Flake, Phillip H.	Co. K, 26th North Carolina	7/29/1843	7/3/1863	Killed in action	Unknown
Flanders, John Mason	Co. F, 14th Georgia	7/26/1833	7/14/1863	Mortally wounded and died at Winchester, VA	Winchester, VA
Fleenor, Isaac Gobble	Co. I, 48th Virginia	Jan. 1840	7/3/1863	Killed in action	Unknown
Fleenor, Robert H.	Co. I, 48th Virginia	1839	7/2/1863	Killed in action	Unknown
Fleming, James B.	Co. I, 12th South Carolina		7/1/1863	Killed in action	Unknown
Fleming, William	Co. F, 26th North Carolina	1828	Jul. 1863	Killed in action	Unknown
Fletcher, Henry Y.	Co. K, 14th Virginia	1841	7/13/1863	Mortally wounded–died at unknown place in Gettysburg	Unknown
Fletcher, Isaiah D.	Co. I, 13th Mississippi	2/26/1842	7/2/1863	Killed in action	Unknown
Fletcher, J.M.	Lt., Co. G, 12th Alabama		7/4/1863	Hollywood Cemetery, Richmond, Va., reburial lists	Richmond, VA
Fletcher, John	Co. G, 49th Virginia		7/3/1863	Killed in action	Unknown
Flincham, Samuel M.	Sgt., Co. H, 53rd North Carolina	1835	7/1/1863	Killed in action	Unknown
Flood, E.T.	Co. G, 3rd Georgia		7/2/1863	Killed in action	Unknown
Florence, Gibson	Co. G, 61st Georgia		7/1/1863	Killed in action	Unknown
Flournoy, Samuel Thomas	Co. K, 31st Georgia	1826	7/3/1863	Killed in action	Unknown
Flowers, David	Co. H, 1st Virginia		7/3/1863	Killed in action	Unknown
Flowers, Thomas	Co. C, 3rd North Carolina	1827	7/2/1863	Killed in action on either July 2nd or 3rd	Unknown

NAME	REGIMENT	BIRTH	DEATH	COMMENT	BURIAL
Flowers, Travis	Co. A, 2nd Florida	1842	7/3/1863	Killed in action	Unknown
Flowers, W.H.	Cpl., Co. C, 4th NC Cavalry		7/4/1863	Killed in action at Monterey, PA	Raleigh, NC
Floyd, Louis J.	Co. C, 61st Georgia		7/1/1863	Killed in action	Unknown
Floyd, William F.	Cpl., Co. F, 4th Texas		7/2/1863	Killed in action	Unknown
Floyd, William W.	Co. K, 61st Georgia		7/1/1863	Killed in action	Unknown
Foley, Green B.	Co. B, 51st Georgia		7/2/1863	Killed in action	Unknown
Fontenot, Horthere	Co. F, 8th Louisiana	1844	7/10/1863	Hollywood Cemetery, Richmond, Va., reburial lists	Richmond, VA
Fonville, Thomas G.	Co. E, 13th North Carolina	1839	7/1/1863	Killed in action	Unknown
Fooshe, James Wesley	Co. A, 3rd South Carolina Battalion	1844	7/2/1863	Killed in action per the Charleston Courier, July 1863	Charleston, SC
Forbes, Wyatt A.	Co. E, 55th North Carolina	1843	8/11/1863	Mortally wounded and died at Chester, PA	Phil. National Cem.
Ford, D.W	Co. H, 23rd North Carolina	1838	7/1/1863	Killed in action	Unknown
Ford, Edward M.	Capt., Co. A, 50th Georgia	1829	7/2/1863	Laurel Grove Cemetery, Savannah, Ga., reburial list	Savannah, GA
Ford, John B.	Lt., Co. G, 16th North Carolina	8/2/1832	Jul. 1863	Killed in action	Unknown
Ford, P. Fletcher	Lt., Co. A, 57th Virginia		Jul. 1863	Killed in action, July 1-3	Unknown
Ford, William	Co. B, 7th Louisiana	1840	8/28/1863	Hollywood Cemetery, Richmond, Va., reburial lists	Richmond, VA
Ford, William	Co. I, 61st Virginia	7/1/1836		Killed in action	Unknown
Forrest, Samuel P.	Cpl., Co. K, 28th North Carolina	1842	9/14/1863	Oakwood Cemetery, Raleigh, NC, reburial list	Raleigh, NC
Forrester, James B.	Co. F, 13th Mississippi	1834	7/2/1863	Mortally wounded and died the same day	Unknown
Forrester, Joel	Co. K, 4th Texas		7/2/1863	Hollywood Cemetery, Richmond, Va., reburial lists	Richmond, VA
Forrester, John B.	Co. I, 4th Alabama		8/11/1863	Mortally wounded-died at unknown place in Gettysburg	Unknown
Forrester, S.B.	Co. I, 24th Georgia		8/11/1863	Laurel Grove Cemetery, Savannah, Ga., reburial list	Savannah, GA
Fortner, Alexander	Co. F, 28th North Carolina	1840	7/3/1863	Killed in action	Unknown
Fortson, Eastin L.	Co. F, 38th Georgia	1845	7/1/1863	Killed in action	Unknown
Fortune, Absalom. M.	Cpl., Co. D, 19th Virginia	1842	7/3/1863	Killed in action per the Richmond Sentinel, August 11, 1863	Unknown
Fortune, Meridith Winston	Sgt., Co. G, 19th Virginia	1823	Jul. 1863	Missing in action and presumed dead	Unknown
Forysthe, James A.B.	Co. F, 2nd Mississippi	1839	7/1/1863	Killed in action	Unknown
Foskey, Manning A.	Co. F, 48th Georgia	1836	7/2/1863	Killed in action	Unknown
Foskey, Stanley Manning	Co. F, 48th Georgia	1/28/1832	7/2/1863	Killed in action	Unknown
Foster, David	Co. E, 26th North Carolina	1834	Jul. 1863	Killed in action	Unknown
Foster, Farris	Co. F, 28th Virginia		7/3/1863	Killed in action	Unknown
Foster, Horace H.	Co. G, 18th Virginia	1831	7/17/1863	Hollywood Cemetery, Richmond, Va., reburial lists	Richmond, VA
Fouche, John H.	Fauquier Artillery (Va.)		Jul. 1863	Mortally wounded and died on unknown date	Unknown
Fouchee, David M.	Cpl., Co. C, 7th Virginia	1841	7/3/1863	Killed in action	Unknown

NAME	REGIMENT	BIRTH	DEATH	COMMENT	BURIAL
Fountain, W.B.	Co. G, 1st Maryland Battalion		Jul. 1863	Mortally wounded and died on unknown date	Unknown
Foushe, John W.	Co. F, 2nd South Carolina	1840	7/22/1863	Magnolia Cemetery, Charleston, SC, reburial list	Charleston, SC
Fowler, Everett	Co. G, 47th North Carolina	1841	7/3/1863	Hollywood Cemetery, Richmond, Va., reburial lists	Richmond, VA
Fowler, John	Lt., Co. C, 26th Alabama		7/3/1863	Killed in action	Unknown
Fowlkes, Andrew J.	Co. C, 18th Virginia	1844	7/3/1863	Killed in action	Unknown
Fox, James F.	Sgt., Co. F, 14th North Carolina		7/30/1863	Died as POW at David's Island, NY	Cypress Hills, NY
Fox, William	Sgt., Co. K, 1st South Carolina		7/30/1863	Died as POW at David's Island, NY	Cypress Hills, NY
Frady, William	Co. G, 12th South Carolina		7/1/1863	Killed in action	Unknown
Fraley, Martin	Co. H, 50th Virginia	7/19/1827	7/3/1863	Killed in action	Unknown
France, James B.	Sgt., Co. F, 3rd Arkansas	1836	7/2/1863	Killed in action	Unknown
Francisco, Charles Lewis	Lt., Co. I, 14th Virginia Cavalry	1840	7/4/1863	Mortally wounded, July 3rd, died the next day. Body returned to Staunton, VA	Staunton, VA
Franklin, Fendall Griffith	Co. B, 1st Virginia	1841	7/3/1863	Killed in action	Unknown
Franklin, George W.	Co. E, 50th Virginia	1844	8/10/1863	Laurel Grove Cemetery, Savannah, Ga., reburial list	Savannah, GA
Franklin, James Cicero	Lt., Co. B, 2nd Georgia		7/1/1863	Killed in action	Unknown
Franks, Rufus B.	Co. I, 4th Alabama		7/2/1863	Hollywood Cemetery, Richmond, Va., reburial lists	Richmond, VA
Fraser, John Couper	Capt., Pulaski Artillery (Ga.)	12/8/1832	7/3/1863	Laurel Grove Cemetery, Savannah, Ga., reburial list	Savannah, GA
Frazor, Francis M.	Co. E, 7th Tennessee		7/11/1863	Hollywood Cemetery, Richmond, Va., reburial lists	Richmond, VA
Free, George Washington, Jr.	Co. K, 14th South Carolina	5/5/1845	7/3/1863	Killed in action	Unknown
Freeman, George W.	Co. C, 13th Alabama		7/2/1863	Killed in action	Unknown
Freeman, J.W.	Co. D, 1st Virginia		7/3/1863	Killed in action	Unknown
Freeman, Jacob. T.	Co. E, 51st Georgia	1833	7/4/1863	Mortally wounded July 2nd	Unknown
Freeman, James	Co. B, 9th Georgia		7/2/1863	Killed in action	Unknown
Freeman, John C.	Co. E, 6th North Carolina	1840	8/21/1863	Oakwood Cemetery, Raleigh, NC, reburial list	Raleigh, NC
Freeman, Thomas S.	Sgt., Co. B, 1st Maryland Battalion		7/3/1863	Killed in action	Unknown
Freeman, William	Cpl., Co. I, 2nd Mississippi	1835	7/20/1863	Hollywood Cemetery, Richmond, Va., reburial lists	Richmond, VA
Freeman, William	Co. C, 2nd South Carolina		7/2/1863	Killed in action	Unknown
French, Edward	Co. I, 8th Florida	1832	7/3/1863	Killed in action	Unknown
French, Junius Butler	Adj., 23rd North Carolina	8/7/1837	7/2/1863	Killed in action	Unknown
Freret, Jules	2nd Co., Washington Arty (La.)	7/18/1838	8/4/1863	Mortally wounded and died at Emmittsburg, MD	Emmittsburg, MD
Freshley, James P.	Cpl., Co. H, 13th South Carolina	1836	7/1/1863	Killed in action	Unknown
Frick, John	Co. H, 23rd North Carolina		7/1/1863	Killed in action	Unknown
Fridley, John H.	Co. K, 28th Virginia		8/13/1863	Mortally wounded and died at Chester, PA	Phil. National Cem.

NAME	REGIMENT	BIRTH	DEATH	COMMENT	BURIAL
Frierson, Thomas H.	Co. K, 3rd Georgia		Jul. 1863	Mortally wounded and died on unknown date	Unknown
Frink, John	Capt., Co. F, 5th Florida	4/9/1826	7/3/1863	Killed in action per the Richmond Sentinel, August 15, 1863	Unknown
Frost, Hezikiah J.	Co. H, 2nd Mississippi	1842	7/1/1863	Killed in action	Unknown
Fry, Eben	Co. I, 52nd North Carolina	1823	7/3/1863	Mortally wounded, July 3rd, and died the same day	Unknown
Fryer, James W.	Co. F, 53rd Georgia		Jul. 1863	Mortally wounded per the Augusta Chronicle & Sentinel, August 13, 1863	Unknown
Fulenwider, Andrew C.	Co. E, 34th North Carolina	1826	Jul. 1863	Hollywood Cemetery, Richmond, Va., reburial lists	Richmond, VA
Fulghum, John Quincy	Co. I, 48th Georgia		7/2/1863	Killed in action	Unknown
Fulks, James M.	Co. G, 19th Virginia		8/6/1863	Mortally wounded and died at Camp Letterman	Unknown
Fuller, Adolphus Augustus	Lt., Co. B, 3rd South Carolina Battalion	3/10/1835	7/16/1863	Magnolia Cemetery, Charleston, SC, reburial list	Charleston, SC
Fuller, Blake J.	Lt., Co. K, 8th Alabama	1835	7/3/1863	Killed in action	Unknown
Fuller, Edward Pickens	Co. B, 3rd South Carolina Battalion	12/15/1843	7/3/1863	Magnolia Cemetery, Charleston, SC, reburial list	Charleston, SC
Fullwood, Thomas C.	Lt., Co. G, 20th North Carolina	1841	7/1/1863	Killed in action	Unknown
Fulmer, William E.C.	Co. F, 3rd South Carolina Battalion	1843	8/14/1863	Magnolia Cemetery, Charleston, SC, reburial list	Charleston, SC
Fulton, Jeremiah	Co. D, 2nd Mississippi	1834	7/25/1863	Died of wounds received July 1 at Martinsburg, VA	Martinsburg, WV
Fulton, Joel	Co. I, 33rd North Carolina	1838	7/3/1863	Killed in action	Unknown
Fuqua, Cornelius Tyree	Co. I, 28th Virginia		7/13/1863	Mortally wounded-died at unknown place in Gettysburg	Unknown
Fuqua, J.C.	Old Virginia			Hollywood Cemetery, Richmond, Va., reburial lists	Richmond, VA
Furgason, John C.	Co. G, 24th Georgia		7/3/1863	Died of wounds received on July 2nd	Unknown
Furr, Henry C.	Cpl., Co. F, 8th Virginia	1843	Jul. 1863	Mortally wounded July 3rd and likely died same day	Unknown
Futch, Charles F.	Co. K, 3rd North Carolina	1831	7/2/1863	Killed in action	Unknown
Futrell, John Allen	Cpl., Co. C, 20th Georgia	9/9/1839	7/13/1863	Mortally wounded-died at unknown place in Gettysburg	Unknown
Futrell, Richard	Co. D, 32nd North Carolina	1827	Jul. 1863	Mortally wounded and died on unknown date	Unknown
Gaddy, David Thomas	Co. D, 37th North Carolina	1841	7/2/1863	Killed in action	Unknown
Gaddy, Elisha D.	Co. K, 26th North Carolina	1839	7/8/1863	Hollywood Cemetery, Richmond, Va., reburial lists	Richmond, VA
Gadsden, Thomas Screven	Co. I, 2nd South Carolina	11/6/1841	7/3/1863	Magnolia Cemetery, Charleston, SC, reburial list	Charleston, SC
Gaff, Dempsey	Co. H, 10th Georgia		7/2/1863	Laurel Grove Cemetery, Savannah, Ga., reburial list	Savannah, GA
Gaffney, Thomas	Co. K, 13th Georgia		7/1/1863	Killed in action	Unknown
Gage, Jeremiah Sanders	Sgt., Co. A, 11th Mississippi	4/19/1840	7/3/1863	Mortally wounded, July 3rd, and died the same day	Picken, MS

NAME	REGIMENT	BIRTH	DEATH	COMMENT	BURIAL
Gaillard, Thomas Edmund	Sgt., Co. I, 2nd South Carolina	1840	10/15/1863	Magnolia Cemetery, Charleston, SC, reburial list	Charleston, SC
Gaines, Albert Broaddus	Co. B, Phillip's Legion (Ga.)	12/24/1831	7/9/1863	Mortally wounded-died at unknown place in Gettysburg	Unknown
Gaither, George Washington	Co. K, 1st Virginia Cavalry	3/11/1838	7/3/1863	Killed in action	Cooksville, MD
Gallimore, Ebenezer	Co. I, 14th North Carolina	1839	7/3/1863	Killed in action	Unknown
Galloway, James S.	Co. A, 11th North Carolina	1837	7/21/1863	Mortally wounded, July 1st, died in Richmond, VA, Chimborazo Hospital, buried Oakwood Cemetery	Richmond, VA
Galloway, John	Co. A, 12th South Carolina	1839	7/6/1863	Mortally wounded-died on unknown date in Gettysburg	Unknown
Galloway, Thomas M.	Co. G, 8th Florida		7/3/1863	Killed in action	Unknown
Gamble, George H.	Sgt., Co. F, 31st Georgia	1837	7/1/1863	Killed in action	Unknown
Gammons, John R.	Co. D, 43rd North Carolina	1847	7/1/1863	Killed in action	Unknown
Ganlan, James	Sgt., Madison Light Artillery (La.)		Jul. 1863	Mortally wounded per the Richmond Sentinel, July 27, 1863	Unknown
Gardner, Francis Marion	Co. E, 12th South Carolina	1846	7/23/1863	Died as POW at David's Island, NY	Cypress Hills, NY
Gardner, Harvey C.	Co. I, 2nd North Carolina	1840	7/2/1863	Killed in action on either July 2nd or 3rd	Unknown
Gardner, Samuel H.	Co. I, 15th Alabama	1845	7/2/1863	Killed in action	Unknown
Gardner, Thomas S.	Co. I, 38th North Carolina	1844	Jul. 1863	Missing in action and presumed dead	Unknown
Gardner, Timothy B.	Co. E, 2nd South Carolina		7/19/1863	Mortally wounded, July 2nd, and died at Staunton, VA	Staunton, VA
Gardner, W.S.	Co. I, 22nd North Carolina	1844	Jul. 1863	Killed in action	Unknown
Gardner, William Carter	Co. C, 55th Virginia	1831	7/1/1863	Killed in action	Unknown
Gardner, William J.	Co. D, 3rd Virginia		7/3/1863	Killed in action	Unknown
Garland, William H.	Sgt., Co. M, 8th South Carolina		7/2/1863	Killed in action per the Charleston Courier, July 1863	Unknown
Garner, James W., Jr.	Co. B, 1st Texas	1839	7/2/1863	Killed in action	Unknown
Garnett, Albert D.	Co. H, 14th Virginia		7/3/1863	Killed in action	Unknown
Garnett, Richard Brooke	Brigadier General	11/21/1817	7/3/1863	Killed in action	Unknown
Garnett, Robert K.	Co. D, 21st Virginia	1826	Jul. 1863	Killed in action, July 1-3	Unknown
Garratt, Esau	Co. G, 11th North Carolina	1843	7/11/1863	Mortally wounded and died at Hagerstown, MD-buried there	Hagerstown, MD
Garrett, C.P.	Co. I, 2nd Louisiana	1839	8/31/1863	Hollywood Cemetery, Richmond, Va., reburial lists	Richmond, VA
Garrett, Henry Baxter	Co. G, 26th North Carolina	10/2/1844	7/1/1863	Killed in action, body recovered and shipped to Liberty, NC	Liberty, N.C
Garrett, James	Cpl., Co. C, 59th Georgia		7/25/1863	Died as POW at David's Island, NY	Cypress Hills, NY
Garrett, Thomas L.	Co. G, 23rd Virginia		7/2/1863	Killed in action	Unknown
Garrett, William Alexander	Co. G, 26th North Carolina	3/10/1843	7/1/1863	Killed in action; brother of Henry Baxter Garrett	Liberty, N.C
Garrison, Edward J.	Lt., Co. F, 3rd North Carolina	1840	7/2/1863	Killed in action, body recovered and shipped to Randolph Co., NC	Randolph Co., NC
Garrison, George R.	Co. K, 47th North Carolina		Jul. 1863	Killed in action	Unknown
Garrison, J.S.	Co. A, 11th North Carolina	1844	7/3/1863	Killed in action	Unknown

NAME	REGIMENT	BIRTH	DEATH	COMMENT	BURIAL
Gaskins, William H.	Sgt., Co. K, 8th Virginia	1843	11/5/1863	Mortally wounded and died at Camp Letterman	Unknown
Gast, William	Co. B, 17th Mississippi	1836	7/2/1863	Killed in action	Unknown
Gaston, James Martin	Capt., Co. G, 42nd Mississippi	1835	7/1/1863	Killed in action	Unknown
Gathings, Thomas C.	Co. K, 26th North Carolina	1832	7/1/1863	Killed in action	Unknown
Gaulden, Jabez Sidney	Co. B, 38th Virginia	1837	7/3/1863	Killed in action per the Richmond Sentinel, August 1, 1863	Unknown
Gay, Gilbert G.	Co. F, 43rd North Carolina	1837	7/1/1863	Killed in action	Raleigh, NC
Gay, James W.	Co. G, 13th Georgia		7/1/1863	Killed in action	Unknown
Gay, Thomas O.	Co. I, 10th Alabama		7/2/1863	Killed in action	Unknown
Gay, William Osborn	Co. B, 47th North Carolina	1830	7/4/1863	Mortally wounded-died at unknown place in Gettysburg	Unknown
Gee, Benjamin C.	Co. B, 56th Virginia		Jul. 1863	Mortally wounded and died on unknown date	Unknown
Gee, Leonidas Irvin	Sgt., Co. B, 56th Virginia	1839	7/17/1863	Hollywood Cemetery, Richmond, Va., reburial lists	Richmond, VA
Gee, Samuel	Co. E, 8th South Carolina	12/26/1835	7/2/1863	Killed in action per the Charleston Courier, July 1863	Unknown
Gee, Spirus W.	Cpl., Pee Dee Artillery (S.C.)		7/2/1863	Killed in action	Unknown
Gee, Theodore W.	Co. I, 21st Mississippi		8/2/1863	Hollywood Cemetery, Richmond, Va., reburial lists	Richmond, VA
Geer, Alexander	Co. C, 57th Virginia	1843	7/7/1863	Mortally wounded-died at unknown place in Gettysburg	Unknown
Geer, Jasper Alvin	Co. E, 47th Alabama	8/5/1838	Jul. 1863	Mortally wounded and captured, July 2nd, died on unknown date	Unknown
Geiger, George Henry, Jr.	Lt., Co. K, 2nd Virginia Cavalry	5/28/1826	7/17/1863	Mortally wounded and captured, July 3rd. reinterred after the war at Grace Episcopal Church	Albemarle Co., VA
Gentry, Allen	Co. F, 44th Alabama	1828	7/2/1863	Killed in action	Unknown
Gentry, M.B.	Co. K, 7th South Carolina		7/2/1863	Killed in action per the Charleston Courier, July 1863	Unknown
Geoghegan, Thomas Quincy	Co. D, 19th Mississippi	7/10/1844	7/18/1863	Hollywood Cemetery, Richmond, Va., reburial lists	Richmond, VA
George, McRae	Co. I, 47th North Carolina	1841	7/5/1863	Mortally wounded-died at unknown place in Gettysburg	Unknown
George, William	Co. E, 57th Virginia	2/27/1824	7/17/1863	Mortally wounded and died at Pittsylvania Co., VA-buried there	Pittsylvania Co., VA
George, William H.	Co. I, 53rd Virginia		7/13/1863	Mortally wounded-died at unknown place in Gettysburg	Unknown
Gerald, William A.	Lt., Co. C, 1st Texas	1838	7/2/1863	Killed in action	Unknown
Geringer, Henry	Co. K, 47th North Carolina	1839	Jul. 1863	Hollywood Cemetery, Richmond, Va., reburial lists	Richmond, VA
Geringer, John H.	Co. H, 1st North Carolina	1829	7/28/1863	Oakwood Cemetery, Raleigh, NC, reburial list	Raleigh, NC
German, John D.	Co. D, 37th North Carolina	1841	Jul. 1863	Missing in action and presumed dead	Unknown
Gerringer, Felty Valentine	Co. E, 13th North Carolina	4/8/1824	7/1/1863	Killed in action	Unknown
Gibbs, Henry	Co. F, 33rd North Carolina		Jul. 1863	Killed in action	Unknown

NAME	REGIMENT	BIRTH	DEATH	COMMENT	BURIAL
Gibbs, Joseph W.	Co. K, 38th Virginia		7/3/1863	Killed in action	Unknown
Gibson, Gustavus A.	Lt., Co. G, 18th Mississippi	1837	7/2/1863	Killed in action	Unknown
Gibson, Hardy V.	Lt., Co. B, 13th Alabama		7/3/1863	Killed in action	Unknown
Gibson, Henry T.	Co. H, 56th Virginia	2/15/1837	8/20/1863	Mortally wounded and died in Baltimore, MD; interred Loudon Park Cemetery	Baltimore, MD
Gibson, Joachim	Sgt., Co. I, 7th Louisiana	1833	7/2/1863	Killed in action	Unknown
Gibson, John R.	Co. G, 22nd Georgia		7/14/1863	Hollywood Cemetery, Richmond, Va., reburial lists	Richmond, VA
Gibson, Robert H.	Co. D, 1st Texas		7/2/1863	Killed in action	Unknown
Gibson, William Henry	Lt., Co. A, 33rd North Carolina	6/2/1837	7/3/1863	Hollywood Cemetery, Richmond, Va., reburial lists	Richmond, VA
Gilbert, Charles Lee	Co. C, 27th Virginia		7/10/1863	Hollywood Cemetery, Richmond, Va., reburial lists	Richmond, VA
Gilbert, George W.	Cpl., Co. I, 11th Georgia		7/2/1863	Laurel Grove Cemetery, Savannah, Ga., reburial list	Savannah, GA
Gilbert, James M.	Co. E, 52nd Virginia	1845	7/5/1863	Oakwood Cemetery, Raleigh, NC, reburial list	Raleigh, NC
Gilbert, John W.	Co. F, 13th Alabama		7/1/1863	Killed in action	Unknown
Gilbert, Samuel S.	Co. I, 24th Virginia		Jul. 1863	Mortally wounded and died on unknown date	Unknown
Gilbert, William	Co. D, 23rd North Carolina	1836	8/15/1863	Oakwood Cemetery, Raleigh, NC, reburial list	Raleigh, NC
Gilbert, Z. Hawkins	Co. D, 26th North Carolina	1840	7/3/1863	Killed in action	Unknown
Gilder, Gifford [Guildford] A.	Co. B, 14th South Carolina	1841	8/23/1863	Died as POW at David's Island, NY	Cypress Hills, NY
Gilder, John C.	Co. A, 47th Alabama		Jul. 1863	Mortally wounded and died on unknown date	Unknown
Giles, Jackson Brown	Co. C, 9th Georgia	7/13/1843	7/2/1863	Killed in action	Unknown
Giles, Richard E.	Co. C, 1st Virginia		8/21/1863	Died as POW at David's Island, NY	Cypress Hills, NY
Giles, W.H.	Co. C, 3rd North Carolina	1841	7/2/1863	Killed in action on either July 2nd or 3rd	Unknown
Gilham, Benjamin F.	Lt., Co. K, 8th Georgia	1836	7/2/1863	Killed in action	Unknown
Gill, James C.	Sgt. Maj., 18th Virginia	1844	7/11/1863	Hollywood Cemetery, Richmond, Va., reburial lists	Richmond, VA
Gill, Nicholas	Co. C, 47th North Carolina	1843	Jul. 1863	Missing in action and presumed dead	Unknown
Gillespie, Richard G.	Co. F, Phillips Legion (Ga.)		7/8/1863	Hollywood Cemetery, Richmond, Va., reburial lists	Richmond, VA
Gillespie, Thomas Ballard	Co. E, 50th Virginia	1843	7/19/1863	Mortally wounded–died at unknown place in Gettysburg	Unknown
Gilliam, Carter M.	Sgt., Co. E, 18th Virginia	1829	7/3/1863	Killed in action	Unknown
Gilliam, Jesse M.	Sgt., Co. K, 47th North Carolina	1834	Jul. 1863	Missing in action and presumed dead	Unknown
Gilliland, Henry D.	Co. C, 27th Virginia		7/3/1863	Killed in action	Unknown
Gilliland, John W.	Sgt., Co. I, 13th Mississippi	1840	7/2/1863	Killed in action	Unknown
Gilmer, Thomas Abner	Co. I, 11th Mississippi	1841	7/3/1863	Killed in action	Unknown
Gilreath, Lawrence P.	Co. B, 2nd South Carolina	9/25/1840	10/2/1863	Mortally wounded, body recovered and shipped to Greenville, SC	Greenville, SC

NAME	REGIMENT	BIRTH	DEATH	COMMENT	BURIAL
Ginn, Jesse G.	Co. G, 16th Georgia	1835	7/2/1863	Killed in action	Unknown
Gist, Gabriel G.	Co. G, 15th South Carolina	1829	7/2/1863	Killed in action per the Charleston Courier, July 1863	Unknown
Gittman, Francis C.	Co. B, 53rd Virginia		7/3/1863	Killed in action	Unknown
Gladden, John Turner William	Co. C, 55th North Carolina	8/10/1836	7/1/1863	Killed in action	Unknown
Gladney, Amos Joseph	Co. E, 15th South Carolina	1/1/1846	7/2/1863	Killed in action per the Charleston Courier, July 1863	Unknown
Glass, John	Co. C, 14th Virginia	1831	7/3/1863	Killed in action	Unknown
Glass, Sanford W.	Capt., Co. E, 53rd Georgia	1834	7/5/1863	Hollywood Cemetery, Richmond, Va., reburial lists	Richmond, VA
Glasscock, John M.	Co. E, 44th Alabama	1841	7/2/1863	Killed in action	Unknown
Glasscock, Stanhope A.	Co. I, 11th North Carolina	1839	7/19/1863	Mortally wounded-died at unknown place in Gettysburg	Unknown
Glasscow, Andrew Jackson	Co. H, 21st North Carolina	1839	10/18/1863	Oakwood Cemetery, Raleigh, NC, reburial list	Raleigh, NC
Glassell, James Somerville	Co. I, 11th Virginia	7/5/1824	7/5/1863	Mortally wounded, July 3rd, and buried on Jacob Schwartz Farm	Unknown
Glazer, Frederick	Co. D, 4th Texas	1839	7/2/1863	Killed in action	Unknown
Gleason, J.	Co. A, 2nd Florida		7/2/1863	Killed in action	Unknown
Glendy, Robert James Larew	Lt., Co. C, 4th Virginia	7/14/1839	7/23/1863	Mortally wounded-died at unknown place in Gettysburg	Unknown
Glenn, Hinton Coslett	Co. C, 6th North Carolina	1840	7/4/1863	Oakwood Cemetery, Raleigh, NC, reburial list	Raleigh, NC
Glenn, Issac Scott	Sgt., Co. D, 18th Virginia	1/4/1843	Jul. 1863	Killed in action, July 1-3	Unknown
Godman, James	Negro		1863	Hollywood Cemetery, Richmond, Va., reburial lists	Richmond, VA
Godsey, Hiram Washington	Sgt., Co. D, 14th Virginia	1838	7/3/1863	Killed in action	Unknown
Godwin, Elza Neal	Co. C, 61st Georgia		7/1/1863	Killed in action	Unknown
Godwin, Perry	Co. I, 43rd North Carolina	1831	7/26/1863	Mortally wounded-died at unknown place in Gettysburg	Unknown
Goetchius, John M.	Co. A, 2nd Georgia Battalion		7/15/1863	Mortally wounded, July 2nd, and buried on Jacob Schwartz Farm	Unknown
Goggins, John	Sgt., Co. A, 31st Georgia		7/14/1863	Mortally wounded-died at unknown place in Gettysburg	Unknown
Going, Perrin	Co. K, 50th Virginia		7/2/1863	Killed in action	Unknown
Gold, Simeon Charles	Co. C, 55th North Carolina	1841	7/3/1863	Mortally wounded, July 3rd, and died the same day	Unknown
Golding, John J., Jr.	Cpl., Co. A, 3rd South Carolina Battalion	1844	7/17/1863	Mortally wounded per the Charleston Mercury, August 28, 1863	Unknown
Goldman, Newton Wilkes	Co. F, 22nd Georgia	1845	7/2/1863	Killed in action	Unknown
Goldsticker, John A.	Co. A, 4th Texas		7/2/1863	Hollywood Cemetery, Richmond, Va., reburial lists	Richmond, VA
Golladay, John Henry	Co. E, 5th Virginia	1/9/1844	7/3/1863	Killed in action	Unknown
Good, Albert H.	Lt., Co. I, 7th Virginia	1843	8/29/1863	Died as POW at David's Island, NY	Cypress Hills, NY
Good, John	Co. B, 6th Louisiana	1833	7/2/1863	Killed in action	Unknown
Good, Marcus L.	Co. G, 16th North Carolina	1837	8/20/1863	Mortally wounded and died at Chester, PA	Phil. National Cem.

NAME	REGIMENT	BIRTH	DEATH	COMMENT	BURIAL
Goode, Thomas Brown	Co. F, 57th Virginia	10/10/1828	Jul. 1863	Killed in action, July 1-3	Unknown
Goodin, John C.	Co. D, 30th North Carolina	1843	7/1/1863	Killed in action	Unknown
Goodman, Alfred	Co. F, 28th Virginia		7/3/1863	Killed in action	Unknown
Goodman, James K.	Co. A, 5th North Carolina	1838	7/11/1863	Mortally wounded-died at unknown place in Gettysburg	Unknown
Goodman, John B.	Co. G, 20th North Carolina	1843	7/1/1863	Killed in action	Unknown
Goodman, John E.	Sgt., Co. E, 11th North Carolina	1829	7/1/1863	Killed in action	Unknown
Goodrum, William J.	Co. A, 11th North Carolina	1845	7/18/1863	Mortally wounded and died at Chester, PA	Phil. National Cem.
Goodson, John H.	Co. B, 18th North Carolina	1835	7/14/1863	Hollywood Cemetery, Richmond, Va., reburial lists	Richmond, VA
Goodson, Matthew	Sgt., Co. A, 52nd North Carolina	2/13/1823	7/12/1863	Hollywood Cemetery, Richmond, Va., reburial lists	Richmond, VA
Goodwin, Charles	Co. G, 1st Texas	1838	7/2/1863	Killed in action	Unknown
Goodwin, Frank Greenwood	Co. B, 8th Georgia	11/13/1846	7/21/1863	Mortally wounded and died at Baltimore, MD-buried there	Baltimore, MD
Goodwin, John R.	Co. K, 17th Mississippi	1836	8/1/1863	Mortally wounded and died at Richmond, VA-interred in Hollywood Cemetery	Richmond, VA
Goodwin, Robert W.	Co. A, 11th Mississippi	1842	12/20/1863	Mortally wounded and died at Baltimore, MD-buried there	Baltimore, MD
Goodwin, William Franklin	Lt., Co. K, 38th Georgia	1828	7/1/1863	Killed in action	Unknown
Goolsby, Pleasant	Lt., Co. E, 11th Mississippi	1837	7/3/1863	Killed in action	Unknown
Gordan, Alexander H.	Cpl., Co. D, 13th North Carolina	1842	7/1/1863	Killed in action	Unknown
Gordon, J.T.	Lt., Co. G, 14th South Carolina	1836	7/1/1863	Killed in action	Unknown
Gordon, James D.	Co. G, 8th Georgia		7/3/1863	Laurel Grove Cemetery, Savannah, Ga., reburial list	Savannah, GA
Gore, Jonathan Linton	Lt., Co. D, 20th North Carolina	1837	7/1/1863	Killed in action	Unknown
Gorley, Andrew William	Co. G, 12th Georgia		7/15/1863	Mortally wounded-died at unknown place in Gettysburg	Unknown
Gornto, John R.	Sgt., Co. E, 3rd North Carolina	1843	8/1/1863	Mortally wounded-died at unknown place in Gettysburg	Unknown
Gorrell, Ralph	Lt., Co. G, 2nd North Carolina Battalion.	2/23/1837	7/1/1863	Killed in action	Unknown
Goss, William Walker	Lt., Co. E, 19th Virginia	1843	7/17/1863	Mortally wounded-died at unknown place in Gettysburg	Unknown
Gossett, Henry	Co. D, 53rd North Carolina	1839	7/7/1863	Mortally wounded and died at Frederick, MD; interred in Mt. Olivet Cemetery	Frederick, MD
Gossom, James H.	Co. G, 1st Maryland Battalion		7/2/1863	Killed in action	Unknown
Gough, Charles A.	3rd Co., Washington Arty. (La.)	1841	7/29/1863	Died as POW at David's Island, NY	Cypress Hills, NY
Gould, James L.	Sgt., Co. G, 4th Texas		7/18/1863	Hollywood Cemetery, Richmond, Va., reburial lists	Richmond, VA
Gouldman, John J.	Co. E, 55th Virginia		7/1/1863	Killed in action per the Richmond Enquirer, July 16, 1863	Unknown
Grady, Preston F.	Blount's Battery (Va.)	1832	Jul. 1863	Died at Camp Curtain while POW at Harrisburg, VA	Harrisburg, PA

NAME	REGIMENT	BIRTH	DEATH	COMMENT	BURIAL
Gragg, Jackson	Co. F, 26th North Carolina	1840	7/1/1863	Killed in action	Unknown
Graham, C.A.	Lt., Co. I, 5th Texas		7/15/1863	Mortally wounded, July 2nd, and died at Winchester, VA	Winchester, VA
Graham, James F.	Co. G, 27th Virginia		7/3/1863	Killed in action	Unknown
Graham, John C.	Co. F, 4th Texas	1833	7/29/1863	Hollywood Cemetery, Richmond, Va., reburial lists	Richmond, VA
Grandstaff, Phillip	Co. C, 33rd Virginia		7/3/1863	Killed in action	Unknown
Granniss, Edward J.	Lt., Co. B, 2nd Georgia Battalion		7/7/1863	Mortally wounded-died at unknown place in Gettysburg	Unknown
Grant, Reuben J.	Co. K, 22nd Georgia		7/2/1863	Killed in action	Unknown
Grant, Willis B.	Co. I, 2nd Mississippi	1841	8/1/1863	Hollywood Cemetery, Richmond, Va., reburial lists	Richmond, VA
Grass, Joseph	Co. H, 5th Virginia		Jul. 1863	Mortally wounded-died at unknown place in Gettysburg	Unknown
Graves, Benjamin Bartholomew	Sgt., Co. H, 53rd Virginia	1/31/1836	7/3/1863	Killed in action per the Richmond Whig August 7, 1863	Unknown
Graves, Hardy G.	Co. C, 6th Alabama	1838	7/26/1863	Hollywood Cemetery, Richmond, Va., reburial lists	Richmond, VA
Graves, Robert H.	Co. C, 9th Virginia		9/10/1863	Died of wounds received July 3rd, in Richmond, VA	Richmond, VA
Graves, Thomas Jefferson	Sgt., Co. I, 21st Georgia	6/29/1829	7/22/1863	Mortally wounded, July 2nd, and died at Hagerstown, MD-buried there	Hagerstown, MD
Gray, Ephraim W.	Co. K, 22nd North Carolina	1834	7/1/1863	Killed in action	Unknown
Gray, Henry D.	Co. G, 1st South Carolina		7/3/1863	Killed in action	Unknown
Gray, Samuel Wiley	Capt., Co. D, 57th North Carolina	7/19/1842	7/2/1863	Killed in action and reinterred in Forysth Co., NC	Forsyth Co., NC
Gray, Thomas W.	Co. K, 38th Virginia	1831	10/4/1863	Hollywood Cemetery, Richmond, Va., reburial lists	Richmond, VA
Gray, William A.	Co. B, 2nd Mississippi	1842	7/1/1863	Killed in action	Unknown
Gray, William G.	Sgt., Co. C, 3rd Virginia	1833	10/6/1863	Hollywood Cemetery, Richmond, Va., reburial lists	Richmond, VA
Gray, William H.	Co. E, 56th Virginia		Jul. 1863	Missing in action and presumed dead	Unknown
Gray, William R.	Co. K, 10th Alabama		7/2/1863	Killed in action	Unknown
Graybill, James Anderson	Lt., Co. K, 28th Virginia	10/18/1839	7/3/1863	Killed in action per the Richmond Sentinel, July 30, 1863	Unknown
Graybill, Madison	Co. K, 28th Virginia		7/3/1863	Killed in action	Unknown
Grayson, Alexander	Capt., Co. F, 8th Virginia		7/3/1863	Killed in action; reinterred at Grayson Plantation, Fauquier Co. Va.	Fauquier Co. VA
Green, Alexander	Co. K, 55th North Carolina		7/1/1863	Killed in action	Unknown
Green, Columbus W.	Co. K, 47th Alabama		7/2/1863	Killed in action	Unknown
Green, David A.	Cpl., Co. A, 38th Georgia		7/1/1863	Killed in action	Unknown
Green, David Howell	Co. D, 55th North Carolina	3/31/1824	7/1/1863	Killed in action	Cleveland Co., NC
Green, Drury A.	Co. D, 55th North Carolina	6/29/1836	7/16/1863	Oakwood Cemetery, Raleigh, NC, reburial list	Raleigh, NC
Green, E.C.N.	Sgt., Co. C, 47th North Carolina	1840	7/1/1863	Killed in action	Unknown

NAME	REGIMENT	BIRTH	DEATH	COMMENT	BURIAL
Green, Eli T.	Co. E, 14th Virginia	1839	8/15/1863	Mortally wounded; buried in Gettysburg National Cemtery as 14th PA	Gettysburg Nat. Cem
Green, George	Co. E, 4th Texas		7/2/1863	Killed in action	Unknown
Green, George M.	Co. H, 28th North Carolina	1843	7/3/1863	Killed in action	Unknown
Green, John Thomas	Capt., Co. I, 8th Virginia		7/3/1863	Killed in action; reinterred at Greenwood Cemetery, Washington, D.C.	Washington, DC
Green, John W.	Co. C, 2nd Mississippi		7/1/1863	Killed in action	Unknown
Green, Thomas	Co. K, 26th North Carolina	1840	7/3/1863	Killed in action	Unknown
Green, Thomas	Co. C, 48th Virginia	1839	7/12/1863	Mortally wounded and reinterred at Washington Co., VA	Wash. Co., VA
Green, W.C.	Co. C, 5th Virginia		7/3/1863	Killed in action	Unknown
Green, W.S.	Co. D, 4th Texas		7/2/1863	Killed in action	Unknown
Green, William A.	Co. K, 22nd Georgia		7/2/1863	Killed in action	Unknown
Green, William Thomas	Co. H, 3rd South Carolina	1842	7/2/1863	Killed in action	Unknown
Greene, John H.	Co. G, 4th Texas		7/2/1863	Hollywood Cemetery, Richmond, Va., reburial lists	Richmond, VA
Greenebaum, Moses	Co. E, 9th Georgia		7/2/1863	Killed in action	Unknown
Greenwood, James A.	Co. G, 13th Georgia		7/1/1863	Killed in action	Unknown
Greer, Augustus A.	Co. F, 11th Mississippi	1841	7/30/1863	Mortally wounded and died at Chester, PA	Phil. National Cem.
Gregory, Benjamin F.	Sgt., Co. G, 3rd Georgia		7/2/1863	Killed in action	Unknown
Gregory, John Branch	Co. B, 38th Virginia	12/15/1829	7/3/1863	Killed in action per the Richmond Sentinel, August 1, 1863	Unknown
Gregory, Richard H.	Co. F, 14th Virginia	1841	7/3/1863	Killed in action	Unknown
Gregory, William L.	Co. C, 11th North Carolina	1837	1863	Mortally wounded and died on unknown date	Unknown
Gregory, William R.	Cpl., Co. G, 3rd Georgia		7/2/1863	Laurel Grove Cemetery, Savannah, Ga., reburial list	Savannah, GA
Gresham, Ferdinand	Co. B, 15th Alabama	1843	7/2/1863	Killed in action	Unknown
Grey, John D.	Co. C, 37th Virginia		Aug. 1863	Mortally wounded and died at unknown place in MD	Maryland
Grier, William J.M.	Co. D, 17th Mississippi	1844	7/2/1863	Killed in action	Unknown
Griffin, Abel	Latham's Battery (NC)		7/26/1863	Mortally wounded, July 3rd, and died at Harrisburg, VA	Harrisburg, PA
Griffin, Andrew J.	Co. G, 14th Virginia		7/3/1863	Killed in action	Unknown
Griffin, David T.	Co. C, 55th North Carolina	1844	7/20/1863	Died as POW at David's Island, NY	Cypress Hills, NY
Griffin, E.J.	Co. I, 1st Virginia	1823	7/18/1863	Mortally wounded-died at unknown place in Gettysburg	Unknown
Griffin, Ellis P.	Sgt., Co. D, 37th North Carolina	1836	7/3/1863	Killed in action	Unknown
Griffin, James T.	Co. D, 37th North Carolina	1842	Jul. 1863	Missing in action and presumed dead	Unknown
Griffin, John	Co. B, 26th North Carolina	1833	7/20/1863	Hollywood Cemetery, Richmond, Va., reburial lists	Richmond, VA
Griffin, Sidney R.	Co. K, 26th North Carolina	1840	7/1/1863	Hollywood Cemetery, Richmond, Va., reburial lists	Richmond, VA

NAME	REGIMENT	BIRTH	DEATH	COMMENT	BURIAL
Griffin, William A.	Co. D, 37th North Carolina	6/6/1839	7/21/1863	Hollywood Cemetery, Richmond, Va., reburial lists	Richmond, VA
Griffith, Aaron E.	Co. K, 30th North Carolina	1843	11/3/1863	Mortally wounded-died at unknown place in Gettysburg	Unknown
Griffith, Elkanah B.	Co. A, 24th Virginia	1835	8/10/1863	Mortally wounded and died at Sulphur Springs, WV	Sulphur Springs, WV
Griffith, Franklin O.	Sgt., Co. A, 60th Georgia		8/20/1863	Died as POW at David's Island, NY	Cypress Hills, NY
Griffith, George W.	Co. C, 3rd South Carolina	1827	7/2/1863	Killed in action	Unknown
Griffith, James A.	Lt., Co. G, 14th North Carolina	1841	7/1/1863	Oakwood Cemetery, Raleigh, NC, reburial list	Raleigh, NC
Griffith, Woodson D.	Co. H, 45th North Carolina	1838	7/1/1863	Killed in action	Unknown
Grigg, William	Co. I, 38th North Carolina	1824	7/21/1863	Mortally wounded-died at unknown place in Gettysburg	Unknown
Griggs, Lewis	Co. K, 43rd North Carolina	1841	7/23/1863	Mortally wounded and died at Frederick, MD; interred in Mt. Olivet Cemetery	Frederick, MD
Grimsley, Colin	Cpl., Co. C, 20th North Carolina	1844	7/1/1863	Killed in action	Unknown
Grinstead, James H.	Lt., Co. K, 19th Virginia	1835	7/3/1863	Killed in action per the Richmond Sentinel, August 11, 1863	Unknown
Grinstead, T.H.	Co. G, 53rd Virginia		7/3/1863	Killed in action	Unknown
Grissom, Alexander M.	Cpl., Co. E, 23rd North Carolina	1838	7/1/1863	Killed in action	Unknown
Grissom, James L.	Co. G, 7th Tennessee		7/3/1863	Killed in action	Unknown
Grogan, John P.	Co. D, 2nd Georgia Battalion.		7/4/1863	Mortally wounded, July 2nd, and died two days later	Unknown
Gross, William H.	Cpl., Co. C, 42nd Virginia		7/23/1863	Mortally wounded-died at unknown place in Gettysburg	Unknown
Groves, James Allston	Surg., F&S, 16th Mississippi		Jul. 1863	Mortally wounded-died at unknown place in Gettysburg	Unknown
Grumbles, Perry Benjamin	Sgt., Co. B, 4th Texas	1831	8/19/1863	Died as POW at David's Island, NY	Cypress Hills, NY
Grutle, Thomas	Co. B, 55th North Carolina		7/1/1863	Killed in action	Unknown
Guerrant, John W.	Sgt., Co. C, 44th Virginia	1835	7/2/1863	Killed in action	Unknown
Guerry, Thomas LeGrande	Co. B, Sumter Artillery BN. (Ga.)	10/26/1846	7/2/1863	Laurel Grove Cemetery, Savannah, Ga., reburial list	Savannah, GA
Guiger, George Henry	Lt., A.D.C. to Genl. J.L. Kemper	5/28/1826	7/17/1863	Mortally wounded, July 3rd, body sent to Albemarle Co., VA	Albemarle Co., VA
Guill, William T.	Cpl., Co. I, 56th Virginia		Jul. 1863	Killed in action, July 1-3	Unknown
Gulledge, Samuel Blackwell	Co. B, 13th Mississippi	2/6/1840	7/5/1863	Mortally wounded-died at unknown place in Gettysburg	Unknown
Gulliver, Thomas	Co. A, 10th Georgia		7/20/1863	Mortally wounded-died at unknown place in Gettysburg	Unknown
Gunn, Radford Greene	Co. A, 17th Mississippi	5/9/1840	7/2/1863	Hollywood Cemetery, Richmond, Va., reburial lists	Richmond, VA
Gunn, Thomas J.	Co. G, 18th Virginia	1837	7/3/1863	Killed in action	Unknown
Gunnell, Joseph L.	Co. A, 38th Virginia		7/3/1863	Killed in action per the Richmond Sentinel, August 1, 1863	Unknown
Gunnell, William A.	Co. H, 24th Virginia		Jul. 1863	Missing in action and presumed dead	Unknown
Gusman, Leon Peter	Cpl., Co. A, 8th Louisiana	1842	7/2/1863	Killed in action	Unknown

NAME	REGIMENT	BIRTH	DEATH	COMMENT	BURIAL
Guthrie, Paul W.	Co. F, 38th Virginia	1838	7/3/1863	Killed in action	Unknown
Guy, Leander	Co. A, 7th North Carolina	1834	7/3/1863	Hollywood Cemetery, Richmond, Va., reburial lists	Richmond, VA
Guy, Robert F.	Lt., Co. B, 3rd Virginia	1840	7/4/1863	Hollywood Cemetery, Richmond, Va., reburial lists	Richmond, VA
Hackett, Francis Marion	Co. D, 56th Virginia		1863	Mortally wounded and died at Williamsport, MD-buried there	Williamsport, MD
Hafner, Adolphus J.	Co. I, 11th North Carolina	1846	7/3/1863	Killed in action	Unknown
Hafner, John	Co. I, 11th North Carolina	1843	7/1/1863	Killed in action	Unknown
Hagans, James W.	Co. B, 33rd North Carolina	1839	7/23/1863	Mortally wounded and died at Chester, PA	Phil. National Cem.
Hager, Brown	Co. K, 23rd North Carolina	1844	7/1/1863	Killed in action	Unknown
Hager, Sidney H.	Co. K, 23rd North Carolina	1843	9/18/1863	Oakwood Cemetery, Raleigh, NC, reburial list	Raleigh, NC
Haggard, S.L.	Co. F, 5th Alabama		7/1/1863	Hollywood Cemetery, Richmond, Va., reburial lists	Richmond, VA
Hagood, John H.	Co. H, 53rd Virginia	1835	7/3/1863	Killed in action	Unknown
Hahn, David Newton	Co. C, 28th North Carolina	7/17/1844	7/3/1863	Killed in action	Unknown
Hailey, William	Co. F, 17th Mississippi	1841	7/2/1863	Killed in action	Unknown
Haines, James D.	Co. C, 6th Louisiana		7/2/1863	Killed in action	Unknown
Hair, W. Jennings	Co. I, 1st South Carolina		9/14/1863	Died as POW at David's Island, NY	Cypress Hills, NY
Halbert, Henry P.	Capt., Co. E, 11th Mississippi	1838	8/9/1863	Hollywood Cemetery, Richmond, Va., reburial lists	Richmond, VA
Hales, E. Frank	Co. I, 11th Georgia	1835	Jul. 1863	Hollywood Cemetery, Richmond, Va., reburial lists	Richmond, VA
Haley, Thomas J.	Co. A, 38th Virginia		7/3/1863	Killed in action	Unknown
Haley, William	Co. I, 5th Texas		7/2/1863	Killed in action	Unknown
Hall, Cary A.	Co. D, 42nd Virginia		7/3/1863	Killed in action	Unknown
Hall, Charles F.	Lt., Co. F, 53rd North Carolina		Jul. 1863	Mortally wounded and died on unknown date	Unknown
Hall, Dennis	Co. I, 8th Alabama		7/2/1863	Hollywood Cemetery, Richmond, Va., reburial lists	Richmond, VA
Hall, Henry	Sgt., Co. H, 18th North Carolina	2/7/1844	7/22/1863	Hollywood Cemetery, Richmond, Va., reburial lists	Richmond, VA
Hall, Henry J.	Co. E, 19th Virginia		7/3/1863	Killed in action	Unknown
Hall, James M.	Co. F, 48th Georgia	1838	7/2/1863	Killed in action	Unknown
Hall, John Archer	Co. A, 14th Virginia	1843	7/3/1863	Killed in action	Unknown
Hall, John H.	King William Artillery (Va.)		7/1/1863	Killed in action	Unknown
Hall, John J.	Sgt., Co. F, 1st Tennessee	1840	7/3/1863	Killed in action	Unknown
Hall, John O.	Co. E, 38th Virginia		7/3/1863	Killed in action per the Richmond Sentinel, August 1, 1863	Unknown
Hall, Joseph B.	Co. F, 48th Georgia	1839	7/2/1863	Killed in action	Unknown
Hall, Nathan C.	Co. F, 52nd North Carolina	1843	10/12/1863	Died as POW at Ft. Delaware	Finn's Point, NJ
Hall, Nicholas	Co. A, 38th North Carolina	1837	Jul. 1863	Mortally wounded and died on unknown date	Unknown
Hall, Pennel P.	Co. K, 12th South Carolina	1827	8/5/1863	Died as POW at David's Island, NY	Cypress Hills, NY

NAME	REGIMENT	BIRTH	DEATH	COMMENT	BURIAL
Hall, Preston	Co. D, 42nd Virginia		7/15/1863	Mortally wounded-died at unknown place in Gettysburg	Unknown
Hall, R.M.	Co. F, 17th Mississippi	1838	7/20/1863	Hollywood Cemetery, Richmond, Va., reburial lists	Richmond, VA
Hall, Robert Y.	Co. I, 47th North Carolina	1839	7/1/1863	Killed in action	Unknown
Hall, T.J.	Co. A, 1st South Carolina		7/3/1863	Mortally wounded, July 3rd, and died the same day	Unknown
Hall, Thomas	Co. E, 53rd North Carolina	1829	7/5/1863	Mortally wounded-died at unknown place in Gettysburg	Unknown
Hall, Thomas M.	Lt., Co. G, 53rd North Carolina	1838	Jul. 1863	Mortally wounded and died at Winchester, VA	Winchester, VA
Hall, William L.J.	Lt., Co. F, 48th Georgia	1845	7/2/1863	Killed in action	Unknown
Hall, William R.	Co. A, 11th Mississippi		11/8/1863	Mortally wounded and died at unknown place in Gettysburg	Unknown
Hallinan, James	Capt., Co. C, 1st Virginia	1841	7/3/1863	Killed in action	Unknown
Hallman, W.M.	Co. A, 33rd North Carolina	1838	7/2/1863	Killed in action	Unknown
Hallowell, Joshua C.	Sgt., Parkers Battery (Va.)	1830	7/20/1863	Mortally wounded and died at Williamsport, MD-reburied in Hollywood Cemetery	Richmond, VA
Haltiwanger, Richard Henry	Lt., Co. E, 3rd South Carolina	2/19/1836	7/6/1863	Mortally wounded, July 2nd, and died four days later	Unknown
Ham, Henry W.	Co. E, 8th South Carolina		7/2/1863	Killed in action per the Charleston Courier, July 1863	Unknown
Hambrick, Abner Pierce	Co. F, 22nd Georgia	1829	7/9/1863	Hollywood Cemetery, Richmond, Va., reburial lists	Richmond, VA
Hambrick, John	Co. A, 24th Georgia		Aug. 1863	Mortally wounded-died at unknown place in Gettysburg	Unknown
Hamby, Andrew J.	Co. G, 42nd Mississippi		7/25/1863	Hollywood Cemetery, Richmond, Va., reburial lists	Richmond, VA
Hamby, Franklin T.	Co. K, 53rd North Carolina	1842	7/1/1863	Killed in action	Unknown
Hamby, James	Co. A, 22nd North Carolina	1840	1863	Missing in action and presumed dead	Unknown
Hames, Andrew Jackson	Sgt., Co. H, 15th South Carolina		7/5/1863	Mortally wounded per the Charleston Mercury, Aug. 28, 1863	Unknown
Hames, Leander A.	Co. F, 15th South Carolina	1842	7/2/1863	Killed in action per the Charleston Courier, July 1863	Unknown
Hamilton, Beale D.	Cpl., Co. C, 1st Maryland Battalion		7/22/1863	Mortally wounded-died at unknown place in Gettysburg	Unknown
Hamilton, Calier G.	Co. H, 38th North Carolina	1841	7/1/1863	Killed in action	Unknown
Hamilton, David G.	Co. E, 15th South Carolina		7/12/1863	Mortally wounded and died at unknown place in MD	Maryland
Hamilton, Francis P.	Cpl., Co. H, 11th Mississippi	1841	7/5/1863	Hollywood Cemetery, Richmond, Va., reburial lists	Richmond, VA
Hamilton, Miles R.	Co. E, 32nd North Carolina	1833	7/2/1863	Mortally wounded, July 2nd, and died the same day	Raleigh, NC
Hamilton, Newton J.	Co. E, 14th Tennessee		7/4/1863	Hollywood Cemetery, Richmond, Va., reburial lists	Richmond, VA
Hamilton, Thomas B.	Co. E, 32nd North Carolina	1843	7/3/1863	Mortally wounded, July 3rd, and died the same day	Unknown

NAME	REGIMENT	BIRTH	DEATH	COMMENT	BURIAL
Hamilton, William M.	Cpl., Co. G, 18th Virginia	1823	7/3/1863	Killed in action	Unknown
Hamilton, William M.	Co. K, 15th South Carolina		7/2/1863	Killed in action per the Charleston Courier, July 1863	Unknown
Hamlet, Henry C.	Co. C, 13th North Carolina	1834	7/1/1863	Killed in action	Unknown
Hamlet, James Marsh	Sgt., Co. H, 18th Virginia	1840	7/3/1863	Killed in action	Unknown
Hammond, Charles	Co. A, 7th South Carolina		7/2/1863	Killed in action	Unknown
Hammond, Christian Valentine	Co. B, 1st S.C. Rifles		7/2/1863	Hollywood Cemetery, Richmond, Va., reburial lists	Richmond, VA
Hammond, Edgar William	Co. C, 1st Maryland Battalion		Jul. 1863	Hollywood Cemetery, Richmond, Va., reburial lists	Richmond, VA
Hammond, William H.	Co. B, 52nd North Carolina	1831	7/22/1863	Mortally wounded and died at Winchester, VA	Winchester, VA
Hammons, T.J.	Co. E, 50th Virginia		Jul. 1863	Killed in action on either July 2nd or 3rd	Unknown
Hampton, Elliott L.	Capt., Co. M, 2nd Florida		7/3/1863	Killed in action	Unknown
Hampton, James M.	Co. F, 16th North Carolina	1840	8/28/1863	Mortally wounded-died at unknown place in Gettysburg	Unknown
Hampton, Thomas S.	Co. H, 8th South Carolina	5/2/1839	7/8/1863	Magnolia Cemetery, Charleston, SC, reburial list	Charleston, SC
Hamrick, David	Co. D, 55th North Carolina		7/3/1863	Killed in action	Unknown
Hamrick, Oliver A.	Co. D, 55th North Carolina		7/3/1863	Killed in action	Unknown
Hance, James Washington	Lt. Col., 53rd Georgia	10/26/1828	7/2/1863	Killed in action; reinterred in summer of 1871	Laurens Co., SC
Hancock, Benjamin L.	Capt., Co. H, 2nd Georgia		7/2/1863	Killed in action	Unknown
Hancock, George	Co. C, 45th Georgia	1838	7/3/1863	Killed in action	Unknown
Hancock, John H. [A.]	Co. D, 52nd North Carolina	1842	7/1/1863	Oakwood Cemetery, Raleigh, NC, reburial list	Raleigh, NC
Hancock, Little Berry	Co. B, Sumter Artillery BN. (Ga.)	1834	7/2/1863	Killed in action per the Richmond Sentinel, July 30, 1863	Unknown
Hancock, Thomas J.	Co. I, 5th North Carolina	1841	7/12/1863	Mortally wounded-died at unknown place in Gettysburg	Unknown
Hand, W. H.	Co. H, 12th South Carolina	1827	7/3/1863	Killed in action	Unknown
Handback, Melmoth	Co. E, 3rd South Carolina Battalion	1827	7/2/1863	Killed in action per the Charleston Courier, July 1863	Unknown
Handley, J.E.	Co. D, 8th Alabama		10/7/1863	Mortally wounded and died at Richmond, VA-interred in Hollywood Cemetery	Richmond, VA
Hanes, Vestine	Co. G, 48th Virginia	1840	7/2/1863	Killed in action	Unknown
Haney, Francis Marion	Co. F, 9th Alabama	1836	7/2/1863	Killed in action	Unknown
Hanigan, T.	Co. A, Phillip's Legion (Ga.)		1863	Laurel Grove Cemetery, Savannah, Ga., reburial list	Savannah, GA
Hanison, James	Co. A, 7th Virginia		7/3/1863	Killed in action	Unknown
Hannah, Edward B.	Co. G, 45th Georgia		7/27/1863	Died as POW at David's Island, NY	Cypress Hills, NY
Hansford, Calvin P.	Sgt., Co. H, 1st Virginia	1837	7/3/1863	Killed in action	Unknown
Hardesty, James Richard	Chesapeake Artillery (Md.)		7/2/1863	Killed in action	Unknown
Hardesty, John W.	Co. A, 1st Maryland Battalion		Jul. 1863	Killed in action, July 1-3	Baltimore, MD

NAME	REGIMENT	BIRTH	DEATH	COMMENT	BURIAL
Hardgrove, John	Co. A, 55th Virginia		7/1/1863	Hollywood Cemetery, Richmond, Va., reburial lists	Richmond, VA
Hardigree, John H.	Co. L, 3rd Georgia	2/22/1843	9/29/1863	Died of wounds received at Ft. Delaware	Finn's Point, NJ
Hardin, Osborn J.	Co. K, 61st Georgia		8/7/1863	Mortally wounded-died at unknown place in Gettysburg	Unknown
Harding, Minor S.	Lt., Co. I, 14th Virginia Cavalry		7/3/1863	Killed in action	Unknown
Hardman, Burton L.	Co. K, 13th Alabama	1836	7/20/1863	Hollywood Cemetery, Richmond, Va., reburial lists	Richmond, VA
Hardwick, William E.G.	Lt., Co. F, 10th Alabama	1836	7/16/1863	Mortally wounded and died at Philadelphia, PA	Philadelphia, PA
Hardwick, William H.	Lt., Co. K, 15th Georgia		7/25/1863	Laurel Grove Cemetery, Savannah, Ga., reburial list	Savannah, GA
Hardy, John R.	Co. I, 28th Virginia		7/3/1863	Hollywood Cemetery, Richmond, Va., reburial lists	Richmond, VA
Hardy, N.P.	Co. H, 14th Alabama		Jul. 1863	Hollywood Cemetery, Richmond, Va., reburial lists	Richmond, VA
Hardy, Presley G.	Co. H, 38th Virginia		10/14/1863	Mortally wounded, July 3rd, and died at Staunton, VA	Staunton, VA
Hardy, William F.	Co. F, 11th Mississippi	1842	7/20/1863	Hollywood Cemetery, Richmond, Va., reburial lists	Richmond, VA
Hardy, William H.	Sgt., Co. K, 11th Virginia	1838	1863	Mortally wounded and died on unknown date	Unknown
Hargroves, James R.	Co. H, 3rd Georgia		7/2/1863	Killed in action	Unknown
Harling, Thomas	Cpl., Co. I, 7th South Carolina		7/2/1863	Hollywood Cemetery, Richmond, Va., reburial lists	Richmond, VA
Harlow, John A.	Capt., Co. D, 48th Georgia	3/18/1823	7/2/1863	Killed in action	Unknown
Harlow, William	Co. G, 19th Virginia	1836	Jul. 1863	Missing in action and presumed dead	Unknown
Harmon, Archibald S.	Co. C, 2nd Georgia Battalion	1844	7/2/1863	Killed in action	Unknown
Harmon, Clark L.	Co. D, 10th Alabama		7/2/1863	Killed in action	Unknown
Harmon, James H.	Co. A, 17th Mississippi	1844	7/2/1863	Killed in action	Unknown
Harmon, James Martin	Co. E, 44th Alabama	4/6/1839	7/2/1863	Killed in action	Unknown
Harmon, Miles Monroe	Co. A, 18th North Carolina	1826	7/3/1863	Killed in action	Unknown
Harmon, Samuel	Cpl., Co. I, 13th South Carolina	1836	7/28/1863	Mortally wounded and died at Chester, PA	Phil. National Cem.
Harmon, William Hardy	Lt., Co. I, 42nd Mississippi	1833	7/14/1863	Mortally wounded-died at unknown place in Gettysburg	Unknown
Harney, Frank M.	Lt., Co. F, 14th North Carolina	1838	7/2/1863	Died of wounds received July 1	Raleigh, NC
Harper, Calvin	Co. D, 8th Florida		7/3/1863	Killed in action	Unknown
Harper, Joseph S.	Co. E, 26th North Carolina	1834	7/1/1863	Killed in action	Unknown
Harper, P.E.	Co. G, 17th Mississippi	1838	7/2/1863	Killed in action	Unknown
Harper, R.A.	Co. H, 53rd Georgia		7/2/1863	Killed in action	Unknown
Harrell, John J.	Co. A, 59th Georgia		7/7/1863	Hollywood Cemetery, Richmond, Va., reburial lists	Richmond, VA
Harrell, John W.	Sgt., Co. B, 26th Alabama	1838	7/21/1863	Hollywood Cemetery, Richmond, Va., reburial lists	Richmond, VA

NAME	REGIMENT	BIRTH	DEATH	COMMENT	BURIAL
Harrell, Leonard B.	Sgt., Co. F, 8th South Carolina	1845	7/3/1863	Hollywood Cemetery, Richmond, Va., reburial lists	Richmond, VA
Harrell, William W.	Co. H, 5th Alabama		7/1/1863	Killed in action	Unknown
Harris, Charles W.S.	Capt., Co. E, 48th Virginia	1837	7/2/1863	Killed in action	Unknown
Harris, James L.	Co. F, 56th Virginia		7/16/1863	Hollywood Cemetery, Richmond, Va., reburial lists	Richmond, VA
Harris, John Vincent	Co. H, 11th Mississippi		7/3/1863	Killed in action	Unknown
Harris, Joseph Q.	Co. I, 4th Texas	1823	7/2/1863	Killed in action	Unknown
Harris, Lewis H.	Co. B, 48th Georgia	1836	7/2/1863	Killed in action	Unknown
Harris, Samuel	Co. F, 45th North Carolina	1834	7/15/1863	Oakwood Cemetery, Raleigh, NC, reburial list	Raleigh, NC
Harris, Thomas J.	Co. B, 9th Georgia	7/1/1842	7/2/1863	Killed in action	Unknown
Harris, Thomas N.	Co. H, 18th North Carolina		8/16/1863	Mortally wounded and died at Chester, PA	Phil. National Cem.
Harris, W. Hudson	Co. F, 47th North Carolina	1812	7/31/1863	Died of wounds at Ft. Delaware, DE	Finn's Point, NJ
Harris, W.T.	Co. F, 7th Virginia		7/3/1863	Hollywood Cemetery, Richmond, Va., reburial lists	Richmond, VA
Harris, William C.	Co. I, 55th North Carolina	1840	7/19/1863	Mortally wouned, July 3rd, and died at Winchester, VA	Winchester, VA
Harris, William E.	Lt., Co. F, 45th North Carolina	1825	7/1/1863	Killed in action	Unknown
Harris, William H.	Co. G, 20th North Carolina	1839	7/1/1863	Killed in action	Unknown
Harris, William Henry	Co. F, 8th Louisiana	1843	1863	Missing in action and presumed dead	Unknown
Harris, William Patton	Capt., Co. E, 48th Virginia	1/4/1841	7/2/1863	Killed in action	Unknown
Harris, William Terrell	Lt. Col., 2nd Georgia	11/29/1829	7/2/1863	Killed in action; reinterred in 1866	Columbus, GA
Harrison, Asbury	Co. G, 8th Virginia		7/3/1863	Killed in action	Unknown
Harrison, Bradford	Co. G, 4th Georgia		7/1/1863	Killed in action	Unknown
Harrison, George W.	Co. I, 11th Georgia	1844	7/20/1863	Hollywood Cemetery, Richmond, Va., reburial lists	Richmond, VA
Harrison, John	Co. B, 59th Georgia		7/6/1863	Mortally wounded-died at unknown place in Gettysburg	Unknown
Harrison, Montgomery	Co. K, 15th Georgia	1838	7/2/1863	Killed in action	Unknown
Harrison, Wayne Crockett	Co. D, 11th Mississippi	1842	7/3/1863	Killed in action	Unknown
Harrison, William Henry	Co. G, 7th Tennessee	1840	7/1/1863	Killed in action	Unknown
Hart, John	Co. E, 26th North Carolina	1843	7/1/1863	Killed in action	Unknown
Hart, Thomas G.	Co. H, 18th Virginia		7/3/1863	Killed in action	Unknown
Hart, William D.	Lt., Co. F, 15th South Carolina	1823	7/2/1863	Killed in action	Unknown
Harter, Peter R.	Co. K, 25th Virginia	1820	7/3/1863	Killed in action	Unknown
Hartsfield, John A.	Co. H, 17th Mississippi	1843	7/11/1863	Hollywood Cemetery, Richmond, Va., reburial lists	Richmond, VA
Hartsock [Heartsock], William	Co. A, 37th Virginia		7/3/1863	Killed in action	Unknown
Hartzog, Daniel	Co. D, 15th Alabama	1834	1863	Missing in action and presumed dead	Unknown
Harvey, Edward B.	Lt., Co. H, 18th Virginia	1828	8/6/1863	Hollywood Cemetery, Richmond, Va., reburial lists	Richmond, VA
Harvey, James Glover	Lt., Co. H, 18th Virginia	2/16/1838	7/3/1863	Killed in action; reinterred in Petersburg, VA	Petersburg, VA

NAME	REGIMENT	BIRTH	DEATH	COMMENT	BURIAL
Harvey, Stephen R.	Co. D, 18th Virginia	1835	7/28/1863	Hollywood Cemetery, Richmond, Va., reburial lists	Richmond, VA
Harvill, David Sanford	Cpl., Co. B, 16th Georgia		7/2/1863	Killed in action per the Augusta Chronicle & Sentinel, August 16, 1863	Unknown
Harville, George A.	Co. K, 38th Virginia	1826	7/3/1863	Killed in action	Unknown
Harwell, Watson A.	Co. C, 28th North Carolina		Jul. 1863	Mortally wounded and "left on the field"	Unknown
Harwell, William S.	Lt., Co. K, 4th Alabama	1842	7/2/1863	Killed in action	Unknown
Harwood, Christopher E.	Sgt., Co. K, 53rd Virginia	1842	8/15/1863	Died at Chimborazo Hospital in Richmond of wounds-buried there in Oakwood Cemetery	Richmond, VA
Haskell, William Thompson	Capt., Co. H, 1st South Carolina	12/12/1837	7/2/1863	Killed in action; reinterred in Abbeville, SC, in1866	Abbeville, SC
Hasten, John C.	Co. E, 28th North Carolina		7/7/1863	Mortally wounded-died at unknown place in Gettysburg	Unknown
Hatfield, James C.	Co. B, 11th Georgia		7/2/1863	Killed in action	Unknown
Hatfield, Joseph W.	Co. B, 11th Georgia		7/2/1863	Killed in action	Unknown
Hathaway, Aaron C.	Sgt., Co. A, 48th Georgia	1842	7/2/1863	Killed in action	Unknown
Hathaway, Henry	Co. F, 30th North Carolina	1842	7/10/1863	Mortally wounded-died at unknown place in Gettysburg	Unknown
Hatley, Alfred	Co. I, 52nd North Carolina	5/4/1834	7/17/1863	Hollywood Cemetery, Richmond, Va., reburial lists	Richmond, VA
Hatley, Daniel A.	Co. K, 28th North Carolina	1844	7/24/1863	Hollywood Cemetery, Richmond, Va., reburial lists	Richmond, VA
Hatley, John M.	Co. D, 28th North Carolina	1832	7/3/1863	Killed in action	Unknown
Hatrick, Pinckney W.	Lt., Co. A, 53rd North Carolina	1837	7/3/1863	Killed in action	Unknown
Hauly, Clairborne	Co. A, 45th North Carolina		7/2/1863	Oakwood Cemetery, Raleigh, NC, reburial list	Raleigh, NC
Haun [Hawn], Newton David	Co. C, 28th North Carolina	7/17/1844	7/3/1863	Killed in action	Unknown
Hawkins, Charles	Woolfolk's Battery (Va.)		7/3/1863	Killed in action per the Richmond Sentinel, July 15, 1863 & July 27, 1863	Unknown
Hawkins, Joseph R.	Co. F, 43rd North Carolina	1832	7/1/1863	Killed in action	Unknown
Hayden, George C.	Cpl., Co. B, 1st Maryland Battalion	6/23/1842	7/7/1863	Mortally wounded and died at Camp Letterman; reinterred after the war in Chaptico, MD	Chaptico, MD
Hayden, John Alexander	Co. B, 1st Maryland Battalion	11/22/1841	7/3/1863	Killed in action	Unknown
Hayden, Joseph S.	Co. E, 13th Georgia	1840	8/30/1863	Laurel Grove Cemetery, Savannah, Ga., reburial list	Savannah, GA
Hayes, Henry Hill	Co. F, 26th North Carolina	1843	10/6/1863	Mortally wounded-died at unknown place in Gettysburg	Unknown
Haynes, Andrew Robert	Sgt., Co. I, 11th North Carolina	1840	7/3/1863	Killed in action	Unknown
Haynes, Daniel Hunter	Co. I, 11th North Carolina	1843	7/1/1863	Killed in action	Unknown
Haynes, Finney	Co. A, 50th Virginia		7/2/1863	Killed in action	Unknown
Haynes, Henry	Co. B, 5th Texas		Jul. 1863	Mortally wounded and died on unknown date	Unknown

NAME	REGIMENT	BIRTH	DEATH	COMMENT	BURIAL
Haynes, John H.	Co. B, 8th Alabama		7/2/1863	Hollywood Cemetery, Richmond, Va., reburial lists	Richmond, VA
Hays, Augustus S.	Co. G, 13th Georgia		7/17/1863	Mortally wounded-died on unknown date in Gettysburg	Unknown
Hays, J.R.	Cpl., Co. G, 17th Georgia		Jul. 1863	Killed in action per the Augusta Chronicle & Sentinel, July 30, 1863	Unknown
Hays, Shelton	Co. B, 26th North Carolina	1838	7/19/1863	Mortally wounded, July 1st, and died at Winchester, VA; Interred Stonewall Cemetery	Winchester, VA
Hays, Thomas	Bachman's Battery (SC)		7/2/1863	Killed in action	Charleston, SC
Hays, Thomas J.	Co. K, 19th Virginia		7/17/1863	Mortally wounded-died at unknown place in Gettysburg	Unknown
Hays, Ulissus A.	Co. K, 13th Mississippi	1822	7/13/1863	Hollywood Cemetery, Richmond, Va., reburial lists	Richmond, VA
Hays, William D.	Co. C, 44th Alabama		Jul. 1863	Missing in action and presumed dead	Unknown
Hazle, Richard H.	Co. K, 10th Virginia		Jul. 1863	Missing in action and presumed dead	Unknown
Head, William H.	Co. K, 12th South Carolina		7/2/1863	Hollywood Cemetery, Richmond, Va., reburial lists	Richmond, VA
Headrick, Jacob	Co. E, 57th Virginia		Jul. 1863	Killed in action, July 1-3	Unknown
Hearn, Joseph L.	Co. C, 35th Georgia		7/5/1863	Laurel Grove Cemetery, Savannah, Ga., reburial list	Savannah, GA
Heath, John R.	Sgt., Co. A, 3rd North Carolina	1838	7/2/1863	Killed in action	Unknown
Heath, Oliver	Co. I, 48th Virginia		7/10/1863	Mortally wounded, July 2nd, and died at Richmond, VA	Richmond, VA
Heath, William D.	Co. I, 53rd Georgia		7/3/1863	Killed in action	Unknown
Heaton, Elijah H.	Co. G, 52nd Virginia	1842	8/9/1863	Hollywood Cemetery, Richmond, Va., reburial lists	Richmond, VA
Hedgecock, Asel	Co. G, 7th North Carolina	1833	7/3/1863	Killed in action	Unknown
Hedgecock, William	Co. G, 2nd North Carolina Battalion.	1843	7/1/1863	Killed in action	Unknown
Hedges, Owen Tuder	Co. D, 2nd Virginia	1816	7/11/1863	Mortally wounded-died at unknown place in Gettysburg; reinterred in WV after the war	Hedgesville, WV
Heenahan, Martin	Co. K, 5th Louisiana		7/3/1863	Killed in action	Unknown
Hefley, Andrew H.	Co. F, 3rd Arkansas	1838	7/2/1863	Killed in action	Unknown
Hefner, Daniel	Co. F, 38th North Carolina	1827	8/17/1863	Mortally wounded-died at unknown place in Gettysburg	Unknown
Hefner, Franklin	Co. F, 32nd North Carolina	1842	10/4/1863	Mortally wounded-died at unknown place in Gettysburg	Unknown
Heggie, Mathew E.	Cpl., Co. F, 8th Georgia		9/9/1863	Hollywood Cemetery, Richmond, Va., reburial lists	Richmond, VA
Heggie, Thomas	Co. F, 45th North Carolina	1838	7/1/1863	Killed in action	Unknown
Heilig, James M.	Co. K, 5th North Carolina	1838	7/1/1863	Killed in action; KIA on Oak Ridge (Iverson's Brigade)	Richmond, VA
Helderman, Rufus M.	Co. H, 52nd North Carolina		7/3/1863	Missing in action and presumed dead	Unknown
Hellard, Thomas	Co. A, 57th North Carolina	1828	7/2/1863	Killed in action	Unknown
Helms, Ezekiel T.	Co. E, 11th North Carolina	1835	7/1/1863	Killed in action	Unknown
Henderson, Daniel T.	Lt., Co. F, 18th Mississippi	1843	7/2/1863	Killed in action	Unknown

NAME	REGIMENT	BIRTH	DEATH	COMMENT	BURIAL
Henderson, David H.	Lt., Co. B, 5th Texas		7/3/1863	Mortally wounded, July 2nd, and died the next day	Unknown
Henderson, Ed	Co. F, 19th Virginia		Jul. 1863	Killed in action, July 1-3	Unknown
Hendren, Jabez E.	Co. F, 52nd North Carolina	1842	7/3/1863	Killed in action	Unknown
Hendrick, David Alexander	Co. K, 2nd Louisiana	4/23/1841	7/2/1863	Killed in action	Unknown
Hendrix, Jesse S.	Co. C, 12th South Carolina		7/29/1863	Mortally wounded per the Richmond Sentinel, August 11, 1863	Charleston, SC
Henkle, John	Co. H, 56th Virginia		Jul. 1863	Killed in action, July 1-3	Unknown
Henkle, Michael P.	Lt., Co. K, 25th Virginia	1825	7/3/1863	Killed in action	Unknown
Henley, John N.	Co. D, 7th Georgia		7/2/1863	Killed in action	Unknown
Henry, Charles	Co. E, 7th Virginia Cavalry		7/5/1863	Hollywood Cemetery, Richmond, Va., reburial lists	Richmond, VA
Henry, Edward Zachary	Co. K, 22nd Georgia	1834	7/2/1863	Killed in action	Unknown
Henry, Z.P	Co. D, 5th Texas		7/11/1863	Mortally wounded and died at Hagerstown, MD-buried there	Hagerstown, MD
Hensley, James O.	Co. K, 37th North Carolina	1842	7/3/1863	Killed in action	Unknown
Herin, R.S.	Co. K, 59th Georgia		7/2/1863	Killed in action	Unknown
Heritage, Furnifold G.	Lt., Co. F, 2nd North Carolina	1841	7/1/1863	Killed in action	Unknown
Herman, Miles Monroe	Co. A, 18th North Carolina	1826	7/3/1863	Killed in action	Unknown
Herndon, Edward J.	Cpl., Co. F, 19th Virginia	1839	7/10/1863	Mortally wounded-died at unknown place in Gettysburg	Unknown
Herndon, Jacob Whiteley	Co. C, 4th Texas	2/7/1845	7/2/1863	Killed in action	Unknown
Herren, S.A.	Co. G, 44th Georgia		7/1/1863	Killed in action	Unknown
Herring, Nimrod B.	Co. I, 7th Virginia		8/1/1863	Mortally wounded-died at unknown place in Gettysburg	Unknown
Herring, W.H.	Co. I, 7th Virginia		7/3/1863	Killed in action	Unknown
Herring, William H.	Co. F, 20th North Carolina	1838	7/20/1863	Mortally wounded-died at unknown place in Gettysburg	Unknown
Herron, Andrew C.	Co. D, 4th Texas	1834	7/2/1863	Killed in action	Unknown
Heslep, Thomas	Sgt., Co. A, 11th Mississippi	1843	7/3/1863	Killed in action	Unknown
Hester, Elias	Co. K, 45th North Carolina	1842	7/26/1863	Mortally wounded-died at unknown place in Gettysburg	Unknown
Hester, W.G.	Co. B, 51st Georgia		Jul. 1863	Missing in action and presumed dead	Unknown
Hethcock, Alexander	Co. D, 3rd North Carolina	1825	7/2/1863	Killed in action	Unknown
Hewett, Samuel M.	Co. C, 30th North Carolina	1839	7/1/1863	Killed in action	Unknown
Hewit, D.H.	Co. E, 5th North Carolina		7/9/1863	Mortally wounded-died at unknown place in Gettysburg	Unknown
Hicks (Hix), John W.	Co. I, 28th Virginia		7/3/1863	Killed in action per the Richmond Sentinel, July 30, 1863	Unknown
Hicks, J.A.	Sgt., Co. I, 47th North Carolina	1836	7/3/1863	Killed in action on or about July 3	Unknown
Hicks, James M.	Cpl., Co. E, 13th North Carolina	1834	7/1/1863	Killed in action	Unknown
Hicks, Jeremiah	Co. C, 24th Virginia		7/26/1863	Mortally wounded and died at Harrisburg, PA; interred Soldiers' Lot, City Cemetery	Harrisburg, PA
Hicks, Polk	Co. E, 2nd North Carolina Battalion		7/2/1863	Killed in action	Unknown

NAME	REGIMENT	BIRTH	DEATH	COMMENT	BURIAL
Hicks, William F.D.	Lt., Co. B, 14th Tennessee	1835	8/10/1863	Mortally wounded and died at Chester, PA	Phil. National Cem.
Higginbotham, James L.	Cpl., Co. G, 19th Virginia	1840	Jul. 1863	Missing in action and presumed dead	Unknown
Higgins, Mills A.	Co. C, 34th North Carolina	1835	7/1/1863	Killed in action	Unknown
Hill, Asaph	Capt., Co. F, 7th Tennessee	1837	7/8/1863	Hollywood Cemetery, Richmond, Va., reburial lists	Richmond, VA
Hill, James E.	Co. I, 44th Alabama	1843	7/2/1863	Killed in action	Unknown
Hill, James W.	Co. E, 57th Virginia		12/22/1863	Died as POW at Pt. Lookout, MD	Pt. Lookout, MD
Hill, John C.	Co. I, 48th Georgia	1828	7/2/1863	Laurel Grove Cemetery, Savannah, Ga., reburial list	Savannah, GA
Hill, Jonathan	Co. D, 43rd North Carolina		8/14/1863	Oakwood Cemetery, Raleigh, NC, reburial list	Raleigh, NC
Hill, Nicholas	Cpl., Co. A, 3rd South Carolina Battalion		8/3/1863	Magnolia Cemetery, Charleston, SC, reburial list	Charleston, SC
Hill, Thomas W.	Lt., Co. H, 11th Mississippi	9/24/1838	7/15/1863	Mortally wounded-died at unknown place in Gettysburg	Unknown
Hill, William	Co. K, 57th Virginia		Jul. 1863	Killed in action, July 1-3	Unknown
Hill, William H.	Cpl., Co. C, 7th Virginia	1842	7/3/1863	Killed in action	Unknown
Hillhouse, Barton Nelson	Co. F, 5th Florida	3/25/1836	7/4/1863	Mortally wounded, July 3rd, and died the next day	Unknown
Hilton, James	Co. H, 44th Georgia		7/1/1863	Killed in action	Unknown
Hindman, N. Bony	Co. A, 13th Mississippi	1836	8/14/1863	Hollywood Cemetery, Richmond, Va., reburial lists	Richmond, VA
Hines, Thomas J.	Co. D, 1st Maryland Battalion	1831	9/15/1863	Mortally wounded-died at unknown place in Gettysburg	Unknown
Hinson, Elijah	Co. H, 2nd South Carolina		7/17/1863	Mortally wounded per Charleston Mercury, August 28, 1863	Unknown
Hinson, George	Co. K, 8th Virginia		Jul. 1863	Missing in action and presumed dead	Unknown
Hinson, Linsey	Co. B, 5th North Carolina	1832	7/1/1863	Hollywood Cemetery, Richmond, Va., reburial lists	Richmond, VA
Hinson, Marion Richard	Lt., Co. H, 2nd South Carolina	1830	7/3/1863	Hollywood Cemetery, Richmond, Va., reburial lists	Richmond, VA
Hinson, McD.	Co. I, 32nd North Carolina	1837	7/3/1863	Killed in action	Unknown
Hinson, W. Brinkley	Co. E, 52nd North Carolina	1842	7/28/1863	Died as POW at David's Island, NY	Cypress Hills, NY
Hipps, John B.	Co. G, 22nd Georgia		7/2/1863	Killed in action	Unknown
Hite, John Pendleton	Co. H, 33rd Virginia	11/15/1840	7/5/1863	Hollywood Cemetery, Richmond, Va., reburial lists	Richmond, VA
Hite, William	Co. B, 47th Alabama		7/2/1863	Killed in action	Unknown
Hitt, Paskill A.	Co. G, 7th Virginia		7/27/1863	Mortally wounded and died at Chester, PA	Phil. National Cem.
Hitt, Peter	Co. B, 3rd South Carolina Battalion	1838	7/3/1863	Magnolia Cemetery, Charleston, SC, reburial list	Charleston, SC
Hobbs, Nathan A.	Co. C, 3rd Georgia		7/2/1863	Killed in action	Unknown
Hobbs, William	Co. A, 3rd North Carolina	1841	7/2/1863	Killed in action	Unknown
Hockman, Whiting F.	Co. F, 10th Virginia	3/5/1839	7/15/1863	Hollywood Cemetery, Richmond, Va., reburial lists	Richmond, VA
Hodge, Isaac B.	Co. D, 2nd South Carolina		7/2/1863	Missing in action and presumed dead	Unknown

NAME	REGIMENT	BIRTH	DEATH	COMMENT	BURIAL
Hodges, Andrew J.	Co. B, 2nd North Carolina Battalion	1817	7/1/1863	Killed in action	Unknown
Hodges, Charles K.	Co. B, 25th Virginia		8/1/1863	Mortally wounded-died at unknown place in Gettysburg	Unknown
Hodges, David	Co. F, 41st Virginia		7/2/1863	Hollywood Cemetery, Richmond, Va., reburial lists	Richmond, VA
Hodges, George R.	Cpl., Co. D, 24th Virginia		Jul. 1863	Missing in action and presumed dead	Unknown
Hodges, James	Co. A, 3rd Georgia		7/2/1863	Laurel Grove Cemetery, Savannah, Ga., reburial list	Savannah, GA
Hodges, James Gregory	Col., 14th Virginia	12/28/1829	7/3/1863	Killed in action	Unknown
Hodges, John D.	Co. E, 1st South Carolina		7/4/1863	Mortally wounded, July 3rd, died the next day	Unknown
Hodges, John F.	Co. D, 9th Louisiana	10/4/1843	7/2/1863	Hollywood Cemetery, Richmond, Va., reburial lists	Richmond, VA
Hodges, Robert W.	Co. C, 1st Tennessee	1835	Jul. 1863	Mortally wounded-died on unknown date in Gettysburg	Unknown
Hodges, Thomas M.	Co. G, 10th Alabama		7/2/1863	Hollywood Cemetery, Richmond, Va., reburial lists	Richmond, VA
Hodges, William C.C.	Lt., Co. B, 7th South Carolina	1835	7/2/1863	Hollywood Cemetery, Richmond, Va., reburial lists	Richmond, VA
Hodges, William R.	Co. G, 57th Virginia		7/3/1863	Killed in action	Unknown
Hodgkins, T.G.	Lt., Co. C, 8th Georgia		7/2/1863	Killed in action	Unknown
Hodnett, Philip	Co. H, 24th Virginia		7/3/1863	Killed in action	Unknown
Hoffman, Addison Clark	Co. A, 18th Mississippi	1840	9/3/1863	Mortally wounded and died at Camp Letterman	Richmond, VA
Hoffman, Charles C.	Marmaduke Johnson's Battery (Va.)	10/21/1838	7/3/1863	Mortally wounded per the Richmond Dispatch, August 12, 1863	Richmond, VA
Hoffner, William Wesley	Reilly's Battery (NC)	3/19/1838	7/2/1863	Killed in action	Unknown
Hogan, William H.	Co. B, 14th Virginia	1836	7/3/1863	Killed in action	Unknown
Hogans, William J.	Co. A, 48th Georgia		7/2/1863	Laurel Grove Cemetery, Savannah, Ga., reburial list	Savannah, GA
Hoge, Andrew Johnston	Cpl., Co. E, 4th Virginia	1843	7/3/1863	Killed in action	Unknown
Hoke, David A.	Cpl., Co. B, 23rd North Carolina	1843	Jul.1863	Missing in action and presumed dead	Unknown
Hoke, Michael	Cpl., Co. B, 23rd North Carolina	1835	7/1/1863	Killed in action	Unknown
Holcomb, Jones	Co. I, 28th North Carolina	1842	7/3/1863	Killed in action	Unknown
Holder, Thomas	Co. C, 11th North Carolina	1844	1863	Mortally wounded-died on unknown date in Gettysburg	Unknown
Holland, James K.	Co. I, 1st Tennessee	1839	11/22/1863	Died as POW at Pt. Lookout, MD	Pt. Lookout, MD
Holland, John	Co. K, 38th Virginia		7/3/1863	Killed in action	Unknown
Holland, William B.	Co. A, 42nd Mississippi		7/4/1863	Mortally wouned, July 3rd, and died the next day	Unknown
Holliday, John D.	Co. D, 17th Georgia		10/26/1863	Mortally wounded, July 2nd, and died at Atlanta, GA	Atlanta, GA
Hollingsworth, H.V.B.	Co. C, 13th Georgia		7/29/1863	Mortally wounded, July 2nd, and died at Staunton, VA	Staunton, VA
Hollingsworth, William J.	Sgt., Co. I, 15th Georgia		7/31/1863	Died as POW at David's Island, NY	Cypress Hills, NY
Hollis, George Washington	Co. H, 47th Alabama	1836	7/17/1863	Mortally wounded-died at unknown place in Gettysburg	Unknown

NAME	REGIMENT	BIRTH	DEATH	COMMENT	BURIAL
Holloway, J.M.	Co. F, 26th North Carolina	1840	10/18/1863	Died as POW at Pt. Lookout, MD	Pt. Lookout, MD
Holloway, John Burton	Lt., Co. F, 26th North Carolina	1/12/1835	7/1/1863	Killed in action	Unknown
Holloway, R.H.	Co. D, 13th North Carolina		7/10/1863	Mortally wounded–died at unknown place in Gettysburg	Unknown
Holloway, Thomas J.	Co. H, 7th Tennessee		7/3/1863	Killed in action	Unknown
Holloway, William R.	Co. G, 15th Alabama	1824	7/3/1863	Killed in action	Unknown
Hollowell, John T.	Co. H, 13th Mississippi		7/12/1863	Hollywood Cemetery, Richmond, Va., reburial lists	Richmond, VA
Holmes, James L.	Co. I, 5th Texas		7/5/1863	Hollywood Cemetery, Richmond, Va., reburial lists	Richmond, VA
Holmes, Rufus	Co. F, 47th North Carolina	1836	7/3/1863	Killed in action	Unknown
Holmes, Rufus B.	Co. F, 57th North Carolina	1838	7/17/1863	Hollywood Cemetery, Richmond, Va., reburial lists	Richmond, VA
Holmes, William M.	Co. K, 53rd Georgia		Jul. 1863	Missing in action and presumed dead	Unknown
Holt, David Joseph	Co. K, 28th North Carolina	1836	7/3/1863	Killed in action	Unknown
Holt, John Lee	Co. I, 56th Virginia	5/31/1829	7/3/1863	Killed in action	Unknown
Holt, John P.	Page's Battery (Va.)		8/4/1863	Mortally wounded–died at unknown place in Gettysburg	Unknown
Holt, William M.	Co. F, 45th North Carolina	1824	7/1/1863	Killed in action	Unknown
Holt, Yancy A.	Co. B, 2nd North Carolina Battalion	1829	7/1/1863	Killed in action	Unknown
Holton, Samuel C.	Co. F, 18th Virginia	1839	7/3/1863	Killed in action	Unknown
Holyfield, Martin R.	Co. B, 2nd North Carolina Battalion	1827	7/1/1863	Killed in action	Unknown
Honeycutt, Franklin L.	Co. B, 26th North Carolina		7/1/1863	Killed in action	Unknown
Honts, George D.	Co. A, 28th Virginia	1840	7/3/1863	Killed in action	Unknown
Hood, J.B.	Co. H, 50th Georgia		7/2/1863	Killed in action; name may be J.R. Hood	Unknown
Hoopaugh, Allen D.	Co. B, 16th Georgia		7/2/1863	Killed in action	Unknown
Hooton, Samuel C.	Co. F, 18th Virginia	1840	7/3/1863	Killed in action	Unknown
Hoover, David M.	Co. I, 11th North Carolina	1842	7/1/1863	Killed in action	Unknown
Hoover, John H.	Co. I, 14th Virginia Cavalry		7/3/1863	Killed in action	Unknown
Hopper, George W.	Co. K, 38th Virginia		7/3/1863	Killed in action	Unknown
Hopper, John T.	Co. K, 38th Virginia	8/25/1829	7/3/1863	Killed in action	Unknown
Horn, William B.	Co. H, 43rd North Carolina	1829	8/18/1863	Oakwood Cemetery, Raleigh, NC, reburial list	Raleigh, NC
Horne, James B.	Co. I, 3rd Georgia		7/2/1863	Killed in action	Unknown
Horney, Elisha Clarkson	Capt., Co. L, 22nd North Carolina	4/4/1843	9/5/1863	Mortally wounded and buried at Franklinville Cem., Randolph Co., NC	Randolph Co., NC
Hornsby, William S.	Sgt., Co. F, 44th Alabama	1838	7/2/1863	Killed in action	Unknown
Horsley, Thomas	Co. G, 57th Virginia		7/5/1863	Mortally wounded, July 3rd, and died two days later	Unknown
Horton, Daniel M.	Co. H, 1st Texas	3/8/1830	7/2/1863	Killed in action	Unknown
Horton, William Columbus	Co. H, 2nd South Carolina	1832	7/5/1863	Hollywood Cemetery, Richmond, Va., reburial lists	Richmond, VA
Hoskins, Blake B.	Lt., Co. F, 11th North Carolina	1839	7/9/1863	Mortally wounded–died at unknown place in Gettysburg	Unknown

NAME	REGIMENT	BIRTH	DEATH	COMMENT	BURIAL
Hough, Joseph A.	Co. E, 9th Georgia		7/9/1863	Hollywood Cemetery, Richmond, Va., reburial lists	Richmond, VA
House, George L.	Co. B, Cobb's Legion	1839	Jul. 1863	Killed in action, July 1-3	Unknown
House, James Pinkney	Co. C, 47th North Carolina	1838	7/20/1863	Hollywood Cemetery, Richmond, Va., reburial lists	Richmond, VA
House, William H.	Cpl., Co. C, 38th North Carolina	1831	7/1/1863	Killed in action	Unknown
Houser, Levi	Co. B, 23rd North Carolina	1825	7/1/1863	Killed in action	Unknown
Houston, David Gardiner	Capt., Co. D, 11th Virginia	3/31/1838	7/3/1863	Killed in action and reinterred in Green Mount Cemetery, Baltimore, MD	Baltimore, MD
Houston, William B.	Co. D, 2nd Mississippi	1843	Jul. 1863	Killed in action either July 1st or July 3rd	Unknown
Howard, Alfred B.	Co. E, 26th North Carolina	1844	7/1/1863	Killed in action	Unknown
Howard, Isaac Adams	Cpl., Co. B, 5th Texas	1845	7/2/1863	Killed in action while carrying the colors	Unknown
Howard, Isom	Co. H, 14th South Carolina	1835	7/1/1863	Killed in action	Unknown
Howard, Joseph	Co. G, 52nd North Carolina	1839	7/3/1863	Killed in action	Unknown
Howard, Thomas W.	Co. G, 28th North Carolina	1826	7/19/1863	Hollywood Cemetery, Richmond, Va., reburial lists	Richmond, VA
Howard, William H.	Co. K, 55th North Carolina	4/22/1826	7/22/1863	Hollywood Cemetery, Richmond, Va., reburial lists	Richmond, VA
Howard, William H.	Co. G, 7th North Carolina	1827	7/3/1863	Killed in action	Unknown
Howel [Howell], Jackson M.	Co. F, 10th Alabama		Jul. 1863	Missing in action and presumed dead. Surname may be Howell	Unknown
Howell, Jackson H.	Co. K, 33rd North Carolina	1836	7/3/1863	Killed in action	Unknown
Howell, Jefferson	Co. C, 37th Virginia		7/3/1863	Killed in action	Unknown
Howell, John T.	Co. K, 28th North Carolina	1839	7/28/1863	Mortally wounded per the Richmond Sentinel, August 11, 1863; died at Chester, PA	Phil. National Cem.
Howell, Joshua	Co. B, 47th Alabama		7/2/1863	Killed in action	Unknown
Howell, N.T.	Co. K, 53rd Georgia		Jul. 1863	Missing in action and presumed dead	Unknown
Howell, Thomas J.	Co. E, 3rd Georgia		7/2/1863	Killed in action	Unknown
Howison, John Hancock	Fredericksburg Artillery (Va.)	7/4/1844	7/18/1863	Died of wounds received July 3rd	Unknown
Howze, George Adrian	Lt., Co. D, 42nd Mississippi	1834	7/1/1863	Killed in action	Unknown
Howze, Thomas	Co. H, Cobb's Legion Cav. (Ga.)		7/2/1863	Laurel Grove Cemetery, Savannah, Ga., reburial list	Savannah, GA
Hoy, James M.	Co. B, 24th Virginia		Jul. 1863	Missing in action and presumed dead	Unknown
Hoyleman, George Washington	2nd Rockbridge Artillery (Va.)	1839	7/3/1863	Killed in action	Unknown
Hubbard, Alexander	Co. C, 28th Virginia	1831	7/9/1863	Mortally wounded-died at unknown place in Gettysburg	Unknown
Hubbard, Thomas J.	Co. B, 7th Tennessee		8/2/1863	Mortally wounded and died at Baltimore, MD-buried there	Baltimore, MD
Hubbard, W.P.	Co. G, 18th Georgia		Jul. 1863	Hollywood Cemetery, Richmond, Va., reburial lists	Richmond, VA
Hubble, William Joshua C.	Co. E, 50th Virginia	1838	7/2/1863	Killed in action	Unknown
Huckaby, Leander	Co. E, 11th Mississippi	1841	8/7/1863	Hollywood Cemetery, Richmond, Va., reburial lists	Richmond, VA

NAME	REGIMENT	BIRTH	DEATH	COMMENT	BURIAL
Hudson, Edward	Co. E, 5th Florida	1837	7/2/1863	Killed in action; buried at Greenhill Cemetery, Martinsburg, WV	Martinsburg, WV
Hudson, Joel J.	Co. I, 13th North Carolina	1840	7/1/1863	Killed in action	Unknown
Hudson, Richard S.	Co. E, 5th Florida		7/3/1863	Killed in action	Unknown
Hudson, Roland	Sgt., Co. C, 59th Georgia		7/2/1863	Killed in action	Unknown
Hudson, William J.	Lt., Co. E, 2nd North Carolina Battalion		8/4/1863	Mortally wounded-died at unknown place in Gettysburg	Unknown
Hudson, William M.	Co. D, 2nd Virginia Cavalry		7/3/1863	Killed in action	Unknown
Huffman, Adison Clark	Co. A, 18th Mississippi	1840	9/5/1863	Hollywood Cemetery, Richmond, Va., reburial lists	Richmond, VA
Huffman, Andrew J.	Co. C, 28th Virginia	1832	7/3/1863	Killed in action	Unknown
Huffman, Jeremiah	Co. C, 28th North Carolina	1838	10/20/1863	Oakwood Cemetery, Raleigh, NC, reburial list	Raleigh, NC
Huffman, Thomas	Co. I, 11th Virginia		Jul. 1863	Missing in action and presumed dead	Unknown
Huffstetler, Jonas L.	Co. M, 16th North Carolina		7/1/1863	Killed in action	Unknown
Huggins, Samuel	Co. F, 20th Georgia		7/2/1863	Killed in action	Unknown
Hughes, Henry H.	Co. D, 19th Virginia		7/3/1863	Killed in action	Unknown
Hughes, James H.	Co. I, 9th Georgia		7/2/1863	Killed in action	Unknown
Hughes, Joseph H.	Co. A, 28th Virginia	1840	7/28/1863	Hollywood Cemetery, Richmond, Va., reburial lists	Richmond, VA
Hughes, Moses P.	Co. G, 19th Virginia	1839	Jul. 1863	Missing in action and presumed dead	Unknown
Hughes, Nicolas Collin	Capt., AAG., Pettigrew's staff	3/10/1840	7/15/1863	Mortally wounded and died at Martinsburg, VA; Removed to New Bern, NC	New Bern, NC
Hughs, Henry T.	Co. A, 26th North Carolina		1863	Missing in action and presumed dead	Unknown
Huie, John Alexander	Lt., Co. G, 44th Georgia		7/6/1863	Died of wounds received July 1st	Unknown
Hulen, Thomas Berry	Co. F, 48th Georgia		7/14/1863	Hollywood Cemetery, Richmond, Va., reburial lists	Richmond, VA
Hulsey, Henry	Co. E, 11th Georgia		7/26/1863	Died as POW at David's Island, NY	Cypress Hills, NY
Humphreys, Charles L.	Cpl., Co. E, 2nd Mississippi	1840	8/9/1863	Mortally wounded-died at unknown place in Gettysburg	Unknown
Humphreys, David W.	Lt. Col., 2nd Mississippi		7/3/1863	Killed in action	Unknown
Humphreys, William H.	Carpenter's Battery (Va.)	11/26/1836	7/6/1863	Mortally wounded-died at unknown place in Gettysburg	Unknown
Hundley, Richard H.	Marmaduke Johnson's Battery		7/2/1863	Hollywood Cemetery, Richmond, Va., reburial lists	Richmond, VA
Hungerpiller, C.	Co. I, 3rd South Carolina		7/2/1863	Killed in action	Unknown
Hunley, Claiborne	Co. A, 45th North Carolina	1820	7/17/1863	Oakwood Cemetery, Raleigh, NC, reburial list	Raleigh, NC
Hunley, John H.	Co. C, 21st North Carolina	1837	7/28/1863	Mortally wounded-died at unknown place in Gettysburg	Unknown
Hunsucker, Thomas	Co. F, 44th Alabama	1828	7/10/1863	Died of wounds received July 2nd	Unknown
Hunt, Barnet B.	Co. K, 11th Virginia		1863	Missing in action and presumed dead	Unknown
Hunt, Elisha B.	Co. F, 18th Virginia		7/3/1863	Killed in action	Unknown
Hunt, John C.	Co. K, 3rd Virginia Cavalry		Jul. 1863	Mortally wounded-died at unknown place in Gettysburg	Unknown

NAME	REGIMENT	BIRTH	DEATH	COMMENT	BURIAL
Hunt, Wiley	Co. C, 59th Georgia		1863	Mortally wounded-died on unknown date in Gettysburg	Unknown
Hunter, James F.	Co. C, 37th North Carolina	1840	7/23/1863	Mortally wounded and died at Chester, PA	Phil. National Cem.
Hunter, Thomas J.	Cpl., Co. D, 26th North Carolina	1832	1863	Missing in action and presumed dead	Unknown
Huntly, George J.	Lt., Co. I, 34th North Carolina	1841	7/3/1863	Killed in action	Unknown
Hurley, M.	Co. B, 5th Texas		7/2/1863	Killed in action	Unknown
Hurley, Marshall	Co. A, 26th North Carolina	1845	7/1/1863	Killed in action	Unknown
Hurst, George Washington	Lt., Co. D, 2nd Georgia	1837	7/2/1863	Killed in action	Unknown
Hurt, Joseph P.	Lt., Co. C, 11th Georgia		7/3/1863	Killed in action	Unknown
Huse, Jesse H.	Co. K, 57th Virginia		10/13/1863	Died of wounds at Ft. Delaware, DE	Finn's Point, NJ
Husky, James P.	Co. A, 13th South Carolina	1843	7/3/1863	Killed in action per the Charleston Courier, July 1863	Unknown
Huson, John C.	Co. F, 1st North Carolina	1841	7/2/1863	Hollywood Cemetery, Richmond, Va., reburial lists	Richmond, VA
Huss, Joseph H.	Sgt., Co. E, 34th North Carolina	1841	7/3/1863	Killed in action	Unknown
Hussey, John M.	Co. E, 1st South Carolina Cav.	1835	7/13/1863	Mortally wounded-died at unknown place in Gettysburg	Unknown
Hutchens, M. Augustus	Co. D, 8th Georgia		7/2/1863	Killed in action	Unknown
Hutchenson, John Floyd	Sgt., Co. F, 24th Virginia	1840	7/3/1863	Killed in action, July 1-3	Unknown
Hutcherson, W.A.	Co. H, 22nd North Carolina	1844	Jul. 1863	Killed in action	Unknown
Hutchins, Andrew Jackson	Co. C, 6th North Carolina	1833	7/1/1863	Killed in action	Unknown
Hutchins, James A.	Sgt., Co. G, 13th Georgia		7/1/1863	Killed in action	Unknown
Hutchinson, George E.	Co. H, 8th South Carolina		7/2/1863	Killed in action	Unknown
Hutchinson, James B.	Co. B, 42nd Virginia	1841	8/19/1863	Hollywood Cemetery, Richmond, Va., reburial lists	Richmond, VA
Hutchison, James H.	Co. A, 11th North Carolina	1838	7/5/1863	Mortally wounded-died at unknown place in Gettysburg	Unknown
Hutchison, William E.	Co. F, 52nd North Carolina	1843	7/3/1863	Killed in action	Unknown
Hutts, John W.T.	Co. G, 57th Virginia		Jul. 1863	Killed in action, July 1-3	Unknown
Hyatt, John Willis	Co. K, 26th North Carolina	4/9/1845	7/1/1863	Killed in action	Unknown
Hyatt, William	Co. B, 33rd North Carolina		1863	Mortally wounded and died on unknown date	Unknown
Hyde, Wesley A.	Co. G, 11th Mississippi	1840	7/3/1863	Killed in action	Unknown
Hyden, Joseph L.	Cpl., Co. F, 24th Virginia	1839	7/3/1863	Killed in action	Unknown
Idol, G.M.	Co. K, 45th North Carolina		7/1/1863	Killed in action	Unknown
Iglehart, James I.	Co. A, 1st Maryland Battalion	1831	7/2/1863	Killed in action	Unknown
Infram, David W.	Co. G, 22nd North Carolina		Jul. 1863	Killed in action, July 1-3	Unknown
Ingle, J.L.	Co. B, 22nd North Carolina	1836	Jul. 1863	Killed in action, July 1-3	Unknown
Ingram, John	Co. K, 15th Alabama	1839	8/3/1863	Hollywood Cemetery, Richmond, Va., reburial lists	Richmond, VA
Inman, Benjamin	Co. H, 5th Florida		7/4/1863	Mortally wounded, July 3rd, and died the next day	Unknown
Irby, Samuel T.	Co. H, 14th Virginia		Jul. 1863	Missing in action and presumed dead	Unknown

NAME	REGIMENT	BIRTH	DEATH	COMMENT	BURIAL
Iredell, Campbell Tredwell	Capt., Co. C, 47th North Carolina	1836	7/1/1863	Mortally wounded July 1, and died the same day; Reinterred in City Cemetery., Raleigh, NC	Raleigh, NC
Irving, John L.	Cpl., Co. F, 45th North Carolina	1838	7/1/1863	Killed in action	Unknown
Irwin, Eli B.	Co. B, 35th Georgia		7/3/1863	Mortally wounded, July 3rd, and died the same day	Unknown
Isbell, Walter D.	Sgt., Co. C, 2nd South Carolina	1836	7/11/1863	Magnolia Cemetery, Charleston, SC, reburial list	Charleston, SC
Iseley, Lewis C.	Co. F, 6th North Carolina	1846	7/16/1863	Oakwood Cemetery, Raleigh, NC, reburial list	Raleigh, NC
Iseley, William	Co. K, 47th North Carolina	1841	8/28/1863	Mortally wounded and died at Staunton, VA-buried there	Staunton, VA
Isom, Dudley Addison	Co. G, 11th Mississippi	1839	Jul. 1863	Hollywood Cemetery, Richmond, Va., reburial lists	Richmond, VA
Ives, Leonard W.	Co. A, 1st Maryland Battalion		1863	Missing in action and presumed dead	Unknown
Ives, Richard W.	Cpl., Co. H, 14th Virginia	1838	Jul. 1863	Mortally wounded and died on unknown date	Unknown
Ives, Walter C.	Lt., Co. E, 61st Virginia		7/2/1863	Killed in action	Unknown
Ivey, Adam	Co. B, 10th Georgia		7/2/1863	Killed in action	Unknown
Ivey, William G.	Cpl., Co. G, 11th North Carolina		8/8/1863	Died as POW at David's Island, NY	Cypress Hills, NY
Ivey, William H.P.	Co. A, 8th Alabama	1839	7/12/1863	Hollywood Cemetery, Richmond, Va., reburial lists	Richmond, VA
Jackson, Andrew	Co. G, 5th Texas	1831	7/23/1863	Mortally wounded-died at unknown place in Gettysburg	Unknown
Jackson, Benjamin E.	Co. D, 8th Virginia	1833	7/3/1863	Killed in action; reinterred in Union Cemetery, Leesburg, VA	Leesburg, VA
Jackson, George H.	Co. G, 18th Virginia	1838	7/20/1863	Mortally wounded, July 3rd, and died at Staunton, VA	Staunton, VA
Jackson, John M.	Co. E, 38th Georgia		7/8/1863	Mortally wounded-died at unknown place in Gettysburg	Unknown
Jackson, Lewis H.	Co. A, 38th Virginia		8/1/1863	Mortally wounded per the Richmond Sentinel, August 1, 1863; died at Chester, PA	Phil. National Cem.
Jackson, Samuel	Co. F, 31st Georgia	1/8/1839	7/1/1863	Killed in action	Unknown
Jackson, W.T.	Co. I, 20th North Carolina	1844	Jul. 1863	Mortally wounded and died on unknown date	Unknown
Jackson, William B.	Co. A, 12th South Carolina	1/21/1844	7/7/1863	Mortally wounded-died at unknown place in Gettysburg	Unknown
Jackson, William H.	Co. B, 5th North Carolina	1836	7/1/1863	Killed in action; KIA on Oak Ridge (Iverson's Brigade)	Richmond, VA
Jacobs, Bailey Shumate	Capt., Co. D, 49th Virginia	1836	7/16/1863	Died of wounds in Winchester, VA; buried in family cemetery	Warren Co., VA
Jacobs, Thomas Pressley	Co. E, 14th South Carolina	1842	7/1/1863	Killed in action	Unknown
James, Richard	Co. G, 14th Virginia		Jul. 1863	Missing in action and presumed dead	Unknown
James, Townsend Asa	Co. A, 8th Virginia		7/3/1863	Killed in action	Unknown
Jamison, George H.	Co. B, 8th Louisiana	1830	7/1/1863	Hollywood Cemetery, Richmond, Va., reburial lists	Richmond, VA

NAME	REGIMENT	BIRTH	DEATH	COMMENT	BURIAL
Jarman, Elijah C.	Co. K, 26th North Carolina	1844	8/1/1863	Hollywood Cemetery, Richmond, Va., reburial lists	Richmond, VA
Jarrell, James W.	Co. E, 2nd North Carolina Battalion		7/1/1883	Killed in action	Unknown
Jarrell, William Garland	Co. D, 1st South Carolina Cavalry	1839	7/1/1863	Killed in action	Unknown
Jarvis, Daniel W.	Lt., Co. G, 48th Georgia		7/2/1863	Killed in action	Unknown
Jarvis, James N.	Co. D, 5th Florida	1844	7/2/1863	Killed in action	Unknown
Jefferson, James T.	Co. E, 57th Virginia		8/16/1863	Hollywood Cemetery, Richmond, Va., reburial lists	Richmond, VA
Jelks, James K.	Co. D, 3rd Virginia	1836	7/3/1863	Killed in action	Unknown
Jenkins, John A.	Lt., Co. E, 5th Florida	1827	7/2/1863	Killed in action	Unknown
Jenkins, John Summerfield	Adj., 14th Virginia	10/29/1832	7/3/1863	Killed in action	Unknown
Jenkins, Richard W.T.	Co. D, 13th Georgia		Jul. 1863	Killed in action	Unknown
Jenkins, Rolla	Co. K, 48th Georgia	1824	7/2/1863	Killed in action	Unknown
Jenkins, W.C.	Co. F, 43rd North Carolina	1836	7/1/1863	Killed in action	Unknown
Jenkins, William	Co. H, 33rd Virginia		7/3/1863	Killed in action	Unknown
Jennings, James	Sgt., Co. I, 18th Virginia	1833	7/10/1863	Mortally wounded-died at unknown place in Gettysburg	Unknown
Jennings, John A.	Co. B, 2nd South Carolina	1835	7/2/1863	Hollywood Cemetery, Richmond, Va., reburial lists	Richmond, VA
Jennings, Thomas	Co. G, 11th Virginia		7/4/1863	Mortally wounded and buried on Jacob Schwartz Farm	Unknown
Jennings, William	Co. G, 11th Virginia		7/4/1863	Killed in action	Unknown
Jerkins, R.Green	Capt., Co. B, 2nd Florida	1833	7/2/1863	Killed in action	Unknown
Jessee, David A.	Co. K, 48th Virginia	1833	7/2/1863	Killed in action per the Abingdon Virginian, Sept. 18, 1863	Unknown
Jessee, Jefferson B.	Co. C, 37th Virginia		7/4/1863	Hollywood Cemetery, Richmond, Va., reburial lists	Richmond, VA
Jett, Thomas Coke	Co. K, 14th Tennessee	1836	7/1/1863	Killed in action	Unknown
Jetton, William H.	Sgt., Co. I, 11th North Carolina	1840	7/3/1863	Killed in action	Unknown
Jimmerson, John A.	Co. A, 21st Virginia	1842	7/18/1863	Mortally wounded-died at unknown place in Gettysburg	Unknown
Jinkins, William S.	Sgt., Co. G, 7th North Carolina	1829	7/3/1863	Killed in action	Unknown
Jinks, Troy	Co. H, 47th North Carolina	1839	7/1/1863	Killed in action	Unknown
Johns, James B.	Co. F, 5th Florida		7/3/1863	Killed in action	Unknown
Johnson, Austin H.	Co. K, 57th Virginia		Jul. 1863	Killed in action, July 1-3	Unknown
Johnson, Charles A.	Co. I, 48th Georgia	1828	1863	Died of wounds received on July 2 on unknown date	Unknown
Johnson, Charles T.	Cpl., Co. A, 49th Georgia	1833	7/2/1863	Killed in action	Unknown
Johnson, Charles W.	Cpl., Co. D, 2nd Florida	1841	7/2/1863	Killed in action	Unknown
Johnson, Daniel J.	Co. H, 20th Georgia		7/2/1863	Killed in action	Unknown
Johnson, Daniel M.	Co. I, 13th Alabama	1837	9/12/1863	Hollywood Cemetery, Richmond, Va., reburial lists	Richmond, VA
Johnson, Edmund	Co. B, 48th Georgia	1840	7/2/1863	Killed in action	Unknown
Johnson, Edward	Co. H, 4th Virginia		7/3/1863	Killed in action	Unknown

NAME	REGIMENT	BIRTH	DEATH	COMMENT	BURIAL
Johnson, Edwin T.	Co. I, 8th Georgia	1844	9/7/1863	Laurel Grove Cemetery, Savannah, Ga., reburial list	Savannah, GA
Johnson, Emerson	Co. D, 47th North Carolina	1838	7/3/1863	Mortally wounded, July 3rd, and died of wounds same day	Unknown
Johnson, H.D.	Co. A, 13th South Carolina	1839	8/15/1863	Mortally wounded-died on unknown date in Gettysburg	Unknown
Johnson, James F.	Co. F, 7th North Carolina	1843	Jul. 1863	Killed in action, July 1-3	Unknown
Johnson, James F.	Co. K, 19th Virginia		Jul. 1863	Missing in action and presumed dead	Unknown
Johnson, James S.	Co. A, 7th South Carolina	1845	7/2/1863	Killed in action per the Edgefield Advertiser, October 7, 1863	Unknown
Johnson, John	Co. C, 47th North Carolina	1844	Jul. 1863	Missing in action and presumed dead	Unknown
Johnson, John J.	Co. E, 8th Alabama		7/3/1863	Killed in action	Unknown
Johnson, John Lewis	Lt., Co. F, 14th Virginia	3/19/1839	7/3/1863	Hollywood Cemetery, Richmond, Va., reburial lists	Richmond, VA
Johnson, John R.	Co. H, 47th North Carolina	1837	7/30/1863	Hollywood Cemetery, Richmond, Va., reburial lists	Richmond, VA
Johnson, John T.	Co. K, 11th Mississippi	1841	8/4/1863	Mortally wounded and buried in Soldiers Cemetery as 11th Mass.	Gettysburg, PA
Johnson, Joseph	Co. H, 12th Georgia		7/12/1863	Died of wounds received July 1st	Unknown
Johnson, Lucanus Adolphus	Cpl., Co. H, 53rd Virginia	12/11/1840	7/3/1863	Killed in action while carrying the colors	Unknown
Johnson, Robert Butler	Co. B, 13th Mississippi	1842	7/2/1863	Killed in action	Unknown
Johnson, Simon P.	Co. I, 26th North Carolina		7/20/1863	Mortally wounded, July 1st, and died at Williamsport, MD	Williamsport, MD
Johnson, Stephen M.	Co. B, 12th South Carolina	1844	7/3/1863	Mortally wounded, July 1st, and died the same day	Unknown
Johnson, Thomas	Co. I, 42nd Mississippi	1825	8/14/1863	Hollywood Cemetery, Richmond, Va., reburial lists	Richmond, VA
Johnson, Thomas	Co. H, 26th North Carolina	1842	7/1/1863	Killed in action	Unknown
Johnson, Whitfield W.	Co. G, 2nd South Carolina		7/2/1863	Killed in action	Unknown
Johnson, William	Co. G, 19th Virginia	1841	Jul. 1863	Missing in action and presumed dead	Unknown
Johnson, William C.	Co. I, 7th Tennessee	1840	8/9/1863	Hollywood Cemetery, Richmond, Va., reburial lists	Richmond, VA
Johnson, William W.	Co. K, 8th Florida	1837	7/12/1863	Mortally wounded-died at unknown place in Gettysburg	Unknown
Johnston, Edwin	Co. H, 4th Virginia	1842	7/3/1863	Killed in action	Unknown
Johnston, H.C.	Co. F, 48th Mississippi		7/2/1863	Hollywood Cemetery, Richmond, Va., reburial lists	Richmond, VA
Johnston, John J.	Co. E, 7th Virginia Cavalry	1842	7/3/1863	Killed in action at Fairfield, PA	Unknown
Johnston, Joseph E.	Capt., Co. B, 47th Alabama	1831	7/19/1863	Mortally wounded-died at unknown place in Gettysburg	Unknown
Johnston, William M.	Co. I, 10th Alabama		Jul. 1863	Missing in action and presumed dead	Unknown
Johnston, William Martin	Co. K, 12th Alabama	5/13/1828	7/7/1863	Mortally wounded-died at unknown place in Gettysburg	Unknown
Jolly, John A.	Cpl., Co. G, 5th Texas		7/2/1863	Killed in action	Unknown
Jolly, Wesley	Co. I, 32nd North Carolina	1837	8/15/1863	Mortally wounded and died at Camp Letterman	Raleigh, NC

NAME	REGIMENT	BIRTH	DEATH	COMMENT	BURIAL
Jones, Charles Mc.	Capt., Co. H, 49th Georgia	1838	7/3/1863	Killed in action	Unknown
Jones, Charles W.	Co. C, 11th Virginia	1836	7/3/1863	Killed in action	Unknown
Jones, Christopher C.	Co. B, 3rd Georgia		7/2/1863	Killed in action	Unknown
Jones, Elisha R.	Co. G, 13th North Carolina	1839	7/3/1863	Mortally wounded, July 3rd, and died the same day	Unknown
Jones, Fabius Haywood	Sgt., Co. G, 7th North Carolina	1831	Jul. 1863	Mortally wounded and died in enemy hands prior to August 1st	Unknown
Jones, Floyd K.	Co. I, 3rd Alabama		7/1/1863	Killed in action	Unknown
Jones, Francis Pendleton	Lt., ADC to Genl. John M. Jones	12/27/1841	9/2/1863	Died of wounds received July 2nd; buried in Louisa Christian Church, Louisa Co., VA	Louisa Co., VA
Jones, G.A.	Co. G, 5th Texas		7/2/1863	Killed in action; brother of W.C. Jones	Unknown
Jones, G.W.	Co. A, 59th Georgia		7/2/1863	Killed in action	Unknown
Jones, Giles W.	Co. I, 13th North Carolina	1841	8/22/1863	Died as POW at David's Island, NY	Cypress Hills, NY
Jones, H.H.	Co. C, 60th Georgia		7/3/1863	Mortally wounded, July 3rd, and died the same day	Unknown
Jones, Henry N.	Lt., Co. I, 1st Texas		7/2/1863	Hollywood Cemetery, Richmond, Va., reburial lists	Richmond, VA
Jones, Isaac N.	Co. B, 45th North Carolina	1839	7/4/1863	Oakwood Cemetery, Raleigh, NC, reburial list	Raleigh, NC
Jones, James W.	Co. A, 14th South Carolina	1837	7/1/1863	Killed in action	Unknown
Jones, Jefferson W.	Co. K, 17th Mississippi	1844	Jul. 1863	Killed in action on July 1st or 2nd	Unknown
Jones, John A.	Cpl., Co. B, 3rd North Carolina	1841	7/2/1863	Killed in action	Unknown
Jones, John A.	Co. C, 2nd Florida	1843	7/3/1863	Mortally wounded, July 3rd, and died the same day	Unknown
Jones, John Augustus	Col., 20th Georgia	2/11/1821	7/2/1863	Killed in action; body lost at sea on return to Georgia	At Sea
Jones, John O.	Co. I, 11th Virginia		7/15/1863	Hollywood Cemetery, Richmond, Va., reburial lists	Richmond, VA
Jones, John Thomas	Co. E, 11th Mississippi	1839	7/15/1863	Hollywood Cemetery, Richmond, Va., reburial lists	Richmond, VA
Jones, Joshua H.	Co. G, 15th Georgia		7/2/1863	Killed in action	Unknown
Jones, Josiah	Co. E, 5th Florida	1836	7/2/1863	Killed in action	Unknown
Jones, Lineous	Co. C, 11th Virginia	1837	7/13/1863	Hollywood Cemetery, Richmond, Va., reburial lists	Richmond, VA
Jones, Lucian H.	Co. C, 5th North Carolina	1835	7/1/1863	Killed in action; KIA on Oak Ridge (Iverson's Brigade)	Richmond, VA
Jones, Lucien S.	Sgt., Co. A, 19th Virginia	1842	7/5/1863	Hollywood Cemetery, Richmond, Va., reburial lists	Richmond, VA
Jones, Noah R.	Co. H, 53rd North Carolina	1846	7/3/1863	Killed in action	Unknown
Jones, Richard Fountain	Adj., 17th Mississipi	6/21/1835	7/3/1863	Killed in action	Unknown
Jones, Robert Williams	Sgt., Co. B, 49th Georgia	1840	7/17/1863	Mortally wounded-died at unknown place in Gettysburg	Unknown
Jones, S.A.	Co. H, 7th South Carolina		8/11/1863	Magnolia Cemetery, Charleston, SC, reburial list	Charleston, SC
Jones, Thomas S.	Co. H, 1st South Carolina		8/10/1863	Magnolia Cemetery, Charleston, SC, reburial list	Charleston, SC

NAME	REGIMENT	BIRTH	DEATH	COMMENT	BURIAL
Jones, W.C.	Co. G, 5th Texas		7/2/1863	Killed in action; brother of G.A. Jones	Unknown
Jones, Walker Wilbur	Co. C, 11th Virginia	1841	7/3/1863	Killed in action	Unknown
Jones, Walter Lenoir	Co. I, 26th North Carolina	12/2/1842	7/9/1863	Mortally wounded; buried at Chapel of Rest Cemetery	Caldwell Co., NC
Jones, William	Co. B, 6th Alabama		10/29/1863	Mortally wounded-died at unknown place in Gettysburg	Unknown
Jones, William	Co. E, 11th Alabama		Jul. 1863	Hollywood Cemetery, Richmond, Va., reburial lists	Richmond, VA
Jones, William Edward	Cpl., Co. D, 56th Virginia	11/1/1840	7/3/1863	Killed in action	Unknown
Jones, William F.	Co. E, 15th Alabama	1844	7/16/1863	Mortally wounded-died at unknown place in Gettysburg	Unknown
Jones, William Levi	Co. C, 5th Florida	9/29/1829	7/3/1863	Killed in action	Unknown
Jones, William P.	Co. D, 2nd Georgia Battalion		7/20/1863	Hollywood Cemetery, Richmond, Va., reburial lists	Richmond, VA
Jones, Williamson C.	Co. I, 40th Virginia	1839	7/1/1863	Killed in action	Unknown
Jordan, Barron Dekalb	Co. B, 47th Alabama	1843	7/2/1863	Killed in action	Unknown
Jordan, Benjamin O.	Co. A, 21st Virginia		7/18/1863	Hollywood Cemetery, Richmond, Va., reburial lists	Richmond, VA
Jordan, David	Co. F, 14th Georgia		7/2/1863	Killed in action	Unknown
Jordan, James A.	Co. G, 38th Georgia		7/1/1863	Killed in action	Unknown
Jordan, John C.	Co. G, 15th Alabama	1838	7/2/1863	Missing in action and presumed dead	Unknown
Jordan, John Chappell	Co. F, 3rd Virginia	1842	7/12/1863	Hollywood Cemetery, Richmond, Va., reburial lists	Richmond, VA
Jordan, Jonathan T.	Lt., Co. G, 14th South Carolina	11/20/1830	7/6/1863	Mortally wounded-died at unknown place in Gettysburg	Unknown
Jordan, Leroy	Co. F, 3rd Georgia		7/12/1863	Mortally wounded and died at Chester, PA	Phil. National Cem.
Jordan, N.C.	Co. G, 11th North Carolina	1834	7/3/1863	Mortally wounded, July 1st, and died of wounds	Unknown
Jordan, William Flemming	Co. G, 19th Virginia	1836	7/3/1863	Missing in action and presumed dead	Unknown
Jordan, William T.	Co. H, 43rd North Carolina	1842	7/1/1863	Killed in action	Unknown
Jourdan, Joseph D.	Co. I, 25th Virginia		7/15/1863	Mortally wounded-died at unknown place in Gettysburg	Unknown
Jowers, Wesley	Co. H, 43rd North Carolina		9/18/1863	Died as POW at David's Island, NY	Cypress Hills, NY
Joyce, Alexander	Co. A, 45th North Carolina	1826	7/1/1863	Killed in action	Unknown
Joyce, Festy	Letcher Artillery (Va.)		7/1/1863	Killed in action	Unknown
Joyce, John R.	Co. A, 45th North Carolina	1842	7/1/1863	Killed in action	Unknown
Joyce, Sullivan	Co. A, 45th North Carolina	1843	8/31/1863	Died as POW at David's Island, NY	Cypress Hills, NY
Joyner, Berry F.	Co. H, 12th North Carolina	1837	Jul. 1863	Killed in action	Unknown
Joyner, Eli	Co A, 47th North Carolina	1839	7/6/1863	Oakwood Cemetery, Raleigh, NC, reburial list	Raleigh, NC
Joyner, James	Co. H, 47th North Carolina	1811	Jul. 1863	Oakwood Cemetery, Raleigh, NC, reburial list	Raleigh, NC
Julius, John	Co. E, 57th Virginia		Jul. 1863	Missing in action and presumed dead	Unknown
Justice, Allen T.	Cpl., Co. B, 16th Georgia		8/5/1863	Mortally wounded per the Augusta Chronicle & Sentinel, August 13, 1863	Unknown

NAME	REGIMENT	BIRTH	DEATH	COMMENT	BURIAL
Justice, Elijah	Co. F, 3rd North Carolina	1843	7/2/1863	Missing in action and presumed dead	Unknown
Kadle, James M.	Co. F, 7th South Carolina	1843	11/5/1863	Died of wounds at Ft. Delaware, DE	Finn's Point, NJ
Kahle, William Henry Harrison	Co. B, 5th Virginia	1837	7/3/1863	Killed in action	Unknown
Kanapaux, Alexander E.	Co. D, 7th North Carolina	1843	1863	Missing in action and presumed dead	Unknown
Karr, James M.	Co. A, 21st Georgia		7/2/1863	Laurel Grove Cemetery, Savannah, Ga., reburial list	Savannah, GA
Katner, J.W.	Co. F, 47th North Carolina	1843	7/3/1863	Killed in action per the Raleigh Observer, July 29, 1863	Unknown
Kean, Charles	Sgt., Co. C, 1st Virginia	1826	1863	Mortally wounded and died on unknown date	Unknown
Kearney, Augustus A.	Co. A, 14th North Carolina	1832	7/1/1863	Killed in action	Unknown
Kearns, Isaac Newton	Lt., Co. H, 38th North Carolina	9/1/1834	7/24/1863	Hollywood Cemetery, Richmond, Va., reburial lists	Richmond, VA
Kearny, Patrick	Co. I, 8th Alabama		7/2/1863	Killed in action	Unknown
Kearse, Francis	Lt. Col., 50th Georgia		7/2/1863	Laurel Grove Cemetery, Savannah, Ga., reburial list	Savannah, GA
Keel, William M.	Sgt., Co. I, 42nd Mississippi		7/26/1863	Hollywood Cemetery, Richmond, Va., reburial lists	Richmond, VA
Keels, John	Co. H, 15th Alabama	1829	7/3/1863	Mortally wounded, July 2nd, and died next day	Unknown
Keenan, Thomas	Co. A, 6th North Carolina	1839	7/2/1863	Killed in action	Unknown
Keeton, Franklin	Co. C, 26th North Carolina	1841	7/1/1863	Killed in action	Unknown
Keeton, James P.	Co. C, 56th Virginia		Jul. 1863	Mortally wounded and died of wounds on an unknown date	Unknown
Keever, George Pinckney	Co. I, 11th North Carolina	1844	7/7/1863	Mortally wounded-died at unknown place in Gettysburg	Unknown
Kehoe, Joseph	Co. F, 7th Louisiana	1841	7/2/1863	Killed in action	Unknown
Keiser, Jacob H.	Lt., Co. H, 5th Virginia	1834	8/1/1863	Hollywood Cemetery, Richmond, Va., reburial lists	Richmond, VA
Keisler, George Albert	Co. K, 13th South Carolina	1835	7/28/1863	Died as POW at David's Island, NY	Cypress Hills, NY
Keith, Anderson C.	Co. I, 3rd North Carolina	1836	8/1/1863	Oakwood Cemetery, Raleigh, NC, reburial list	Raleigh, NC
Keith, George	Co. K, 5th North Carolina	1834	7/1/1863	Killed in action; KIA on Oak Ridge (Iverson's Brigade)	Richmond, VA
Kellam, Franklin	Co. H, 22nd North Carolina	1827	7/1/1863	Killed in action	Unknown
Kellam, Jonathan F.	Co. E, 22nd North Carolina	1841	Jul. 1863	Killed in action, July 1-3	Unknown
Kelley, William M.	Co. E, 13th Alabama		7/25/1863	Mortally wounded-died at unknown place in Gettysburg	Unknown
Kellis, Josiah	Co. E, 27th North Carolina		7/25/1863	Hollywood Cemetery, Richmond, Va., reburial lists	Richmond, VA
Kelly, Gersham P.	Sgt., Co. B, 10th Alabama	1831	7/2/1863	Hollywood Cemetery, Richmond, Va., reburial lists	Richmond, VA
Kelly, Mordecai A.	King William Artillery (Va.)		7/19/1863	Mortally wounded and died at Winchester, VA; interred Stonewall Cemetery	Winchester, VA
Kelly, Richard	Co. I, 6th Louisiana	1837	7/13/1863	Mortally wounded and died at Williamsport, MD-buried there	Williamsport, MD

NAME	REGIMENT	BIRTH	DEATH	COMMENT	BURIAL
Kelly, Samuel L.	Co. F, 1st South Carolina		7/6/1863	Mortally wounded and died at Williamsport, MD-buried there	Williamsport, MD
Kelly, Thomas J.	Lt., Co. B, 3rd North Carolina		7/9/1863	Hollywood Cemetery, Richmond, Va., reburial lists	Richmond, VA
Kemp, G.E.	Co. C, 26th North Carolina	1836	7/1/1863	Killed in action	Unknown
Kemp, William Merideth	Cpl., Co. K, 44th Alabama	1840	Jul. 1863	Mortally wounded, July 2nd, and died on unknown date	Unknown
Kendall, Julius A.	Co. I, 52nd North Carolina	1829	Jul. 1863	Mortally wounded, July 3rd, and died on unknown date	Unknown
Kendley, Columbus C.	Co. A, 20th North Carolina	1845	Jul. 1863	Killed in action	Unknown
Kendrick, Benjamin E.	Co. B, 15th Alabama	1838	7/2/1863	Killed in action	Unknown
Kendrick, Henry Christopher	Sgt., Co. E, 9th Georgia	Dec. 1840	7/2/1863	Killed in action	Unknown
Kendrick, J.C.	Sgt., Co. E, 9th Georgia		7/2/1863	Killed in action	Unknown
Kendrick, Linwood	Co. H, 38th Virginia		7/3/1863	Killed in action	Unknown
Kennedy, Alsey	Co. B, 15th Alabama	1840	7/2/1863	Killed in action	Unknown
Kennedy, Arthur T.	Co. A, 1st Maryland Battalion		7/2/1863	Killed in action	Unknown
Kennedy, Hugh Reid	Brooks Artillery (S.C.)		7/15/1863	Mortally wounded-died on unknown date in Gettysburg	Unknown
Kennedy, Isaac	Co. F, 13th Alabama		7/1/1863	Killed in action	Unknown
Kennedy, J.V.	Sgt., Co. G, 2nd North Carolina Battalion.	1833	7/7/1863	Mortally wounded-died at unknown place in Gettysburg	Unknown
Kennedy, Jabez F.	Co. E, 20th Georgia		7/5/1863	Mortally wounded-died at unknown place in Gettysburg	Unknown
Kennedy, John S.	Co. A, 3rd Georgia		7/2/1863	Killed in action	Unknown
Kennedy, Patrick	Co. C, 59th Georgia		8/23/1863	Died as POW at David's Island, NY	Cypress Hills, NY
Kennedy, William D.	Co. A, 2nd Florida	1841	8/10/1863	Hollywood Cemetery, Richmond, Va., reburial lists	Richmond, VA
Kenner, Henry W.	Co. H, 40th Virginia	1836	7/7/1863	Mortally wounded-died at unknown place in Gettysburg	Unknown
Kenney [Kenny], Bernard	Co. C, 1st Maryland Battalion		7/2/1863	Killed in action	Unknown
Kenney, James	Co. G, 24th Virginia		7/31/1863	Mortally wounded-died at unknown place in Gettysburg	Unknown
Kenney, Nicholas J.	Cpl., Co. C, 24th Virginia		Jul. 1863	Missing in action and presumed dead	Unknown
Kent, James W.	Cpl., Co. C, 19th Virginia	1835	Jul. 1863	Missing in action and presumed dead	Unknown
Kerbow, Doctor Singleton	Co. B, 16th Georgia	1831	7/3/1863	Killed in action	Unknown
Kercheval, John W.	Co. F, 8th Virginia		7/3/1863	Killed in action	Unknown
Kerns, Cornelius	Co. D, 1st Maryland Battalion		Jul. 1863	Killed in action, July 1-3	Unknown
Kersey, Jackson	Co. D, 6th Alabama		7/1/1863	Killed in action	Unknown
Kesler, Peter	Co. E, 57th Virginia		7/3/1863	Killed in action	Unknown
Kestler, Noah	Co. B, 23rd North Carolina	1840	7/1/1863	Killed in action	Unknown
Ketterman, Joseph	Co. K, 25th Virginia	1842	Jul. 1863	Killed in action, July 1-3	Unknown
Key, Hugh	Co. C, 17th Georgia	1838	8/5/1863	Hollywood Cemetery, Richmond, Va., reburial lists	Richmond, VA
Key, John Oliver	Co. A, 1st South Carolina		7/1/1863	Killed in action	Unknown
Key, John Thomas	Lt., Co. E, 10th Georgia	1841	7/2/1863	Killed in action	Unknown

NAME	REGIMENT	BIRTH	DEATH	COMMENT	BURIAL
Kidd, Green L.	Co. G, 2nd Mississippi	1817	7/1/1863	Killed in action	Unknown
Kidd, Thomas J.	Co. B, 16th Georgia		1863	Mortally wounded per the Augusta Chronicle & Sentinel, August 13, 1863	Unknown
Kiger, Franklin T.	Cpl., Co. I, 33rd North Carolina	1844	7/3/1863	Killed in action	Unknown
Kilgore, Andrew J.	Cpl., Co. E, 8th Florida	1843	7/24/1863	Hollywood Cemetery, Richmond, Va., reburial lists	Richmond, VA
Kilgore, Wilson	Sgt., Co. A, 35th Georgia		7/3/1863	Killed in action	Unknown
Kilpatrick, Henry C.	Sgt., Co. A, 3rd North Carolina	1840	7/2/1863	Killed in action	Unknown
Kimbrell, Archibald	Co. G, 10th Alabama		7/2/1863	Killed in action	Unknown
Kimbrell, James L.	Co. B, 13th North Carolina	1841	7/1/1863	Killed in action	Unknown
Kinard, Walter J.	Co. D, 13th South Carolina	1842	7/1/1863	Killed in action	Unknown
Kincaid, George W.	Lt., Co. D, 11th North Carolina	1839	7/3/1863	Killed in action	Unknown
Kincaid, J.W.	Co. D, 11th North Carolina	1832	7/1/1863	Killed in action	Unknown
Kincaid, James Monroe	Capt., Co. G, 52nd North Carolina	1838	8/27/1863	Oakwood Cemetery, Raleigh, NC, reburial list	Raleigh, NC
Kindall, J.A.	Co. I, 52nd North Carolina	1829	7/3/1863	Killed in action	Unknown
King, Allen	Co. K, 14th South Carolina	1827	7/1/1863	Killed in action	Unknown
King, Daniel C.	Lt., Co. D, 16th North Carolina	1841	7/28/1863	Mortally wounded and died at Mt. Jackson, VA; interred Our Soldiers' Cemetery	Mt. Jackson, VA
King, Daniel S.	Co. A, 17th Mississippi	1839	Jul. 1863	Hollywood Cemetery, Richmond, Va., reburial lists	Richmond, VA
King, George A.	Co. G, 7th North Carolina	1839	7/3/1863	Killed in action	Unknown
King, George H.	Co. D, 21st Virginia	1838	Jul. 1863	Killed in action, July 1-3	Unknown
King, James M.D.	Capt., Co. K, 9th Virginia		11/4/1863	Mortally wounded, July 5th, died as POW at Johnson's Island, OH	Johnson's Island, OH
King, John	Co. B, 5th North Carolina		7/1/1863	Killed in action; KIA on Oak Ridge (Iverson's Brigade)	Richmond, VA
King, John C.	Cpl., Co. C, 38th North Carolina	1844	8/18/1863	Died as POW at David's Island, NY	Cypress Hills, NY
King, M.S.	Co. C, 38th North Carolina	1826	7/1/1863	Killed in action	Unknown
King, Madison	Co. G, 44th Georgia		8/21/1863	Died as POW at David's Island, NY	Cypress Hills, NY
King, Milton S.	Co. C, 13th Georgia		7/18/1863	Mortally wounded-died at unknown place in Gettysburg	Unknown
King, Samuel H.	Co. B, 7th Tennessee	8/3/1841	7/3/1863	Killed in action	Unknown
King, William	Co. I, 21st North Carolina		1863	Missing in action and presumed dead	Unknown
King, William Albert	Sgt., Co. K, 8th Georgia	1841	7/4/1863	Hollywood Cemetery, Richmond, Va., reburial lists	Richmond, VA
Kinney, James	Co. G, 24th Virginia		7/3/1863	Killed in action	Unknown
Kinney, Thomas Colston	Lt., Engineering Officer	4/27/1841	7/28/1863	Mortally wounded and died at Staunton, VA-buried there	Staunton, VA
Kinsey, James E.	Co. B, 11th Georgia		7/2/1863	Mortally wounded, July 2nd, and died the same day	Unknown
Kirby, Andrew	Co. I, 13th South Carolina	1840	Jul. 1863	Mortally wounded and died on unknown date	Unknown
Kirby, Calvin	Co. F, 42nd Mississippi		7/7/1863	Mortally wounded-died at unknown place in Gettysburg	Unknown

NAME	REGIMENT	BIRTH	DEATH	COMMENT	BURIAL
Kirk, George E.	Co. K, 28th North Carolina	1843	7/3/1863	Missing in action and presumed dead	Unknown
Kirk, Parham S.	Co. I, 52nd North Carolina	1829	7/3/1863	Mortally wounded, July 3rd, and died the same day	Unknown
Kirkland, Caleb	Co. E, 59th Georgia		8/12/1863	Mortally wounded-died at unknown place in Gettysburg	Unknown
Kirkman, George E. Badger	Co. G, 26th North Carolina	1844	7/2/1863	Killed in action	Unknown
Kirkman, Henry Clay Bascom	Co. G, 26th North Carolina	2/27/1844	9/1/1863	Oakwood Cemetery, Raleigh, NC, reburial list	Raleigh, NC
Kirkman, William D.	Co. C, 45th North Carolina	1839	7/1/1863	Killed in action	Unknown
Kirkman, William Preston	Sgt., Co. G, 26th North Carolina	1838	Jul. 1863	Missing in action and presumed dead	Unknown
Kiser, Eli	Sgt., Co. H, 23rd North Carolina	1834	7/1/1863	Killed in action	Unknown
Kiser, William A.	Co. G, 21st North Carolina	1842	7/16/1863	Mortally wounded-died at unknown place in Gettysburg	Unknown
Kistler, William N.	Co. D, 7th North Carolina	1836	7/3/1863	Killed in action	Unknown
Kitchen, James Smith	Co. H, 48th Georgia	1834	7/2/1863	Killed in action	Unknown
Klutts, J.W.	Co. F, 57th North Carolina		7/1/1863	Killed in action	Unknown
Knabe, Benjamin	Sgt., Co. D, 18th Mississippi		7/5/1863	Hollywood Cemetery, Richmond, Va., reburial lists	Richmond, VA
Knight, D.M.	Co. A, 2nd Florida	1842	7/2/1863	Killed in action	Unknown
Knight, Daniel Colwell	Cpl., Co. H, 19th Virginia	11/9/1843	7/3/1863	Killed in action	Unknown
Knight, Dempsey	Co. B, 5th North Carolina	1838	7/10/1863	Mortally wounded-died at unknown place in Gettysburg	Unknown
Knight, Robert H.	Co. B, 5th North Carolina	1843	7/6/1863	Mortally wounded-died at unknown place in Gettysburg	Unknown
Knott, James C.	Co. K, 55th North Carolina		7/1/863	Killed in action	Unknown
Knott, Minion F.	Co. F, 1st Maryland Battalion.	1840	8/24/1863	Mortally wounded; buried at Gettysburg National Cemetery as 1st MD (US)	Gettysburg Nat. Cem.
Knox, John N.	Sgt., Co. B, 13th North Carolina	1830	7/1/1863	Killed in action	Unknown
Knox, Joseph A.	Co. A, 7th North Carolina	1842	7/3/1863	Killed in action	Unknown
Kone, Benjamin A.	Cpl., Co. A, 13th Virginia Cavalry		7/3/1863	Killed in action	Unknown
Koon, Walter William	Co. I, 15th South Carolina	10/5/1837	7/10/1863	Magnolia Cemetery, Charleston, SC, reburial list	Charleston, SC
Koonce, Elijah B.	Co. G, 2nd North Carolina	1843	7/7/1863	Mortally wounded-died at unknown place in Gettysburg	Unknown
Kyle, James	Co. C, 11th Mississippi	1844	7/16/1863	Mortally wounded-died at unknown place in Gettysburg	Unknown
Kyzer, Paul Harris	Co. B, 44th Alabama	5/30/1841	7/2/1863	Killed in action	Unknown
Lackey, George	Co. B, 57th Virginia	4/3/1841	7/3/1863	Killed in action	Unknown
Lackey, John C.	Co. G, 38th North Carolina	1841	8/1/1863	Mortally wounded-died at unknown place in Gettysburg	Unknown
Lackey, William N.	Co. I, 4th Virginia	1838	7/9/1863	Hollywood Cemetery, Richmond, Va., reburial lists	Richmond, VA
Lackey, William S.	Co. F, 38th North Carolina	1842	7/1/1863	Killed in action	Unknown
Lackman, E.	Co. D, 5th Texas		7/16/1863	Mortally wounded and buried on Jacob Schwartz Farm	Unknown

NAME	REGIMENT	BIRTH	DEATH	COMMENT	BURIAL
Ladd, Henry L.	Co. K, 53rd Virginia	1842	7/3/1863	Killed in action	Unknown
Lafan, W.J.	Co. I, 9th Alabama		Jul. 1863	Missing in action and presumed dead	Unknown
Lafargue, Bernard	Co. G, 10th Louisiana	1837	7/26/1863	Mortally wounded-died on unknown date in Gettysburg	Unknown
Lafler, W.R.	Co. C, 23rd North Carolina		7/1/1863	Killed in action	Unknown
Lague, Aristide	Co. F, 8th Louisiana	1843	Jul. 1863	Killed in action	Unknown
LaHue, Isaac Newton	Co. A, 4th Virginia		7/3/1863	Killed in action	Unknown
Lale, Jacob	Co. F, 38th North Carolina	2/7/1832	7/1/1863	Killed in action	Unknown
Lamb, James	Co. C, 2nd Mississippi	1818	7/3/1863	Killed in action	Unknown
Lamb, James	Co. C, 20th North Carolina	1833	7/1/1863	Killed in action	Unknown
Lamb, Nicholas P.	Co. I, 17th Georgia		7/19/1863	Mortally wounded-died on unknown date in Gettysburg	Unknown
Lamb, William P.	Co. E, 25th Virginia	1842	Jul. 1863	Killed in action, exact date not given in compiled service record	Unknown
Lambert, Exekiel G.	Co. A, 3rd Georgia		1863	Mortally wounded, July 2nd, and died on unknown date	Unknown
Lambert, Hugh	Co. K, 7th North Carolina	1835	7/3/1863	Killed in action	Unknown
Lambert, John D.	Co. H, 3rd North Carolina	1844	7/2/1863	Killed in action	Unknown
Lambert, Lewis F.	Co. C, 12th North Carolina	1837	7/23/1863	Mortally wounded and died at Staunton, VA-buried there	Staunton, VA
Lamberth, William S.	Co. H, 14th Alabama	11/12/1843	7/3/1863	Killed in action	Unknown
Lamm, Elias	Co. E, 43rd North Carolina	1821	7/10/1863	Mortally wounded-died at unknown place in Gettysburg	Unknown
Lancaster, William Thomas	Cpl., Co. F, 3rd Virginia	1839	8/11/1863	Mortally wounded and died at Baltimore, MD-buried there	Baltimore, MD
Land, William B.	Co. K, 55th North Carolina	1840	7/3/1863	Hollywood Cemetery, Richmond, Va., reburial lists	Richmond, VA
Landingham, James J.	Co. B, 45th North Carolina		7/1/1863	Killed in action	Unknown
Landis, James M.	Co. G, 10th Virginia		7/3/1863	Killed in action	Unknown
Landrum, James E.	Lt., Co. H, 19th Virginia	1841	7/3/1863	Missing in action and presumed dead	Unknown
Lane, John T.	Capt., Co. G, 4th Georgia	1833	7/25/1863	Mortally wounded and died at Frederick, MD; interred in Mt. Olivet Cemetery	Frederick, MD
Lane, John W.	Co. A, 26th Alabama		Jul. 1863	Killed in action, July 1-3	Unknown
Lane, William George	Co. C, 14th Virginia	1835	7/3/1863	Killed in action	Unknown
Laney, Eli B.	Co. B, 26th North Carolina	1840	Jul. 1863	Missing in action and presumed dead	Unknown
Laney, Levi	Co. I, 26th North Carolina	1841	7/1/1863	Killed in action	Unknown
Laney, William B.	Co. B, 26th North Carolina	1841	7/10/1863	Hollywood Cemetery, Richmond, Va., reburial lists	Richmond, VA
Lanford, Francis Marion	Sgt., Co. K, 3rd South Carolina	1839	7/2/1863	Killed in action	Unknown
Langford, Etheldred	Lt., Co. D, 50th Georgia	1842	7/2/1863	Killed in action	Unknown
Langford, John	Cpl. Co. E, 60th Georgia	1827	8/10/1863	Mortally wounded and died at Frederick MD; interred in Mt. Olivet Cemetery	Frederick, MD
Langford, Pickens Butler	Lt., Co. E, 3rd South Carolina	1842	7/2/1863	Magnolia Cemetery, Charleston, SC, reburial list	Charleston, SC

NAME	REGIMENT	BIRTH	DEATH	COMMENT	BURIAL
Langley, William S.	Co. D, 1st Texas		7/2/1863	Killed in action	Unknown
Langston, Alexander L.	Cpl., Co. C, 3rd Georgia	1841	7/2/1863	Killed in action	Unknown
Langston, David Henry Mason	Capt., Co. I, 3rd South Carolina	11/3/1833	7/2/1863	Killed in action	Unknown
Langston, F.M.	Co. D, 26th North Carolina	1840	7/3/1863	Killed in action	Unknown
Langston, Jacob	Co. A, 22nd Georgia		7/2/1863	Killed in action	Unknown
Langston, Reuben Young	Co. I, 51st Georgia	2/14/1839	7/3/1863	Killed in action	Unknown
Lanham, Benjamin Lewis	Co. C, 1st Maryland Battalion	8/3/1844	7/3/1863	Killed in action	Unknown
Lanier, Hosea W.	Cpl., Co. A, 38th North Carolina	1839	8/13/1863	Mortally wounded and died at Chester, PA	Phil. National Cem.
Lanier, J.T.	Co. I, 52nd North Carolina	1842	7/3/1863	Mortally wounded, July 3rd, and died the same day	Unknown
Lanier, Thomas H.	Co. F, 4th Alabama		7/2/1863	Killed in action	Unknown
Lantz, Joseph T. Van	Taylor's Battery (Va.)		7/2/1863	Killed in action; reinterred at Greenhill Cemetery, Martinsburg, VA	Martinsburg, WV
Laprade, Cornelius	Co. I, 14th Virginia	1841	7/3/1863	Killed in action	Unknown
Larew, James M.	Co. E, 1st Virginia Cavalry	1843	7/3/1863	Killed in action	Unknown
Lashmit, Francis M.	Co. I, 33rd North Carolina	1842	Jul. 1863	Killed in action	Unknown
Lassiter, Ezekial	Co. H, 38th North Carolina	1834	7/1/1863	Hollywood Cemetery, Richmond, Va., reburial lists	Richmond, VA
Lassiter, Wesley	Co. I, 3rd North Carolina	1828	7/3/1863	Killed in action	Unknown
Latch, John H.	Co. C, 11th Georgia		7/22/1863	Mortally wounded-died at unknown place in Gettysburg	Unknown
Latimer, Joseph White	Major of Artillery	8/27/1843	8/1/1863	Mortally wounded and died at Harrisonburg, VA-buried there in Woodbine Cemetery	Harrisonburg, VA
Latta, John P.	Co. A, 53rd Georgia		7/4/1863	Killed in action	Unknown
Lattimer, John William	Co. G, 9th Virginia	8/15/1839	9/18/1863	Hollywood Cemetery, Richmond, Va., reburial lists	Richmond, VA
Lauderdale, John C.	Lt., Co. B, 2nd Mississippi	1833	7/1/1863	Killed in action	Unknown
Laughlin, John	Co. K, 15th Georgia		7/3/1863	Hollywood Cemetery, Richmond, Va., reburial lists	Richmond, VA
Laughlin, Thomas	Co. H, 29th Virginia	1843	7/31/1863	Hollywood Cemetery, Richmond, Va., reburial lists	Richmond, VA
Laughrun, Hugh W.	Co. B, 22nd North Carolina	1834	Jul. 1863	Killed in action	Unknown
Law, George W.	Co. H, 38th Virginia		Jul. 1863	Missing in action and presumed dead	Unknown
Law, Josiah H.	Co. B, 4th Georgia		7/2/1863	Laurel Grove Cemetery, Savannah, Ga., reburial list	Savannah, GA
Law, Nathaniel C.	Co. D, 24th Virginia		9/18/1863	Mortally wounded-died at unknown place in Gettysburg	Unknown
Law, Samuel S.	Co. E, 53rd Virginia		7/3/1863	Killed in action	Unknown
Lawhorn, Alexander	Co. E, 44th Alabama	1843	7/2/1863	Killed in action	Unknown
Lawhorn, William	Co. A, 17th Mississippi	1829	Jul. 1863	Killed in action on July 1st or 2nd	Unknown
Lawhorne, Isham	Co. I, 19th Virginia		7/3/1863	Killed in action	Unknown
Lawhorne, Thomas	Co. I, 49th Virginia		7/14/1863	Mortally wounded-died at unknown place in Gettysburg	Unknown
Lawless, George W.	Co. I, 24th Virginia	1840	7/3/1863	Missing in action and presumed dead	Unknown

NAME	REGIMENT	BIRTH	DEATH	COMMENT	BURIAL
Lawrence, G.A.	Co. G, 24th Georgia	1832	8/19/1863	Laurel Grove Cemetery, Savannah, Ga., reburial list	Savannah, GA
Lawrence, Ira L.	Cpl., Co. I, 35th Georgia		8/23/1863	Died as POW at David's Island, NY	Cypress Hills, NY
Lawrence, Louis A.	Co. B, 11th Mississippi	1828	7/3/1863	Killed in action	Unknown
Lawson, James	Co. H, 53rd North Carolina	1841	7/3/1863	Mortally wounded, July 3rd, and died the same day	Unknown
Lawson, James A.	Cpl., Co. C,1st Maryland Battalion		Jul. 1863	Mortally wounded-died at unknown place in Gettysburg	Unknown
Lawson, John O.	Co. H, 38th Virginia		7/3/1863	Killed in action	Unknown
Lawson, William A.	Co. C, 27th Virginia		7/3/1863	Killed in action	Unknown
Lawson, William Spencer	Co. E, 22nd Georgia		9/6/1863	Mortally wounded and died at Baltimore, MD-buried there	Baltimore, MD
Layman, William	2nd Co., Washington Arty (La.)	1836	7/18/1863	Mortally wounded per the Richmond Sentinel, July 17, 1863	Unknown
Layne, Robert Carson	Co. H, 56th Virginia	1834	7/3/1863	Killed in action per the Richmond Sentinel, July 29, 1863	Unknown
Layton, William P.	Co. E, 12th North Carolina	1842	7/1/1863	Killed in action	Unknown
Leach, E.E.	Co. K, 5th North Carolina	1827	7/15/1863	Mortally wounded-died at unknown place in Gettysburg	Unknown
Leach, Julius M.	Co. H, 8th South Carolina		7/2/1863	Killed in action	Unknown
Leaman , James D.	Co. D, 52nd North Carolina	1827	7/1/1863	Oakwood Cemetery, Raleigh, NC, reburial list	Raleigh, NC
Leatherwood, George C.	Co. G, 11th Georgia		7/17/1863	Mortally wounded-died at unknown place in Gettysburg	Unknown
Leavell, John K.G.	Sgt., Co. I, 2nd Mississippi	1839	7/2/1863	Killed in action	Unknown
Ledbetter, William	Co. D, 55th North Carolina	1832	7/1/1863	Killed in action	Unknown
Ledford, Samuel	Co. D, 55th North Carolina		7/1/1863	Killed in action; reinterred at Poplar Springs Cemetery, Cleveland Co., NC	Cleveland Co., NC
Lee, Benjamin H.	Co. A, 5th Florida		7/18/1863	Mortally wounded and died at Winchester, VA; interred Stonewall Cemetery	Winchester, VA
Lee, Berry B.	Co. D, 47th North Carolina	1828	8/4/1863	Mortally wounded and died at Chester, PA	Phil. National Cem.
Lee, Daniel W.	Co. C, 5th North Carolina	1831	7/1/1863	Killed in action	Unknown
Lee, Elisha L.	Co. K, 11th Mississippi	1837	7/10/1863	Hollywood Cemetery, Richmond, Va., reburial lists	Richmond, VA
Lee, George P.C.	Co. I, 44th Alabama	1842	7/2/1863	Killed in action	Unknown
Lee, James G.	Co. A, 57th Virginia	1843	7/2/1863	Killed in action	Unknown
Lee, James Hanson	Co. B, 47th Viginia	1840	7/3/1863	Killed in action	Unknown
Lee, John W.	Co. H, 28th North Carolina	1842	7/3/1863	Killed in action	Unknown
Lee, Joseph I.	Co. K, 26th North Carolina	1839	7/1/1863	Killed in action	Unknown
Lee, Richard Henry Guy	Co. I, 57th Virginia		7/11/1863	Hollywood Cemetery, Richmond, Va., reburial lists	Richmond, VA
Lee, Watson E.	Co. H, 28th North Carolina	1839	7/3/1863	Killed in action	Unknown
Lee, William A.	Co. A, 57th Virginia	1842	Jul. 1863	Killed in action, July 1-3	Unknown
Lee, William Joel	Capt., Co. E, 4th Alabama	1/9/1829	7/3/1863	Killed in action	Unknown

NAME	REGIMENT	BIRTH	DEATH	COMMENT	BURIAL
Lee, William M.	Co. A, 23rd North Carolina		7/1/1863	Killed in action	Unknown
Lefler, Eli	Co. C, 13th North Carolina	12/8/1825	7/1/1863	Killed in action	Unknown
Leftwich, James P.	Sgt., Co. G, 28th Virginia		Jul. 1863	Died as POW at Ft. Delaware	Unknown
Leftwich, William W.	Capt., Co. F, 4th Alabama	1840	7/3/1863	Hollywood Cemetery, Richmond, Va., reburial lists	Richmond, VA
Legg, Alexander F.	Co. E, 7th Virginia		7/3/1863	Killed in action	Unknown
Legrand, Peter A.	Cpl., Co. C, 11th Virginia		7/3/1863	Killed in action	Unknown
Leigh, Benjamin Watkins	Maj., AAG, Genl. Edward Johnson	1/18/1831	7/3/1863	Killed in action; reinterred at Richmond, VA-Shockoe Cemetery	Richmond, VA
Leitzey, David Martin	Lt., Co. H, 13th South Carolina		7/2/1863	Killed in action	Unknown
Lemerieux, Francis M.	Sgt., Co. G, 15th South Carolina	1838	7/27/1873	Mortally wounded per the Charleston Mercury, August 28, 1863	Unknown
Lemmon, Robert	Acting Lt., Volunteer with 42nd Virginia		7/2/1863	Killed in action	Unknown
Lemon, William	Co. K, 57th Virginia		8/24/1863	Died as POW at David's Island, NY	Cypress Hills, NY
Lemons, Milton J.	Co. E, 45th North Carolina	1842	7/1/1863	Killed in action	Unknown
Lenhardt, Cameron L.	Co. I, 11th North Carolina	1843	7/30/1863	Mortally wounded and initially buried on George Spangler Farm	Unknown
Leonard, Emanuel	Co. F, 13th North Carolina	1833	7/1/1863	Killed in action	Unknown
Leonard, Jeff W.	Capt., Co. D, 22nd Georgia		7/2/1863	Laurel Grove Cemetery, Savannah, Ga., reburial list	Savannah, GA
Leonhardt, Jacob M.	Co. I, 11th North Carolina		7/3/1863	Killed in action	Unknown
Lesley, James N.	Co. C, 2nd Mississippi	1843	10/5/1863	Hollywood Cemetery, Richmond, Va., reburial lists	Richmond, VA
Leslie, William Atwell	Co. A, 8th Virginia		7/3/1863	Killed in action; reinterred at Arnold Grove Cemetery, Loudoun, Co., VA	Loudoun Co., VA
LeTellier, William Borchers	Lt., Co. E, 19th Virginia	1839	8/11/1863	Mortally wounded and died at Chester, PA	Phil. National Cem.
Lewie, Emanuel W.	Sgt., Co. C, 15th South Carolina	4/5/1844	7/2/1863	Magnolia Cemetery, Charleston, SC, reburial list	Charleston, SC
Lewis, Angus	Co. E, 1st South Carolina		7/17/1863	Mortally wounded-died at unknown place in Gettysburg	Unknown
Lewis, B.F.	Co. C, 26th North Carolina	1832	7/1/1863	Killed in action	Unknown
Lewis, Daniel Mills	Sgt., Co. F, 5th Florida	1830	7/2/1863	Killed in action	Unknown
Lewis, Frank M.	Co. I, 9th Louisiana	1842	9/19/1863	Died as POW at Ft. Delaware	Finn's Point, NJ
Lewis, Gilbert	Co. A, 47th North Carolina	1841	7/3/1863	Killed in action	Unknown
Lewis, J. Richard	Co. B, 8th Georgia		7/1/1863	Killed in action	Unknown
Lewis, J. Robert	Co. G, 53rd Georgia	1831	7/10/1863	Mortally wounded-died at unknown place in Gettysburg	Unknown
Lewis, James Kent	Co. I, 16th North Carolina	1839	7/1/1863	Killed in action	Unknown
Lewis, James P.	Co. D, 2nd Mississippi	1842	7/20/1863	Died as POW at David's Island, NY	Cypress Hills, NY
Lewis, John C.	Co. F, 26th North Carolina	1839	7/1/1863	Killed in action	Unknown
Lewis, John H.	Co. K, 44th Georgia		Sept. 1863	Mortally wounded-died at unknown place in Gettysburg	Unknown
Lewis, Josiah Daniel	Co. H, 18th Virginia		7/3/1863	Killed in action	Unknown

NAME	REGIMENT	BIRTH	DEATH	COMMENT	BURIAL
Lewis, Miles W.	Co. D, 22nd Georgia		7/22/1863	Laurel Grove Cemetery, Savannah, Ga., reburial list	Savannah, GA
Lewis, Patrick Henry	Co. C, 45th North Carolina	1837	7/1/1863	Killed in action	Unknown
Lewis, Samuel M.	Co. A, 57th Virginia		Jul. 1863	Killed in action, July 1-3	Unknown
Lewis, Tillman J.	Co. K, 9th Georgia		7/5/1863	Mortally wounded, July 3rd, and died two days later	Unknown
Lewis, Trevanion Dudley	Col., 8th Louisiana	1837	7/2/1863	Killed in action	Unknown
Lewis, W.F.	Co. B, 28th North Carolina	1842	7/17/1863	Hollywood Cemetery, Richmond, Va., reburial lists	Richmond, VA
Lewis, William M.	Co. D, 17th Georgia		7/19/1863	Laurel Grove Cemetery, Savannah, Ga., reburial list	Savannah, GA
Liddell, Joseph W.	Co. K, 11th Mississippi	1844	7/3/1863	Killed in action	Unknown
Liddell, Samuel Bailis	Sgt., Co. F, 2nd Mississippi	12/27/1840	7/1/1863	Killed in action	Unknown
Light, Charles M.	Co. F, 38th Virginia		7/30/1863	Died as POW at David's Island, NY	Cypress Hills, NY
Light, George W.	Co. H, 14th Virginia	1835	7/16/1863	Mortally wounded and died at Baltimore, MD-buried there	Baltimore, MD
Light, George W.	Co. E, 14th Georgia	1837	7/3/1863	Killed in action	Unknown
Ligon, William Davis	Co. D, 52nd North Carolina	1842	7/3/1863	Missing in action and presumed dead	Unknown
Lile, William H.	Co. I, 11th Mississippi	1839	8/1/1863	Hollywood Cemetery, Richmond, Va., reburial lists	Richmond, VA
Liles, Joseph G.	Co. K, 26th North Carolina	1844	7/3/1863	Killed in action	Unknown
Lilly, William M.	Co. D, 53rd North Carolina		7/20/1863	Mortally wounded-died at unknown place in Gettysburg	Unknown
Lindamood, James	Co. B, 7th Virginia Cavalry		7/5/1863	Hollywood Cemetery, Richmond, Va., reburial lists	Richmond, VA
Lindsey, James A.	Sgt., Co. I, 3rd Georgia	1837	7/24/1863	Mortally wounded-died at unknown place in Gettysburg	Unknown
Lindsey, John	Co. A, 38th Virginia		7/3/1863	Killed in action	Unknown
Lindsey, Pickens Butler	Co. I, 12th South Carolina		7/1/1863	Killed in action	Unknown
Lindsey, William	Co. F, 15th Alabama	1842	7/2/1863	Killed in action	Unknown
Linebarger, Jacob A.	Co. C, 28th North Carolina	1842	7/5/1883	Mortally wounded-died at unknown place in Gettysburg	Unknown
Link, Ephraim Michael	Co. C, 28th North Carolina	2/17/1832	7/3/1863	Killed in action	Unknown
Linn, Henry V.	Cpl., Co. E, 32nd North Carolina		Jul. 1863	Killed in action	Unknown
Linton, Hugh	Co. E, 5th Florida		7/2/1863	Killed in action	Unknown
Lipscomb, James H.	Capt., Co. K, 53rd Virginia	1831	7/3/1863	Killed in action	Unknown
Lisenby, Green	Co. A, 31st Georgia		7/1/1863	Killed in action	Unknown
Litchfield, James D.	Co. E, 4th North Carolina	1845	Jul. 1863	Died on either July 2nd or 3rd of wounds	Unknown
Little, Ellis P.	Co. D, 37th North Carolina	1837	7/23/1863	Hollywood Cemetery, Richmond, Va., reburial lists	Richmond, VA
Little, Green	Co. F, 2nd North Carolina Battalion	1813	7/1/1863	Killed in action	Unknown
Little, Hugh	Cpl., Co. K, 23rd North Carolina		7/1/1863	Killed in action	Unknown
Little, William	Co. D, 42nd Virginia	1816	7/2/1863	Killed in action	Unknown
Littleford, John Thomas	Co. G, 1st Maryland Battalion		Jul. 1863	Mortally wounded and died on unknown date	Unknown

NAME	REGIMENT	BIRTH	DEATH	COMMENT	BURIAL
Littlejohn, J.B.	Co. F, 26th North Carolina	1841	7/3/1863	Mortally wounded, July 1st, and died two days later	Unknown
Littleton, Elisha A.	Co. G, 3rd North Carolina	1839	7/2/1863	Hollywood Cemetery, Richmond, Va., reburial lists	Richmond, VA
Littleton, Matthew H.	Lt., Co. H, 22nd Georgia	12/9/1839	7/2/1863	Killed in action	Unknown
Littrell, Murray M.	Cpl., Co. A, 47th Virginia	1840	7/3/1863	Mortally wounded, July 3rd, and died the same day	Unknown
Livingston, J.B.	Sgt., Co. A, 2nd South Carolina		7/2/1863	Mortally wounded, July 2nd, and died the same day	Unknown
Livingston, Lewis A.	Capt., Co. F, 8th Alabama	1836	9/27/1863	Mortally wounded-died at unknown place in Gettysburg	Unknown
Livingston, M.A.	Co. G, 20th Georgia		7/2/1863	Killed in action	Unknown
Lloyd, Charles Tilghman	Co. A, 1st Maryland Battalion	10/22/1842	7/3/1863	Killed in action	Unknown
Lloyd, Lucian	Co. G, 28th North Carolina	1840	7/17/1863	Mortally wounded-died at unknown place in Gettysburg	Unknown
Locke, John J.	Co. G, 5th North Carolina	1826	7/18/1863	Mortally wounded-died at unknown place in Gettysburg	Unknown
Lockett, S.S.	Co. E, 5th Texas		7/6/1863	Mortally wounded, July 2nd, and died four days later	Unknown
Locklin, Jesse Daniel	Co. G, 5th Texas	10/10/1833	Jul. 1863	Missing in action, July 2nd, and presumed dead	Unknown
Locklin, Minor B.	Co. K, 3rd Georgia	1843	7/15/1863	Mortally wounded, July 2nd, and died at Mercersburg, PA	Mercersburg, PA
Lockman, Elihu P.	Cpl., Co. K, 23rd North Carolina	1845	7/1/1863	Killed in action	Unknown
Logan, G.M.	Co. B, 28th North Carolina		8/15/1863	Died as POW at David's Island, NY	Cypress Hills, NY
Logan, John S.	Co. I, 19th Mississippi		Jul. 1863	Mortally wounded per the Richmond Enquirer, July 16, 1863	Unknown
Logan, Richard	Capt., Co. H, 14th Virginia	12/3/1829	7/3/1863	Killed in action	Unknown
Lollar, R.E.A.	Co. K, 18th North Carolina		9/21/1863	Died as POW at David's Island, NY	Cypress Hills, NY
Lomax, William George	Co. F, 2nd South Carolina	9/15/1840	7/2/1863	Magnolia Cemetery, Charleston, SC, reburial list	Charleston, SC
Long, Calvin J.	Co. G, 47th North Carolina	1826	10/14/1863	Mortally wounded and died at Richmond, VA-interred in Hollywood Cemetery	Richmond, VA
Long, D.L.	Co. H, 23rd North Carolina	1837	7/1/1863	Killed in action	Unknown
Long, John E.	Co. G, 42nd Mississippi		7/1/1863	Killed in action	Unknown
Long, Noah J.	Co. K, 33rd Virginia		Jul. 1863	Missing in action and presumed dead	Unknown
Long, Simon	Co. K, 5th Louisiana	1837	9/11/1863	Died as POW at David's Island, NY	Cypress Hills, NY
Longis, John C.	King William Artillery (Va.)		7/31/1863	Mortally wounded-died at unknown place in Gettysburg	Unknown
Longstreet, George	Co. D, 4th Texas		7/27/1863	Mortally wounded-died at unknown place in Gettysburg	Unknown
Looney, James M.	Co. C, 28th Virginia	1837	7/3/1863	Killed in action	Unknown
Looney, Richmond Duncan	Co. C, 10th Alabama	10/8/1841	Jul.1863	Hollywood Cemetery, Richmond, Va., reburial lists	Richmond, VA
Loos, Earnest	Co. A, 12th Alabama		7/3/1863	Killed in action	Unknown
Lopez, Antonio	Co. G, 10th Louisiana	1826	7/3/1863	Killed in action on Culp's Hill	Unknown

NAME	REGIMENT	BIRTH	DEATH	COMMENT	BURIAL
Lord, James H.	Co. F, 3rd Georgia	1835	7/2/1863	Killed in action	Unknown
Lott, John Bolivar	Co. H, 7th South Carolina	1842	7/2/1863	Killed in action	Unknown
Loughridge, James B.	Cpl., Parker's Battery (Va.)	1840	7/3/1863	Killed in action	Unknown
Love, Joseph A.	Co. E, 7th Tennessee		7/15/1863	Hollywood Cemetery, Richmond, Va., reburial lists	Richmond, VA
Love, Joseph E.	Co. A, 5th Texas	1832	8/22/1863	Mortally wounded and died at Baltimore, MD-buried there	Baltimore, MD
Love, McDuffie Rutledge	Co. G, 2nd South Carolina	1839	7/2/1863	Killed in action	Charleston, SC
Love, S.C.	Co. H, 1st Texas		7/2/1863	Killed in action	Unknown
Love, Thomas R.	Capt., Co. B, 8th Florida	7/3/1841	7/3/1863	Killed in action	Unknown
Lovelace, Charles M.	Co. C, 38th Virginia		Jul. 1863	Mortally wounded per the Richmond Sentinel, August 1, 1863	Unknown
Lovelady, Noah H.	Co. K, 11th Alabama		Jul. 1863	Hollywood Cemetery, Richmond, Va., reburial lists	Richmond, VA
Loving, Cleophas A.	Co. C, 8th Virginia		7/7/1863	Mortally wounded-died at unknown place in Gettysburg	Unknown
Lovins, Arthur J.	Co. I, 24th Virginia	Nov. 1833	8/7/1863	Mortally wounded and died at Lynchburg, VA-buried there	Lynchburg, VA
Lovvorn, Thomas J.	Co. E, 13th Alabama		7/2/1863	Killed in action either July 2nd or July 3rd	Unknown
Lowder, E.M.	Co. B, 5th North Carolina	1831	7/1/1863	Hollywood Cemetery, Richmond, Va., reburial lists	Richmond, VA
Lowder, Jacob W.	Co. B, 20th North Carolina	1831	7/10/1863	Oakwood Cemetery, Raleigh, NC, reburial list	Raleigh, NC
Lowe, Samuel P.	Co. F, 3rd Alabama		7/29/1863	Mortally wounded-died at unknown place in Gettysburg	Unknown
Lowman, Levi	Co. C, 6th North Carolina	1828	7/8/1863	Mortally wounded-died at unknown place in Gettysburg	Unknown
Lowrie, James B.	Lt., Co. H, 11th North Carolina	1838	7/1/1863	Killed in action; reinterred at Greenmount Cemetery, Baltimore, MD	Baltimore, MD
Lowry, William J.	Co. B, 45th North Carolina	1839	7/2/1863	Killed in action	Unknown
Loyd, David	Co. I, 23rd North Carolina	1843	7/1/1863	Killed in action	Unknown
Lucas, Henderson C.	Adj., 11th North Carolina		7/25/1863	Mortally wounded and died at Martinsburg, VA; interred Green Hill Cemetery	Martinsburg, WV
Lucas, Thomas Hendrix [Hendrick]	Co. H, 13th South Carolina		7/1/1863	Killed in action	Unknown
Lummas, John G.	Co. B, 53rd Georgia		7/2/1863	Hollywood Cemetery, Richmond, Va., reburial lists	Richmond, VA
Lummas, William D.	Co. B, 53rd Georgia	4/21/1841	7/15/1863	Hollywood Cemetery, Richmond, Va., reburial lists	Richmond, VA
Lumpkin, Robert M.	Co. A, 55th Virginia		7/1/1863	Killed in action	Unknown
Lumpkin, Samuel P.	Col., 44th Georgia	12/5/1833	9/11/1863	Mortally wounded and died at Hagerstown, MD-reinterred after the war in GA	Buena Vista, GA
Luna, James W.	Co. F, 2nd Mississippi	1831	7/1/1863	Killed in action	Unknown
Lupo, Thomas	Co. F, 31st Georgia	1836	7/1/1863	Killed in action	Unknown
Luther, B.F.	Co. H, 38th North Carolina	1843	7/1/1863	Killed in action	Unknown

NAME	REGIMENT	BIRTH	DEATH	COMMENT	BURIAL
Luther, Franklin	Cpl., Co. B, 52nd North Carolina	1830	9/14/1863	Oakwood Cemetery, Raleigh, NC, reburial list	Raleigh, NC
Lutz, Wade D.	Co. A, 22nd North Carolina	1844	8/9/1863	Mortally wounded and died at Chester, PA	Phil. National Cem.
Lyday, Thomas L.	Co. B, 9th Georgia	1838	7/2/1863	Hollywood Cemetery, Richmond, Va., reburial lists	Richmond, VA
Lyerly, Christopher Columbus	Co. F, 5th North Carolina	12/22/1832	7/1/1863	Hollywood Cemetery, Richmond, Va., reburial lists	Richmond, VA
Lyerly, Henry	Co. A, 57th North Carolina	1841	7/12/1863	Mortally wounded-died at unknown place in Gettysburg	Unknown
Lynch, Christopher	Co. B, 24th Virginia		12/20/1863	Mortally wounded-died at unknown place in Gettysburg	Unknown
Lynch, J. Pinkney	Co. F, 13th Georgia		7/1/1863	Killed in action	Unknown
Lynch, Jerry	Co. I, 7th Louisiana	1827	7/2/1863	Killed in action	Unknown
Lynch, John S.	Co. I, 3rd Alabama	1844	8/1/1863	Hollywood Cemetery, Richmond, Va., reburial lists	Richmond, VA
Lynch, Robert	Co. G, 8th Georgia		7/3/1863	Killed in action	Unknown
Lynn, Joseph F.	Sgt., Co. G, 8th Virginia		7/3/1863	Killed in action	Unknown
Lyon, George W.	Co. H, 6th North Carolina	1842	7/1/1863	Killed in action	Unknown
Lyon, Robert Newton	Sgt., Co. H, 11th Mississippi	9/13/1841	7/15/1863	Mortally wounded-died at unknown place in Gettysburg	Unknown
Lyons, B.F.	Co. E, 15th Georgia		7/2/1863	Killed in action	Unknown
Mackey, John H.	Co. C, 9th Virginia		7/3/1863	Killed in action	Unknown
Mackey, Thomas	Co. D, 10th Alabama		7/2/1863	Hollywood Cemetery, Richmond, Va., reburial lists	Richmond, VA
Mackie, Jonas	Co. I, 28th North Carolina	1844	7/3/1863	Killed in action	Unknown
Macklin, James J.	Co. E, 27th Virginia		Jul. 1863	Missing in action and presumed dead	Unknown
Macy, Shubal	Co. K, 45th North Carolina	1840	7/1/1863	Killed in action	Unknown
Madden, Daniel	Sgt., Co. C, 21st Mississippi	1836	7/2/1863	Hollywood Cemetery, Richmond, Va., reburial lists	Richmond, VA
Maddox, John B.	Co. F, 44th Georgia		7/1/1863	Killed in action	Unknown
Madower, -	Co. I, 5th Alabama		7/12/1863	Mortally wounded-died at unknown place in Gettysburg	Unknown
Magee, Mildridge	Cpl., Co. D, 9th Louisiana	1835	7/21/1863	Mortally wounded-died at unknown place in Gettysburg	Unknown
Magruder, John Bowie	Col., 57th Virginia	11/24/1839	7/5/1863	Mortally wounded, July 3rd, and died two days later; reinterred in Charlottesville, VA	Charlottesville, VA
Magruder, William Thomas	Capt., AAG, Genl. Joseph Davis	1/16/1825	7/3/1863	Killed in action; reinterred at Green Mount Cemetery, Baltimore, MD	Baltimore, MD
Mahone, Edward B.	Co. K, 57th Virginia		Jul. 1863	Killed in action, July 1-3	Unknown
Mahorner, Bernard	Co. F, 11th Mississippi	1842	12/1/1863	Died as POW at Pt. Lookout, MD	Pt. Lookout, MD
Mahorner, Harris	Co. F, 11th Mississippi	1844	7/27/1863	Hollywood Cemetery, Richmond, Va., reburial lists	Richmond, VA
Maier, John	Co. E, 11th Virginia		7/3/1863	Killed in action	Unknown
Mains, John	Co. F, 22nd North Carolina	1841	7/2/1863	Killed in action	Unknown
Mallis, James M.	Co. K, 23rd North Carolina	1840	7/1/1863	Killed in action	Unknown

NAME	REGIMENT	BIRTH	DEATH	COMMENT	BURIAL
Malloy, John Thomas	Co. E, 45th North Carolina	1842	8/12/1863	Oakwood Cemetery, Raleigh, NC, reburial list	Raleigh, NC
Malone, Daniel	Co. H, 26th North Carolina		7/1/1863	Killed in action	Unknown
Malone, Matthew J.	Lt., Co. D, 5th North Carolina	1839	7/1/1863	Hollywood Cemetery, Richmond, Va., reburial lists	Richmond, VA
Malone, Patrick	Madison Light Artillery (La.)		Jul. 1863	Mortally wounded per the Richmond Sentinel, July 27, 1863	Unknown
Malone, William Herbert	Co. F, 9th Alabama	1825	7/2/1863	Killed in action	Unknown
Maner, James	Co. E, 52nd North Carolina	1828	7/3/1863	Mortally wounded, July 3rd, and died same day	Unknown
Mangum, Jason D.	Co. E, 47th North Carolina		7/3/1863	Killed in action	Unknown
Manley, James M.	Lt., Co. G, 1st Tennessee	1835	8/12/1863	Hollywood Cemetery, Richmond, Va., reburial lists	Richmond, VA
Manley, John W.	Cpl., Co. K, 53rd North Carolina	1835	9/25/1863	Oakwood Cemetery, Raleigh, NC, reburial list	Raleigh, NC
Mann, James W.	Co. D, 9th Georgia		7/2/1863	Killed in action	Unknown
Mann, William C.	Co. K, 48th Alabama		Jul. 1863	Killed in action while carrying the colors	Unknown
Manning, Abram	Co. D, 3rd North Carolina	1826	7/3/1863	Killed in action on Culp's Hill	Unknown
Manning, Benjamin L.	Co. B, 5th Alabama Battalion	1843	7/3/1863	Killed in action while carrying the colors	Unknown
Manning, Samuel H.	Co. K, 4th Alabama		7/22/1863	Mortally wounded-died at unknown place in Gettysburg	Unknown
Mansel, Amos P.	Co. C, 15th Alabama	1843	7/2/1863	Killed in action	Unknown
Mansfield, James D.	Sgt., Co. B, 24th Virginia		Jul. 1863	Missing in action and presumed dead	Unknown
Manuel, Gideon H.	Co. H, 53rd North Carolina	1843	7/2/1863	Mortally wounded, July 2nd, and died the same day	Unknown
Marable, William H.	Co. H, 11th Mississippi	1840	7/3/1863	Killed in action	Unknown
Marbry, James E.	Co. I, 52nd North Carolina	1835	7/27/1863	Mortally wounded and died at Baltimore, MD-buried there	Baltimore, MD
Marcom, William B.	Co. E, 47th North Carolina	1827	7/16/1863	Hollywood Cemetery, Richmond, Va., reburial lists	Richmond, VA
Marcus, William A.	Co. E, 44th Alabama	1843	Jul. 1863	Missing in action and presumed dead	Unknown
Markley, Charles A.	Co. B, 2nd South Carolina	1840	7/2/1863	Hollywood Cemetery, Richmond, Va., reburial lists	Richmond, VA
Marks, Thomas Elijah [Elisha]	Co. B, 53rd North Carolina		7/3/1863	Killed in action	Unknown
Marley, John	Co. K, 53rd North Carolina	1834	9/25/1863	Oakwood Cemetery, Raleigh, NC, reburial list	Raleigh, NC
Marley, John R.	Co. G, 26th North Carolina	1843	7/1/1863	Killed in action	Unknown
Marlin, David	Lt., Co. H, 2nd Mississippi	1835	7/3/1863	Killed in action	Unknown
Marlow, David F.	Co. B, 55th North Carolina		7/1/1863	Killed in action	Unknown
Marlow, Edmund	Co. A, 37th North Carolina	1834	7/3/1863	Killed in action	Unknown
Marlow, Noah	Co. E, 11th Georgia		7/3/1863	Killed in action	Unknown
Maroney, William M.	Cpl., Co. C, 10th Alabama		7/3/1863	Killed in action	Unknown
Marsh, Solomon F.	Co. D, 37th North Carolina	1837	Jul. 1863	Missing in action and presumed dead	Unknown
Marsh, William G.	Cpl., Co. H, 48th Georgia	1834	7/2/1863	Killed in action	Unknown

NAME	REGIMENT	BIRTH	DEATH	COMMENT	BURIAL
Marshall, Ballard P.	Co. C, 24th Virginia	1843	7/10/1863	Mortally wounded-died at unknown place in Gettysburg	Unknown
Marshall, Isaac Perry	Sgt., Co. A, 7th North Carolina	1837	7/3/1863	Killed in action	Unknown
Marshall, James A.	Co. C, 2nd Mississippi	1843	7/1/1863	Killed in action	Unknown
Marshall, James Keith	Col., 52nd North Carolina	4/17/1839	7/2/1863	Killed in action	Unknown
Marshall, Laurister Lafayette	Cpl., Co. E, 53rd North Carolina	1840	7/3/1863	Oakwood Cemetery, Raleigh, NC, reburial list	Raleigh, NC
Marshall, William O.	Co. G, 4th Alabama		7/2/1863	Killed in action	Unknown
Marshbourn, Joseph J.	Cpl., Co. A, 55th North Carolina	1840	7/14/1863	Hollywood Cemetery, Richmond, Va., reburial lists	Richmond, VA
Martholomew, John	Co. E, 23rd North Carolina	1846	7/25/1863	Mortally wounded-died at unknown place in Gettysburg	Unknown
Martin, Andrew	Cpl., Brooks Artillery (S.C.)		7/3/1863	Killed in action per the Richmond Sentinel, July 27, 1863	Unknown
Martin, Andrew Jackson	Co. K, 9th Alabama	2/2/1839	7/15/1863	Hollywood Cemetery, Richmond, Va., reburial lists	Richmond, VA
Martin, George F.	Co. D, 3rd Georgia		7/2/1863	Killed in action	Unknown
Martin, James B.	Cpl., Co. C, 14th Virginia	1839	7/10/1863	Mortally wounded-died at unknown place in Gettysburg	Unknown
Martin, James F.	Co. K, 2nd South Carolina	1828	8/6/1863	Hollywood Cemetery, Richmond, Va., reburial lists	Richmond, VA
Martin, John	Sgt., Co. C, 2nd Georgia Battalion		7/2/1863	Killed in action	Unknown
Martin, John	Co. F, 3rd South Carolina Battalion	1828	7/2/1863	Killed in action per the Charleston Courier, July 1863	Unknown
Martin, John B.	Co. H, 26th North Carolina	1835	8/3/1863	Mortally wounded and died at Winchester, VA	Winchester, VA
Martin, John C.	Sgt., Co. C, 7th South Carolina	1838	9/17/1863	Died of Wounds after POW exchange. in Petersburg, VA	Petersburg, VA
Martin, Joseph B.	Lt., Co. E, 15th South Carolina	1831	7/2/1863	Killed in action	Unknown
Martin, Liberty Smith	Co. E, 11th Mississippi	1840	7/3/1863	Killed in action	Unknown
Martin, M.P.	Cpl., Co. F, 23rd North Carolina	1842	7/1/1863	Killed in action	Unknown
Martin, Nathan Green	Co. B, 1st North Carolina	2/9/1819	7/4/1863	Mortally wounded, July 2nd, and died two days later	Unknown
Martin, Raleigh H.	Co. H, 22nd North Carolina	1844	7/1/1863	Killed in action	Unknown
Martin, Richard	Co. E, 56th Virginia		10/12/1863	Mortally wounded per the Richmond Sentinel, July 27, 1863	Unknown
Martin, T.J.	Co. C, 18th North Carolina	1838	Jul. 1863	Mortally wounded and died on unknown date	Unknown
Martin, Van Buren	Co. C, 11th Georgia		7/2/1863	Killed in action	Unknown
Martin, W.H.	Co. I, 3rd North Carolina	1829	7/3/1863	Killed in action	Unknown
Martin, William P.	Co. H, 11th Mississippi	1843	7/3/1863	Killed in action	Unknown
Mason, Israel H.	Co. D, 30th North Carolina	1841	7/16/1863	Mortally wounded and died prior to July 16th	Unknown
Mason, John E.	Cpl., Co. F, 44th Alabama	1833	7/4/1863	Mortally wounded, July 2nd, and died on the 3rd or 4th	Unknown
Mason, John R.	Co. I, 56th Virginia		Jul. 1863	Missing in action and presumed dead	Unknown

NAME	REGIMENT	BIRTH	DEATH	COMMENT	BURIAL
Mason, Joseph L.	Co. I, 17th Mississippi	1842	9/12/1863	Hollywood Cemetery, Richmond, Va., reburial lists	Richmond, VA
Mason, Joseph W.	Co. I, 17th Mississippi	1838	8/12/1863	Mortally wounded-died at unknown place in Gettysburg	Unknown
Mason, Maurice W.	Co. C, 11th Virginia		7/3/1863	Killed in action; given name may be Morris	Unknown
Mason, Miles Milas	Co. G, 5th North Carolina	1829	7/19/1863	Oakwood Cemetery, Raleigh, NC, reburial list	Raleigh, NC
Mason, Richard	Co. F, 1st Tennessee		Jul. 1863	Missing in action and presumed dead	Unknown
Mason, William D.A.	Cpl., Co. I, 52nd North Carolina	1836	7/3/1863	Killed in action	Unknown
Massey, Jacob W.	Co. A, 4th North Carolina	1840	9/2/1863	Oakwood Cemetery, Raleigh, NC, reburial list	Raleigh, NC
Massey, William	Sgt., Co. C, 45th North Carolina	1840	7/1/1863	Killed in action	Unknown
Massie, John W.	Co. I, 19th Virginia	11/8/1840	7/10/1863	Mortally wounded-died at unknown place in Gettysburg	Unknown
Matherby, William T.	Co. E, 7th Tennessee		9/10/1863	Died as POW at Ft. Delaware	Finn's Point, NJ
Matheson, Alexander C.	Co. H, 55th North Carolina		7/1/1863	Killed in action	Unknown
Matheson, Eli	Co. H, 55th North Carolina		7/1/1863	Killed in action	Unknown
Mathews, James S.	Co. C, 44th Alabama	1831	7/2/1863	Killed in action	Unknown
Mathis [Mathews], W.W.	Co. H, 8th Georgia		Jul. 1863	Hollywood Cemetery, Richmond, Va., reburial lists	Richmond, VA
Mathis, James M.	Co. E, 13th North Carolina	1833	8/6/1863	Died as POW at David's Island, NY	Cypress Hills, NY
Mathis, Joab	Co. G, 13th South Carolina	11/16/1835	7/1/1863	Killed in action per the Charleston Mercury, August 28, 1863	Unknown
Mathis, William Henry	Co. I, 7th South Carolina	10/10/1843	7/2/1863	Hollywood Cemetery, Richmond, Va., reburial lists	Richmond, VA
Matney, John W.	Co. I, 26th North Carolina	1827	7/1/1863	Killed in action	Unknown
Matthews, Andrew J.	Co. C, 28th Virginia	1842	7/23/1863	Hollywood Cemetery, Richmond, Va., reburial lists	Richmond, VA
Matthews, B.C.	Co. A, 1st South Carolina	1843	7/1/1863	Killed in action	Unknown
Matthews, Barnaba B.	Co. F, 9th Virginia		7/3/1863	Killed in action	Unknown
Matthews, Elijah	Co. A, 1st South Carolina	1841	7/27/1863	Died as POW at David's Island, NY	Cypress Hills, NY
Matthews, John H.	Co. C, 56th Virginia		Jul. 1863	Killed in action per the Richmond Sentinel, July 29, 1863, exact date not known	Unknown
Matthews, T.G.	Co. K, 5th Texas		7/2/1863	Killed in action	Unknown
Maupin, Carson Barnett	Co. H, 56th Virginia	1835	Jul. 1863	Missing in action and presumed dead	Unknown
Maupin, David G.	Co. H, 56th Virginia		Jul. 1863	Missing in action and presumed dead	Unknown
Maupin, James Rawlings	2nd Co., Richmond Howitzers	1/30/1833	7/2/1863	Killed in action	Charlottesville, VA
Maxey, Frederick C.	Co. A, 57th Virginia	1843	7/9/1863	Mortally wounded-died at unknown place in Gettysburg	Unknown
Maxey, Travis R.	Sgt., Co. K, 8th Georgia	1826	Jul. 1863	Killed in action, July 1-3	Unknown
Maxwell, James D.	Co. A, 43rd North Carolina	1831	7/25/1863	Mortally wounded-died at unknown place in Gettysburg	Unknown
May, Edmund G.	Fraser's Battery (Ga.)	1842	7/2/1863	Killed in action	Unknown

NAME	REGIMENT	BIRTH	DEATH	COMMENT	BURIAL
May, John	Co. E, 22nd North Carolina	1817	1863	Mortally wounded-died on unknown date in Gettysburg	Unknown
May, John D.	Co. E, 22nd North Carolina		7/31/1863	Died as POW at David's Island, NY	Cypress Hills, NY
Mayeux, Octave	Co. E, 2nd Louisiana		8/10/1863	Mortally wounded and died at Chester, PA	Phil. National Cem.
Mayhew, Moses B.	Co. A, 4th North Carolina	1835	7/1/1863	Killed in action	Unknown
Maynard, John H.	Sgt., Co. K, 6th North Carolina	1837	7/4/1863	Oakwood Cemetery, Raleigh, NC, reburial list	Raleigh, NC
Maynard, Sidney	Co. E, 47th North Carolina	1837	7/3/1863	Killed in action	Unknown
Maynard, William M.	Co. B, 11th Mississippi	1844	7/3/1863	Killed in action	Unknown
Maynor, Laban Franklin	Co. F, 6th Alabama	1842	Jul. 1863	Killed in action, July 1-3	Unknown
Mayo, James L.	Co. A, 2nd Mississippi	1843	7/20/1863	Mortally wounded-died at unknown place in Gettysburg	Unknown
Mayo, Thomas	Cpl., Co. I, 17th Georgia		Jul. 1863	Mortally wounded per the Augusta Chronicle & Sentinel, July 30, 1863	Unknown
Mays, Anderson	Co. I, 19th Virginia		Jul. 1863	Missing in action and presumed dead	Unknown
Mays, G.W.	Co. G, 2nd Georgia		7/2/1863	Killed in action	Unknown
Mays, J. Nelson	Co. D, 4th Texas		7/2/1863	Killed in action	Unknown
Mays, James	Co. A, 17th Mississippi	1840	Jul. 1863	Killed in action on July 1st or 2nd	Unknown
Mays, John C.	Sgt., Co. G, 1st South Carolina		7/3/1863	Magnolia Cemetery, Charleston, SC, reburial list	Charleston, SC
Mays, Leland C.	Co. F, 15th South Carolina	1842	10/3/1863	Mortally wounded- sent home and died of wounds there	Union C.H., SC
McAfee, Charles A.	Lt., Co. I, 22nd Georgia	2/2/1841	7/2/1863	Killed in action	Unknown
McAfee, David Roe	Phillip's Legion (Ga.)	4/1/1838	11/14/1863	Mortally wounded-died at unknown place in Gettysburg	Unknown
McAfee, Watson Green	Co. I, 22nd Georgia	12/18/1845	7/2/1863	Killed in action	Unknown
McArtor, John Robert	Sgt., Co. B, 8th Virginia	2/19/1842	7/3/1863	Killed in action	Unknown
McAuley, Auley M.	Sgt., Co. H, 26th North Carolina	1840	7/1/1863	Killed in action	Unknown
McCain, George C.	Capt., Co. I, 52nd North Carolina	1832	7/1/1863	Hollywood Cemetery, Richmond, Va., reburial lists	Richmond, VA
McCain, John Christian	Capt., Co. I, 52nd North Carolina	6/2/1831	7/1/1863	Killed in action	Unknown
McCall, Martin Crawford	Cpl., Co. K, 8th South Carolina	1843	7/2/1863	Killed in action per the Charleston Courier, July 1863	Richmond, VA
McCargo, Samuel J.	Co. B, 14th Virginia Cavalry		7/3/1863	Killed in action	Unknown
McCarley, Green	Co. B, 2nd Mississippi	1839	10/13/1863	Died as POW at David's Island, NY	Cypress Hills, NY
McCarroll, Samuel	Co. E, 13th Georgia		7/1/1863	Killed in action	Unknown
McCarty, Joseph M.	Sgt., Co. F, 2nd Virginia	1843	Jul. 1863	Missing in action and presumed dead	Unknown
McCarty, Thomas	Co. I, 8th Louisiana	1823	7/2/1863	Mortally wounded, July 2nd, and died the same day	Unknown
McCarty, W.C.	Co. B, 4th Texas		7/20/1863	Mortally wounded-died at unknown place in Gettysburg	Unknown
McCaskill, D.C.	Sgt., Co. K, 38th North Carolina	1834	7/4/1863	Died of wounds received on July 2nd or 3rd	Unknown
McCaskill, Daniel	Co. H, 26th North Carolina	1839	11/17/1863	Mortally wounded and died at Baltimore, MD-buried there	Baltimore, MD

NAME	REGIMENT	BIRTH	DEATH	COMMENT	BURIAL
McCaslan, William E.	Capt., Co. E, 2nd Florida	1833	7/3/1863	Killed in action	Unknown
McClannahan, John H.	Co. D, 9th Louisiana	1838	7/2/1863	Killed in action	Unknown
McClelland, Rudolphus Henry	Cpl., Co. A, 5th Florida	9/25/1843	7/5/1863	Mortally wounded, July 2nd or 3rd	Unknown
McClelland, William K.	Co. D, 1st Texas		7/2/1863	Killed in action	Unknown
McClendon, W.F.	Co. A, 1st Texas		7/2/1863	Killed in action	Unknown
McClenny, Josiah	Co. G, 55th North Carolina	1841	7/1/1863	Killed in action	Unknown
McClenny, Walter Montague	Co. D, 47th North Carolina	7/8/1845	7/3/1863	Killed in action	Unknown
McCleskey, Francis C.	Sgt., Co. B, 38th Georgia		7/1/1863	Killed in action	Unknown
McCloud, Samuel M.	Co. C, 37th Virginia		7/5/1863	Mortally wounded-died at unknown place in Gettysburg	Unknown
McClure, James H.	Co. H, 14th North Carolina	1836	7/5/1863	Died of wounds received on July 2nd or 3rd	Unknown
McClure, John J.	Co. I, 5th Alabama	1834	7/3/1863	Killed in action	Unknown
McClure, John S.	Co. F, 1st Tennessee	1829	7/3/1863	Killed in action	Unknown
McClure, S.L.	Co. H, 23rd North Carolina		7/5/1863	Mortally wounded, July 3rd, and died two days later	Unknown
McConchie, William	Co. I, 11th Virginia	1838	Jul. 1863	Missing in action and presumed dead	Unknown
McConnel, John F.	Co. A, 11th North Carolina		1863	Mortally wounded-died on unknown date in Gettysburg	Unknown
McConnell, Richmond T.	Co. G, 11th Georgia	1834	7/30/1863	Died as POW at David's Island, NY	Cypress Hills, NY
McCormick, Henry Alexander	Co. A, 1st Maryland Battalion		Jul. 1863	Mortally wounded-died at unknown place in Gettysburg	Unknown
McCormick, John (James)	Co. H, 38th Virginia		7/23/1863	Hollywood Cemetery, Richmond, Va., reburial lists	Richmond, VA
McCorquodale, William T.	Cpl., Co. E, 51st Georgia	1840	1863	Mortally wounded, July 2nd, and died at home of wounds	Georgia
McCowan, William C.	Co. B, 2nd Mississippi	1844	7/3/1863	Killed in action	Richmond, VA
McCowen, Benjamin Butler	Lt., Co. K, 53rd Georgia		7/2/1863	Magnolia Cemetery, Charleston, SC, reburial list	Charleston, SC
McCoy, John F.	Co. C, 37th North Carolina	9/5/1830	7/3/1863	Killed in action; reinterred at Hopewell Cemetery	Mecklenburg Co., NC
McCracken, Robert Hayne	Co. D, 13th South Carolina	1839	8/4/1863	Magnolia Cemetery, Charleston, SC, reburial list	Charleston, SC
McCrary, Alexander A.	Co. E, 9th Georgia		7/5/1863	Hollywood Cemetery, Richmond, Va., reburial lists	Richmond, VA
McCrary, John V.	Sgt., Co. B, 20th Georgia		7/2/1863	Killed in action	Unknown
McCrea, William H.	Richmond Fayette Artillery (Va.)		7/3/1863	Hollywood Cemetery, Richmond, Va., reburial lists	Richmond, VA
McCreery, William Westwood	Capt., AIG, Gen. Pettigrew's staff	Sept 1836	7/1/1863	Killed in action per the Richmond Sentinel, July 18, 1863; reinterred in Oakwood Cemetery	Raleigh, NC
McCrimmon, Farquhar	Lt., Co. H, 20th Georgia	1838	7/2/1863	Killed in action	Unknown
McCrum, Hugh A.	Co. B, 53rd North Carolina	1826	7/1/1863	Killed in action	Unknown
McCullar, Jesse C.	Co. F, 9th Georgia		7/2/1863	Hollywood Cemetery, Richmond, Va., reburial lists	Richmond, VA
McCulloch, William H.	Co. H, 14th Tennessee	1842	7/3/1863	Killed in action; reinterred in Riverview Cemetery, Clarksville, TN	Clarksville, TN

NAME	REGIMENT	BIRTH	DEATH	COMMENT	BURIAL
McCullough, John T.	Sgt., Co. A, 3rd Georgia		7/27/1863	Mortally wounded and died at Camp Letterman	Unknown
McCurley, David	Co. E, 47th Alabama	1818	9/8/1863	Died as POW at David's Island, NY	Cypress Hills, NY
McCurley, Joseph	Co. A, 2nd Louisiana	1837	7/28/1863	Hollywood Cemetery, Richmond, Va., reburial lists	Richmond, VA
McCurry, John S.	Co. I, 14th South Carolina	1840	9/12/1863	Died as POW at David's Island, NY	Cypress Hills, NY
McCurry, William L.	Sgt., Co. D, 7th South Carolina		7/2/1863	Hollywood Cemetery, Richmond, Va., reburial lists	Richmond, VA
McCutcheon, John Davis	Co. F, 48th Alabama	1828	7/2/1863	Killed in action	Unknown
McDade, James Alexander	Co. D, 5th Texas	1843	7/2/1863	Killed in action	Unknown
McDade, John Henderson	Lt., Co. G, 11th North Carolina		7/1/1863	Killed in action; reinterred Green Mount Cem., Area R/63	Baltimore, MD
McDaniel, Charles T.	Co. D, 28th Virginia	1840	7/3/1863	Missing in action and presumed dead	Unknown
McDaniel, David E.	Co. K, 24th Virginia		7/31/1863	Died as POW at David's Island, NY	Cypress Hills, NY
McDaniel, William	Co. C, 6th North Carolina	1839	7/28/1863	Mortally wounded-died at unknown place in Gettysburg	Unknown
McDermott, William	Co. A, 10th Louisiana	1840	7/14/1863	Mortally wounded-died at unknown place in Gettysburg	Unknown
McDonald, Henry C.	Sgt., Co. D, 2nd Georgia Battalion		7/8/1863	Mortally wounded-died at unknown place in Gettysburg	Unknown
McDonald, Joseph W.	Co. D, 2nd Georgia Battalion	4/24/1843	7/2/1863	Missing in action and presumed dead	Unknown
McDonnell, Daniel	Co. E, 9th Louisiana	1839	7/2/1863	Killed in action	Unknown
McDonnell, John F.	Sgt., Co. H, 5th Texas	1833	7/2/1863	Killed in action	Unknown
McDougald, Dougald A.	Cpl., Co. K, 38th North Carolina	1835	7/1/1863	Killed in action	Unknown
McDowall, George Marshall	Capt., Co. F, 2nd South Carolina	3/8/1838	7/3/1863	Magnolia Cemetery, Charleston, SC, reburial list	Charleston, SC
McDowell, P.H.	Co. E, 17th Georgia		7/2/1863	Killed in action	Unknown
McDowell, Robert B.	Co. K, 38th Virginia		7/22/1863	Mortally wounded-died at unknown place in Gettysburg	Unknown
McDowell, Thomas E.	Sgt., Co. D, 9th Georgia		7/2/1863	Killed in action	Unknown
McDowell, William	Co. A, 5th Texas	1829	Jul. 1863	Mortally wounded and died at Baltimore, MD-buried there	Baltimore, MD
McDuffie, Daniel	Co. G, 26th Alabama		7/1/1863	Killed in action	Unknown
McDuffie, Daniel	Co. K, 38th North Carolina	1835	7/2/1863	Killed in action	Unknown
McDuffie, Daniel Q.	Sgt., Co. I, 8th South Carolina		7/3/1863	Magnolia Cemetery, Charleston, SC, reburial list	Charleston, SC
McDuffie, Norman L.	Capt., Co. F, 18th Mississippi	1838	7/2/1863	Hollywood Cemetery, Richmond, Va., reburial lists	Richmond, VA
McElroy, J.H.	Co. F, 10th Louisiana		7/3/1863	Mortally wounded, July 3rd, and died on the same say	Unknown
McElroy, James H.	Co. A, 1st Louisiana	1838	7/2/1863	Hollywood Cemetery, Richmond, Va., reburial lists	Richmond, VA
McElroy, James W.	Co. B, 53rd North Carolina	1834	7/7/1863	Mortally wounded-died at unknown place in Gettysburg	Unknown
McFarland, Walker	Co. D, 13th North Carolina	1842	7/10/1863	Mortally wounded-died at unknown place in Gettysburg	Unknown

NAME	REGIMENT	BIRTH	DEATH	COMMENT	BURIAL
McGahee, Stephen	Co. K, 48th Georgia	1838	1863	Mortally wounded and left on the field	Unknown
McGahee, William H.	Co. K, 48th Georgia	1841	Jul. 1863	Killed in action	Georgia
McGarie, A.J.	Co. I, 26th North Carolina		7/1/1863	Killed in action	Unknown
McGee, Franklin M.	Co. I, 32nd North Carolina	1841	7/11/1863	Oakwood Cemetery, Raleigh, NC, reburial list	Raleigh, NC
McGee, U.G.	Co. E, 7th South Carolina		7/2/1863	Killed in action	Unknown
McGee, William Butler	Co. C, 17th Mississippi	1841	8/6/1863	Hollywood Cemetery, Richmond, Va., reburial lists	Richmond, VA
McGehee, J.G.	Lt., Co. C, 2nd Georgia	1843	7/2/1863	Killed in action	Unknown
McGill, John	Co. K, 38th North Carolina	1843	7/22/1863	Mortally wounded-died at unknown place in Gettysburg	Unknown
McGinnis, James L.B.	Co. H, 28th North Carolina	1845	9/5/1863	Mortally wounded and died at Chester, PA	Phil. National Cem.
McGinnis, John W.	Sgt., Co. E, 53rd Georgia		8/27/1863	Mortally wounded-died at unknown place in Gettysburg	Unknown
McGinnis, Michael	Co. I, 1st South Carolina		7/2/1863	Killed in action	Unknown
McGlemre, John W.	Sgt., Co. K, 12th Virginia	1836	8/5/1863	Mortally wounded and died at Hagerstown, MD-buried there	Hagerstown, MD
McGough, Christopher Columbus	Lt., Co. B, 45th Georgia	1833	7/2/1863	Killed in action	Unknown
McGrady, Jacob	Co. K, 37th North Carolina	1834	7/14/1863	Oakwood Cemetery, Raleigh, NC, reburial list	Raleigh, NC
McGrath, John	Co. B, 6th North Carolina	1838	7/2/1863	Killed in action	Unknown
McGraw, William H.	Sgt., Co. H, 8th Alabama		7/2/1863	Killed in action	Unknown
McGregor, Archibald W.	Lt., Co. F, 18th North Carolina	1839	7/3/1863	Killed in action	Unknown
McGuinn, Patrick	Sgt., Co. B, 6th Louisiana	1838	7/2/1863	Killed in action	Unknown
McGuire, Benjamin Harrison	Lt., Co. D, 22nd Virginia Battalion	10/20/1843	7/1/1863	Killed in action; reinterred in Old Chapel Cemetery, Millwood, VA	Millwood, VA
McHenry, Alkana	Co. B, 11th Mississippi	1838	8/23/1863	Died as POW at David's Island, NY	Cypress Hills, NY
McHone, Micajah	Co. C, 24th Virginia		7/23/1863	Hollywood Cemetery, Richmond, Va., reburial lists	Richmond, VA
McIivane, Daniel M.	Sgt., Co. I, 11th Georgia		7/22/1863	Mortally wounded and died at Richmond, VA-interred in Hollywood Cemetery	Richmond, VA
McInnis, Allen M.	Co. K, 34th North Carolina	1839	7/1/1863	Killed in action	Unknown
McInnis, Evander J.	Co. E, 28th North Carolina	1842	7/12/1863	Mortally wounded and died at Chester, PA	Phil. National Cem.
McIntosh, Alexander	Cpl., Co. G, 8th South Carolina		7/2/1863	Hollywood Cemetery, Richmond, Va., reburial lists	Richmond, VA
McIntosh, Samuel Jackson	Co. H, 26th North Carolina	1840	7/1/1863	Killed in action	Unknown
McIntosh, Thomas Rose	Garden's Battery (S.C.)	11/9/1836	7/4/1863	Hollywood Cemetery, Richmond, Va., reburial lists	Richmond, VA
McInturff, Franklin	Co. B, 33rd Virginia	5/12/1833	7/12/1863	Hollywood Cemetery, Richmond, Va., reburial lists	Richmond, VA
McIntyre, George W.	Co. A, 1st Maryland Battalion		Jul. 1863	Mortally wounded-died on unknown date in Gettysburg	Unknown

NAME	REGIMENT	BIRTH	DEATH	COMMENT	BURIAL
McIver, John Kolb	Capt., Co. F, 8th South Carolina	9/1/1835	10/13/1863	Mortally wounded-died at unknown place in Gettysburg	Unknown
McKay, Lauchlin L.	Co. E, 52nd North Carolina	1811	7/3/1863	Killed in action	Unknown
McKay, Tristram Bethea	Co. B, 2nd Mississippi	11/14/1839	7/1/1863	Killed in action	Unknown
McKee, Levi T.	Co. G, 42nd Mississippi		8/13/1863	Mortally wounded and died at Frederick, MD; interred in Mt. Olivet Cemetery	Frederick, MD
McKenzie, Alfred D.	Sgt., Co. D, 17th Georgia		7/3/1863	Died of wounds received July 2nd	Unknown
McKerrell, James	Co. K, 3rd Alabama	1840	7/4/1863	Mortally wounded, July 2nd, and died two days later; reinterred in Magnolia Cemetery, Mobile, AL	Mobile, AL
McKethan, J.A.	Co. L, 1st South Carolina		8/3/1863	Died as POW at David's Island, NY	Cypress Hills, NY
McKie, Thomas Fondren	Co. A, 11th Mississippi	11/2/1845	7/4/1863	Died of wounds received July 3rd	Unknown
McKinney, David	Sgt., Co. B, 2nd North Carolina Battalion	1842	7/1/1863	Oakwood Cemetery, Raleigh, NC, reburial list	Raleigh, NC
McKinney, George W.	Co. K, 3rd Virginia		7/3/1863	Mortally wounded, July 3rd, and died the same day	Unknown
McKinney, Moses J.	Sgt., Co. E, 6th North Carolina	1837	Jul. 1863	Oakwood Cemetery, Raleigh, NC, reburial list	Raleigh, NC
McKinnon, Colin B.	Co. H, 26th North Carolina	1839	7/1/1863	Killed in action	Unknown
McKinnon, John	Cpl., Co. H, 26th North Carolina	1836	7/1/1863	Killed in action	Unknown
McKnight, James	Co. E, 8th Alabama		7/2/1863	Killed in action	Unknown
McLacklan, Edward T.	Cpl., Co. I, 2nd North Carolina	1841	7/2/1863	Killed in action	Unknown
McLaughlin, Hugh	Co. I, 1st Virginia	1817	7/3/1863	Killed in action	Unknown
McLaughlin, James	Co. A, 8th Florida	1838	8/1/1863	Mortally wounded and died at Winchester, VA; buried Oak City Cemetery, Bainbridge, Ga.	Bainbridge, Ga.
McLaughlin, James	Sgt., Co. I, 21st Mississippi		7/2/1863	Killed in action	Unknown
McLaurine, Richard Lewis	Cpl., Co. A, 18th Mississippi	2/28/1838	7/12/1863	Hollywood Cemetery, Richmond, Va., reburial lists	Richmond, VA
McLean, A.L.	Cpl., Co. G, 44th Alabama	1842	7/2/1863	Killed in action	Unknown
McLean, J.R.	Sgt., Co. A, 9th Alabama		Jul. 1863	Hollywood Cemetery, Richmond, Va., reburial lists	Richmond, VA
McLendon, Dennis	Co. B, 11th Georgia		7/10/1863	Mortally wounded-died at unknown place in Gettysburg	Unknown
McLendon, V.F.	Co. A, 1st Texas		7/2/1863	Killed in action	Unknown
McLeod, Donald McDairmed	Maj., 8th South Carolina	12/18/1823	7/5/1863	Mortally wounded, July 2nd, and died at Cashtown, PA; Reinterred in SC	Marlboro Co., SC
McLeod, James A.N.	Sgt., Co. H, 26th North Carolina		7/1/1863	Killed in action	Unknown
McLeod, Norman J.	Sgt., Co. K, 34th North Carolina	1839	7/1/1863	Killed in action	Unknown
McLeod, William H.H.	Sgt., Co. I, 2nd Florida		1863	Mortally wounded-died on unknown date in Gettysburg	Unknown
McLeod, William L.	Capt., Co. C, 38th Georgia	5/6/1842	7/1/1863	Killed in action; reinterred family cemetery, Swainsboro, GA in 1865	Emanuel Co., GA
McLucas, Hugh	Sgt., Co. K, 8th South Carolina	1841	7/2/1863	Hollywood Cemetery, Richmond, Va., reburial lists	Richmond, VA

NAME	REGIMENT	BIRTH	DEATH	COMMENT	BURIAL
McMakin, John B.	Co. A, 13th Mississippi		8/3/1863	Hollywood Cemetery, Richmond, Va., reburial lists	Richmond, VA
McMellon, William H.	Co. B, 57th Virginia		Jul. 1863	Killed in action, July 1-3	Unknown
McMillan, A.P.	Co. B, 15th Alabama	1840	7/2/1863	Killed in action	Unknown
McMillan, John C.	Co. A, 22nd North Carolina	1840	7/1/1863	Killed in action	Unknown
McMiller, Joseph	Co. A, 52nd North Carolina	1831	7/21/1863	Hollywood Cemetery, Richmond, Va., reburial lists	Richmond, VA
McNair, James L.	Co. C, 31st Georgia		7/25/1863	Mortally wounded and died at Frederick, MD; interred in Mt. Olivet Cemetery	Frederick, MD
McNeely, Thomas V.	Co. G, 17th Mississippi	1844	7/2/1863	Killed in action on July 1st or 2nd	Unknown
McNeil, Patrick	Parker's Battery (Va.)	1827	7/3/1863	Mortally wounded, July 3rd, and died the same day	Unknown
McNeill, George Hector	Cpl., Co. K, 38th North Carolina	1842	7/1/1863	Killed in action	Unknown
McNeill, John	Co. B, 55th North Carolina		7/1/1863	Killed in action	Unknown
McNeill, Robert G.	Sgt., Co. G, 14th South Carolina	1842	7/3/1863	Killed in action	Unknown
McNeily, Samuel	Co. F, 55th North Carolina		8/3/1863	Died as POW at David's Island, NY	Cypress Hills, NY
McNinch, William C.	Lt., Co. G, 13th South Carolina	1841	7/1/1863	Killed in action	Unknown
McPherson, Angus M.	Co. K, 8th South Carolina	1838	7/2/1863	Hollywood Cemetery, Richmond, Va., reburial lists	Richmond, VA
McPherson, Malcom	Co. K, 8th South Carolina	1836	7/2/1863	Hollywood Cemetery, Richmond, Va., reburial lists	Richmond, VA
McPherson, Norvel J.	Co. A, 42nd Mississippi	1832	7/21/1863	Hollywood Cemetery, Richmond, Va., reburial lists	Richmond, VA
McQuay, James	Co. E, 11th North Carolina	1827	7/3/1863	Killed in action	Unknown
McQuay, William H.	Co. E, 11th North Carolina	1842	7/7/1863	Died of wounds received July 1st	Unknown
McRae, Montford Stokes	Sgt. Maj., 26th North Carolina	1837	8/2/1863	Mortally wounded and died at Camp Letterman	Unknown
McRaven, William T.	Co. B, 17th Mississippi	1843	7/2/1863	Killed in action	Unknown
McReed, William	Co. K, 11th North Carolina	1845	7/15/1863	Died of wounds received July 1st	Unknown
McSwain, Doctor T.J.M.	Co. D, 55th North Carolina	1844	7/1/1863	Killed in action	Unknown
McWhirter, John	Co. A, 11th North Carolina	1842	1863	Mortally wounded-died at unknown place in Gettysburg	Unknown
McWhorter, John	Co. B, 26th North Carolina	3/20/1843	7/1/1863	Killed in action	Unknown
McWilliams, David W.	Co. B, 17th Mississippi	1829	9/8/1863	Hollywood Cemetery, Richmond, Va., reburial lists	Richmond, VA
McWilliams, James	Co. C, 1st Maryland Battalion	1844	7/2/1863	Killed in action	Unknown
Meacham, R.W.	Lt., Co. B, 13th Georgia		7/1/1863	Killed in action	Unknown
Meaders, James Turner	Lt., Co. G, 24th Georgia	1/25/1839	7/2/1863	Killed in action	Unknown
Meador, Calvin H.	Co. F, 53rd Virginia		7/3/1863	Killed in action	Unknown
Meador, Jesse Lee	Co. A, 57th Virginia	1839	7/9/1863	Hollywood Cemetery, Richmond, Va., reburial lists	Richmond, VA
Meadors, William C.	Co. B, 24th Virginia		Jul. 1863	Missing in action and presumed dead	Unknown
Meadows, Jerre [John] Spicer	Co. H, 55th North Carolina	1835	7/3/1863	Killed in action	Unknown
Meadows, John Wash	Co. G, 61st Georgia		7/1/1863	Laurel Grove Cemetery, Savannah, Ga., reburial list	Savannah, GA

NAME	REGIMENT	BIRTH	DEATH	COMMENT	BURIAL
Meadows, Thomas P.	Co. D, 12th North Carolina	1837	7/1/1863	Killed in action	Unknown
Meares, John A.	Sgt., Co. E, 14th South Carolina	1842	7/2/1863	Killed in action	Unknown
Mears, Goldsborough B.	Capt., Co. K, 42nd Mississippi	1833	7/3/1863	Killed in action	Unknown
Mears, William B.	Co. K, 42nd Mississippi	1836	7/3/1863	Killed in action	Unknown
Mears, Woodson B.	Co. C, 17th Mississippi	1833	7/30/1863	Mortally wounded-died at unknown place in Gettysburg	Unknown
Medlin, Thomas L.	Co. E, 47th North Carolina	1841	Jul. 1863	Oakwood Cemetery, Raleigh, NC, reburial list	Raleigh, NC
Medlin, W.A.	Co. E, 47th North Carolina	1845	Jul. 1863	Killed in action	Unknown
Medlin, William C.	Co. E, 47th North Carolina	1835	7/16/1863	Hollywood Cemetery, Richmond, Va., reburial lists	Richmond, VA
Meece, John [James] F. [Pinkney]	Co. K, 5th Texas	1841	7/10/1863	Hollywood Cemetery, Richmond, Va., reburial lists	Richmond, VA
Meekins, John Roderick	Co. B, 1st Texas		7/2/1863	Killed in action	Unknown
Megahee, William H.	Cpl., Co. K, 48th Georgia	1841	7/2/1863	Killed in action	Unknown
Megehee, John H.	Co. G, 7th North Carolina	1836	Jul. 1863	Mortally wounded-died on unknown date in Gettysburg	Unknown
Mellhausen, Theo. H.	Co. L, 1st Texas	1843	7/2/1863	Killed in action	Unknown
Melton, Joshua Garner	Co. K, 44th Virginia		7/2/1863	Killed in action	Unknown
Melton, Robert Bolling	Co. D, 47th North Carolina	1843	7/25/1863	Mortally wounded-died at unknown place in Gettysburg	Unknown
Melton, William G.	Co. H, 57th Virginia		Jul. 1863	Killed in action, July 1-3	Unknown
Melvin, John	Co. B, 45th North Carolina	1840	7/1/1863	Killed in action	Unknown
Mendenhall, Joseph W.	Co. K, 45th North Carolina	1833	7/11/1863	Mortally wounded-died at unknown place in Gettysburg	Unknown
Menefee, James Willis	Sgt., Co. H, 33rd Virginia	6/5/1837	7/3/1863	Killed in action	Unknown
Mercer, Oliver Evans	Capt., Co. G, 20th North Carolina	1/23/1842	7/1/1863	Killed in action	Unknown
Meredith, Wilson Cable	Co. D, 18th Virginia	1843	1863	Hollywood Cemetery, Richmond, Va., reburial lists	Richmond, VA
Meret, Lewis R.	Co. C, 2nd South Carolina		7/9/1863	Mortally wounded-died at unknown place in Gettysburg	Unknown
Merriman, James A.	Co. A, 57th Virginia		Jul. 1863	Killed in action, July 1-3	Unknown
Merriman, John E.	Cpl., Blount's Battery (Va.)		7/3/1863	Killed in action	Unknown
Merritt, Robert V.	Sgt., Co. F, 43rd North Carolina	1839	7/1/1863	Killed in action	Unknown
Mester, Joel	Co. K, 4th Texas		7/2/1863	Killed in action	Unknown
Michael, Thomas	Co. C, 9th Georgia		7/20/1863	Mortally wounded, July 2nd, and died at Martinsburg, VA	Martinsburg, WV
Michie, Orin G.	Co. H, 56th Virginia	1/29/1839	9/27/1863	Mortally wounded-died at unknown place in Gettysburg	Unknown
Mickey, James W.	Co. I, 21st North Carolina	1842	Jul. 1863	Killed in action on either July 2nd or 3rd	Unknown
Mickey, Thomas J.	Co. K, 52nd North Carolina	1831	7/24/1863	Hollywood Cemetery, Richmond, Va., reburial lists	Richmond, VA
Mickle, William N.	Lt., Co. K, 37th North Carolina	1843	7/3/1863	Killed in action	Unknown
Middleton, Frank W. "Bud"	Capt., Co. H, 17th Mississippi	1838	Jul. 1863	Mortally wounded and died at Winchester, VA	Winchester, VA

NAME	REGIMENT	BIRTH	DEATH	COMMENT	BURIAL
Midkiff, E.P.	Co. G, 4th Texas		1863	Hollywood Cemetery, Richmond, Va., reburial lists	Richmond, VA
Midkiff, Levi Thomas	Co. A 18th Virginia		7/3/1863	Killed in action per the Richmond Sentinel, July 29, 1863	Unknown
Milam, James C.	Sgt. Maj., Co. A, 5th Virginia		7/3/1863	Hollywood Cemetery, Richmond, Va., reburial lists	Richmond, VA
Miles, D.D.	Co. C, 6th Alabama	1834	Jul. 1863	Killed in action, July 1-3	Unknown
Miles, Drury L.	Co. A, 57th Virginia		Jul. 1863	Killed in action, July 1-3	Unknown
Miles, J. Foster	Co. D, 1st Texas		7/2/1863	Killed in action	Unknown
Miles, Micagah	Co. H, 6th North Carolina	1839	Jul. 1863	Missing in action and presumed dead	Unknown
Miles, Septimus Charles	Co. I, 2nd South Carolina	1836	7/2/1863	Killed in action	Charleston, SC
Miles, Thomas C.	Co. H, 6th North Carolina	1838	7/2/1863	Killed in action	Unknown
Millam, James E.	Sgt., Co. G, 53rd Virginia		8/6/1863	Mortally wounded and died at Chester, PA	Phil. National Cem.
Miller, Alexander	Maj., 21st North Carolina	5/29/1833	8/2/1863	Hollywood Cemetery, Richmond, Va., reburial lists	Richmond, VA
Miller, Alexander	Co. D, 21st North Carolina	1841	7/31/1863	Mortally wounded-died at unknown place in Gettysburg	Unknown
Miller, Alfred	Co. B, 37th North Carolina	1834	7/3/1863	Missing in action and presumed dead	Unknown
Miller, Houston A.	Co. G, 2nd Mississippi	1842	7/1/1863	Killed in action	Unknown
Miller, Hugh Reid	Col., 42nd Mississippi	5/14/1812	7/19/1863	Mortally wounded; funeral at 1st Presbyterian Church, July 29th, Richmond, VA-reinterred in MS	Aberdeen, MS
Miller, Ibsom A.	Co. D, 34th North Carolina	1840	7/3/1863	Killed in action	Unknown
Miller, James Ball	Lt., Co. A, 18th Virginia	1836	8/5/1863	Mortally wounded and died at Chester, PA	Phil. National Cem.
Miller, Jeremiah	Co. E, 5th North Carolina	1839	7/1/1863	Hollywood Cemetery, Richmond, Va., reburial lists	Richmond, VA
Miller, Joel	Co. M, 7th South Carolina		7/8/1863	Mortally wounded per the Charleston Mercury, August 28, 1863	Charleston, SC
Miller, John S.	Cpl., Co. B, 5th Texas		7/2/1863	Killed in action	Unknown
Miller, John T.	Co. E, 45th North Carolina	1841	7/20/1863	Oakwood Cemetery, Raleigh, NC, reburial list	Raleigh, NC
Miller, Jonathan	Co. A, 26th North Carolina	12/11/1829	7/3/1863	Killed in action	Unknown
Miller, Joseph Mc.	Co. A, 52nd North Carolina	1831	7/21/1863	Hollywood Cemetery, Richmond, Va., reburial lists	Richmond, VA
Miller, Thomas H.	Co. B, 14th South Carolina	1845	7/2/1863	Killed in action	Unknown
Miller, William B.	Co. K, 11th Alabama		7/3/1863	Killed in action	Unknown
Miller, William J.	Co. C, 28th North Carolina		7/3/1863	Killed in action	Unknown
Miller, William J.	Capt., Co. K, 53rd North Carolina	1838	7/1/1863	Killed in action	Unknown
Miller, William Preston	Co. B, 3rd South Carolina Battalion	1838	7/2/1863	Killed in action per the Charleston Courier, July 1863	Charleston, SC
Miller, William T.	Cpl., Co. G, 1st Virginia	1839	Jul. 1863	Mortally wounded, July 3rd, and died on unknown date	Unknown
Millican, Joseph B.	Co. F, 1st South Carolina		7/3/1863	Killed in action	Unknown
Millican, P.B.	Co. B, 9th Georgia		7/2/1863	Killed in action	Unknown

NAME	REGIMENT	BIRTH	DEATH	COMMENT	BURIAL
Mills, Edmund James	Co. I, 2nd South Carolina	12/11/1841	7/2/1863	Killed in action	Charleston, SC
Mills, Jefferson	Co. H, 47th North Carolina	1843	Jul. 1863	Missing in action and presumed dead	Unknown
Mills, John	Co. G, 9th Georgia		Dec. 1863	Laurel Grove Cemetery, Savannah, Ga., reburial list	Savannah, GA
Mills, William H.	Co. E, 49th Virginia		7/3/1863	Killed in action	Unknown
Millwood, Edward B.	Co. H, 15th South Carolina	1844	7/2/1863	Killed in action per the Charleston Courier, July 1863	Unknown
Milton, H.H.	Co. F, 5th North Carolina	1819	7/1/1863	Hollywood Cemetery, Richmond, Va., reburial lists	Richmond, VA
Milton, Joseph R.	Co. G, 5th Florida		8/7/1863	Mortally wounded, July 2nd, and died at Winchester, VA	Winchester, VA
Milton, William L.	Co. K, 8th Virginia		Jul. 1863	Missing in action and presumed dead	Unknown
Mimms, Thomas P.	Lt., Co. E, 11th Mississippi	1836	7/6/1863	Hollywood Cemetery, Richmond, Va., reburial lists	Richmond, VA
Mims, Robert L.	Sgt., Co. A, 7th South Carolina	1840	7/2/1863	Killed in action	Unknown
Minchew, Isaac	Co. E, 49th Georgia	1840	7/2/1863	Killed in action	Unknown
Minnick, Daniel B.	Co. B, 4th Virginia		Jul. 1863	Missing in action and presumed dead	Unknown
Minor, Peter H.	Co. E, 19th Virginia	10/1/1837	7/3/1863	Killed in action per the Richmond Sentinel, August 11, 1863	Unknown
Minton, Columbus	Co. D, 15th South Carolina		7/2/1863	Killed in action per the Charleston Courier, July 1863	Unknown
Mintz, Peter L.	Cpl., Co. D, 16th North Carolina	1832	7/3/1863	Hollywood Cemetery, Richmond, Va., reburial lists	Richmond, VA
Misenheimer, James M.	Co. A, 52nd North Carolina	1833	7/3/1863	Mortally wounded, July 3rd, and died the same day	Unknown
Misenhimer, Jacob	Co. A, 20th North Carolina	1844	Jul. 1863	Killed in action	Unknown
Mitchel, William	Co. D, 1st Virginia	1847	7/3/1863	Killed in action while carrying the colors	Unknown
Mitchell, David H.	Brooks Artillery (S.C.)		7/3/1863	Killed in action	Unknown
Mitchell, George William	Lt., Co. H, 3rd Virginia	1834	7/3/1863	Killed in action	Unknown
Mitchell, Goodrich	Lt., Co. C, 49th Virginia		7/3/1863	Killed in action	Unknown
Mitchell, Jacob	Co. D, 1st Tennessee	1840	7/3/1863	Hollywood Cemetery, Richmond, Va., reburial lists	Richmond, VA
Mitchell, James W.	Co. H, 18th North Carolina		Jul. 1863	Missing in action and presumed dead	Unknown
Mitchell, Jeremiah P.	Co. C, 11th North Carolina	1843	7/1/1863	Killed in action	Unknown
Mitchell, Paul M.	Co. E, 7th South Carolina		7/2/1863	Killed in action	Unknown
Mitchell, Thomas J.	Co. G, 32nd North Carolina	1837	7/8/1863	Oakwood Cemetery, Raleigh, NC, reburial list	Raleigh, NC
Mitchell, William L.	Co. D, 11th Georgia		8/7/1863	Died as POW at David's Island, NY	Cypress Hills, NY
Mitchell, Young A.	Co. B, 20th Georgia		7/2/1863	Killed in action	Unknown
Mizell, Thomas E.C.	Sgt., Co. K, 8th Florida	1842	Jul. 1863	Missing in action and presumed dead	Unknown
Moat, David	Co. B, 22nd Georgia		7/2/1863	Killed in action	Unknown
Mobley, Edwin Ruthven S.	Sgt., Co. K, 14th South Carolina	8/26/1843	7/2/1863	Killed in action	Unknown
Mobley, John	Co. E, 26th North Carolina	1842	Jul. 1863	Killed in action	Unknown
Mobley, W.A.J.	Co. G, 13th Georgia		7/1/1863	Laurel Grove Cemetery, Savannah, Ga., reburial list	Savannah, GA

NAME	REGIMENT	BIRTH	DEATH	COMMENT	BURIAL
Mock, Jacob D.	Co. E, 14th South Carolina	1843	7/29/1863	Magnolia Cemetery, Charleston, SC, reburial list	Charleston, SC
Mock, Lewis	Co. G, 2nd North Carolina Battalion.	1841	7/10/1863	Hollywood Cemetery, Richmond, Va., reburial lists	Richmond, VA
Moffatt, H.D.	Co. H, 8th Alabama	1846	9/19/1863	Hollywood Cemetery, Richmond, Va., reburial lists	Richmond, VA
Moncrief, David Harvey	Sgt., Co. K, 3rd Georgia	1837	7/12/1863	Laurel Grove Cemetery, Savannah, Ga., reburial list	Savannah, GA
Money, Edward Francis	Sgt., Co. G, 8th Virginia	3/15/1842	7/3/1863	Hollywood Cemetery, Richmond, Va., reburial lists	Richmond, VA
Monroe, Nelson	Sgt., Co. G, 19th Virginia	1823	Jul. 1863	Missing in action and presumed dead	Unknown
Monte, William G.	Co. G, 9th Virginia	1832	7/3/1863	Killed in action	Unknown
Montford, Thomas	Co. K, 5th Florida	1832	7/3/1863	Killed in action	Unknown
Montgomery, Daniel J.	Cpl., Co. C, 3rd North Carolina	1843	Jul. 1863	Killed in action on either July 2nd or 3rd	Unknown
Montgomery, Green B.W.	Lt., Co. F, 3rd South Carolina Battalion	1826	7/2/1863	Hollywood Cemetery, Richmond, Va., reburial lists	Richmond, VA
Monts, Walter F.	Lt., Co. I, 15th South Carolina	1839	7/2/1863	Killed in action	Unknown
Moody, John Littleberry	Co. C, 22nd Georgia		7/2/1863	Killed in action	Unknown
Moody, John W.	Co. I, 8th Georgia		7/6/1863	Hollywood Cemetery, Richmond, Va., reburial lists	Richmond, VA
Moody, Joseph O.	Taylor's Battery (Va.)		11/12/1863	Mortally wounded-died at unknown place in Gettysburg	Unknown
Moody, William H.	Lt., Co. A, 2nd Mississippi	1840	7/3/1863	Killed in action	Unknown
Moon, Julian K.	Co. C, 14th Virginia	1838	8/17/1863	Hollywood Cemetery, Richmond, Va., reburial lists	Richmond, VA
Moon, William W.	Co. I, 18th Virginia		7/3/1863	Killed in action	Unknown
Moore, Bishop M.	Co. G, 59th Georgia		7/2/1863	Killed in action	Unknown
Moore, Caswell D.	Co. K, 43rd North Carolina	1830	7/2/1863	Killed in action	Unknown
Moore, Charles	Co. F, 13th Mississippi		7/7/1863	Hollywood Cemetery, Richmond, Va., reburial lists	Richmond, VA
Moore, Dan Patrick	Co. F, 48th Virginia	1839	7/2/1863	Killed in action	Unknown
Moore, David T.	Co. A, 9th Louisiana	1841	7/1/1863	Killed in action	Unknown
Moore, Gabe E.	Co. Co. G, 1st Tennessee		9/10/1863	Died as POW at David's Island, NY	Cypress Hills, NY
Moore, George T.	Cpl., Co. D, 14th Virginia		7/3/1863	Killed in action	Unknown
Moore, George W.	Co. F, 6th North Carolina	1842	7/4/1863	Oakwood Cemetery, Raleigh, NC, reburial list	Raleigh, NC
Moore, Henry M.	Co. G, 14th Virginia		8/17/1863	Hollywood Cemetery, Richmond, Va., reburial lists	Richmond, VA
Moore, Isaac	Co. B, 2nd North Carolina Battalion	1828	7/1/1863	Killed in action	Unknown
Moore, James M.	Co. G, 11th Virginia		7/19/1863	Mortally wounded and buried on Jacob Schwartz Farm	Unknown
Moore, Jameson H.	Capt., Co. H, 11th Mississippi	1838	7/5/1863	Hollywood Cemetery, Richmond, Va., reburial lists	Richmond, VA
Moore, John L.	Co. A, 40th Virginia		Jul. 1863	Mortally wounded and died on unknown date	Unknown

NAME	REGIMENT	BIRTH	DEATH	COMMENT	BURIAL
Moore, John R.	Lt., Co. D, 48th Virginia	1835	7/2/1863	Hollywood Cemetery, Richmond, Va., reburial lists	Richmond, VA
Moore, L.D.	Co. E, 48th Georgia		1863	Mortally wounded—died on unknown date in Gettysburg	Unknown
Moore, Lewis M.	Lt., Co. E, 17th Mississippi		8/2/1863	Hollywood Cemetery, Richmond, Va., reburial lists	Richmond, VA
Moore, M.P.	Co. H, 2nd North Carolina Battalion.		11/16/1863	Died as POW at David's Island, NY	Cypress Hills, NY
Moore, Percolus M.	Sgt., Co. E, 1st Maryland Battalion		7/11/1863	Hollywood Cemetery, Richmond, Va., reburial lists	Richmond, VA
Moore, Robert Brown	Co. G, 13th South Carolina	1826	7/1/1863	Killed in action	Unknown
Moore, Samuel	Co. B, 16th Georgia		7/2/1863	Killed in action per the Augusta Chronicle & Sentinel, August. 13, 1863	Unknown
Moore, Samuel B.	King William Artillery (Va.)		7/1/1863	Killed in action	Unknown
Moore, Warren Francis	Co. B, 1st Maryland Battalion	10/17/1844	7/2/1863	Killed in action on Culp's Hill; reinterred at Our Lady's Cemetery	Medley Neck, MD
Moore, William A.	Cpl., Co. H, 2nd Mississippi	1834	7/3/1863	Killed in action	Unknown
Moore, William M.	Co. H, 34th North Carolina	1834	7/1/1863	Killed in action	Unknown
Moorehead, James H.	Co. E, 11th Mississippi	1815	7/6/1863	Killed in action	Unknown
Moorer, Jacob F.	Capt., Co. K, 2nd South Carolina		7/27/1863	Mortally wounded, July 2nd, and died at Hagerstown, MD	Hagerstown, MD
Moores, Jordan R.	Lt., Co. E, 42nd Mississippi	1820	7/3/1863	Killed in action	Unknown
Moorhead, James H.	Lt., Co. H, 11th Alabama		7/6/1863	Hollywood Cemetery, Richmond, Va., reburial lists	Richmond, VA
Moorman, Samuel Edward	Co. B, 11th Virginia	1835	7/17/1863	Mortally wounded—died at unknown place in Gettysburg	Unknown
Moose, Edmund	Lt., Co. D, 28th North Carolina	1833	9/27/1863	Mortally wounded and died at Chester, PA	Phil. National Cem.
Moran, John A.J.	Cpl., Co. G, 26th North Carolina		8/22/1863	Died as POW at David's Island, NY	Cypress Hills, NY
Moran, William	Co. C, 57th Virginia		7/30/1863	Mortally wounded and died at G.H. no. 1, Richmond, Va. -interred Hollywood Cemetery	Richmond, VA
Moreland, Levi	Co. C, 33rd Virginia		7/3/1863	Killed in action	Unknown
Morgan, David	Sgt., Co. C, 45th North Carolina	1819	7/1/1863	Killed in action	Unknown
Morgan, George	Co. F, 26th North Carolina	1837	7/31/1863	Oakwood Cemetery, Raleigh, NC, reburial list	Raleigh, NC
Morgan, James Thomas	Cpl., Co. B, 5th North Carolina	1843	7/1/1863	Hollywood Cemetery, Richmond, Va., reburial lists	Richmond, VA
Morgan, John G.	Sgt., Co. D, 49th Georgia		7/2/1863	Killed in action	Unknown
Morgan, John William Sharp	Color Sgt., 35th Georgia	1/21/1834	7/2/1863	Hollywood Cemetery, Richmond, Va., reburial lists	Richmond, VA
Morgan, Lafayette	Sgt., Co. D, 42nd Mississippi	1827	7/1/1863	Killed in action	Unknown
Morgan, Lycurgus W.	Co. I, 11th Mississippi	1840	7/3/1863	Killed in action	Unknown
Morgan, Miles P.	Co. G, 5th North Carolina	1831	7/1/1863	Hollywood Cemetery, Richmond, Va., reburial lists	Richmond, VA
Morgan, Robert Whitfield	Lt., Co. K, 16th North Carolina	1835	7/3/1863	Killed in action	Unknown
Morgan, Samuel	Co. F, 24th Georgia		7/18/1863	Mortally wounded, July 2nd, and died at Hagerstown, Md	Hagerstown, MD

NAME	REGIMENT	BIRTH	DEATH	COMMENT	BURIAL
Morgan, Samuel	Co. E, 53rd North Carolina	1840	7/20/1863	Mortally wounded-died at unknown place in Gettysburg	Unknown
Morgan, Solomon Goodlow	Co. I, 45th North Carolina	3/14/1843	7/1/1863	Killed in action	Unknown
Morgan, T.B.	Cpl., Co. I, 23rd North Carolina	1834	7/1/1863	Killed in action	Unknown
Morris, Abel	Co. B, 19th Virginia		Jul. 1863	Killed in action, July 1-3	Unknown
Morris, Albert J.	Co. D, 8th Virginia		7/3/1863	Killed in action per the Richmond Sentinel, July 28, 1863	Unknown
Morris, Haley	Co. H, 33rd Virginia		7/3/1863	Killed in action	Unknown
Morris, James E.	Co. B, 19th Virginia	1838	Jul. 1863	Missing in action and presumed dead	Unknown
Morris, John	Lt., Ordnance Off., Pegram's Battalion	12/2/1838	7/2/1863	Hollywood Cemetery, Richmond, Va., reburial lists	Richmond, VA
Morris, John A.	Co. G, 28th North Carolina	1841	7/3/1863	Killed in action	Unknown
Morris, John B.	Co. K, 48th Alabama		7/2/1863	Killed in action	Unknown
Morris, Lewis M.	Co. D, 44th Georgia	1842	7/3/1863	Killed in action	Unknown
Morris, Patrick	Co. B, 5th Louisiana	1833	7/3/1863	Killed in action	Unknown
Morrison, A.H.	Co. B, 11th North Carolina	1844	7/1/1863	Killed in action	Unknown
Morrison, H. Wilbur	Co. A, 1st Maryland Battalion		Jul. 1863	Killed in action, July 1-3	Unknown
Morrison, John A.	Co. A, 6th North Carolina		7/1/1863	Killed in action	Unknown
Morrison, William A.	Co. K, 18th Virginia	1842	7/3/1863	Killed in action per the Richmond Sentinel, July 29, 1863	Unknown
Morrison, William Varick	Co. K, 11th North Carolina	1845	7/1/1863	Killed in action	Unknown
Morriss, Simon	Sgt., Co. D, 1st Texas		7/2/1863	Killed in action	Unknown
Morrow, Elijah Graham	Capt., Co. G, 28th North Carolina	1832	7/27/1863	Hollywood Cemetery, Richmond, Va., reburial lists	Richmond, VA
Morrow, Harry Augustus	Co. E, 10th Georgia	1843	7/2/1863	Killed in action	Unknown
Mortimer, LaBruce	Sgt., Co. I, 2nd South Carolina	10/26/1842	7/4/1863	Mortally wounded per the Charleston Mercury, August 28, 1863	Unknown
Morton, Allan Waller	Cpl., 1st Co., Richmond Howitzers	4/4/1842	7/2/1863	Killed in action per the Richmond Sentinel, July 15, 1863	Richmond, VA
Morton, Ezekiel	Co. I, 52nd North Carolina	4/12/1832	7/3/1863	Killed in action	Unknown
Morton, James W.	Co. E, 18th Virginia		7/23/1863	Hollywood Cemetery, Richmond, Va., reburial lists	Richmond, VA
Moseley, John Winn	Sgt., Co. G, 4th Alabama	8/2/1832	7/5/1863	Mortally wounded, July 2nd, and died three days later	Unknown
Mosely, W.B.	Co. F, 15th South Carolina	1833	7/2/1863	Killed in action	Unknown
Moser, Henry S.	Co. B, 13th North Carolina	1838	7/1/1863	Killed in action	Unknown
Moser, Miles	Co. F, 38th North Carolina	1842	7/1/1863	Killed in action	Unknown
Moss, Roland	Co. C, 12th South Carolina		7/2/1863	Killed in action	Unknown
Moss, U.S.	Co. K, 13th Georgia		7/27/1863	Mortally wounded-died at unknown place in Gettysburg	Unknown
Moss, Wiley J.	Co. B, 53rd Georgia		7/2/1863	Killed in action	Unknown
Mote, S.M.P.	Co. D, 60th Georgia		Jul. 1863	Killed in action	Unknown
Motherly, Henry	Co. A, 21st North Carolina	1843	7/31/1863	Mortally wounded, July 2nd, and died in Richmond, VA; interred in Hollywood Cemetery	Richmond, VA

NAME	REGIMENT	BIRTH	DEATH	COMMENT	BURIAL
Mott, Moses D.	Co. K, 3rd North Carolina	1839	7/2/1863	Killed in action	Unknown
Mounger, John Clark	Lt. Col., 9th Georgia	1812	7/2/1863	Laurel Grove Cemetery, Savannah, Ga., reburial list	Savannah, GA
Mowyer, Andrew J.	Marmaduke Johnson's Battery (Va.)		8/7/1863	Mortally wounded, July 3rd, and died in Nelson Co, VA	Nelson Co., VA
Moxley, James H.	Co. I, 7th Tennessee		7/16/1863	Mortally wounded and died in Jordan Springs Hopital, Winchester, VA; interred Stonewall Cemetery	Winchester, VA
Moye, Marion	Co. B, 47th North Carolina	1845	7/3/1863	Killed in action	Unknown
Moylan [Maylan], Peter A.	Cpl., Co. I, 3rd South Carolina		7/5/1863	Mortally wounded-died at unknown place in Gettysburg	Unknown
Mozo, George G.	Sgt., Co. B, 61st Georgia		7/1/1863	Killed in action	Unknown
Mull, David	Co. D, 6th North Carolina	5/20/1834	7/6/1863	Mortally wounded-died at unknown place in Gettysburg	Unknown
Mull, Jacob M.	Co. F, 11th Georgia		8/6/1863	Died as POW at David's Island, NY	Cypress Hills, NY
Mullen, Andrew Jackson	Co. H, 27th Virginia	9/13/1843	7/12/1863	Hollywood Cemetery, Richmond, Va., reburial lists	Richmond, VA
Mullen, John L.	Co. H, 27th Virginia		7/3/1863	Killed in action; brother of Andrew J. Mullen	Unknown
Mullens, James H.	Co. G, 57th North Carolina	1836	7/13/1863	Hollywood Cemetery, Richmond, Va., reburial lists	Richmond, VA
Mullin, Montgomery	Co. I, 50th Virginia		Jul. 1863	Mortally wounded-died on unknown date in Gettysburg	Unknown
Mullins, Martin V.	Co. E, 13th Georgia		7/1/1863	Killed in action	Unknown
Munday, George	Co. E, 37th North Carolina	1841	7/5/1863	Mortally wounded-died at unknown place in Gettysburg	Unknown
Munday, William M.	Lt., Co. K, 23rd North Carolina	1838	7/1/1863	Killed in action	Unknown
Mundle, William W.	Co. F, 12th South Carolina		7/2/1863	Killed in action	Unknown
Mundy, Thomas W.	Sgt., Co. E, 19th Virginia		Jul. 1863	Missing in action and presumed dead	Unknown
Munn, David D.	Sgt. Maj., 17th Georgia		7/7/1863	Mortally wounded-died at unknown place in Gettysburg	Unknown
Murden, Joshua	Co. B, 3rd Virginia	1836	7/4/1863	Mortally wounded while carrying the colors	Unknown
Murphy, Enoch E.	Co. E, 15th South Carolina	1843	9/2/1863	Died as POW at David's Island, NY	Cypress Hills, NY
Murphy, Mortimer	Co. I, 1st Texas		7/2/1863	Killed in action	Unknown
Murphy, Thomas	Co. F, 7th Louisiana	1835	Jul. 1863	Killed in action	Unknown
Murphy, Thompson A.	Co. B, 49th Virginia	1833	8/18/1863	Mortally wounded and died at Petersburg, VA	Petersburg, VA
Murrah, John W.	Lt., Co. C, 15th Georgia		7/2/1863	Killed in action	Unknown
Murray, Elisha	Co. F, 3rd Virginia	1833	7/21/1863	Mortally wounded-died at unknown place in Gettysburg	Unknown
Murray, R.A.	Co. G, 14th Virginia		7/3/1863	Killed in action	Unknown
Murray, William	Co. F, 6th Louisiana	1836	7/29/1863	Mortally wounded-died at unknown place in Gettysburg	Unknown
Murray, William Henry	Capt., Co. A, 1st Maryland Battalion	4/30/1839	7/3/1863	Killed in action; reinterred after the war at Christ Episcopal Church	West River, MD
Murray, William W.	Co. E, 13th North Carolina	1840	7/1/1863	Killed in action	Unknown

NAME	REGIMENT	BIRTH	DEATH	COMMENT	BURIAL
Murrell, Benjamin Perry	Sgt., Co. G, 8th Louisiana	1837	7/2/1863	Mortally wounded, July 2nd, and believed to have died the same day	Unknown
Muse, Ashley F.	Co. H, 26th North Carolina	1841	7/1/1863	Killed in action	Unknown
Muse, Thomas H.	Co. G, 2nd Georgia		7/2/1863	Killed in action	Unknown
Musgraves, Thomas D.	Co. B, 11th Mississippi	1844	7/3/1863	Killed in action	Unknown
Mustain, Creed G.	Co. D, 57th Virginia		7/23/1863	Mortally wounded-died at unknown place in Gettysburg	Unknown
Myers, Alfred	Co. B, 28th Virginia		10/12/1863	Mortally wounded-died at unknown place in Gettysburg	Unknown
Myers, George Matthews	Lt., Co. H, 8th South Carolina	10/2/1837	7/2/1863	Hollywood Cemetery, Richmond, Va., reburial lists	Richmond, VA
Myers, Jacob W.	Co. B, 28th Virginia	1844	1863	Hollywood Cemetery, Richmond, Va., reburial lists	Richmond, VA
Myers, Joseph S.	Co. F, 11th Virginia	1840	Jul. 1863	Missing in action and presumed dead	Unknown
Myrick, Edward L.	Co. H, 1st Tennessee		7/3/1863	Killed in action	Unknown
Nabers, Austin	Lt., Co. G, 2nd S.C. Cavalry	1843	9/5/1863	Magnolia Cemetery, Charleston, SC, reburial list	Charleston, SC
Nail, James M.	Lt., Co. C, 42nd Mississippi	1834	7/2/1863	Killed in action	Unknown
Nance, M.C.	Co. H, 38th North Carolina	1839	Jul. 1863	Missing in action and presumed dead	Unknown
Nance, Obediah	Co. A, 45th North Carolina	1841	7/3/1863	Killed in action	Unknown
Nash, James	Co. C, 1st Maryland Battalion		7/16/1863	Hollywood Cemetery, Richmond, Va., reburial lists	Richmond, VA
Nash, John Miles	Cpl., Co. D, 38th Georgia		Jul. 1863	Laurel Grove Cemetery, Savannah, Ga., reburial list	Savannah, GA
Nash, Nimrod Newton	Co. I, 13th Mississippi	2/15/1833	7/2/1863	Killed in action	Unknown
Nash, Richard James	Co. G, 9th Virginia	1836	8/16/1863	Hollywood Cemetery, Richmond, Va., reburial lists	Richmond, VA
Nash, William Franklin	Co. G, 9th Georgia	3/10/1843	8/18/1863	Laurel Grove Cemetery, Savannah, Ga., reburial list	Savannah, GA
Neal, David Wesley	Co. G, 44th Alabama	10/10/1837	7/2/1863	Killed in action	Unknown
Neal, Green Berry	Co. D, 37th North Carolina	1838	8/27/1863	Mortally wounded and died at Chester, PA	Phil. National Cem.
Neal, Joseph	Sgt., Co. H, 53rd North Carolina	1825	7/7/1863	Mortally wounded-died at unknown place in Gettysburg	Unknown
Neal, William F.	Co. K, 17th Mississippi	1838	Jul. 1863	Killed in action on July 1st or 2nd	Unknown
Nelms, William C.D.	Co. C, 21st Georgia		7/19/1863	Mortally wounded, July 2nd, and died at Hagerstown, MD	Hagerstown, MD
Nelms, William F.	Co. B, 5th Texas	1846	7/9/1863	Hollywood Cemetery, Richmond, Va., reburial lists	Richmond, VA
Nelson, John	Co. K, 28th North Carolina	1831	7/3/1863	Killed in action	Unknown
Nelson, John	Co. K, 15th Alabama	1838	7/2/1863	Killed in action	Unknown
Nelson, John H.	Sgt., Co. D, 52nd North Carolina	1844	7/5/1863	Mortally wounded-died at unknown place in Gettysburg	Unknown
Nelson, John Samuel	Co. H, 22nd North Carolina	1834	7/1/1863	Killed in action	Unknown
Nettles, F.L.	Sgt., Co. E, 8th South Carolina	1842	8/18/1863	Magnolia Cemetery, Charleston, SC, reburial list	Charleston, SC
Neuffer, Charles E.	Co. A, 2nd South Carolina		7/3/1863	Killed in action	Unknown

NAME	REGIMENT	BIRTH	DEATH	COMMENT	BURIAL
Neverson, Cornelius	Co. A, 47th Alabama		8/25/1863	Mortally wounded and died at Camp Letterman	Unknown
New, James B.	Co. I, 55th Virginia		7/3/1863	Killed in action per the Richmond Enquirer, July 16, 1863	Unknown
Newell, Joseph	Co. D, 32nd North Carolina	1841	7/1/1863	Killed in action	Unknown
Newlon, James M.	Cpl., Co. B, 8th Virginia		7/31/1863	Mortally wounded-died at unknown place in Gettysburg	Unknown
Newman, William Robert	Co. D, 8th Virginia	4/15/1843	7/3/1863	Killed in action	Unknown
Newson, John S.	Co. B, 2nd Georgia Battalion		7/2/1863	Killed in action	Unknown
Newton, Ezra	Co. A, 50th Georgia		7/2/1863	Laurel Grove Cemetery, Savannah, Ga., reburial list	Savannah, GA
Newton, John	Sgt., Hart's Battery (S.C)		7/2/1863	Mortally wounded, July 1st, and died the next day	Unknown
Nichols, Anderson	Co. C, 26th North Carolina	1840	7/3/1863	Killed in action	Unknown
Nichols, Charles	Co. C, 57th Virginia	1840	9/11/1863	Hollywood Cemetery, Richmond, Va., reburial lists	Richmond, VA
Nichols, James Riley	Co. H, 13th Mississippi	1836	7/2/1836	Killed in action	Unknown
Nichols, John B.	Sgt., Co. H, 1st Texas	1833	7/2/1863	Killed in action	Unknown
Nichols, John G.	Co. I, 28th Virginia		7/18/1863	Mortally wounded-died at unknown place in Gettysburg	Unknown
Nichols, John W.	Cpl., Co. I, Cobb's Legion Cavalry	1838	Jul. 1863	Missing in action and presumed dead	Unknown
Nichols, Thomas	Co. I, 8th Georgia		7/3/1863	Killed in action	Unknown
Nichols, Thomas H.B.	Co. H, 16th Georgia		7/6/1863	Laurel Grove Cemetery, Savannah, Ga., reburial list	Savannah, GA
Nichols, William L.	Co. C, 1st Maryland Battalion	1844	7/31/1863	Mortally wounded, July 2nd, and died at Camp Letterman; interred in Soldier's Cemetery	Gettysburg, PA
Nicholson, Anderson	Co. C, 26th North Carolina	1842	7/1/1863	Killed in action	Unknown
Nicholson, J.T.S.	Co. H, 14th Tennessee	1823	7/3/1863	Killed in action	Unknown
Nicholson, Richard H.	Co. F, 14th Virginia	1840	7/3/1863	Killed in action	Unknown
Nicholson, W.H.	Co. K, 32nd North Carolina		Jul. 1863	Killed in action	Unknown
Nicholson, William Hannah	Co. G, 50th Virginia		Jul. 1863	Killed in action on July 1st or 2nd	Unknown
Nickols, James Riley	Co. H, 13th Mississippi	1836	7/2/1863	Killed in action	Unknown
Nicolai, Herman	Co. A, 1st Maryland Battalion		Jul. 1863	Killed in action, July 1-3	Unknown
Nicolson, William Hannah	Co. G, 50th Virginia		7/3/1863	Killed in action	Unknown
Niemeyer, John Chandler	Lt., Co. I, 9th Virginia	10/5/1842	7/3/1863	Killed in action	Unknown
Nixon, Archibald	Co. G, 52nd North Carolina	1823	7/19/1863	Hollywood Cemetery, Richmond, Va., reburial lists	Richmond, VA
Nixon, George	Co. G, 52nd North Carolina	1828	7/20/1863	Hollywood Cemetery, Richmond, Va., reburial lists	Richmond, VA
Nixon, William Green	Lt., Co. G, 18th North Carolina	1841	Jul. 1863	Missing in action and presumed dead	Unknown
Noble, James Samuel	Co. K, 3rd Arkansas	10/18/1847	7/7/1863	Hollywood Cemetery, Richmond, Va., reburial lists	Richmond, VA
Nolan, Michael	Lt. Col., 1st Louisiana	1821	7/3/1863	Killed in action	Unknown
Noles, Lawrence	Co. E, 45th North Carolina		7/1/1863	Killed in action	Unknown
Nolly, William B.	Co. F, 4th North Carolina	1843	7/1/1863	Killed in action	Unknown

NAME	REGIMENT	BIRTH	DEATH	COMMENT	BURIAL
Norman, Anthony	Co. D, 13th North Carolina	1842	7/1/1863	Killed in action	Unknown
Norman, William H.	Co. B, 38th North Carolina	1840	7/1/1863	Killed in action	Unknown
Norman, William Y.	Co. G, 3rd Alabama		7/21/1863	Mortally wounded and died at Harrisburg, PA; interred Soldiers' Lot, City Cemetery	Harrisburg, PA
Normant, A.A.	Co. B, 53rd North Carolina		7/1/1863	Killed in action	Unknown
Norred, Preston Byrd	Lt., Co. I, 44th Alabama	1827	7/2/1863	Killed in action	Unknown
Norris, Hardy R.	Co. B, 15th Alabama	1840	8/27/1863	Hollywood Cemetery, Richmond, Va., reburial lists	Richmond, VA
Norris, Moses T.	Sgt., Co. B, 4th Texas		7/2/1863	Hollywood Cemetery, Richmond, Va., reburial lists	Richmond, VA
Norris, Samuel	Co. G, 17th Mississippi	1843	7/2/1863	Killed in action	Unknown
Norvell, Joseph B.	Co. E, 19th Virginia		Jul. 1863	Missing in action and presumed dead	Unknown
Norwood, Fletcher	Co. E, 11th Mississippi	1844	7/3/1863	Killed in action	Unknown
Norwood, Nathaniel	Co. G, 26th North Carolina	1842	7/1/1863	Killed in action	Unknown
Norwood, William J.	Co. D, 47th North Carolina	1839	Jul. 1863	Killed in action, July 1-3	Unknown
Nowell, Ransom Green	Co. K, 14th North Carolina	1842	7/1/1863	Oakwood Cemetery, Raleigh, NC, reburial list	Raleigh, NC
Nuchols, James A.	Co. B, 38th Virginia	1841	9/2/1863	Hollywood Cemetery, Richmond, Va., reburial lists	Richmond, VA
Nuckles, William N.	Lt., Co. F, 1st Tennessee	1832	7/1/1863	Killed in action	Unknown
Nuckolds, David R.	Co. B, 38th Virginia	1843	9/17/1863	Hollywood Cemetery, Richmond, Va., reburial lists	Richmond, VA
Nuckols, E.G.	Co. H, 1st Virginia		7/3/1863	Killed in action	Unknown
Null, Erastus J.	Sgt., Co. H, 53rd North Carolina	1842	7/23/1863	Mortally wounded-died at unknown place in Gettysburg	Unknown
Nunn, Calton	Co. K, 13th North Carolina	1839	7/24/1863	Mortally wounded and died at Chester, PA	Phil. National Cem.
Nunn, William David	Capt., Co. B, 11th Mississippi	1842	7/13/1863	Mortally wounded-died at unknown place in Gettysburg	Unknown
Nunn, William E.	Co. E, 3rd Georgia		7/2/1863	Killed in action	Unknown
Nunnally, Edward J.	Co. H, 12th Virginia		7/2/1863	Killed in action	Unknown
Nunnally, Matthew Talbot	Capt., Co. H, 11th Georgia	3/18/1839	7/2/1863	Killed in action; reinterred at Rest Haven Cemetery	Monroe, GA
Nunnally, Virgil T.	Capt., Co. G, 13th Georgia		7/1/1863	Killed in action	Unknown
Nunnally, William Mills	Lt., Co. K, 13th North Carolina	1/3/1835	7/1/1863	Killed in action	Unknown
Nutting, George W.	Co. D, 5th Alabama		7/1/1863	Hollywood Cemetery, Richmond, Va., reburial lists	Richmond, VA
Oakes, James Allen	Co. B, 38th Virginia	1822	7/15/1863	Mortally wounded-died at unknown place in Gettysburg	Unknown
Oakes, Thomas Clement	Sgt., Co. B. 38th Virginia	7/23/1832	8/2/1863	Hollywood Cemetery, Richmond, Va., reburial lists	Richmond, VA
Oakley, Aaron	Co. A, 45th North Carolina		7/3/1863	Killed in action	Unknown
Oakley, William R.	Co. D, 13th North Carolina	1837	7/1/1863	Killed in action	Unknown
Oakman, Raymond H.	Co. D, 2nd Georgia	7/29/1839	Jul. 1863	Missing in action and presumed dead	Unknown

NAME	REGIMENT	BIRTH	DEATH	COMMENT	BURIAL
Oates, John Alvin	Lt., Co. G, 15th Alabama	12/24/1835	7/23/1863	Hollywood Cemetery, Richmond, Va., reburial lists	Richmond, VA
O'Banion, John	Co. D, 48th Georgia	11/1/1830	7/2/1863	Killed in action	Unknown
O'Brien, Patrick John	Co. C, 10th Louisiana	1837	7/2/1863	Killed in action on Culp's Hill	Unknown
O'Brien, William	Co. C, 11th Mississippi		7/3/1863	Killed in action	Unknown
O'Bryant, John D.	Co. K, 55th North Carolina		7/3/1863	Killed in action	Unknown
O'Byrn, John T.	Co. C, 1st Maryland Battalion		Jul. 1863	Killed in action, July 1-3	Unknown
Odom, Elkanah	Co. A, 5th Florida		7/25/1863	Mortally wounded-died at unknown place in Gettysburg	Unknown
Odum, J.C.	Co. G, 18th Georgia		7/12/1863	Laurel Grove Cemetery, Savannah, Ga., reburial list	Savannah, GA
Ogden, Dewees	1st Co., Richmond Howitzers	8/5/1839	7/3/1863	Killed in action per the Richmond Sentinel, July 28, 1863	Unknown
Ogilvie, James Polk	Co. F, 17th Mississippi	1/6/1841	Jul. 1863	Killed in action on July 1st or 2nd ; brother of William B. Ogilvie	Unknown
Ogilvie, William Brumfield	Co. F, 17th Mississippi	8/20/1838	7/2/1863	Killed in action	Unknown
Oglesby Edward	Co. C, 4th Alabama	1826	Jul. 1863	Mortally wounded-died at unknown place in Gettysburg	Unknown
Oglesby, John	Lt., Co. H, 38th Georgia	8/10/1831	7/2/1863	Killed in action	Unknown
Oldner, Philip	Chesapeake Artillery (Md.)		7/2/1863	Hollywood Cemetery, Richmond, Va., reburial lists	Richmond, VA
Oliver, Alvin	Co. C, 5th Florida		7/2/1863	Killed in action	Unknown
Oliver, Andrew G.	Co. C, 18th Georgia		7/2/1863	Laurel Grove Cemetery, Savannah, Ga., reburial list	Savannah, GA
Oliver, Caleb R.	Co. L, 3rd Alabama		8/16/1863	Mortally wounded-died at unknown place in Gettysburg	Unknown
Oliver, John C.	Sgt., Co. F, 11th Georgia		Jul. 1863	Hollywood Cemetery, Richmond, Va., reburial lists	Richmond, VA
Oliver, John J.	Co. F, 38th Virginia		7/3/1863	Killed in action	Unknown
Oliver, Thomas	Co. D, 26th North Carolina	1842	Jul. 1863	Killed in action	Unknown
O'Mearra, William	Co. F, 5th Alabama		7/1/1863	Hollywood Cemetery, Richmond, Va., reburial lists	Richmond, VA
O'Neal, James	Co. H, 21st North Carolina	1836	9/7/1863	Mortally wounded and died at Chester, PA	Phil. National Cem.
O'Neill, John	Co. B, 5th Texas		7/2/1863	Killed in action	Unknown
Orander, Lewis R.	Co. I, 2nd South Carolina		7/27/1863	Mortally wounded-died at unknown place in Gettysburg	Unknown
Osborn, John Pinckney	Lt., Co. D, 24th Georgia	12/29/1837	7/2/1863	Killed in action; reinterred at Osborn Cemetery, Towns Co., GA	Towns Co., GA
Osborn, S.W.	Sgt., Co. A, 14th Louisiana		7/25/1863	Mortally wounded and died at Baltimore, MD-buried there	Baltimore, MD
Osborn, William D.	Co. C, 49th Georgia		7/10/1863	Mortally wounded-died at unknown place in Gettysburg	Unknown
Osborne, William A.	Lt., Co. G, 11th Mississippi	1838	7/3/1863	Killed in action	Unknown
Oswalt, David Wilson	Co. C, 15th South Carolina	1830	7/4/1863	Mortally wounded, July 2nd, and died two days later	Unknown
Oswalt, Simeon O.	Co. C, 15th South Carolina		7/31/1863	Died as POW at David's Island, NY	Cypress Hills, NY

NAME	REGIMENT	BIRTH	DEATH	COMMENT	BURIAL
Otey, John M.	Co. B, 57th Virginia		Jul. 1863	Died of wounds received July 3rd	Unknown
Otrick, Henry C.	Co. H, 55th North Carolina		7/1/1863	Killed in action	Unknown
Oursler, Robert A.	Sgt., Co. F, 17th Mississippi	1839	7/2/1863	Killed in action; given name may be Richard	Unknown
Oursler, William R.	Lt., Co. F, 17th Mississippi	1841	Jul. 1863	Hollywood Cemetery, Richmond, Va., reburial lists	Richmond, VA
Ousby, William Clark	Capt., Co. F, 43rd North Carolina	1833	7/3/1863	Killed in action	Unknown
Outlaw, John J.	Co. A, 43rd North Carolina	1844	7/1/1863	Killed in action	Unknown
Outlaw, W.G.	Co. F, 48th Georgia		7/2/1863	Killed in action	Unknown
Outlaw, William L.	Co. F, 48th Georgia		7/2/1863	Killed in action	Unknown
Ouzts, George Martin	Co. K, 14th South Carolina	1842	7/15/1863	Mortally wounded-died at unknown place in Gettysburg	Unknown
Ouzts, James	Co. K, 14th South Carolina	1845	7/2/1863	Killed in action	Unknown
Overbey, Patrick Henry	Co. H, 14th Virginia	1833	7/3/1863	Killed in action	Unknown
Overby, Henry	Co. G, 18th Virginia	1840	7/3/1863	Killed in action	Unknown
Overcash, Aaron J.	Co. B, 57th North Carolina	1831	7/2/1863	Killed in action	Unknown
Overcash, Samuel C.	Co. I, 7th North Carolina	1843	7/3/1863	Killed in action	Unknown
Overstreet, Alex	Co. G, 11th Virginia	10/7/1820	7/3/1863	Killed in action	Unknown
Overstreet, Jesse W.	Cpl., Co. B, 14th Virginia		7/29/1863	Mortally wounded and died at Winchester, VA; interred Stonewall Cemetery	Winchester, VA
Overstreet, Jesse Ward	Co. G, 28th Virginia		7/23/1863	Mortally wounded and died at Chester, PA	Phil. National Cem.
Owen, Beverly B.	Co. A, 38th Virginia		7/3/1863	Killed in action	Unknown
Owen, Isaac Wilson	Co. H, 38th Virginia	1807	7/3/1863	Killed in action	Unknown
Owen, James P.	Co. D, 17th Mississippi	1839	7/7/1863	Hollywood Cemetery, Richmond, Va., reburial lists	Richmond, VA
Owen, Jesse	Co. B, 3rd Arkansas	1844	Jul. 1863	Missing in action and presumed dead	Unknown
Owen, Pleasant D.	Sgt., Co. I, 18th Virginia	1843	Jul. 1863	Missing in action and presumed dead	Unknown
Owens, Albert Preston	Cpl., Co. E, 1st South Carolina	1/17/1841	8/6/1863	Died as POW at David's Island, NY	Cypress Hills, NY
Owens, Dempsey	Co. G, 3rd North Carolina	1837	7/2/1863	Killed in action	Unknown
Owens, Henry W.	Reilly's Battery (NC)	1843	7/2/1863	Killed in action	Unknown
Owens, Jesse	Co. C, 3rd Arkansas	1842	7/2/1863	Killed in action	Unknown
Owens, John	Co. I, 20th Georgia		7/2/1863	Killed in action	Unknown
Owens, John Crowder	Maj., 9th Virginia	3/19/1830	7/4/1863	Mortally wounded; reinterred in Cedar Grove Cemetery after the war	Portsmouth, VA
Owens, Thomas C.	Co. G, 9th Virginia	5/8/1837	7/12/1863	Mortally wounded; reinterred in Cedar Grove Cemetery after the war	Portsmouth, VA
Owens, Thomas E.	Co. F, 8th Virginia		Jul. 1863	Missing in action and presumed dead	Unknown
Owens, Thomas Rutledge	Sgt., Co. F, 14th South Carolina	1843	7/1/1863	Killed in action	Unknown
Owings, J.W.	Co. E, 14th South Carolina		7/2/1863	Killed in action	Unknown
Owings, Joshua	Cpl., Co. D, 1st Maryland Battalion	1834	7/19/1863	Mortally wounded-died at unknown place in Gettysburg	Unknown
Pace, Archibald B.	Co. C, 14th Virginia		7/3/1863	Killed in action	Unknown
Padget, James L.	Co. A, 43rd North Carolina	1846	7/1/1863	Killed in action	Unknown

NAME	REGIMENT	BIRTH	DEATH	COMMENT	BURIAL
Padgett, Ellis	Co. E, 8th Florida	1840	7/30/1863	Hollywood Cemetery, Richmond, Va., reburial lists	Richmond, VA
Padgett, Wesley P.	Co. B, 14th South Carolina	1845	7/31/1863	Killed in action	Unknown
Padley, Merritt P.	Co. E, 6th North Carolina		8/18/1863	Oakwood Cemetery, Raleigh, NC, reburial list	Raleigh, NC
Page, Aaron	Cpl., Co. F, 11th Georgia	1840	7/2/1863	Killed in action	Unknown
Page, Everet C.	Co. E, 26th North Carolina	1838	7/28/1863	Hollywood Cemetery, Richmond, Va., reburial lists	Richmond, VA
Page, John C.	Co. A, 52nd North Carolina	1842	7/3/1863	Missing in action and presumed dead	Unknown
Page, Solomon S.	Cpl., Co. D, 59th Georgia		8/7/1863	Mortally wounded and died at Harrisburg, PA; Interred in Soldiers' Lot at City Cemetery	Harrisburg, PA
Paggett, Wiley	Co. H, 47th North Carolina	1811	Jul. 1863	Missing in action and presumed dead	Unknown
Paine, John W.	Co. H, 1st Virginia		7/3/1863	Killed in action	Unknown
Painter, George	Co. K, 16th North Carolina	1842	12/5/1863	Mortally wounded-died at unknown place in Gettysburg	Unknown
Painter, James Barnabas	Cpl., Co. K, 28th Virginia	1844	7/3/1863	Killed in action per the Richmond Sentinel, July 30, 1863	Unknown
Palmer, John R.	Lt., Co. I, 22nd North Carolina	10/21/1837	7/1/1863	Killed in action; remains returned home	Randolph Co., NC
Palmer, Samuel D.	Sgt., Co. A, 3rd Georgia		Jul. 1863	Died of wounds received July 2nd on unknown date	Unknown
Palmer, William T.	King William Artillery (Va.)		7/1/1863	Hollywood Cemetery, Richmond, Va., reburial lists	Richmond, VA
Palmer, William Thomas	Co. E, 42nd Mississippi	6/2/1837	7/3/1863	Killed in action	Unknown
Palmore, Charles	Co. C, 9th Louisiana	1839	7/2/1863	Killed in action	Unknown
Pardue, Franklin C.	Sgt., Co. D, 33rd North Carolina	1836	7/3/1863	Killed in action	Unknown
Parham, Frederick L.	Co. C, 13th South Carolina	1822	7/3/1863	Killed in action	Unknown
Parish, John	Co. C, 43rd North Carolina	1828	7/1/1863	Killed in action	Unknown
Parish, Samuel	Co. E, 28th Virginia		7/3/1863	Killed in action	Unknown
Parish, Stephen	Co. C, 21st North Carolina	1827	Jul. 1863	Missing in action and presumed dead	Unknown
Park, William A.	Co. K, 13th Mississippi	1841	8/18/1863	Hollywood Cemetery, Richmond, Va., reburial lists	Richmond, VA
Parker, Angus M.	Lt., Co. B, 11th Georgia		7/21/1863	Hollywood Cemetery, Richmond, Va., reburial lists	Richmond, VA
Parker, Cader Atkins, Jr.	Sgt., Co. B, 15th Alabama	2/14/1841	7/21/1863	Mortally wounded-died at unknown place in Gettysburg	Unknown
Parker, Calihan	Co. I, 3rd Arkansas		7/30/1863	Mortally wounded and died at Chester, PA	Phil. National Cem.
Parker, Dorson	Cpl., Co. H, 5th North Carolina	1839	7/23/1863	Mortally wounded-died at unknown place in Gettysburg	Unknown
Parker, George W.	Co. F, 1st South Carolina		7/10/1863	Died of wounds received July 3rd	Unknown
Parker, James O.	Co. H, 17th Mississippi	1836	7/2/1863	Killed in action	Unknown
Parker, John	Co. B, 5th North Carolina	1841	7/1/1863	Hollywood Cemetery, Richmond, Va., reburial lists	Richmond, VA
Parker, John C.	Co. E, 28th North Carolina	1838	7/3/1863	Missing in action and presumed dead	Unknown

NAME	REGIMENT	BIRTH	DEATH	COMMENT	BURIAL
Parker, Peter W.	Co. I, 7th North Carolina	1829	Jul. 1863	Mortally wounded-died on unknown date in Gettysburg	Unknown
Parker, Thaddeus Marion	Chesapeake Artillery (Md.)	Feb. 1838	7/2/1863	Killed in action; reinterred in Baltimore, MD	Baltimore, MD
Parker, William George	Sgt., Co. C, 11th North Carolina	6/1/1819	7/20/1863	Mortally wounded, July 1st, and died at Winchester, VA	Winchester, VA
Parker, William J.	Sgt., Co. A, 17th Mississippi	1837	7/29/1863	Hollywood Cemetery, Richmond, Va., reburial lists	Richmond, VA
Parkerson, Mills D.	Co. I, 3rd Virginia	1836	7/3/1863	Killed in action	Unknown
Parkman, Jesse	Co. K, 14th South Carolina	1841	7/1/1863	Killed in action	Unknown
Parks, Andrew P.	Co. C, 17th Mississippi	1843	7/8/1863	Hollywood Cemetery, Richmond, Va., reburial lists	Richmond, VA
Parks, Charles Samuel	Cpl., Co. K, 11th Virginia	6/3/1842	Jul. 1863	Missing in action and presumed dead	Unknown
Parks, Henry Harrison	Cpl., Co. B, 11th North Carolina		7/3/1863	Missing in action and presumed dead	Unknown
Parks, Hiram	Co. H, 17th Georgia		7/8/1863	Hollywood Cemetery, Richmond, Va., reburial lists	Richmond, VA
Parks, John K.	Sgt., Co. G, 15th Georgia		7/5/1863	Died of wounds received July 3rd	Unknown
Parks, Virgil A.S.	Capt., Co. D, 17th Georgia		7/2/1863	Killed in action	Unknown
Parr, William P.	Lt., Co. H, 15th South Carolina	11/4/1826	7/2/1863	Killed in action	Unknown
Parrish, James Madison	Sgt., Co. C, 48th Alabama		7/26/1863	Mortally wounded-died at unknown place in Gettysburg	Unknown
Parrish, John	Co. C, 43rd North Carolina	1837	7/1/1863	Killed in action	Unknown
Parrish, Samuel	Co. E, 57th Virginia		7/17/1863	Hollywood Cemetery, Richmond, Va., reburial lists	Richmond, VA
Parrish, Uriah R.	Co. K, 2nd North Carolina Cav.	1838	8/3/1863	Oakwood Cemetery, Raleigh, NC, reburial list	Raleigh, NC
Parrott, George W.	Sgt., Co. D, 19th Virginia		7/24/1863	Mortally wounded and died at Gordonsville, VA	Gordonsville, VA
Parrott, James	Co. K, 14th Virginia	1836	7/3/1863	Killed in action	Unknown
Parsel, Isaiah	Cpl., Co. G, 57th Virginia		Jul. 1863	Killed in action, July 1-3	Unknown
Partin, Daniel Wilson	Co. D, 14th Virginia	6/6/1840	7/23/1863	Hollywood Cemetery, Richmond, Va., reburial lists	Richmond, VA
Partin, William M.	Co. H, 11th Georgia		7/2/1863	Killed in action	Unknown
Partridge, H.H.	Co. G, 8th Alabama		Jul. 1863	Missing in action and presumed dead	Unknown
Pate, Thomas Benton	Co. A, 9th Louisiana	1843	7/28/1863	Hollywood Cemetery, Richmond, Va., reburial lists	Richmond, VA
Patenco. John A.	Co. F, 10th Louisiana		7/14/1863	Mortally wounded-died at unknown place in Gettysburg	Unknown
Patrick, James M.	Co. A, 2nd Mississippi	1839	7/3/1863	Hollywood Cemetery, Richmond, Va., reburial lists	Richmond, VA
Patten, Lewis M.	Co. K, 47th North Carolina	1843	Jul. 1863	Killed in action	Unknown
Patterson, Benjamin F.	Co. C, 47th Alabama		8/10/1863	Mortally wounded, July 2nd, and died at Staunton, VA	Staunton, VA
Patterson, William B.	Lt., Co. E, 31st Georgia	1832	7/1/1863	Laurel Grove Cemetery, Savannah, Ga., reburial list	Savannah, GA
Patterson, William D.	Co. E, 52nd North Carolina		10/18/1863	Mortally wounded, July 3rd, and died in Winder Hospital, Richmond, VA	Richmond, VA

NAME	REGIMENT	BIRTH	DEATH	COMMENT	BURIAL
Patterson, William M.	Co. B, 8th Georgia	1845	7/2/1863	Laurel Grove Cemetery, Savannah, Ga., reburial list	Savannah, GA
Patteson, George T.	Co. D, 48th Mississippi		7/2/1863	Killed in action per the Richmond Enquirer, July 16, 1863	Unknown
Patteson, John M.	Co. D, 19th Virginia		7/3/1863	Killed in action	Unknown
Patton, Dudley F.	Co. C, 49th Virginia		7/3/1863	Killed in action	Unknown
Patton, Henry	Sgt. Maj., 44th Virginia		Jul. 1863	Missing in action and presumed dead	Unknown
Patton, Waller Tazewell	Col., 7th Virginia	7/15/1835	7/21/1863	Mortally wounded and died at Winchester, VA; interred Stonewall Cemetery	Winchester, VA
Patty, James H.	Co. B, 7th Tennessee	1838	7/3/1863	Killed in action; surname may be Patey or Paty	Unknown
Paulett, Andrew J.	Co. H, 18th Virginia	1839	7/3/1863	Killed in action per the Richmond Sentinel, July 29,1863	Unknown
Paull, William Cornelius	Co. D, 1st North Carolina	1843	7/11/1863	Hollywood Cemetery, Richmond, Va., reburial lists	Richmond, VA
Payne, Benjamin	Co. C, 1st Maryland Battalion		Jul. 1863	Killed in action, July 1-3	Unknown
Payne, Fielding F.	Lt., Co. F, 8th Virginia	1839	7/13/1863	Hollywood Cemetery, Richmond, Va., reburial lists	Richmond, VA
Payne, John F.	Co. A, 18th Virginia		7/3/1863	Hollywood Cemetery, Richmond, Va., reburial lists	Richmond, VA
Payne, Joseph Thomas	Co. C, 38th Virginia	7/24/1828	7/22/1863	Mortally wounded and died at US II Corps Hospital, Gettysburg	Unknown
Payne, Thomas M.	Sgt., Co. C, 3rd Arkansas		7/2/1863	Killed in action	Unknown
Paysinger, Henry M.	Sgt., Co. C, 3rd South Carolina	1840	9/5/1863	Magnolia Cemetery, Charleston, SC, reburial list	Charleston, SC
Peach, William	Co. G, 2nd South Carolina		7/2/1863	Killed in action	Unknown
Peacock, E.L.	Co. A, 1st South Carolina		7/1/1863	Killed in action	Unknown
Pearce, Thomas	Co. D, 22nd Georgia		7/2/1863	Killed in action	Unknown
Pearson, Richard	Co. G, 47th North Carolina		7/3/1863	Killed in action	Unknown
Pearson, Robert Raiford	Co. C, 2nd South Carolina	1843	7/28/1863	Magnolia Cemetery, Charleston, SC, reburial list	Charleston, SC
Pearson, William	Co. B, 55th North Carolina		7/1/1863	Killed in action	Unknown
Pease, John Q.	Co. D, 3rd South Carolina Battalion	1843	7/25/1863	Died as POW at David's Island, NY	Cypress Hills, NY
Peck, Benjamin Wallace	Sgt., Co. G, 24th Virginia		7/3/1863	Killed in action	Unknown
Peck, Julius	Co. F, 5th North Carolina	1/16/1834	7/6/1863	Mortally wounded-died at unknown place in Gettysburg	Unknown
Pedigo, Elisha F.	Co. H, 24th Virginia	1834	7/3/1863	Killed in action	Unknown
Peed, John F.	Co. I, 3rd Georgia		7/2/1863	Killed in action	Unknown
Peel, Eli H.	Sgt., Co. C, 11th Mississippi	1840	7/3/1863	Killed in action	Unknown
Peele, Thomas H.	Co. C, 11th North Carolina	1842	Jul. 1863	Killed in action	Unknown
Pegram, Joseph E.	Co. K, 52nd North Carolina	1839	8/1/1863	Died as POW at David's Island, NY	Cypress Hills, NY
Pelt, James A.	Co. K, 20th North Carolina	1836	7/22/1863	Mortally wounded-died at unknown place in Gettysburg	Unknown
Pender, William Dorsey	Major General	1834	7/18/1863	Mortally wounded and died at Staunton, VA; body removed to Tarboro, NC	Tarboro, NC

NAME	REGIMENT	BIRTH	DEATH	COMMENT	BURIAL
Pendergrass, William	Co. G, 11th North Carolina	1836	7/1/1863	Killed in action	Unknown
Pendleton, Hugh Thomas	2nd Co., Richmond Howitzers	1841	7/3/1863	Killed in action; reinterred in Hollywood Cemetery, Nov. 5, 1866	Richmond, VA
Pendleton, Joseph R.	Co. F, 11th Mississippi	1833	7/3/1863	Killed in action	Unknown
Pendley, Merrit B.	Sgt., Co. E, 6th North Carolina	1830	9/18/1863	Oakwood Cemetery, Raleigh, NC, reburial list	Raleigh, NC
Penn, H.C.	Co. C, 3rd Alabama		7/28/1863	Mortally wounded-died at unknown place in Gettysburg	Unknown
Pennington, John	Co. B, 8th Virginia		7/3/1863	Killed in action	Unknown
Pennington, Levi	Co. B, 8th Virginia		7/3/1863	Killed in action	Unknown
Penny, Henry Frank	Co. F, 12th Georgia		7/23/1863	Laurel Grove Cemetery, Savannah, Ga., reburial list	Savannah, GA
Penry, William H.	Co. F, 13th North Carolina	1836	7/1/1863	Killed in action	Unknown
Perkins, Edward W.	Co. C, 20th Georgia		7/5/1863	Mortally wounded, July 3rd, and died two days later	Unknown
Perrin, John J.	Lt., Co. A, 14th Virginia	1838	7/3/1863	Killed in action	Unknown
Perry, Benjamin	Co. D, 28th North Carolina	1843	8/30/1863	Mortally wounded, July 3rd, and died at Petersburg, VA	Petersburg, VA
Perry, Chesley	Co. B, 47th North Carolina	1835	7/3/1863	Killed in action	Unknown
Perry, Henry H.	Co. E, 26th North Carolina	1840	7/1/1863	Killed in action	Unknown
Perry, Hezekiah D.	Cpl., Co. I, 22nd North Carolina	1839	7/3/1863	Killed in action	Unknown
Perry, James	Co. I, 52nd North Carolina	1841	7/3/1863	Mortally wounded, July 3rd, and died the same day	Unknown
Perry, Joseph E.	Co. G, 32nd North Carolina	1845	8/27/1863	Oakwood Cemetery, Raleigh, NC, reburial list	Raleigh, NC
Perryman, Harvey	Co. K, 14th Alabama	1800	7/12/1863	Hollywood Cemetery, Richmond, Va., reburial lists	Richmond, VA
Person, Jesse H.H.	Lt., Co. E, 1st NC Cavalry	1842	7/3/1863	Killed in action near Hunterstown, PA	Hunterstown, PA
Persons, William M.	Co. H, 26th North Carolina		8/2/1863	Died of wounds received July 1st	Unknown
Peters, Reason L.	Co. A, 42nd Mississippi	1844	7/14/1863	Mortally wounded-died at unknown place in Gettysburg	Unknown
Peters, Samuel W.	Co. A, 50th Virginia	1844	7/17/1863	Hollywood Cemetery, Richmond, Va., reburial lists	Richmond, VA
Peters, William Edward	Co. C, 57th Virginia	10/2/1835	7/4/1863	Mortally wounded, July 3rd, and died the next day	Unknown
Petrie, George H.	Co. C, 33rd North Carolina	1/10/1824	7/26/1863	Mortally wounded-died at unknown place in Gettysburg	Unknown
Petrovich, George	Cpl., Co. D, 10th Louisiana	1833	7/2/1863	Killed in action	Unknown
Pettigrew, John J.	Co. F, 6th North Carolina	1842	7/2/1863	Killed in action	Unknown
Petty, Robert J.	Co. H, 14th Virginia		7/3/1863	Killed in action	Unknown
Phelps, James H.	Sgt. Maj., 28th Virginia	1825	7/3/1863	Killed in action per the Richmond Sentinel, August 12, 1863	Unknown
Phillippa, William A.	Co. A, 53rd North Carolina	1841	7/3/1863	Killed in action	Unknown
Phillips, Benjamin H.	Co. E, 8th Alabama		Jul. 1863	Missing in action and presumed dead	Unknown
Phillips, Claudius Crawley	Capt., Co. F, 3rd Virginia	1835	7/3/1863	Killed in action	Unknown
Phillips, John	Co. I, 32nd North Carolina	1843	7/3/1863	Killed in action	Unknown

NAME	REGIMENT	BIRTH	DEATH	COMMENT	BURIAL
Phillips, John Horace	Cpl., Co. E, 26th North Carolina	1833	Jul. 1863	Killed in action, July 1-3	Unknown
Phillips, John N.	Co. B, 11th Virginia		Jul. 1863	Missing in action and presumed dead	Unknown
Phillips, Joseph	Co. A, 53rd Georgia		7/2/1863	Killed in action	Unknown
Phillips, Joseph	Co. F, 26th North Carolina		7/1/1863	Killed in action; twin brother of W.E. Phillips	Unknown
Phillips, Levi J.	Co. K, 7th North Carolina	1838	Jul. 1863	Missing in action and presumed dead	Unknown
Phillips, Thomas H.	Co. E, 26th North Carolina	1842	7/1/1863	Killed in action	Unknown
Phillips, W.E.	Co. F, 26th North Carolina		7/1/1863	Killed in action; twin brother of Joseph Phillips	Unknown
Phillips, William	Co. E, 28th North Carolina	1842	7/3/1863	Missing in action and presumed dead	Unknown
Phlegar, George Washington	Sgt., Co. G, 4th Virginia	3/19/1838	7/3/1863	Mortally wounded, July 3rd, and died the same day	Unknown
Pickett, Jacob W.	Co. G, 13th Alabama	9/20/1831	7/28/1863	Hollywood Cemetery, Richmond, Va., reburial lists	Richmond, VA
Pickett, Jeptha S.	Co. E, 3rd Arkansas	1843	7/2/1863	Killed in action	Unknown
Pickett, John M.	Co. G, 31st Georgia	1836	7/2/1863	Killed in action	Unknown
Pickett, William	Co. F, 1st North Carolina	7/22/1832	7/2/1863	Killed in action	Unknown
Pierce, D.H.	Co. K, 14th Tennessee	1836	7/3/1863	Killed in action	Unknown
Pierce, James H.	Co. C, 11th North Carolina	1840	7/1/1863	Killed in action	Unknown
Pierce, Richard R.	Co. F, 11th Mississippi	1840	7/3/1863	Killed in action	Unknown
Pigg, Amos	Co. B, 26th North Carolina		Jul. 1863	Killed in action, July 1-3	Unknown
Pike, John	Co. G, 26th North Carolina	2/27/1833	7/15/1863	Mortally wounded and reinterred in Rocky River Friends Cemetery after the war	Chatham Co., NC
Pillow, Daniel A.	Co. C, 11th Virginia	1838	7/3/1863	Killed in action	Unknown
Pindell, Philip [Smith]	Co. A, 1st Maryland Battalion	6/18/1839	8/2/1863	Mortally wounded and died at Chester, PA; reinterred in Pindell Cemetery	Lothian, MD
Pinson, Allen	Co. G, 14th Virginia	1838	7/4/1863	Mortally wounded, July 3rd, and died the next day	Unknown
Pinson, Harrison H.	Co. C, 14th South Carolina	11/7/1835	7/12/1863	Mortally wounded and died at Hagerstown, MD-buried there	Hagerstown, MD
Piper, George	Co. I, 45th North Carolina	1845	8/11/1863	Oakwood Cemetery, Raleigh, NC, reburial list	Raleigh, NC
Pitcock, Robert	Co. D, 33rd Virginia		7/15/1863	Hollywood Cemetery, Richmond, Va., reburial lists	Richmond, VA
Piterit, Adolph	Co. D, 5th Lousiana		7/2/1863	Killed in action	Unknown
Pittman, Benjamin Franklin	Co. C, 1st North Carolina	1835	9/14/1863	Oakwood Cemetery, Raleigh, NC, reburial list	Raleigh, NC
Pittman, Jesse Ricks	Sgt., Co. I, 11th Georgia	1840	7/2/1863	Hollywood Cemetery, Richmond, Va., reburial lists	Richmond, VA
Pittman, William H.	Co. A, 17th Mississippi		Jul. 1863	Killed in action on July 1st or 2nd	Unknown
Player, Thomas G.	Co. E, 49th Georgia		7/2/1863	Killed in action	Unknown
Pleasant, Anderson M.	Co. H, 6th North Carolina	1838	Aug. 1863	Mortally wounded, July 1st, and died at Hagerstown, MD	Hagerstown, MD
Plott, Valentine	Sgt., Co. C, 33rd North Carolina	1837	7/3/1863	Killed in action	Unknown

NAME	REGIMENT	BIRTH	DEATH	COMMENT	BURIAL
Plumer, James M.	Sgt., Co. B, 1st South Carolina	1838	9/4/1863	Mortally wounded and died at Chester, PA	Charleston, SC
Plummer, Mitchel M.	Co. A, 26th North Carolina	1839	7/16/1863	Mortally wounded-died at unknown place in Gettysburg	Unknown
Poag, Alonzo Walker	Lt., Co. H, 12th South Carolina	1839	7/3/1863	Killed in action	Unknown
Poindexter, William G.W.	Co. G, 28th North Carolina	8/2/1835	7/5/1863	Mortally wounded, July 3rd, and died two days later	Yadkin Co., NC
Polhill, Thomas N.	Capt., Co. E, 48th Georgia	1840	7/2/1863	Killed in action	Unknown
Polk, J.W.	Co. E, 2nd South Carolina		7/2/1863	Magnolia Cemetery, Charleston, SC, reburial list	Charleston, SC
Pollard, Wiley	Co. G, 7th North Carolina	1841	Jul. 1863	Mortally wounded and died on unknown date	Unknown
Pollock, Allen G.	Co. D, 1st Tennessee	1840	7/4/1863	Mortally wounded, July 3rd, and died the next day	Unknown
Pollock, Thomas Gordon	Capt., AIG, Gen. Pickett's staff	9/27/1838	7/3/1863	Killed in action; reinterred near Wm. E. Myer's Home, Warrenton, VA	Warrenton, VA
Pomeroy, William S.	Co. C, 47th Virginia		Jul. 1863	Killed in action, July 1-3	Unknown
Pool, Hansel	Co. C, 47th North Carolina	1836	7/1/1863	Killed in action	Unknown
Pool, James H.	Co. C, 5th Texas	1843	7/3/1863	Died of wounds received July 2nd	Unknown
Pool, James W.	Co. B, 16th Georgia		7/6/1863	Mortally wounded-died at unknown place in Gettysburg	Unknown
Pool, John E.P.	Sgt., Co. E, 14th Virginia	12/4/1842	7/3/1863	Killed in action	Unknown
Pool, John H.	Cpl., Co. K, 44th Alabama	1839	7/2/1863	Killed in action	Unknown
Pool, Robert W.	Sgt., Co. B, 2nd South Carolina		7/3/1863	Hollywood Cemetery, Richmond, Va., reburial lists	Richmond, VA
Pool, William David	Co. C, 6th North Carolina	1836	7/1/1863	Killed in action	Unknown
Poole, George H.	Co. F, 17th Mississippi	1843	Jul. 1863	Hollywood Cemetery, Richmond, Va., reburial lists	Richmond, VA
Poole, William H.	Cpl., Co. H, 9th Louisiana	1842	7/3/1863	Killed in action; body exhumed to Louisiana by parents	Brush Valley, LA
Poore, Robert Henry	Maj., 14th Virginia	5/31/1823	7/3/1863	Killed in action	Unknown
Pooser, George E.	Lt., Co. F, 2nd Florida		7/3/1863	Killed in action	Unknown
Poovey, David A.	Co. C, 28th North Carolina	1840	7/3/1863	Mortally wounded, July 3rd, and died the same day	Unknown
Poovey, Henry Franklin	Co. C, 28th North Carolina	11/9/1824	7/3/1863	Killed in action	Unknown
Pope, George M.	Co. F, 38th North Carolina	1832	7/1/1863	Killed in action	Unknown
Pope, Joseph W.	Cpl., Co. G, 3rd Virginia	1836	7/11/1863	Hollywood Cemetery, Richmond, Va., reburial lists	Richmond, VA
Porter, Algernon Chastain	3rd Co., Richmond Howitzers	3/21/1831	7/3/1863	Killed in action; reinterred in Hollywood Cemetery, Nov. 5, 1866	Richmond, VA
Porter, John F.M.	Co. I, 9th Alabama	1840	Jul. 1863	Killed in action, July 1-3	Unknown
Porter, Joseph M.	Lt., Co. H, 15th South Carolina	1841	7/2/1863	Magnolia Cemetery, Charleston, SC, reburial list	Charleston, SC
Porter, William H.	Sgt., Co. L, 1st Texas	1816	7/2/1863	Killed in action	Unknown
Porter, William S.	Sgt., Co. I, 11th Virginia	1841	Jul. 1863	Missing in action and presumed dead	Unknown
Porterfield, David Harrison	Co. F, 24th Virginia	1842	7/3/1863	Mortally wounded, July 3rd, and died the same day	Unknown

NAME	REGIMENT	BIRTH	DEATH	COMMENT	BURIAL
Poteet, W.G.	Co. B, 22nd North Carolina	1835	Jul. 1863	Killed in action	Unknown
Potter, George W.	Lt., Co. F, 17th Georgia		7/5/1863	Hollywood Cemetery, Richmond, Va., reburial lists	Richmond, VA
Potter, Henry W.	Lt., Co. F, 3rd North Carolina	1836	7/2/1863	Killed in action	Unknown
Pounders, Albert H.	Co. C, 42nd Mississippi	1834	7/3/1863	Killed in action	Unknown
Pounds, Alva P.	Co. I, 48th Alabama	3/22/1837	7/22/1863	Mortally wounded-died at unknown place in Gettysburg	Unknown
Powe, Hugh Torrence	Sgt., Co. K, 5th North Carolina	1829	7/16/1863	Mortally wounded, July 1st, and died at Baltimore, MD	Baltimore, MD
Powe, Thomas Erasmus	Capt., Co. C, 8th South Carolina	3/21/1838	7/22/1863	Hollywood Cemetery, Richmond, Va., reburial lists	Richmond, VA
Powell, Andrew Jackson	Co. F, 34th North Carolina		8/2/1863	Died as POW at David's Island, NY	Cypress Hills, NY
Powell, Cornelius	Cpl., Co. A, 9th Virginia	1843	7/21/1863	Mortally wounded-died at unknown place in Gettysburg	Unknown
Powell, Daniel	Co. A, 11th North Carolina	1835	7/1/1863	Killed in action	Unknown
Powell, Gaither	Co. E, 16th North Carolina	1836	7/3/1863	Killed in action	Unknown
Powell, George B.	Co. C, 14th Tennessee		7/3/1863	Killed in action	Unknown
Powell, James R.	Sgt., Co. H, 5th North Carolina	1838	7/7/1863	Mortally wounded-died at unknown place in Gettysburg	Unknown
Powell, Jesse Rigdon	Co. D, 13th Georgia	1830	7/1/1863	Killed in action	Unknown
Powell, Leonard A.	Co. D, 56th Virginia	1837	7/3/1863	Killed in action	Unknown
Powell, Stephen	Co. F, 48th Georgia	1832	7/2/1863	Killed in action	Unknown
Powell, William E.	Co. K, 1st North Carolina	1816	Jul. 1863	Killed in action	Unknown
Powell, William Joseph	Cpl., Co. F, 38th Georgia	1840	7/1/1863	Laurel Grove Cemetery, Savannah, Ga., reburial list	Savannah, GA
Powell, William M.	Co. C, 13th North Carolina	1842	7/3/1863	Mortally wounded, July 3rd, and died the same day	Unknown
Powers, James E.	Co. K, 52nd North Carolina	1839	7/3/1863	Killed in action	Unknown
Powers, William	Co. K, 7th Louisiana	1839	Jul. 1863	Killed in action	Unknown
Powers, Wilson	Co. B, 32nd North Carolina	1842	Jul. 1863	Killed in action	Unknown
Poynor, William Henry	Co. H, 53rd Virginia	1844	7/3/1863	Killed in action per the Richmond Whig, August 7, 1863	Unknown
Pratt, Henry	Co. B, 5th Texas		10/23/1863	Mortally wounded-died at unknown place in Gettysburg	Unknown
Pratt, Thomas	Sgt., Co. K, 52nd North Carolina	1841	7/3/1863	Killed in action	Unknown
Pratt, Thomas Henry	Co. K, 45th North Carolina	1832	7/26/1863	Died as POW at David's Island, NY	Cypress Hills, NY
Prescott, William C.	Co. A, 22nd Georgia		7/2/1863	Killed in action	Unknown
Presgraves, John Richard	Lt., Co. I, 8th Virginia	1836	7/15/1863	Mortally wounded and reinterred after the war at Sharon Cemetery	Middleburg, VA
Preskitt, John	Co. F, 12th Alabama		7/1/1863	Mortally wounded, July 1st, and died the same day	Unknown
Presley, Thomas N.	Co. I, 7th South Carolina	1841	7/3/1863	Hollywood Cemetery, Richmond, Va., reburial lists	Richmond, VA
Presnell, Daniel	Sgt., Co. H, 3rd North Carolina	1830	7/2/1863	Killed in action	Unknown
Presnell, James Madison	Co. B, 52nd North Carolina	5/27/1828	7/3/1863	Killed in action	Unknown

NAME	REGIMENT	BIRTH	DEATH	COMMENT	BURIAL
Presson, John A.	Cpl., Co. B, 53rd Georgia		7/15/1863	Hollywood Cemetery, Richmond, Va., reburial lists	Richmond, VA
Price, Charles	Madison Light Artillery (La.)		Jul. 1863	Killed in action, July 1-3	Unknown
Price, George H.	Cpl., Co. F, 24th Virginia		Jul. 1863	Mortally wounded-died on unknown date in Gettysburg	Unknown
Price, James Green	Co. D, 12th South Carolina	1833	7/1/1863	Killed in action	Unknown
Price, John E.	Co. D, 6th Alabama	3/25/1843	7/2/1863	Killed in action	Unknown
Price, John H.	Co. C, 45th North Carolina	1826	7/11/1863	Mortally wounded-died at unknown place in Gettysburg	Unknown
Price, John W.	Co. E, 17th Mississippi	1834	Jul. 1863	Mortally wounded-died on unknown date in Gettysburg	Unknown
Price, William Franklin	Co. H, 2nd North Carolina Battalion.	1837	7/1/1863	Killed in action	Unknown
Pridgen, Hinton Haywood	Co. E, 18th North Carolina	4/19/1840	7/5/1863	Hollywood Cemetery, Richmond, Va., reburial lists	Richmond, VA
Prillaman, Isaac C.	Lt., Co. B, 57th Virginia		Jul. 1863	Killed in action, July 1-3	Unknown
Prim, Thomas A.	Co. A, 11th North Carolina	1845	Jul. 1863	Mortally wounded-died on unknown date in Gettysburg	Unknown
Prince, Ephraim	Co. C, 9th Georgia	1837	7/17/1863	Mortally wounded-died at unknown place in Gettysburg	Unknown
Prince, William H.	Sgt., Co. A, 5th Virginia	1843	7/3/1863	Killed in action; reinterred at Winchester, VA	Winchester, VA
Pritchard, Barton R.	Co. C, 3rd Arkansas	1837	7/2/1863	Killed in action	Unknown
Pritchett, Stephen D.	Co. F, 2nd Florida		7/3/1863	Killed in action	Unknown
Pritchett, William Messer	Co. D, 11th Georgia		7/2/1863	Killed in action	Unknown
Proctor, John R.	Co. F, 11th North Carolina	1844	Aug. 1863	Mortally wounded, July 1st, and died after August 1st at Williamsport. MD	Williamsport, MD
Proctor, Sterling Yancy	Co. C, 6th North Carolina	1838	7/2/1863	Missing in action and presumed dead	Unknown
Proctor, Thomas D.	Co. A, 45th North Carolina		8/16/1863	Died as POW at David's Island, NY	Cypress Hills, NY
Propst, Mathias	Co. G, 7th North Carolina	1842	7/5/1863	Mortally wounded, July 3rd, and died to days later	Unknown
Prue, Marshal	Co. F, 5th Texas		7/2/1863	Killed in action	Unknown
Pruitt, John	Co. G, 3rd Georgia		7/2/1863	Killed in action	Unknown
Pruitt, Thomas J.	Co. F, 47th North Carolina	1840	7/3/1863	Missing in action, July 3rd, and presumed dead	Unknown
Pryor, David	Co. C, 28th North Carolina		7/3/1863	Missing in action, July 3rd, and presumed dead	Unknown
Pryor, William	Co. C, 28th North Carolina		7/3/1863	Missing in action, July 3rd, and presumed dead	Unknown
Pucket, Jimesson	Co. B, 47th North Carolina		7/3/1863	Killed in action	Unknown
Puckett, Emerson	Co. A, 47th North Carolina	1830	7/1/1863	Killed in action	Unknown
Puckett, William A.	Co. K, 55th North Carolina		7/23/1863	Hollywood Cemetery, Richmond, Va., reburial lists	Richmond, VA
Puckett, William T.	Co. D, 41st Virginia		Jul. 1863	Killed in action, July 1-3	Unknown
Pugh, Nathan S.	Lt., Co. I, Cobb's Legion Cav. (Ga.)		7/2/1863	Laurel Grove Cemetery, Savannah, Ga., reburial list	Savannah, GA
Pugh, Whitson	Co. B, 15th Alabama	1839	7/2/1863	Killed in action	Unknown

NAME	REGIMENT	BIRTH	DEATH	COMMENT	BURIAL
Pugh, William Eli	Co. D, 50th Virginia		8/8/1863	Died as POW at David's Island, NY	Cypress Hills, NY
Pullen, J.E.	Co. C, 13th Georgia		7/22/1863	Mortally wounded-died at unknown place in Gettysburg	Unknown
Pulley, E.P.	Co. B, 3rd South Carolina Battalion		7/2/1863	Magnolia Cemetery, Charleston, SC, reburial list	Charleston, SC
Pulliam, Robert Campbell	Capt., Co. B, 2nd South Carolina	1828	7/3/1863	Magnolia Cemetery, Charleston, SC, reburial list	Charleston, SC
Purdham, William	Co. H, 33rd Virginia	1826	7/8/1863	Mortally wounded-died at unknown place in Gettysburg	Unknown
Purdue [Perdew], James M.	Co. A, 15th Alabama	1830	Jul. 1863	Missing in action and presumed dead	Unknown
Purvis, James Edward	Co. B, 1st North Carolina	8/5/1843	7/3/1863	Killed in action	Unknown
Quaintance, William Henry	Unspecfied Confederate Unit		8/23/1863	Died of wounds in a private residence in Mercersburg, PA	Mercersburg, PA
Quick, Jesse	Co. E, 12th Georgia		7/1/1863	Killed in action	Unknown
Quinn, Charles H.	Sgt., Co. B, Phillips Legion (Ga.)		7/2/1863	Killed in action	Unknown
Quinn, Hillery L.	Co. E, 18th Mississippi	1843	9/1/1863	Hollywood Cemetery, Richmond, Va., reburial lists	Richmond, VA
Quinton, John B.	Co. B, 12th South Carolina	1843	7/3/1863	Killed in action	Unknown
Raber, Henry L.	Co. A, 8th Virginia		8/14/1863	Mortally wounded and died at Baltimore, MD-buried there	Baltimore, MD
Rabon, Calvin	Co. E, 47th North Carolina		7/1/1863	Killed in action	Unknown
Rabon, Willis H.	Co. B, 9th Louisiana	1841	7/2/1863	Killed in action	Unknown
Racer, James O.B.	Sgt., Co. K, 7th Virginia	1841	7/15/1863	Hollywood Cemetery, Richmond, Va., reburial lists	Richmond, VA
Ragan, Cornelius H.	Co. C, 9th Georgia		7/2/1863	Killed in action	Unknown
Ragan, James	Co. K, 10th Louisiana	1831	7/2/1863	Killed in action	Unknown
Ragan, James H.	Co. K, 22nd Georgia		7/2/1863	Killed in action	Unknown
Ragland, Francis Marion	Sgt., Co. K, 17th Mississippi	1838	7/7/1863	Hollywood Cemetery, Richmond, Va., reburial lists	Richmond, VA
Raines, Burton	Co. I, 61st Georgia		7/2/1863	Killed in action	Unknown
Rainey, Joseph Henry	Co. B, 56th Virginia	2/26/1836	7/3/1863	Killed in action per the Richmond Sentinel, July 29, 1863	Unknown
Rainey, P.L.	Co. F, 14th Virginia		7/3/1863	Killed in action	Unknown
Rainey, Silas	Co. F, 61st Georgia		7/30/1863	Mortally wounded-died at unknown place in Gettysburg	Unknown
Rainey, William Wirt	Capt., Co. C, 13th North Carolina	7/6/1838	7/9/1863	Killed in action and reinterred at Red House Presbyterian Church	Caswell Co., NC
Rains, Anthony	Co. C, 12th South Carolina	1843	7/2/1863	Killed in action whiled carrying the colors	Unknown
Raley, James W.	Co. B, 22nd Georgia		7/2/1863	Killed in action	Unknown
Ralston, Green G.	Lt., Co. A, 2nd Mississippi	1834	7/30/1863	Mortally wounded and died at Chester, PA	Phil. National Cem.
Ramseur, Alfred A.	Co. A, 33rd North Carolina	1828	7/3/1863	Killed in action	Unknown
Ramsey, R. Nelson	Co. I, 11th North Carolina	1843	7/1/1863	Killed in action	Unknown
Ramsey, Richard	Co. K, 13th North Carolina	1841	7/1/1863	Killed in action	Unknown
Ramsey, Robert A.	Co. F, 5th Virginia	1838	7/3/1863	Killed in action	Unknown

NAME	REGIMENT	BIRTH	DEATH	COMMENT	BURIAL
Ramsey, Thomas J.	Co. I, 38th North Carolina	1830	7/1/1863	Killed in action	Unknown
Ramsey, W. Frank	Manly's Battery (NC)	1838	7/2/1863	Oakwood Cemetery, Raleigh, NC, reburial list	Raleigh, NC
Ramsey, William B.	Co. E, 14th Virginia	1838	7/25/1863	Mortally wounded-died at unknown place in Gettysburg	Unknown
Ramsour, Martin	Sgt., Co. B, 23rd North Carolina	10/27/1842	7/1/1863	Killed in action	Unknown
Randle, John W.	Capt., Co. D, 28th North Carolina	1838	7/10/1863	Mortally wounded-died at unknown place in Gettysburg	Unknown
Randleman, Augustus T.	Co. F, 28th North Carolina	1841	7/23/1863	Died as POW at David's Island, NY	Cypress Hills, NY
Randolph, Auguste	Lt., Co. D, 8th Louisiana	1825	7/2/1863	Killed in action	Unknown
Randolph, R.J.	Co. B, 16th Georgia		7/6/1863	Hollywood Cemetery, Richmond, Va., reburial lists	Richmond, VA
Randolph, William	Co. D, 44th Alabama		7/2/1863	Killed in action	Unknown
Rank, Eugene R.	Co. I, 33rd North Carolina	1840	Jul. 1863	Killed in action, July 1-3	Unknown
Ransdall, B.L.F.	Co. K, 32nd North Carolina		Aug. 1863	Mortally wounded-died on unknown date in Gettysburg	Unknown
Ransom, John H.	Co. E, 20th Georgia	1834	8/23/1863	Died as POW at David's Island, NY	Cypress Hills, NY
Ransom, Pleiades Orion	Sgt., Co. G, 1st South Carolina	1842	7/31/1863	Mortally wounded, July 1st, and died at Staunton, VA	Staunton, VA
Raper, William Martin	Co. K, 42nd Mississippi	1827	7/11/1863	Mortally wounded-died at unknown place in Gettysburg	Unknown
Rash, William H.	Co. B, 53rd Virginia		7/3/1863	Killed in action	Unknown
Rathbert, Henry	Co. K, 7th Louisiana	1838	7/2/1863	Killed in action	Unknown
Ratteree, James	Co. H, 12th South Carolina	1844	7/1/1863	Killed in action	Unknown
Raugh, Henry Joseph, Jr.	Lt., Co. B, 14th South Carolina	Aug. 1842	7/16/1863	Mortally wounded-died at unknown place in Gettysburg	Unknown
Raulerson, Aaron	Cpl., Co. C, 2nd Florida		7/2/1863	Killed in action	Unknown
Rawlings, Benjamin Caleb	Crenshaw Battery (Va.)	12/5/1845	7/4/1863	Died of wounds at Williamsport, MD	Williamsport, MD
Rawls, Charles Cross	Lt., Co. G, 5th North Carolina	12/30/1833	7/3/1863	Killed in action	Unknown
Rawls, Thomas F.	Lt., Co. G, 53rd Georgia	1842	7/28/1863	Mortally wounded and died at Richmond, VA; interred in Hollywood Cemetery	Richmond, VA
Rawson, John C.	Co. K, 13th Mississippi	1843	7/11/1863	Hollywood Cemetery, Richmond, Va., reburial lists	Richmond, VA
Ray, Andrew	Lt., Co. E, 47th Alabama		7/22/1863	Mortally wounded-died at unknown place in Gettysburg	Unknown
Ray, Joseph A.	Co. K, 34th North Carolina	1837	7/31/1863	Died as POW at David's Island, NY	Cypress Hills, NY
Ray, Thomas N.	Co. K, 22nd Georgia		7/10/1863	Hollywood Cemetery, Richmond, Va., reburial lists	Richmond, VA
Ray, William Griffin	Sgt., Co. B, 6th North Carolina	7/7/1841	7/1/1863	Killed in action	Unknown
Ray, William P.	Co. F, 50th Virginia	1844	7/3/1863	Killed in action	Unknown
Ray, William P.	Cpl., Taylor's Battery (Va.)		7/2/1863	Killed in action per the Richmond Sentinel, July 27, 1863	Unknown
Ray, Willis	Co. I, 3rd North Carolina		7/7/1863	Mortally wounded-died at unknown place in Gettysburg	Unknown
Read, James W.	Co. D, 38th Virginia		7/25/1863	Mortally wounded-died at unknown place in Gettysburg	Unknown

NAME	REGIMENT	BIRTH	DEATH	COMMENT	BURIAL
Readling, James M.	Co. B, 20th North Carolina	1836	7/1/1863	Killed in action	Unknown
Reagan, J.R.	Co. E, 60th Georgia		7/3/1863	Killed in action	Unknown
Reaves, Charles Williams	Cpl., Co. E, 1st South Carolina	1844	7/1/1863	Killed in action	Unknown
Reaves, William Henry Clay	Co. G, 26th North Carolina	1844	9/22/1863	Mortally wounded, July 3rd, died at home in NC per the Fayetteville Observer, August 22, 1864	North Carolina
Reddick, George	Co. K, 2nd Florida		7/3/1863	Killed in action	Unknown
Reddick, Peter	Cpl., Co. K, 2nd Florida	1839	7/3/1863	Killed in action	Unknown
Redding, Charles R.	Capt., Co. C, 2nd Georgia Battalion		7/2/1863	Killed in action	Unknown
Redeau, Henry	3rd Co., Washington Arty. (La.)	1846	7/3/1863	Killed in action	Unknown
Redman, Stephen	Co. K, 57th Virginia		7/9/1863	Died of wounds received, July 3, at Ft. Delaware	Finn's Point, NJ
Redman, Thomas Conway	Lt., Co. C, 40th Virginia	3/27/1837	8/2/1863	Died as POW at David's Island, NY	Cypress Hills, NY
Reed, Charles William	Sgt., Co. G, 8th Virginia	2/25/1820	7/17/1863	Mortally wounded and reinterred in Union Cemetery, Leesburg, VA	Leesburg, VA
Reed, Joseph D.	Co. C, 16th Georgia		1863	Missing in action and presumed dead per the Augusta Chronicle & Sentinel, August 13, 1863	Savannah, GA
Reed, Robert E.	Co. D, 9th Virginia	1838	7/3/1863	Killed in action	Unknown
Reedy, Elias	Co. D, 50th Virginia	1832	7/13/1863	Mortally wounded-died at unknown place in Gettysburg	Unknown
Reese, Albert Jeremiah	Co. F, 10th Georgia		7/2/1863	Killed in action	Unknown
Reeves, George R.	Co. H, 20th Georgia		7/2/1863	Killed in action	Unknown
Reeves, Isaac	Cpl., Co. K, 10th Louisiana	1838	9/2/1863	Hollywood Cemetery, Richmond, Va., reburial lists	Richmond, VA
Reeves, John A.	Co. D, 13th Georgia		7/13/1863	Laurel Grove Cemetery, Savannah, Ga., reburial list	Savannah, GA
Reeves, Malachai	Co. K, 3rd Arkansas	9/26/1843	7/18/1863	Hollywood Cemetery, Richmond, Va., reburial lists	Richmond, VA
Reeves, William R.	Co. E, 16th Mississippi		7/19/1863	Mortally wounded and died at Hagerstown, MD-buried there	Hagerstown, MD
Reid, Calvin Henry	Sgt., Co. F, 7th North Carolina	1841	8/13/1863	Oakwood Cemetery, Raleigh, NC, reburial list	Raleigh, NC
Reily, Bartly	Co. A, 12th Alabama		7/3/1863	Killed in action	Unknown
Reinhardt, Alexander Sidney	Co. A, 3rd Arkansas	9/1/1838	7/2/1863	Killed in action	Unknown
Reinhardt, Elsie T.	Co. F, 23rd North Carolina	7/15/1843	7/1/1863	Killed in action	Unknown
Rentfrow, Calvin	Co. C, 43rd North Carolina	1837	7/3/1863	Killed in action	Unknown
Revells, Rilery	Co. E, 5th Florida		7/3/1863	Killed in action	Unknown
Reynolds, Alonzo	Co. K, 8th Alabama		7/3/1863	Killed in action	Unknown
Reynolds, Coleman	Co. B, 38th Virginia	1830	7/30/1863	Mortally wounded and reinterred in Pittsylvania, Co., VA	Pittsylvania Co., VA
Reynolds, James A.	Co. E, 11th Georgia		7/3/1863	Killed in action	Unknown
Reynolds, James A.	Co. C, 28th North Carolina		Jul. 1863	Missing in action and presumed dead	Unknown
Reynolds, John H.	Co. B, 16th Georgia	1826	7/2/1863	Killed in action per the Augusta Chronicle & Sentinel, August 13, 1863	Unknown
Reynolds, John McKellar	Co. F, 2nd South Carolina	9/6/1844	7/2/1863	Killed in action	Charleston, SC

NAME	REGIMENT	BIRTH	DEATH	COMMENT	BURIAL
Reynolds, William	Unknown Co., 42nd Mississippi		7/19/1863	Hollywood Cemetery, Richmond, Va., reburial lists	Richmond, VA
Reynolds, William Chappel	Co. A, 14th South Carolina	1838	7/1/1863	Killed in action	Unknown
Reynolds, William H.	Co. K, 19th Mississippi	1834	7/2/1863	Killed in action per the Richmond Enquirer, July 16, 1863	Unknown
Rhidenhour, John W.	Co. F, 13th North Carolina	1828	8/12/1863	Mortally wounded and died at Chester, PA	Phil. National Cem.
Rhodes, Aaron E.	Co. I, 28th Virginia		7/3/1863	Killed in action	Unknown
Rhodes, Edward Averett	Lt., Co. C, 11th North Carolina	6/15/1841	7/1/1863	Killed in action; reinterred April 1866 at Baltimore, MD-Green Mount, Cemetery	Baltimore, MD
Rhodes, John Dawsey	Co. F, 8th South Carolina	1841	7/2/1863	Hollywood Cemetery, Richmond, Va., reburial lists	Richmond, VA
Rhodes, Samuel	Co. B, 33rd Virginia	1836	7/3/1863	Killed in action	Unknown
Rhodes, Theodore Augustus	Sgt., Co. H, 1st South Carolina	1/18/1832	7/3/1863	Magnolia Cemetery, Charleston, SC, reburial list	Charleston, SC
Rhodes, William Burton	Co. C, 6th North Carolina	1840	7/2/1863	Killed in action	Unknown
Rice, Benjamin F.	Sgt., Co. C, 58th Virginia		10/22/1863	Mortally wounded and died at Harrisburg, PA; Interred in Soldiers' Lot at City Cemetery	Harrisburg, PA
Rice, James P.	Sgt., Co. E, 38th Virginia	,	7/3/1863	Killed in action per the Richmond Sentinel, August 1, 1863	Unknown
Rice, Napoleon B.	Co. C, 11th North Carolina	1842	7/17/1863	Mortally wounded and died at Winchester, VA; interred Stonewall Cemetery	Winchester, VA
Rice, Stephen H.	Lt., Co. F, 61st Georgia		7/1/1863	Laurel Grove Cemetery, Savannah, Ga., reburial list	Savannah, GA
Rice, Wilkinson	Co. K, 14th South Carolina	1843	7/1/1863	Killed in action	Unknown
Rice, William	Co. A, 52nd North Carolina	1833	8/20/1863	Mortally wounded and died at Chester, PA	Phil. National Cem.
Richards, Daniel M.	Co. F, 14th South Carolina	1827	7/2/1863	Killed in action	Unknown
Richards, King David	Co. A, 57th Virginia	1832	7/3/1863	Killed in action	Unknown
Richards, Randle	Co. G, 2nd North Carolina Battalion.	1833	7/1/1863	Killed in action	Unknown
Richardson, Benjamin F.	Lt., Co. E, 2nd Mississippi	1836	7/3/1863	Killed in action	Unknown
Richardson, Elisha N.	Co. B, 11th Mississippi	1844	7/3/1863	Killed in action	Unknown
Richardson, Elwood	Co. F, 2nd North Carolina Battalion	1842	7/1/1863	Killed in action	Unknown
Richardson, Frederick	Capt., Co. F, 5th Louisiana	1837	7/4/1863	Killed in action	Unknown
Richardson, George	Co. A, 10th Georgia		7/2/1863	Killed in action	Unknown
Richardson, Hopkins R.	Co. B, 11th Mississippi	1842	7/3/1863	Killed in action	Unknown
Richardson, James E.	Sgt., Co. K, 18th North Carolina	1833	7/3/1863	Killed in action	Unknown
Richardson, Jesse C.	Co. C, 3rd Arkansas		7/2/1863	Killed in action	Baltimore, MD
Richardson, John Quincy Adams	Maj., 52nd North Carolina	1836	7/3/1863	Killed in action	Unknown
Richardson, John S.	Co. C, 14th Virginia	1842	7/3/1863	Killed in action	Cypress Hills, NY
Richardson, Robert Norsworthy	Co. K, 53rd Georgia	1822	8/7/1863	Died as POW at David's Island, NY	Cypress Hills, NY

NAME	REGIMENT	BIRTH	DEATH	COMMENT	BURIAL
Richardson, Samuel R.	Co. B, 17th Georgia		Jul. 1863	Hollywood Cemetery, Richmond, Va., reburial lists	Richmond, VA
Richardson, T.J.	Co. D, 11th Mississippi		7/27/1863	Mortally wounded, July 3rd, and died at Jerusalem, VA	Raleigh, NC
Richardson, William W.	Lt., Co. B, 26th North Carolina	1835	7/1/1863	Oakwood Cemetery, Raleigh, NC, reburial list	Raleigh, NC
Richerson, William A.	Co. B, 9th Virginia Cavalry	1841	7/5/1863	Hollywood Cemetery, Richmond, Va., reburial lists	Richmond, VA
Richey, William F.	Co. E, 11th North Carolina	1838	Jul. 1863	Mortally wounded and died between July 6th-9th	Unknown
Richmond, Thomas S.	Co. H, 6th North Carolina	1842	7/1/1863	Killed in action	Unknown
Richmond, William B.	Co. K, 50th Virginia	1841	Jul. 1863	Killed in action on either July 2nd or 3rd	Unknown
Ricks, Guilford	Co. C, 43rd North Carolina	1823	7/2/1863	Hollywood Cemetery, Richmond, Va., reburial lists	Richmond, VA
Ridenour, Amos	Carpenter's Battery (Va.)	1820	7/2/1863	Hollywood Cemetery, Richmond, Va., reburial lists	Richmond, VA
Rider, James Whaley	Co. K, 1st Virginia Cavalry	1841	8/13/1863	Mortally wounded and died after POW exchange	Whaleyville, MD
Ridgell, Felix	Co. D, 14th South Carolina	1844	7/1/1863	Killed in action	Unknown
Ridgeway, S.C.	Co. I, 7th South Carolina		7/2/1863	Hollywood Cemetery, Richmond, Va., reburial lists	Richmond, VA
Ridgway, John Caldwell	Co. B, 11th Alabama	1838	7/3/1863	Killed in action	Unknown
Ridlehuber, William F.	Cpl., Co. H, 13th South Carolina	1842	7/1/1863	Killed in action	Unknown
Rigdon, Berry George	Co. F, 49th Georgia	1840	7/2/1863	Killed in action	Unknown
Rigdon, Daniel R.	Co. I, 9th Georgia	12/13/1839	7/2/1863	Killed in action	Unknown
Riggs, Augustus L.	Co. K, 2nd Mississippi	1829	12/5/1863	Died as POW at David's Island, NY	Cypress Hills, NY
Riggs, Richard	Co. B, 32nd North Carolina	1/3/1840	7/3/1863	Killed in action	Unknown
Rikard, John A.	Co. G, 13th South Carolina		7/1/1863	Killed in action	Unknown
Rikard, Miles M.	Co. D, 11th Mississippi	1841	7/3/1863	Killed in action	Unknown
Riley, Bartholomew	Co. A, 12th Alabama		Jul. 1863	Killed in action, July 1-3	Unknown
Riley, Henry F.	Lt., Co. A, 2nd Florida	1837	7/3/1863	Killed in action	Unknown
Riley, James A.	Co. B, 2nd Mississippi	1826	Jul. 1863	Mortally wounded-died on unknown date in Gettysburg	Unknown
Riley, Stephen	Co. I, 5th North Carolina	1837	1863	Mortally wounded-died on unknown date in Gettysburg	Unknown
Riley, William Newton	Co. F, 2nd South Carolina	1841	7/2/1863	Magnolia Cemetery, Charleston, SC, reburial list	Charleston, SC
Rinehardt, Abraham	Co. F, 23rd North Carolina	1831	7/1/1863	Killed in action	Unknown
Rinehardt, E.T.	Cpl., Co. F, 23rd North Carolina	1843	7/1/1863	Killed in action	Unknown
Rison, Henry C.	Co. B, 7th Tennessee	1842	8/1/1863	Hollywood Cemetery, Richmond, Va., reburial lists	Richmond, VA
Ritchie, John D.	Co. B, 20th North Carolina	1843	7/1/1863	Killed in action	Unknown
Ritchie, John Robert	Sgt., Co. E, 4th Alabama	2/28/1836	7/2/1863	Killed in action	Unknown
Ritenour, Hiram	Co. B, 33rd Virginia		7/3/1863	Killed in action	Unknown

NAME	REGIMENT	BIRTH	DEATH	COMMENT	BURIAL
Riveer, Abner	Cpl., Co. I, 40th Virginia	1830	7/2/1863	Mortally wounded, July 2nd, and died the same day	Unknown
Rives [Rieves], William Henry C.	Co. G, 26th North Carolina	1843	9/22/1863	Mortally wounded, July 1st, and died at Chatham Co., NC	North Carolina
Riviere, Joseph H.	Lt., Co. K, 4th Georgia		7/1/1863	Killed in action	Unknown
Roach, Thomas J.	Co. K, 11th Mississippi	1843	7/3/1863	Killed in action	Unknown
Roach, William J.	Co. A, 2nd South Carolina		7/2/1863	Magnolia Cemetery, Charleston, SC, reburial list	Charleston, SC
Roark, Walter	Co. F, 5th Alabama	1842	7/1/1863	Hollywood Cemetery, Richmond, Va., reburial lists	Richmond, VA
Robbins, Daniel	Co. B, 53rd Virginia	1841	7/29/1863	Hollywood Cemetery, Richmond, Va., reburial lists	Richmond, VA
Robbins, Isaiah Spurgeon	Lt., Co. I, 22nd North Carolina	5/30/1837	7/1/1863	Hollywood Cemetery, Richmond, Va., reburial lists	Richmond, VA
Robbins, Jackson	Co. I, 34th North Carolina	1838	Jul. 1863	Killed in action	Unknown
Robbins, James P.	Co. H, 53rd Virginia	1841	7/20/1863	Hollywood Cemetery, Richmond, Va., reburial lists	Richmond, VA
Robbins, John B.	Cpl., Co. I, 8th South Carolina		7/2/1863	Hollywood Cemetery, Richmond, Va., reburial lists	Richmond, VA
Robbins, Robert F.	Co. F, 3rd North Carolina	1840	Jul.1863	Mortally wounded, July 3rd, and died on unknown date	Unknown
Robbins, Rufus A.	Co. C, 17th Mississippi	1838	7/3/1863	Hollywood Cemetery, Richmond, Va., reburial lists	Richmond, VA
Roberson, James	Co. B, 45th North Carolina	1824	8/4/1863	Oakwood Cemetery, Raleigh, NC, reburial list	Raleigh, NC
Roberts, Atlas K.	Lt., Co. H, 2nd Mississippi	1842	7/1/1863	Killed in action	Unknown
Roberts, Benjamin G.	Lt., Chesapeake Artillery (Md.)		7/2/1863	Killed in action	Baltimore, MD
Roberts, David C.	Co. I, 48th Virginia	11/23/1840	7/2/1863	Killed in action	Unknown
Roberts, Franklin	Co. I, 45th North Carolina	1841	7/1/1863	Killed in action	Unknown
Roberts, James F.	Co. A, 2nd South Carolina		7/2/1863	Killed in action	Charleston, SC
Roberts, James M.	Co. A, 45th North Carolina	1841	7/1/1863	Mortally wounded and died the same day	Unknown
Roberts, John	Co. G, 7th Tennessee		7/3/1863	Killed in action	Unknown
Roberts, John Thomas	Co. B, 14th Virginia Cavalry		7/18/1863	Mortally wounded and died at Staunton, VA-buried there	Staunton, VA
Roberts, Jones W.	Lt., Co. F, 45th North Carolina	1815	7/1/1863	Killed in action	Unknown
Roberts, Melville C.	Cpl., Co. C, 35th Georgia	9/28/1834	7/3/1863	Killed in action	Unknown
Roberts, Robert S.	Co. A, 45th North Carolina	1839	Jul. 1863	Mortally wounded and died sometime after July 22nd	Unknown
Roberts, Ruffin A.	Sgt., Co. C, 2nd Mississippi	1839	7/1/1863	Killed in action	Unknown
Roberts, Whitmel P.	Co. I, 42nd Mississippi		8/5/1863	Mortally wounded and died at Chester, PA	Phil. National Cem.
Robertson, Abiah E.	Co. H, 11th Mississippi	1840	7/3/1863	Killed in action	Unknown
Robertson, Henry H.	Co. K, 38th Virginia		8/5/1863	Mortally wounded, July 3rd, and died at Richmond, VA; interred in Hollywood Cemetery	Richmond, VA

NAME	REGIMENT	BIRTH	DEATH	COMMENT	BURIAL
Robertson, James M.	Co. B, 2nd Mississippi	1844	7/1/1863	Oakwood Cemetery, Raleigh, NC, reburial list	Raleigh, NC
Robertson, John	Co. A, 13th North Carolina	1840	7/2/1863	Killed in action	Unknown
Robertson, John H.	Lt., Co. B, 5th Alabama Battalion		7/9/1863	Hollywood Cemetery, Richmond, Va., reburial lists	Richmond, VA
Robertson, John J.	Co. F, 57th Virginia		Jul. 1863	Killed in action, July 1-3	Unknown
Robertson, Robert A.	Cpl., Co. C, 18th Virginia	1838	7/24/1863	Mortally wounded per the Richmond Sentinel, July 29, 1863	Unknown
Robins, Seaborn	Co. B, Phillips Legion (Ga.)	1843	7/2/1863	Killed in action	Unknown
Robinson, Calvin	Co. C, 56th Virginia		7/4/1863	Hollywood Cemetery, Richmond, Va., reburial lists	Richmond, VA
Robinson, Charles	Co. E, 52nd North Carolina		7/5/1863	Mortally wounded, July 3rd, and died two days later	Unknown
Robinson, Hugh Y.	Sgt., Co. E, 15th South Carolina	1839	7/6/1863	Magnolia Cemetery, Charleston, SC, reburial list	Richmond, VA
Robinson, J.W.	Co. D, 17th Mississippi	1836	1863	Missing in action and presumed dead	Unknown
Robinson, Jacob T.	Co. G, 53rd Virginia		7/3/1863	Killed in action	Unknown
Robinson, Joseph B.	Cpl., Co. G, 52nd North Carolina	1839	9/9/1863	Oakwood Cemetery, Raleigh, NC, reburial list	Raleigh, NC
Robinson, William A.	Co. C, 11th Mississippi	1841	7/10/1863	Died of wounds received on July 3rd	Unknown
Robinson, William H.	Co. A, 22nd Georgia		7/2/1863	Killed in action	Unknown
Robnett, Jesse A.	Sgt., Co. G, 37th North Carolina	1842	7/22/1863	Hollywood Cemetery, Richmond, Va., reburial lists	Richmond, VA
Robnett, Lawson C.	Sgt., Co. G, 37th North Carolina	1843	8/9/1863	Died as POW at David's Island, NY	Cypress Hills, NY
Roby, William C.	Co. F, 44th Georgia		7/1/1863	Killed in action	Unknown
Rodden, W.R.	Co. B, 53rd North Carolina	1841	7/15/1863	Mortally wounded-died at unknown place in Gettysburg	Unknown
Rodgers, John H.	Co. I, 52nd North Carolina		7/1/1863	Killed in action	Unknown
Rodgers, John J.	Co. I, 3rd Alabama		7/7/1863	Mortally wounded-died at unknown place in Gettysburg	Unknown
Rodgers, Joseph	Cpl., Co. G, 48th Georgia		7/2/1863	Killed in action	Unknown
Rodgers, William G.S.	Co. D, 20th Georgia		7/2/1863	Killed in action	Unknown
Rodgers, William J.	Co. G, 12th Alabama		Jul. 1863	Missing in action and presumed dead	Unknown
Rogers [Rodgers], James D.	Co. E, 13th Alabama		7/3/1863	Killed in action	Unknown
Rogers, Ebenezer	Sgt., Co. L, 8th South Carolina		7/8/1863	Mortally wounded per the Charleston Mercury, August 28, 1863	Unknown
Rogers, Henry M.	Co. E, 26th North Carolina	1838	7/1/1863	Killed in action	Unknown
Rogers, John C.	Co. I, 9th Louisiana	1841	7/2/1863	Killed in action	Unknown
Rogers, John D.	Co. F, 9th Louisiana	1842	7/2/1863	Killed in action	Unknown
Rogers, John H.	Co. I, 52nd North Carolina	1833	7/1/1863	Killed in action	Unknown
Rogers, Robert	Co. B, 26th North Carolina	1843	8/21/1863	Mortally wounded-died at unknown place in Gettysburg	Unknown
Rogers, Warrenton	Co. C, 9th Georgia	1842	7/2/1863	Killed in action	Unknown
Rogers, William M.	Sgt., Co. A, 42nd Mississippi	8/31/1837	7/1/1863	Killed in action	Unknown
Roller, Jacob	Co. A, 33rd Virginia	11/27/1835	7/27/1863	Mortally wounded-died at unknown place in Gettysburg	Unknown

NAME	REGIMENT	BIRTH	DEATH	COMMENT	BURIAL
Rollins, Alfred F.	Co. A, 8th Virginia		7/3/1863	Killed in action	Unknown
Rollins, James J.	Sgt., Co. H, 28th North Carolina	1834	7/22/1863	Oakwood Cemetery, Raleigh, NC, reburial list	Raleigh, NC
Rollins, John W.	Lt., Co. E, 47th Virginia		7/3/1863	Killed in action	Unknown
Rolls, Landon	Co. B, 49th Virginia		7/3/1863	Killed in action	Unknown
Rominger, Reuben	Co. G, 2nd North Carolina Battalion.	1826	8/3/1863	Died as POW at David's Island, NY	Cypress Hills, NY
Roney, L.H.	Lt., Co. I, 57th North Carolina	1830	7/1/1863	Oakwood Cemetery, Raleigh, NC, reburial list	Raleigh, NC
Rorex, James Adgate	Sgt., Co. E, 60th Georgia	1843	7/2/1863	Killed in action	Unknown
Rose, Joseph	Sgt., Co. C, 12th South Carolina	1840	7/2/1863	Killed in action	Unknown
Rose, William A.	Co. I, 7th North Carolina	1826	7/21/1863	Hollywood Cemetery, Richmond, Va., reburial lists	Richmond, VA
Rosenberger, Erasmus	Co. C, 7th Virginia Cavalry	1/14/1835	7/4/1863	Mortally wounded, July 3rd, died the next day; reinterred in Zion Cemetery	Hamburg, VA
Rosenberger, John Wesley	Sgt., Co. H, 33rd Virginia	1831	7/3/1863	Killed in action	Unknown
Rosenfeld, Jacob	Co. C, 2nd Georgia Battalion		7/3/1863	Mortally wounded, July 2nd, and died the next day	Unknown
Ross, Benjamin F.	Cpl., Co. F, 6th North Carolina		9/28/1863	Died of wounds at Raleigh, NC-buried there	Raleigh, NC
Ross, Egbert A.	Maj., 11th North Carolina	1842	7/1/1863	Killed in action; reinterred at Charlotte, NC	Charlotte, NC
Ross, Elisha	Cpl., Co. K, 22nd North Carolina	1833	Jul. 1863	Killed in action, July 1-3	Unknown
Ross, Frank S.	Co. B, 17th Mississippi	1846	7/2/1863	Killed in action	Unknown
Ross, George Washington	Maj., 2nd Georgia Battalion	11/22/1825	8/2/1863	Died of wounds received July 2nd; interred Rose Hill Cemetery, Macon, GA	Macon, GA
Ross, James M.	Co. D, 44th Alabama	1827	7/3/1863	Mortally wounded, July 2nd, died the next day	Unknown
Ross, Thomas H.	Co. I, 47th North Carolina	1824	7/3/1863	Killed in action	Unknown
Rosser, E.A.	Co. C, 10th Georgia		7/6/1863	Mortally wounded-died at unknown place in Gettysburg	Unknown
Rost, John C.	Cpl., Co. A, 4th Alabama	1839	Jul. 1863	Killed in action	Unknown
Roten, Solomon	Co. A, 26th North Carolina	1832	7/3/1863	Killed in action	Unknown
Rothschild, Albert	Cpl., Co. G, 8th Alabama		7/17/1863	Hollywood Cemetery, Richmond, Va., reburial lists	Richmond, VA
Roughton, Charles H.	Co. A, 32nd North Carolina	1833	7/10/1863	Mortally wounded-died at unknown place in Gettysburg	Unknown
Roundtree, John M.	Sgt., Co. E, 3rd Georgia		7/2/1863	Mortally wounded, July 2nd, and died the same day	Unknown
Rountree, Gordon	Co. A, 55th North Carolina		Jul. 1863	Killed in action	Unknown
Rountree, Reuben	Sgt., Co. A, 61st Georgia		7/1/1863	Laurel Grove Cemetery, Savannah, Ga., reburial list	Savannah, GA
Rouse, Daniel H.	Co. I, 48th Georgia		7/2/1863	Killed in action	Unknown
Rowan, Timothy	Co. G, 10th Louisiana		7/6/1863	Mortally wounded-died at unknown place in Gettysburg	Unknown
Rowe, John	Co. F, 8th Florida		7/3/1863	Killed in action	Unknown

NAME	REGIMENT	BIRTH	DEATH	COMMENT	BURIAL
Rowell, James H.	Co. E, 42nd Mississippi	1836	7/3/1863	Killed in action	Hagerstown, MD
Rowen, S. Tim	Cpl., Co. G, 14th Louisiana		7/2/1863	Hollywood Cemetery, Richmond, Va., reburial lists	Richmond, VA
Rowland, Jeremiah W.	Sgt., Co. G, 13th Georgia		7/10/1863	Mortally wounded-died at unknown place in Gettysburg	Unknown
Royall, Henry C.	Co. K, 11th Mississippi	1835	7/3/1863	Killed in action	Unknown
Royster, Iowa Michigan	Lt., Co. G, 37th North Carolina	1840	7/14/1863	Oakwood Cemetery, Raleigh, NC, reburial list	Raleigh, NC
Royster, James M.	Co. C, 47th North Carolina	1834	7/29/1863	Mortally wounded, July 1st, and died at Frederick, MD; interred Mt. Olivet Cem., grave #209	Frederick, MD
Rozzell, William F.	Lt., Co. E, 11th North Carolina	1840	7/10/1863	Hollywood Cemetery, Richmond, Va., reburial lists	Richmond, VA
Rudacillar, George W.	Co. D, 49th Virginia		7/3/1863	Killed in action	Unknown
Ruddell, Michael	Co. I, 28th Virginia		7/19/1863	Mortally wounded, July 3rd, and died at Lynchburg, VA-buried there	Lynchburg, VA
Rudisill, Martin	Co. B, 23rd North Carolina	1844	7/1/1863	Killed in action	Unknown
Ruleau, Felix	3rd Co., Washington Arty. (La.)	1837	7/28/1863	Mortally wounded-died at unknown place in Gettysburg	Unknown
Runyan, James Madison	Cpl., Co. D, 55th North Carolina	1836	7/1/1863	Killed in action	Unknown
Rush, Joseph B.	Sgt., Co. E, 10th Virginia		7/14/1863	Mortally wounded-died at unknown place in Gettysburg	Unknown
Rushing, Andrew Paul	Co. A, 23rd North Carolina	1843	7/1/1863	Killed in action	Unknown
Rushing, Harrison	Co. D, 61st Georgia	1840	7/1/1863	Killed in action; given name may be William	Unknown
Russell, Abednego	Co. K, 53rd North Carolina		9/20/1863	Died as POW at David's Island, NY	Cypress Hills, NY
Russell, Benjamin	Co. K, 53rd North Carolina		Jul. 1863	Mortally wounded-died on unknown date in Gettysburg	Unknown
Russell, Harvey T.	Co. B, 53rd North Carolina	1839	7/3/1863	Killed in action	Unknown
Russell, John W.	Co. I, 8th Florida	1816	8/8/1863	Hollywood Cemetery, Richmond, Va., reburial lists	Richmond, VA
Russell, John W.	Co. E, 26th North Carolina	1836	7/1/1863	Killed in action	Unknown
Russell, M.B.	Co. F, 12th South Carolina	1838	7/31/1863	Mortally wounded an died at Baltimore, MD-buried there	Baltimore, MD
Rutland, John B.	Co. H, 7th Tennessee		Jul. 1863	Missing in action and presumed dead	Unknown
Rutland, William A.	Lt., Co. E, 7th South Carolina		7/8/1863	Mortally wounded and died at Williamsport, MD-buried there	Williamsport, MD
Rutledge, James H.	Co. K, 50th Virginia	1812	7/2/1863	Killed in action	Unknown
Ryan, Carroll	Co. H, 12th Alabama		7/1/1863	Killed in action	Unknown
Ryan, David Rogers [Rodes]	Sgt., Co. E, 2nd South Carolina	1838	7/2/1863	Killed in action	Charleston, SC
Ryan, John	Co. H, 8th Alabama		7/2/1863	Killed in action	Unknown
Ryan, Thomas	Co. I, 12th Georgia		7/1/1863	Killed in action	Unknown
Rye, James J.	Co. B, 26th Alabama	1842	7/4/1863	Mortally wounded, July 1st, and died three days later	Unknown
Rykard, James R.	Sgt., Co. B, 5th Florida	1835	7/2/1863	Killed in action	Unknown
Safrit, Moses	Co. K, 5th North Carolina	1826	7/17/1863	Mortally wounded-died at unknown place in Gettysburg	Unknown

NAME	REGIMENT	BIRTH	DEATH	COMMENT	BURIAL
Saintsing, James	Co. G, 43rd North Carolina	1835	1863	Mortally wounded-died on unknown date in Gettysburg	Unknown
Sale, William Augustus	Co. G, 1st South Carolina		10/23/1863	Died as POW at David's Island, NY	Cypress Hills, NY
Sams, George W.	Co. F, 45th North Carolina	1834	7/17/1863	Mortally wounded-died at unknown place in Gettysburg	Unknown
Sanchez, Manuel	Co. H, 2nd Florida	6/17/1835	Jul. 1863	Mortally wounded, July 2nd, died on either July 10th or July 17th	Unknown
Sanchez, Simeon J.	Co. B, 2nd Florida	1830	7/17/1863	Mortally wounded-died at unknown place in Gettysburg	Unknown
Sandbower, John	Co. B, 7th Virginia		7/3/1863	Killed in action	Unknown
Sanders, Adam	Co. I, 3rd Georgia		7/16/1863	Hollywood Cemetery, Richmond, Va., reburial lists	Richmond, VA
Sanders, Andrew J.	Co. I, 5th Alabama		7/2/1863	Mortally wounded, July 1st, and died the next day	Unknown
Sanders, Jacob E.	Co. H, 38th Georgia		7/6/1863	Died of wounds received July 1st	Unknown
Sanders, Robert D.	Co. F, 11th Mississippi	1840	7/3/1863	Killed in action	Unknown
Sanderson, Daniel B.	Co. H, 42nd Mississippi		7/16/1863	Hollywood Cemetery, Richmond, Va., reburial lists	Richmond, VA
Sanderson, Frank Henry	Co. A, 1st Maryland Battalion		Jul. 1863	Mortally wounded-died on unknown date in Gettysburg	Unknown
Sanderson, John	Co. C, 3rd North Carolina	1836	7/2/1863	Killed in action	Unknown
Sandridge, George W.	Co. H, 56th Virginia		Jul. 1863	Missing in action and presumed dead	Unknown
Sandridge, James J.	Cpl., Co. E, 19th Virginia		7/3/1863	Killed in action	Unknown
Sanford, J.A.	Co. E, 48th Georgia		1863	Mortally wounded-died on unknown date in Gettysburg	Unknown
Sanford, John T.	Co. I, 23rd North Carolina	1839	7/14/1863	Mortally wounded-died at unknown place in Gettysburg	Unknown
Sansom, John	Co. D, 42nd Mississippi		8/29/1863	Hollywood Cemetery, Richmond, Va., reburial lists	Richmond, VA
Sapp, F.M.	Co. F, 8th Alabama		8/28/1863	Died as POW at David's Island, NY	Cypress Hills, NY
Sapp, Judson Cormick "Elisha"	Co. D, 2nd Georgia	10/27/1838	10/19/1863	Mortally wounded, July 2nd, and died at Martinsburg, WV; interred Green Hill Cem.	Martinsburg, WV
Satterfield, Edward Fletcher	Capt., Co. H, 55th North Carolina	6/17/1837	7/3/1863	Killed in action	Unknown
Sauls, Richard	Co. E, 51st Georgia		8/7/1863	Laurel Grove Cemetery, Savannah, Ga., reburial list	Savannah, GA
Saunders, Aaron	Co. H, 45th North Carolina	1840	7/25/1863	Died of wounds at Ft. Delaware, DE	Finn's Point, NJ
Saunders, Albert P.	King William Artillery (Va.)		8/3/1863	Mortally wounded and died at Winchester, VA; interred Stonewall Cemetery	Winchester, VA
Saunders, Edmond	Co. K, 55th Virginia		7/1/1863	Killed in action per the Richmond Enquirer, July 16, 1863	Unknown
Saunders, James	Co. H, 52 North Carolina	1844	7/19/1863	Hollywood Cemetery, Richmond, Va., reburial lists	Richmond, VA
Saunders, Joseph	Co. I, 48th Georgia	1837	7/2/1863	Killed in action	Unknown
Saunders, Randle	Co. C, 2nd North Carolina Battalion.	1843	7/1/1863	Killed in action	Unknown

NAME	REGIMENT	BIRTH	DEATH	COMMENT	BURIAL
Saunders, Richard A.	Co. B, 5th North Carolina	1829	7/21/1863	Mortally wounded-died at unknown place in Gettysburg	Unknown
Saunders, Thomas J.	Co. B, 2nd Mississippi	1841	7/1/1863	Killed in action	Unknown
Savage, Braxton	Co. B, 53rd Georgia		7/22/1863	Died as POW at David's Island, NY	Cypress Hills, NY
Savage, David W.	Co. C, 52nd North Carolina		7/3/1863	Missing in action and presumed dead	Unknown
Savage, Edward	Co. H, 4th Texas		Jul. 1863	Missing in action and presumed dead	Unknown
Sawyer, Richard L.	Cpl., Co. K, 3rd Arkansas	1837	7/2/1863	Killed in action	Unknown
Sawyer, Tillman T.	Co. A, 32nd North Carolina	1837	7/1/1863	Killed in action	Unknown
Sayers, Abner	Cpl., Co. C, 4th Virginia	1843	7/3/1863	Killed in action	Unknown
Scales, Peter Perkins	Capt., Co. C, 45th North Carolina	1/1/1835	7/18/1863	Mortally wounded and died at Winchester, VA; interred Stonewall Cemetery	Winchester, VA
Scammel, John E.	Co. C, 1st Virginia		7/5/1863	Mortally wounded and buried on Jacob Schwartz Farm	Unknown
Scarboro, James Newton	Co. K, 61st Georgia		7/1/1863	Laurel Grove Cemetery, Savannah, Ga., reburial list	Savannah, GA
Scarborough, J.S.	Cpl., Co. A, 2nd Louisiana		7/3/1863	Hollywood Cemetery, Richmond, Va., reburial lists	Richmond, VA
Scarborough, James Brannon	Co. K, 26th North Carolina	1/31/1835	7/3/1863	Killed in action	Unknown
Schoonover, John	Unknown Co., 48th Virginia		7/4/1863	Mortally wounded, July 3rd, and died the next day	Unknown
Schrader, Samuel Erza	Cpl., Co. K, 25th Virginia		8/9/1863	Died as POW at David's Island, NY	Cypress Hills, NY
Schwartz, John Benedict	Co. C, 12th South Carolina	1844	7/1/1863	Killed in action	Unknown
Schwarz, George	Lt., Co. G, 8th Alabama		7/2/1863	Killed in action	Unknown
Sclater, Robert J.	Co. F, 44th Virginia		7/28/1863	Mortally wounded and died at Chester, PA	Phil. National Cem.
Sclater, William A.	Co. H, 44th Virginia		7/3/1863	Killed in action	Unknown
Scogin, Monroe Vines	Co. A, 13th Mississippi	1844	7/2/1863	Killed in action	Unknown
Scott, David W.	Co. A, 5th Florida		7/2/1863	Killed in action	Unknown
Scott, Elijah	Co. E, 45th North Carolina	1822	Jul. 1863	Mortally wounded-died on unknown date in Gettysburg	Unknown
Scott, Franklin	Fraser's Battery (Ga.)		7/6/1863	Mortally wounded-died at unknown place in Gettysburg	Unknown
Scott, James Monroe	Co. A, 14th Virginia		7/3/1863	Killed in action	Unknown
Scott, James Thornwell	Lt., Co. C, 2nd South Carolina		7/2/1863	Killed in action	Unknown
Scott, John B.	Cpl., Co. G, 53rd Virginia		7/3/1863	Killed in action	Unknown
Scott, Robert Graham	Co. E, 14th Virginia	1843	7/3/1863	Killed in action	Unknown
Scott, Robert R.	Lt., Co. H, 8th Alabama	1828	7/22/1863	Hollywood Cemetery, Richmond, Va., reburial lists	Richmond, VA
Scott, William Alfred	Cpl., Co. K, 12th Alabama	8/13/1831	7/3/1863	Killed in action	Unknown
Scott, William W.	Co. K, 57th Virginia		Jul. 1863	Killed in action, July 1-3	Unknown
Scruggs, Drury	Co. D, 16th North Carolina	1840	7/3/1863	Killed in action	Unknown
Scruggs, J.J.	Co. D, 16th North Carolina	1843	7/20/1863	Mortally wounded-died at unknown place in Gettysburg	Unknown
Scruggs, Powhatan B.	Sgt., Co. H, 38th Virginia	1840	7/3/1863	Killed in action	Unknown

NAME	REGIMENT	BIRTH	DEATH	COMMENT	BURIAL
Seagle, George	Co. B, 23rd North Carolina	1823	7/1/1863	Killed in action	Unknown
Seagle, John	Co. B, 23rd North Carolina	1826	7/1/1863	Killed in action	Unknown
Seagler, Alfred A.	Co. I, 11th North Carolina	1816	7/1/1863	Killed in action	Unknown
Seals, James M.	Lt., Co. F, 42nd Mississippi	1833	7/20/1863	Hollywood Cemetery, Richmond, Va., reburial lists	Richmond, VA
Seay, Franklin	Co. F, 13th South Carolina		7/1/1863	Killed in action	Unknown
Seay, John R.	Sgt., Co. A, 57th Virginia		Jul. 1863	Killed in action, July 1-3	Unknown
Seay, William B. Jr.	Co. A, 57th Virginia	8/27/1841	7/3/1863	Killed in action	Unknown
Seay, William B. Sr.	Co. A, 57th Virginia		Jul. 1863	Killed in action	Unknown
Sebastian, William G.	Co. F, 52nd North Carolina	1841	7/2/1863	Killed in action	Unknown
Seitz, George Louis	Cpl., Co. F, 23rd North Carolina		8/5/1863	Mortally wounded and died at Staunton, VA-buried there	Staunton, VA
Self, William J.	Co. F, 55th North Carolina		7/1/1863	Killed in action	Unknown
Sell, Jacob	Co. I, 52nd North Carolina	1844	7/3/1863	Killed in action	Unknown
Sell, John	Co. I, 52nd North Carolina	1825	7/3/1863	Mortally wounded, July 3rd, and died the same day	Unknown
Sell, William Wesley	Co. K, 45th North Carolina	1827	7/1/1863	Killed in action	Unknown
Sellars, Benjamin Franklin	Co. E, 13th Mississippi	1843	7/3/1863	Killed in action	Unknown
Sellars, Calvin S.	Co. H, 3rd North Carolina	1843	7/2/1863	Killed in action	Unknown
Sellars, Ramon Franklin	Co. F, 48th Georgia	1828	7/2/1863	Killed in action	Unknown
Sellers, Samuel H.	Co. A, 47th North Carolina	1842	7/3/1863	Mortally wounded, July 3rd, and died the same day	Unknown
Semmes, Paul Jones	Brigadier General	1815	7/9/1863	Mortally wounded and died at Martinsburg, VA; reinterred in Linwood Cemetery after the war	Columbus, GA
Semones, William G.	Co. D, 24th Virginia		7/3/1863	Killed in action	Unknown
Senice, B.	Co. E, 5th Florida		7/3/1863	Killed in action	Unknown
Senn, Ketcham M.	Co. D, 13th South Carolina	1842	7/1/1863	Killed in action	Unknown
Sensebaugh, William	Co. E, 5th Texas		7/21/1863	Hollywood Cemetery, Richmond, Va., reburial lists	Richmond, VA
Sessoms, Micajah A.	Sgt., Co. F, 20th North Carolina	1838	Jul. 1863	Killed in action	Unknown
Setser, Joseph	Co. F, 26th North Carolina	1843	7/17/1863	Mortally wounded-died at unknown place in Gettysburg	Unknown
Setser, W.E.	Co. F, 26th North Carolina	1844	7/4/1863	Mortally wounded, July 1st, and died three days later	Unknown
Settle, John S.	Lt., Co. D, 14th Tennessee		7/12/1863	Mortally wounded-died at unknown place in Gettysburg	Unknown
Setzer, George M.	Co. F, 18th Virginia		7/3/1863	Killed in action	Unknown
Sexton, Solomon McDonald	Sgt., Co. D, 4th Virginia	3/20/1842	7/3/1863	Killed in action	Unknown
Shackleford, Francis S.	Co. E, 38th Virginia		7/3/1863	Killed in action per the Richmond Sentinel, August 1,1863	Unknown
Shackleford, Robert A.	Co. A, 14th Tennessee		Jul. 1863	Killed in action	Unknown
Shacklett, Edward P.	Cpl., Co. G, 10th Virginia		7/3/1863	Killed in action	Unknown
Shadrack, Abraham Wilhoit	Co. C, 7th Virginia	6/22/1838	8/30/1863	Mortally wounded and died at Culpeper, VA-buried there	Culpeper Co., VA

NAME	REGIMENT	BIRTH	DEATH	COMMENT	BURIAL
Shaffer, John C.	Co. G, 1st South Carolina	1838	7/3/1863	Killed in action	Unknown
Shankle, James W.	Co. I, 52nd North Carolina	1845	7/6/1863	Hollywood Cemetery, Richmond, Va., reburial lists	Richmond, VA
Shaon, Singleton	Co. F, 57th Virginia		Jul. 1863	Killed in action, July 1-3	Unknown
Sharp, Elias P.	Sgt., Co. F, 11th Georgia		7/4/1863	Hollywood Cemetery, Richmond, Va., reburial lists	Richmond, VA
Sharp, F. Marion	Co. K, 1st Tennessee	1840	7/1/1863	Killed in action	Unknown
Sharpless, William J.	Co. A, 43rd North Carolina	1835	7/1/1863	Killed in action	Unknown
Shaver, Noah	Co. I, 52nd North Carolina	1829	7/3/1863	Killed in action	Unknown
Shaw, Charles	Sgt., Co. E, 48th Alabama		7/20/1863	Mortally wounded-died at unknown place in Gettysburg	Unknown
Shaw, George Turner	Co. H, 11th Mississippi	4/17/1843	7/3/1863	Killed in action	Unknown
Shaw, N.M.	Co. B, 44th Georgia		7/1/1863	Hollywood Cemetery, Richmond, Va., reburial lists	Richmond, VA
Shealey, P.	Lt., Co. C, 2nd Florida	1834	7/3/1863	Killed in action	Unknown
Shearley, Nathan	Co. F, 43rd North Carolina	1839	7/1/1863	Killed in action	Unknown
Sheets, Jacob	Co. H, 5th Virginia		7/3/1863	Killed in action	Unknown
Sheffield, James S.	Cpl., Co. E, 10th Louisiana	1836	7/2/1863	Killed in action on Culp's Hill	Unknown
Sheffield, John C.	Cpl., Co. C, 45th Georgia		7/10/1863	Mortally wounded, July 2nd, and died at unknown place in Georgia	Georgia
Sheffield, John C.	Co. C, 61st Georgia		7/1/1863	Killed in action	Unknown
Shelton, Charles L.	Co. K, 10th Virginia		7/3/1863	Killed in action	Unknown
Shelton, Edward Franklin	Co. I, 21st North Carolina	2/5/1841	7/1/1863	Killed in action	Unknown
Shelton, Josiah W.	Co. B, 57th Virginia	1841	7/27/1863	Mortally wounded-died at unknown place in Gettysburg	Unknown
Shepard, John M. W.	Co. D, 11th Mississippi	1829	7/3/1863	Killed in action	Unknown
Shepard, Samuel Monroe	Co. A, 57th Virginia	1842	7/3/1863	Killed in action	Unknown
Shepherd, James N.	Co. G, 15th Alabama	1839	8/26/1863	Hollywood Cemetery, Richmond, Va., reburial lists	Richmond, VA
Sheppard, Josiah	Cpl., Co. D, 18th Virginia	1837	7/3/1863	Killed in action	Unknown
Sherbert, William F.	Co. B, 44th Alabama	1842	7/2/1863	Killed in action	Unknown
Sherrill, Rufus R.	Co. F, 32nd North Carolina	1841	Jul. 1863	Killed in action	Unknown
Shields, Allen R.	Co. E, 26th North Carolina	1837	7/29/1863	Mortally wounded and died at Chester, PA	Phil. National Cem.
Shields, K.	Co. K, 6th North Carolina		7/29/1863	Mortally wounded and died at Chester, PA	Phil. National Cem.
Shields, Robert W.	Sgt., Co. A, 33rd North Carolina	1842	7/3/1863	Killed in action	Unknown
Shifflett, Octavius M.	Sgt., Co. H, 57th Virginia	1841	7/13/1863	Hollywood Cemetery, Richmond, Va., reburial lists	Richmond, VA
Shiflet, William J.	Co. F, 38th Georgia		7/1/1863	Killed in action	Unknown
Shiplett, W.	Co. K, 57th Virginia		7/13/1863	Mortally wounded-died at unknown place in Gettysburg	Unknown
Shireman, John	Sgt., Co. K, 33rd Virginia		Jul. 1863	Killed in action	Unknown
Shirer, William David	Co. E, 1st South Carolina Cav.	1842	8/14/1863	Mortally wounded-died at unknown place in Gettysburg	Unknown

NAME	REGIMENT	BIRTH	DEATH	COMMENT	BURIAL
Shirley, John Patrick	Co. F, 3rd South Carolina	11/18/1840	7/3/1863	Killed in action	Unknown
Shirley, Newton N.	Co. I, 2nd Mississippi	1835	7/1/1863	Killed in action	Unknown
Shirley, William R.	Co. I, 48th Georgia	1840	7/18/1863	Mortally wounded, July 2nd, and died at Hagerstown, MD-buried there	Hagerstown, MD
Shoaf, William N.	Co. H, 33rd North Carolina		8/3/1863	Mortally wounded and died at Chester, PA	Phil. National Cem.
Shockley, William	Co. C, 24th Virginia		11/19/1863	Mortally wounded and died at home in Carroll Co., VA	Carroll Co. VA
Shofutt, John H.	Co. E, 13th Alabama	1844	11/2/1863	Mortally wounded-died at unknown place in Gettysburg	Unknown
Shook, Joseph P.	Co. F, 26th North Carolina	1831	7/1/1863	Killed in action	Unknown
Short, Augustus L.	Cpl., Co. C, 17th Georgia		7/2/1863	Killed in action	Unknown
Short, Samuel P.	Cpl., Co. H, 26th North Carolina	1843	7/1/1863	Killed in action	Unknown
Shorter, James Thomas	Co. B, 16th Mississippi	1841	Jul. 1863	Missing in action and presumed dead	Unknown
Shoup, Jacob Gochenour	Lt., Co. H, 7th Virginia Cavalry	4/16/1835	7/3/1863	Hollywood Cemetery, Richmond, Va., reburial lists	Richmond, VA
Shrigley, Jacob Reasoner	Co. A, 8th Virginia	1838	7/3/1863	Killed in action	Unknown
Shufflebarger, Jackson	Co. I, 50th Virginia		7/12/1863	Mortally wounded-died at unknown place in Gettysburg	Unknown
Sibert, David M.	Co. B, 33rd Virginia		7/3/1863	Killed in action	Unknown
Sibert, Onesimus	Co. F, 2nd Virginia		7/9/1863	Hollywood Cemetery, Richmond, Va., reburial lists	Richmond, VA
Sikes, S. Thomas	Sgt., Co. H, 43rd North Carolina	1846	7/3/1863	Killed in action	Unknown
Siler, Wesley C.	Cpl., Co. M, 22nd North Carolina	1840	Jul. 1863	Killed in action, July 1-3	Unknown
Siler, William J.	Co. I, 26th North Carolina	1838	7/3/1863	Killed in action	Unknown
Simmerman, George David	Co. A, 4th Virginia	11/19/1843	7/3/1863	Killed in action	Unknown
Simmons, George A.	Co. A, 2nd North Carolina Battalion.	1843	10/26/1863	Mortally wounded-died at unknown place in Gettysburg	Unknown
Simmons, Henry D.	Lt., Co. B, 47th Alabama	1840	7/2/1863	Killed in action	Unknown
Simmons, Jarred	Co. H, 1st Tennessee	1845	7/6/1863	Mortally wounded, July 3rd, and died three days later	Unknown
Simmons, John Lowery	Co. G, 8th Louisiana		7/1/1863	Hollywood Cemetery, Richmond, Va., reburial lists	Richmond, VA
Simmons, Stephen A.	Lt., Co. H, 28th North Carolina	1843	7/3/1863	Killed in action	Unknown
Simmons, Thomas	Co. C, 26th North Carolina	1839	7/1/1863	Killed in action	Unknown
Simmons, Thomas N.	Cpl., Co. C, 14th Tennessee	1839	7/16/1863	Hollywood Cemetery, Richmond, Va., reburial lists	Richmond, VA
Simmons, William J.	Sgt., Co. K, 7th North Carolina	1842	7/3/1863	Killed in action	Unknown
Simms, Alexander	Co. G, 28th Virginia		7/20/1863	Mortally wounded and died at Chester, PA	Phil. National Cem.
Simms, William Henry	Co. H, 18th Virginia		7/3/1863	Killed in action	Unknown
Simonton, Theophilus J.	Co. C, 44th Georgia	1806	7/2/1863	Laurel Grove Cemetery, Savannah, Ga., reburial list	Savannah, GA
Simpkins, Robert B.	Co. K, 22nd Georgia	1842	7/2/1863	Killed in action	Unknown
Simpson, Archer M.	Co. C, 38th Virginia		7/6/1863	Mortally wounded, July 3rd, and died three days later	Unknown

NAME	REGIMENT	BIRTH	DEATH	COMMENT	BURIAL
Simpson, Elijah M.	Co. F, 5th Florida	1841	7/2/1863	Killed in action	Unknown
Simpson, G.S.	Co. A, 13th South Carolina	1840	7/2/1863	Killed in action	Unknown
Simpson, Wiley G.	Co. A, 48th Georgia	1844	7/2/1863	Killed in action	Unknown
Simpson, William J.	Co. I, 28th Virginia		7/3/1863	Killed in action	Unknown
Sims, Benjamin Augustus	Sgt., Co. B, 11th Mississippi	1/10/1833	7/5/1863	Mortally wounded, July 3rd, and died two days later	Unknown
Sims, E.B.	Cpl., Co. E, 10th Alabama		9/19/1863	Mortally wounded, July 3rd, and died at Harrisburg, PA; interred Soldiers' Lot	Harrisburg, PA
Sims, Theophrastus	Co. C, 18th Mississippi	1845	7/2/1863	Killed in action	Unknown
Sims, William B.	Co. B, 14th Virginia		7/3/1863	Killed in action	Unknown
Singon, John	Co. G, 20th Georgia		7/2/1863	Killed in action	Unknown
Sink, John H.	Cpl., Co. B, 24th Virginia		Jul. 1863	Killed in action, July 1-3	Unknown
Sipe, David	Co. C, 28th North Carolina	9/9/1829	7/3/1863	Killed in action	Unknown
Sisk, William H.	Co. H, 22nd North Carolina	1845	7/1/1863	Killed in action	Unknown
Sizemore, Maston T.	Co. A, 5th North Carolina	1827	7/7/1863	Mortally wounded-died at unknown place in Gettysburg	Unknown
Skeen, Charles Ira J.	Carpenter's Battery (Va.)	4/16/1844	Jul. 1863	Killed in action and reinterred in Cedar Hill Cemetery, Covington, VA	Covington, VA
Skelton, Charles L.	Co. K, 10th Virginia		7/3/1863	Killed in action	Unknown
Skinner, Evander	Co. A, 6th Alabama		Jul. 1863	Killed in action	Unknown
Skinner, Uriah L.	Capt., Co. D, 48th Georgia	1837	7/2/1863	Killed in action	Unknown
Skipper, Silas	Co. G, 9th Alabama		7/14/1863	Hollywood Cemetery, Richmond, Va., reburial lists	Richmond, VA
Slade, Jesse Franklin	Co. K, 13th North Carolina	1824	7/1/1863	Killed in action	Unknown
Slaughter, William	Co. C, 8th Florida	1836	7/2/1863	Killed in action	Unknown
Sligh, Thomas W.	Co. E, 3rd South Carolina	1841	7/2/1863	Magnolia Cemetery, Charleston, SC, reburial list	Charleston, SC
Sloan, A.G.	Co. B, 5th Texas		7/2/1863	Killed in action	Unknown
Sloan, Samuel H.	Co. C, 1st Virginia		11/29/1863	Died as POW at Ft. Delaware	Finn's Point, NJ
Slough, James W.	Co. H, 4th Virginia	1837	7/3/1863	Killed in action	Unknown
Small, James M.	Cpl., Co. H, 2nd South Carolina		7/18/1863	Mortally wounded per the Charleston Mercury, August 28, 1863	Unknown
Small, Robert F.	Cpl., Garden's Battery (S.C.)	1843	7/7/1863	Mortally wounded, July 3rd, and died at Hagerstown, Md-buried there	Hagerstown, MD
Smallwood, Jacob H.	Co. E, 6th North Carolina	1836	7/29/1863	Mortally wounded-died at unknown place in Gettysburg	Unknown
Smiley, Alonzo N.	Co. K, 3rd North Carolina	1836	7/2/1863	Killed in action	Unknown
Smiley, Jefferson P.	Sgt., Co. K, 8th Louisiana	1838	7/1/1863	Killed in action	Unknown
Smith, Albert	Co. A, 13th South Carolina	1842	7/1/1863	Killed in action	Newberry, SC
Smith, Alexander E.	Co. A, 18th Virginia		7/3/1863	Killed in action per the Richmond Sentinel, August 29, 1863	Unknown
Smith, Angus	Co. C, 3rd North Carolina		10/8/1863	Died as POW at Ft. Delaware	Finn's Point, NJ
Smith, Benjamin H.	Lt., Co. B, 14th Virginia		7/3/1863	Hollywood Cemetery, Richmond, Va., reburial lists	Richmond, VA

NAME	REGIMENT	BIRTH	DEATH	COMMENT	BURIAL
Smith, Benjamin R.	Co. M, 7th South Carolina		7/2/1863	Hollywood Cemetery, Richmond, Va., reburial lists	Richmond, VA
Smith, Benjamin W.	Co. H, 7th South Carolina		7/2/1863	Killed in action	Unknown
Smith, David G.	Co. I, 11th North Carolina		7/20/1863	Mortally wounded and died at Chambersburg, PA	Chambersburg, PA
Smith, David N.	Co. H, 11th Mississippi	1838	7/8/1863	Mortally wounded-died at unknown place in Gettysburg	Unknown
Smith, David P.	Co. A, 28th North Carolina	1842	7/3/1863	Killed in action	Unknown
Smith, Doctor E.	Co. D, 28th North Carolina	1844	8/21/1863	Mortally wounded and died at Chester, PA	Phil. National Cem.
Smith, Ebenezer F.	Cpl., Co. F, Cobb's Legion	1839	7/2/1863	Laurel Grove Cemetery, Savannah, Ga., reburial list	Savannah, GA
Smith, Elijah	Co. H, 11th Georgia	11/27/1835	718/1863	Died of wounds received July 2nd; interred Bennett Family Cemetery, Walton Co., GA	Walton Go., GA
Smith, Frank	Co. F, 14th Virginia		8/8/1863	No service record-died at Camp Letterman and reinterred in Hollywood Cemetery	Richmond, VA
Smith, George A.	Co. H, 20th North Carolina		8/12/1863	Died as POW at David's Island, NY	Cypress Hills, NY
Smith, George Washington	Jordan's Battery (Va.)		7/3/1863	Hollywood Cemetery, Richmond, Va., reburial lists	Richmond, VA
Smith, Green B.	Co. E, 26th North Carolina	1837	7/1/1863	Killed in action	Unknown
Smith, Isaac L.	Co. G, 17th Mississippi	1842	7/2/1863	Killed in action	Unknown
Smith, J.H.	Co. D, 12th South Carolina		8/2/1863	Died as POW at David's Island, NY	Cypress Hills, NY
Smith, J.W.	Co. A, 49th Georgia		7/3/1863	Killed in action	Unknown
Smith, Jackson L.	Co. A, 45th North Carolina	1841	7/3/1863	Mortally wounded, July 3rd, and died the same day	Unknown
Smith, James A.	Capt., Co. B, 14th Virginia	1837	7/3/1863	Killed in action	Unknown
Smith, James M.	Co. I, 22nd North Carolina	1827	Jul. 1863	Killed in action	Unknown
Smith, James S.	Co. M, 16th North Carolina	1841	7/1/1863	Killed in action	Unknown
Smith, Jefferson B.	Sgt., Co. K, 8th Louisiana		7/1/1863	Killed in action	Unknown
Smith, Joe C.	Lt., Co. E, 4th Texas		7/2/1863	Killed in action	Unknown
Smith, John	Co. E, 14th Tennessee		Jul. 1863	Grave still marked in July 1866 on Jacob Schwartz Farm	Unknown
Smith, John	Co. G, 48th Georgia	1845	7/2/1863	Killed in action	Unknown
Smith, John A.	Co. I, 47th North Carolina	1844	7/3/1863	Killed in action	Unknown
Smith, John Edward	Co. A, 17th Mississippi	1830	Jul. 1863	Killed in action on July 1st or 2nd	Unknown
Smith, John H.	Capt., Co. B, 57th Virginia		7/3/1863	Killed in action	Unknown
Smith, John S.	Co. A, 11th North Carolina	1827	7/15/1863	Hollywood Cemetery, Richmond, Va., reburial lists	Richmond, VA
Smith, John W.	Co. A, 57th Virginia		Jul. 1863	Killed in action	Unknown
Smith, Joseph Henry	Lt., Co. C, 56th Virginia	3/30/1842	7/3/1863	Killed in action per the Richmond Sentinel, July 29, 1863	Unknown
Smith, Joshua	Co. H, 20th Georgia		7/4/1863	Mortally wounded, July 2nd, and died two days later	Unknown
Smith, Leroy	Co. B, 52nd North Carolina	1843	10/7/1863	Died as POW at Ft. Delaware	Finn's Point, NJ

NAME	REGIMENT	BIRTH	DEATH	COMMENT	BURIAL
Smith, Lewis R.	Co. B, 2nd South Carolina	1836	8/8/1863	Mortally wounded per the Charleston Mercury, August 28, 1863	Unknown
Smith, M.C.	Co. C, 55th North Carolina		7/1/1863	Killed in action	Unknown
Smith, Maurice Thompson	Lt. Col., 55th North Carolina	1828	7/2/1863	Killed in action; reinterred at Smith Farm in NC	Granville Co., NC
Smith, Perry L.	Co. I, 13th South Carolina	1840	7/1/1863	Killed in action	Unknown
Smith, Richard T.	Co. H, 17th Mississippi	1838	Jul. 1863	Killed in action on July 1st or 2nd	Unknown
Smith, Robert	Co. G, 3rd Arkansas	1842	7/2/1863	Killed in action	Unknown
Smith, Russell P.	Co. E, Cobb's Legion		7/9/1863	Laurel Grove Cemetery, Savannah, Ga., reburial list	Savannah, GA
Smith, Stephen	Co. E, 9th Louisiana	1837	7/3/1863	Killed in action	Unknown
Smith, Thomas	Co. H, 14th Louisiana		8/16/1863	Hollywood Cemetery, Richmond, Va., reburial lists	Richmond, VA
Smith, Thomas J.	Co. H, 7th South Carolina		7/2/1863	Killed in action	Unknown
Smith, Thomas J.	Co. A, 44th Alabama	1838	7/2/1863	Killed in action	Unknown
Smith, Tillman	Co. H, 31st Georgia		7/7/1863	Mortally wounded-died at unknown place in Gettysburg	Unknown
Smith, W.A.	Co. E, 28th North Carolina	1830	7/11/1863	Mortally wounded-died at unknown place in Gettysburg	Unknown
Smith, Wiley R.	Co. E, 26th North Carolina	1838	1863	Mortally wounded, July 1st, and died at Winchester, VA on an unknown date-buried there	Winchester, VA
Smith, William A.	Co. B, 11th North Carolina		10/1/1863	Died as POW at David's Island, NY	Cypress Hills, NY
Smith, William F.	Co. H, 2nd Mississippi	1843	7/1/1863	Killed in action	Unknown
Smith, William H.	Co. G, 47th North Carolina	1841	7/3/1863	Killed in action	Unknown
Smith, William Hutchinson	Sgt., Co. K, 26th North Carolina	12/2/1830	7/18/1863	Hollywood Cemetery, Richmond, Va., reburial lists	Richmond, VA
Smith, William J.	Cpl., Co. K, 1st Louisiana	1845	11/3/1863	Hollywood Cemetery, Richmond, Va., reburial lists	Richmond, VA
Smith, William J.	Co. G, 17th Mississippi	1836	7/2/1863	Killed in action	Unknown
Smith, William J.	Co. F, 11th North Carolina	1836	7/3/1863	Killed in action	Unknown
Smith, William J. J.	Co. C, 35th Georgia		7/2/1863	Killed in action	Unknown
Smith, William Lee	Co. I, 56th Virginia	1835	Jul. 1863	Killed in action, July 1-3	Unknown
Smith, William P.	Co. C, 10th Alabama		Jul. 1863	Hollywood Cemetery, Richmond, Va., reburial lists	Richmond, VA
Smith, William T.	Co. I, 4th Texas		7/2/1863	Killed in action	Unknown
Smith, William T.	Co. H, 22nd North Carolina	1826	Jul. 1863	Missing in action and presumed dead	Unknown
Smither, George W.	Co. F, 55th Virginia		7/1/1863	Hollywood Cemetery, Richmond, Va., reburial lists	Richmond, VA
Smoot, Joshua	Lt., Co. M, 8th South Carolina		7/2/1863	Killed in action	Unknown
Snead, James	Co. E, 47th North Carolina		7/1/1863	Killed in action	Unknown
Snead, Pleasant A.	Co. C, 19th Virginia		Jul. 1863	Missing in action and presumed dead	Unknown
Snelgrove, Francis Marion	Co. B, 14th South Carolina	1843	7/7/1863	Mortally wounded-died at unknown place in Gettysburg	Unknown
Snellgrove, John C.	Co. M, 6th Alabama		8/20/1863	Hollywood Cemetery, Richmond, Va., reburial lists	Richmond, VA

NAME	REGIMENT	BIRTH	DEATH	COMMENT	BURIAL
Snider, J.A.	Co. H, 11th North Carolina	1826	7/3/1863	Killed in action	Unknown
Snider, William E.	Co. B, 27th Virginia		7/3/1863	Killed in action	Unknown
Snipes, Jeter J.	Cpl., Co. G, 11th North Carolina	1842	7/19/1863	Mortally wounded and died at Chester, PA	Phil. National Cem.
Snoddy, Lorenzo L.	Co. A, 57th Virginia		Jul. 1863	Killed in action, July 1-3	Unknown
Snuggs, P.S.	Co. B, 51st Georgia		Jul. 1863	Mortally wounded, July 2nd, and died at Martinsburg, VA-buried there	Martinsburg, WV
Snyder, Wesley	Co. G, 2nd North Carolina Battalion.	1837	7/17/1863	Mortally wounded-died at unknown place in Gettysburg	Unknown
Solley, Seabron G.	Co. C, 47th Alabama		7/4/1863	Hollywood Cemetery, Richmond, Va., reburial lists	Richmond, VA
Somerville, Robert Briggs	Co. C, 7th Virginia	1841	7/3/1863	Killed in action	Unknown
Sorey, Dorsey W.	Cpl., Co. H, 12th North Carolina	1841	7/11/1863	Oakwood Cemetery, Raleigh, NC, reburial list	Raleigh, NC
South, Levi A.	Co. I, 42nd Mississippi	1845	9/6/1863	Died as POW at Ft. Delaware	Finn's Point, NJ
Southall, Jeremiah W.	Co. K, 10th Georgia		7/2/1863	Killed in action	Unknown
Southall, Valentine W.	Lt., Co. B, 23rd Virginia	1839	7/20/1863	Mortally wounded and reinterred on family plantation after the war	Amelia Co., VA
Southerds, D.	Co. B, 48th Virginia		7/15/1863	Mortally wounded-died at unknown place in Gettysburg	Unknown
Southwick, J.W.	Sgt., Co. L, 1st Texas	1837	7/2/1863	Killed in action	Unknown
Sowers, John S.	Co. L, 4th Virginia		7/3/1863	Hollywood Cemetery, Richmond, Va., reburial lists	Richmond, VA
Spain, William G.	Co. G, 47th North Carolina	1839	7/23/1863	Mortally wounded-died at unknown place in Gettysburg	Unknown
Spainhower, Jacob Peter	Co. D, 53rd North Carolina	1841	7/25/1863	Oakwood Cemetery, Raleigh, NC, reburial list	Raleigh, NC
Sparks, Champ C.	Cpl., Co. G, 7th Virginia	1837	10/3/1863	Died as POW at Ft. Delaware	Finn's Point, NJ
Sparks, Hiram	Co. H, 17th Georgia		7/8/1863	Mortally wounded-died at unknown place in Gettysburg	Unknown
Sparks, Stephen Smiley	Co. B, 59th Georgia	9/8/1841	7/4/1863	Hollywood Cemetery, Richmond, Va., reburial lists	Richmond, VA
Speagle, Logan Monroe	Co. I, 11th North Carolina	1845	7/1/1863	Killed in action	Unknown
Spears, J.T.	Sgt., Co. H, 15th South Carolina	1842	7/2/1863	Magnolia Cemetery, Charleston, SC, reburial list	Charleston, SC
Spears, Jesse	Co. D, 13th South Carolina	1842	7/1/1863	Killed in action	Unknown
Speer, John H.	Co. C, 13th Alabama	1840	7/3/1863	Killed in action	Unknown
Speir, Henry Harris	Co. H, 42nd Mississippi	1833	7/1/1863	Killed in action	Unknown
Speissegger, Samuel L.M.	Sgt., Fraser's Battery (Ga.)		7/2/1863	Killed in action	Unknown
Spell, William	Co. F, 14th Georgia		7/3/1863	Killed in action	Unknown
Spencer, James W.	Co. D, 56th Virginia		7/3/1863	Killed in action	Unknown
Spencer, John Montgomery	Lt., Co. G, 42nd Mississippi	2/17/1833	7/5/1863	Mortally wounded, July 3rd, and died two days later	Unknown
Spencer, Samuel T.	Co. K, 18th Virginia	1833	7/3/1863	Killed in action	Unknown
Spencer, William A.	Blount's Battery (Va.)		7/3/1863	Killed in action	Unknown

NAME	REGIMENT	BIRTH	DEATH	COMMENT	BURIAL
Spessard, Hezekiah Casper	Co. C, 28th Virginia	1/8/1845	7/19/1863	Mortally wounded, July 3rd, and died at 1st Div., 3rd Corps Hospital	Unknown
Spicer, Joseph Henry	Sgt., Co. A, 44th Virginia		7/3/1863	Missing in action and presumed dead	Unknown
Spivey, Ephraim	Co. B, 12th Alabama		7/8/1863	Mortally wounded-died at unknown place in Gettysburg	Unknown
Sprawls, John F.	Sgt., Co. A, 1st South Carolina	1836	7/25/1863	Died as POW at David's Island, NY	Cypress Hills, NY
Sprayberry, Ferdinand G.	Co. K, 22nd Georgia		7/2/1863	Killed in action	Unknown
Spruill, Henry W.	Co. A, 32nd North Carolina	1830	7/10/1863	Mortally wounded-died at unknown place in Gettysburg	Unknown
St. Clair, B.S.	Co. H, 1st Virginia		7/3/1863	Killed in action	Unknown
St. John, Alexander A.	Co. I, 56th Virginia		7/26/1863	Mortally wounded, July 2nd, and died in 1st Corps Hospital	Unknown
St. Martin, Victor Joseph	Capt., Co. K, 8th Louisiana	8/2/1838	7/2/1863	Killed in action; VA marker located in area K, Lot 21, Green Mount Cemetery, Baltimore, MD	Baltimore, MD
Staggers, William J.	Co. E, 6th Alabama	1841	7/3/1863	Killed in action	Unknown
Stallings, F.M.	Cpl., Co. B, 53rd Georgia		7/2/1863	Killed in action	Unknown
Stallings, Hosea	Co. F, 26th North Carolina	1843	8/26/1863	Died as POW at David's Island, NY	Cypress Hills, NY
Stallings, Joseph T.	Co. B, 47th North Carolina	1831	Jul. 1863	Hollywood Cemetery, Richmond, Va., reburial lists	Richmond, VA
Stallings, Richard J.	Sgt., Co. G, 13th North Carolina	1836	7/3/1863	Killed in action	Unknown
Stalnaker, Samuel	Co. G, 14th South Carolina	1838	7/10/1863	Mortally wounded-died at unknown place in Gettysburg	Unknown
Staly, Thomas	Co. K, 7th North Carolina	1844	7/22/1863	Died as POW at David's Island, NY	Cypress Hills, NY
Stampley, George	Co. F, 48th Mississippi		7/2/1863	Killed in action per the Richmond Enquirer, July 16, 1863	Unknown
Stamps, Isaac Davis	Capt., Co. E, 21st Mississippi	4/23/1828	7/3/1863	Killed in action; reinterred in Woodbine, Mississippi in the 1870's	Woodbine, MS
Stancill, John	Sgt., Co. C, 8th South Carolina		7/25/1863	Magnolia Cemetery, Charleston, SC, reburial list	Charleston, SC
Stanford, Samuel	Co. K, 48th Georgia		7/3/1863	Killed in action	Unknown
Stanley, J.G.	Co. K, 22nd Georgia		7/2/1863	Killed in action	Unknown
Stanley, William Penn	Co. B, 45th North Carolina	11/12/1839	7/1/1863	Killed in action	Unknown
Stanly, James	Co. I, 3rd North Carolina	1829	7/16/1863	Mortally wounded-died at unknown place in Gettysburg	Unknown
Starlings, George Columbus	Co. A, 1st Maryland Battalion		7/3/1863	Killed in action	Unknown
Starnes, Henry R.	Co. H, 5th North Carolina	1833	7/1/1863	Hollywood Cemetery, Richmond, Va., reburial lists	Richmond, VA
Starnes, Thomas	Co. B, 26th North Carolina	1840	7/24/1863	Mortally wounded-died at unknown place in Gettysburg	Unknown
Starns, A.H.	Co. D, 3rd South Carolina	1833	7/2/1863	Killed in action	Unknown
Staton, Malachi	Co. D, 37th North Carolina	1835	8/16/1863	Died as POW at David's Island, NY	Cypress Hills, NY
Steadman, John Rowan	Co. I, 34th North Carolina	1846	1863	Mortally wounded-died on unknown date in Gettysburg	Unknown
Steed, Collier A.	Co. C, 35th Georgia	1843	7/3/1863	Killed in action	Unknown
Steel, O. Frank	Co. G, 8th Virginia		7/3/1863	Killed in action	Unknown

NAME	REGIMENT	BIRTH	DEATH	COMMENT	BURIAL
Steel, Robert C.	Co. I, 7th North Carolina	1833	8/27/1863	Oakwood Cemetery, Raleigh, NC, reburial list	Raleigh, NC
Steele, Robert	Sgt., Co. E, 5th Virginia	1837	7/18/1863	Hollywood Cemetery, Richmond, Va., reburial lists	Richmond, VA
Steele, William	Sgt., Co. E, 5th North Carolina	1824	7/1/1863	Hollywood Cemetery, Richmond, Va., reburial lists	Richmond, VA
Steger, Thomas E.	Sgt., Co. F, 17th Mississippi	1843	9/8/1863	Hollywood Cemetery, Richmond, Va., reburial lists	Richmond, VA
Stein, John	Co. B, 14th Louisiana	1843	7/30/1863	Mortally wounded and died at Chester, PA	Phil. National Cem.
Stennis, J. Dudley	Co. C, 13th Mississippi	1842	7/18/1863	Mortally wounded-died at unknown place in Gettysburg	Unknown
Stephens, Andrew W.	Co. D, 13th North Carolina	1831	7/1/1863	Killed in action	Unknown
Stephens, Armistead	Co. I, 45th North Carolina	1809	7/1/1863	Killed in action	Unknown
Stephens, C.A.T.	Co. K, 9th Georgia		8/1/1863	Died as POW at David's Island, NY	Cypress Hills, NY
Stephens, John F.	Co. C, 9th Georgia		7/2/1863	Killed in action	Unknown
Stephens, Lewis F.	Sgt., Co. A, 20th Georgia		7/2/1863	Killed in action	Unknown
Stephens, Thomas Jefferson	Co. E, 3rd Arkansas	1835	7/2/1863	Killed in action	Unknown
Stephens, William O.	Co. C, 24th Georgia		7/3/1863	Killed in action	Unknown
Stevens, James W.	Co. F, 38th Virginia		7/29/1863	Hollywood Cemetery, Richmond, Va., reburial lists	Richmond, VA
Stevens, M.Wesley	Co. K, 14th South Carolina	1840	7/1/1863	Killed in action	Unknown
Stevens, Thomas M.	Co. C, 42nd Virginia		7/3/1863	Killed in action	Unknown
Stevens, William E.	Co. E, 5th Texas	1845	9/4/1863	Hollywood Cemetery, Richmond, Va., reburial lists	Richmond, VA
Stevenson, S.V.	Co. H, 5th Texas	1833	8/7/1863	Mortally wounded, July 3rd, and died at Baltimore, MD-buried there	Baltimore, MD
Stewart, Charles Judson	Co. F, 11th Mississippi	3/3/1845	7/3/1863	Killed in action	Unknown
Stewart, George	Co. G, 1st Tennessee		7/3/1863	Missing in action and presumed dead	Unknown
Stewart, J. Rial	Co. G, 23rd North Carolina		7/1/1863	Killed in action	Unknown
Stewart, John Walter	Lt., Co. F, 18th North Carolina	1840	7/19/1863	Hollywood Cemetery, Richmond, Va., reburial lists	Richmond, VA
Stewart, Joseph W.	Co. E, 3rd South Carolina Battalion	1826	7/2/1863	Killed in action per the Charleston Courier, July 1863	Charleston, SC
Stewart, Philip H.	Co. A, 11th Virginia		7/3/1863	Killed in action	Unknown
Stewart, S.W.	Co. G, 22nd Georgia		7/2/1863	Laurel Grove Cemetery, Savannah, Ga., reburial list	Savannah, GA
Stewart, Thomas J.	Co. D, 2nd North Carolina Battalion		7/2/1863	Killed in action	Unknown
Stewart, Thomas W.	Co. H, 52nd North Carolina	1842	7/3/1863	Killed in action	Unknown
Stewart, William B.	Lt., Co. I, 47th Virginia	1830	7/1/1863	Killed in action	Unknown
Stewart, William Marvin	Lt., Co. F, 24th Georgia		7/2/1863	Killed in action	Unknown
Stinnett, Paulus Percival	Co. H, 19th Virginia		7/3/1863	Killed in action	Unknown
Stinson, George M.	Co. A, 57th Virginia		7/15/1863	Mortally wounded-died at unknown place in Gettysburg	Unknown
Stockton, John B.	Lt., Co. H, 4th North Carolina	1844	7/1/1863	Killed in action	Unknown

NAME	REGIMENT	BIRTH	DEATH	COMMENT	BURIAL
Stokes, Ellwood R.	Sgt., Co. F, 3rd South Carolina Battalion	1840	7/2/1863	Killed in action per the Charleston Courier, July 1863	Unknown
Stokes, John W.	Capt., Co. B, 11th Georgia		7/2/1863	Killed in action	Unknown
Stokes, Thomas	Co. F, 8th Georgia		7/2/1863	Killed in action	Unknown
Stone, Benjamin H.	Page's Artillery (Va.)	1842	7/2/1863	Hollywood Cemetery, Richmond, Va., reburial lists	Richmond, VA
Stone, David G.	Co. C, 11th North Carolina	1841	7/1/1863	Killed in action	Unknown
Stone, Enoch Mattison	Sgt., Co. I, 21st North Carolina	6/10/1835	7/1/1863	Killed in action	Unknown
Stone, Henry D.	Co. B, 15th Alabama	1836	7/2/1863	Killed in action	Unknown
Stone, J. Henry	Cpl., Co. G, 13th Georgia		7/1/1863	Killed in action	Unknown
Stone, Joseph A.	Page's Artillery (Va.)		7/11/1863	Mortally wounded-died at unknown place in Gettysburg	Unknown
Stone, William R.	Co. A, 57th Virginia	1838	7/3/1863	Killed in action, July 1-3	Unknown
Storey, Henry H.	Co. C, 2nd Mississippi	1841	7/3/1863	Killed in action	Unknown
Storey, John F.	Co. C, 2nd Mississippi	1837	7/3/1863	Killed in action	Unknown
Storie, Jesse P.	Sgt., Co. B, 37th North Carolina	1833	8/1/1863	Mortally wounded and died at Lynchburg, VA-buried there	Lynchburg, VA
Story, Columbus	Lt., Co. G, 7th Virginia	1843	7/3/1863	Mortally wounded and died the same day	Unknown
Stott, John A.	Co. A, 33rd North Carolina	1839	7/3/1863	Killed in action	Unknown
Stoudemire, A.B.	Co. H, 13th South Carolina	1838	7/1/1863	Killed in action	Unknown
Stout, William A.	Co. H, 53rd North Carolina	1841	7/15/1863	Died as POW at Ft. Delaware	Finn's Point, NJ
Stout, William L.	Co. G, 48th Virginia	1839	7/3/1863	Killed in action	Unknown
Stovall, Charles L.	Cpl., Co. K, 55th North Carolina		7/31/1863	Mortally wounded and died at Mt. Jackson, VA; interred Our Soldiers' Cemetery	Mt. Jackson, VA
Stowe, J.N.	Sgt., Co. H, 23rd North Carolina		8/3/1863	Died as POW at David's Island, NY	Cypress Hills, NY
Strader, John A.	Co. H, 45th North Carolina	1844	7/20/1863	Oakwood Cemetery, Raleigh, NC, reburial list	Raleigh, NC
Street, Edward	Brooks Arty. (S.C) Rhett's		7/2/1863	Killed in action per the Richmond Sentinel, July 27, 1863	Unknown
Street, Silas	Co. D, 10th Alabama		7/2/1863	Killed in action	Unknown
Stricker, Daniel F.	Co. B, 20th North Carolina	1836	7/1/1863	Killed in action	Unknown
Stricker, John M.	Sgt., Co. E, 21st Mississippi		7/2/1863	Killed in action	Unknown
Strickland, Marcus T.S.	Co. A, 47th North Carolina	1841	7/3/1863	Killed in action	Unknown
Strickland, Noah C.	Co. C, Cobb's Legion Cav. (Ga.)		7/3/1863	Laurel Grove Cemetery, Savannah, Ga., reburial list	Savannah, GA
Strickland, Stephen B.	Co. F, 28th North Carolina	1842	7/3/1863	Killed in action	Unknown
Strong, Charles	Co. I, 11th Mississippi	1839	7/3/1863	Killed in action	Unknown
Strong, William M.	Cpl., Co. I, 44th Alabama	1835	7/2/1863	Killed in action	Unknown
Stroud, Joseph Dewitt	Co. H, 13th Mississippi	1840	7/2/1863	Killed in action	Unknown
Stroud, William	Co. H, 8th Alabama		7/21/1863	Mortally wounded and buried on Jacob Schwartz Farm	Unknown
Stroup, Rufus	Co. D, 38th North Carolina	1835	7/31/1863	Mortally wounded-died at unknown place in Gettysburg	Unknown

NAME	REGIMENT	BIRTH	DEATH	COMMENT	BURIAL
Stroup, William J.	Co. K, 11th North Carolina	1836	7/3/1863	Killed in action	Unknown
Strutt, Pinkney S.	Co. I, 11th North Carolina	1843	8/18/1863	Died as POW at David's Island, NY	Cypress Hills, NY
Stuart, William Dabney	Col., 56th Virginia	9/30/1830	7/29/1863	Mortally wounded, July 3rd, and died at Staunton, VA-buried there	Staunton, VA
Stuck, Jacob Barnett	Co. H, 13th South Carolina	1826	7/1/1863	Killed in action	Unknown
Stunz, Charles W.	Co. H, 24th Virginia		7/3/1863	Killed in action	Unknown
Styne, Andrew Jackson	Lt., Co. K, 57th Virginia	1836	7/3/1863	Killed in action	Unknown
Styne, James M.	Lt., Co. K, 57th Virginia	1841	7/3/1863	Killed in action	Unknown
Sublett, John P.	Co. D, 7th Virginia		7/3/1863	Killed in action	Unknown
Sublett, John S.	Co. K, 4th Alabama		7/2/1863	Killed in action	Unknown
Sudderth, E.M.	Co. D, 11th North Carolina	1825	7/3/1863	Killed in action	Unknown
Sudderth, George H.	Co. I, 26th North Carolina	1839	7/1/1863	Oakwood Cemetery, Raleigh, NC, reburial list	Raleigh, NC
Suddith, Oscar F.	Co. C, 8th Virginia		Jul. 1863	Missing in action and presumed dead	Unknown
Suit, Johnson	Co. D, 6th Alabama	1845	8/28/1863	Mortally wounded, July 1st and died at Frederick, MD; interred in Mt. Olivet Cemetery	Frederick, MD
Sullens, James Willis	Co. D, 53rd Virginia		7/3/1863	Killed in action	Unknown
Sullivan, Cornelius	Sgt., Co. B, 10th Louisiana		7/3/1863	Killed in action	Unknown
Sullivan, John E.	Co. E, 1st Maryland Battalion		8/15/1863	Hollywood Cemetery, Richmond, Va., reburial lists	Richmond, VA
Summers, John Henry Pickard	Co. K, 47th North Carolina	1841	7/1/1863	Killed in action	Unknown
Summers, Peter Riley	Co. A, 53rd North Carolina	1/17/1825	7/3/1863	Killed in action	Unknown
Summers, William Rufus	Co. A, 7th North Carolina	3/30/1843	Jul. 1863	Missing in action and presumed dead	Unknown
Surber, Levi	Co. B, 28th Virginia	1833	7/3/1863	Killed in action	Unknown
Suther, Robert J.	Co. C, 33rd North Carolina	1836	7/3/1863	Killed in action	Unknown
Sutton, Francis M.	Co. K, 2nd Mississippi	1839	7/19/1863	Mortally wounded and died at Hagerstown, MD-buried there	Hagerstown, MD
Sutton, Isaac	Co. G, 3rd North Carolina	1838	7/2/1863	Killed in action	Unknown
Sutton, James H.	Co. F, 7th Tennessee		7/3/1863	Killed in action	Unknown
Sutton, Jordan M.	Co. H, 48th Georgia	1833	7/2/1863	Killed in action	Unknown
Sutton, Richard Sherod	Co. I, 3rd Georgia		7/2/1863	Killed in action	Unknown
Sutton, Stephen A.	Co. A, 4th Georgia		7/2/1863	Killed in action	Unknown
Sutton, William	Co. I, 50th Virginia	1844	7/3/1863	Killed in action	Unknown
Swain, George Thomas	Co. C, 30th North Carolina	1842	7/1/1863	Killed in action	Unknown
Swain, Joseph J.	Co. D, 17th Georgia		7/2/1863	Killed in action	Unknown
Swan, Hugh Brown	Sgt., Co. H, 18th Virginia	1836	7/3/1863	Killed in action	Unknown
Swann, Benjamin	Marmaduke Johnson's Battery (Va.)		8/17/1863	Mortally wounded, July 2nd, and died at Martinsburg, VA	Martinsburg, WV
Swanner, James	Co. A, 5th Alabama		8/15/1863	Hollywood Cemetery, Richmond, Va., reburial lists	Richmond, VA
Swaringen, Henry C.	Co. K, 28th North Carolina	1844	Jul. 1863	Killed in action	Unknown
Sweetland, William Albert	Lt., Co. K, 16th Virginia Cavalry	4/27/1829	7/3/1863	Hollywood Cemetery, Richmond, Va., reburial lists	Richmond, VA

NAME	REGIMENT	BIRTH	DEATH	COMMENT	BURIAL
Swilley, Jack	Co. D, 50th Georgia		7/2/1863	Killed in action	Unknown
Swinson, John A.	Cpl., Co. G, 11th Georgia	1844	7/10/1863	Mortally wounded-died at unknown place in Gettysburg	Unknown
Swofford, Robert	Co. F, 55th North Carolina	9/16/1844	7/1/1863	Missing in action and presumed dead	Unknown
Sydnor, Samuel	Co. E, 40th Virginia		7/3/1863	Missing in action and presumed dead	Unknown
Sykes, John W.	Co. F, 59th Georgia		7/2/1863	Killed in action	Unknown
Sykes, Joseph	Co. A, 61st Virginia		7/2/1863	Killed in action	Unknown
Taber, Ferdinand D.	Co. A, 1st Louisiana	1836	8/10/1863	Hollywood Cemetery, Richmond, Va., reburial lists	Richmond, VA
Taggart, James S.	Co. I, 37th North Carolina	1842	7/1/1863	Killed in action	Unknown
Talbot, Wallace P.	Lt., Co. E, 7th Louisiana	1835	7/3/1863	Killed in action	Unknown
Taliaferro, Edwin	Co. I, 1st Virginia	1842	7/3/1863	Killed in action	Unknown
Taliaferro, James Ed	Lt., Co. K, 42nd Virginia	1841	Jul. 1863	Killed in action commanding company July 2nd or 3rd	Unknown
Taliaferro, John W.	Sgt., Co. A, 42nd Mississippi		7/3/1863	Killed in action	Unknown
Talleen, Joseph B.	Sgt., Co. C, 8th Alabama		7/2/1863	Killed in action	Unknown
Tally, James Ruffin	Co. E, 26th North Carolina	1842	7/8/1863	Hollywood Cemetery, Richmond, Va., reburial lists	Richmond, VA
Tally, William F.	Co. F, 45th North Carolina	1836	7/3/1863	Killed in action	Unknown
Tart, J.E.	Co. D, 5th North Carolina		7/5/1863	Mortally wounded, July 1st, died four days later	Unknown
Tate, Enos R.	Co. C, 15th Georgia		8/5/1863	Hollywood Cemetery, Richmond, Va., reburial lists	Richmond, VA
Tate, Hugh Alexander	Co. D, 11th North Carolina	6/6/1841	8/25/1863	Mortally wounded and died at Camp Letterman; reinterred after the war in Morganton, NC	Morganton, NC
Taylor, A. John	Co. F, 26th North Carolina	1843	7/1/1863	Killed in action	Unknown
Taylor, Adam	Co. A, 37th Virginia		7/3/1863	Hollywood Cemetery, Richmond, Va., reburial lists	Richmond, VA
Taylor, Benjamin	Co. G, 12th Alabama		Jul. 1863	Missing in action and presumed dead	Unknown
Taylor, Brooks	Co. G, 12th Alabama		Jul. 1863	Missing in action and presumed dead	Unknown
Taylor, Callaway	Co. A, 26th North Carolina	1843	7/1/1863	Killed in action	Unknown
Taylor, Henry G.	Co. F, 1st Maryland Battalion		Jul. 1863	Killed in action, July 1-3	Unknown
Taylor, J.H.	Co. H, 12th South Carolina	1843	7/1/1863	Killed in action	Unknown
Taylor, Jacob S.	Cpl., Co. C, 28th Virginia	1828	7/3/1863	Killed in action	Unknown
Taylor, James	Co. I, 34th North Carolina	1836	7/1/1863	Killed in action	Unknown
Taylor, James F.	Co. F, 19th Virginia	1829	Jul. 1863	Mortally wounded per the Richmond Sentinel, August 11, 1863	Unknown
Taylor, James W.	Co. I, 49th Virginia	1837	7/3/1863	Mortally wounded, July 3rd, and died the same day	Unknown
Taylor, John	Co. H, 48th Virginia		7/2/1863	Killed in action	Unknown
Taylor, John	Co. G, 55th North Carolina	1826	7/1/1863	Killed in action	Unknown
Taylor, John	Co. C, 2nd Virginia		Jul. 1863	Missing in action and presumed dead	Unknown
Taylor, John Rice	Co. E, 19th Virginia	1/26/1838	7/3/1863	Killed in action	Unknown
Taylor, John W.	Co. B, 53rd North Carolina		7/3/1863	Killed in action	Unknown

NAME	REGIMENT	BIRTH	DEATH	COMMENT	BURIAL
Taylor, John Wade	Co. F, 11th Virginia	1844	9/28/1863	Mortally wounded-died at unknown place in Gettysburg	Unknown
Taylor, Miles	Co. I, 26th North Carolina	1838	7/3/1863	Killed in action	Unknown
Taylor, Nicholas Harrison	Co. E, 22nd Georgia		7/15/1863	Mortally wounded and died in unknown hospital, Richmond, VA	Richmond, VA
Taylor, Robert	Cpl., Co. E, 14th Virginia	1842	7/3/1863	Killed in action	Unknown
Taylor, Robert J.	Co. B, 56th Virginia		7/3/1863	Missing in action and presumed dead	Unknown
Taylor, Roland S.	Co. G, 5th North Carolina		7/10/1863	Mortally wounded-died at unknown place in Gettysburg	Unknown
Taylor, William A.	Co. F, 3rd Arkansas		7/2/1863	Killed in action	Unknown
Taylor, William E.S.	Co. C, 2nd Georgia Battalion		7/2/1863	Killed in action	Unknown
Taylor, Wilson G.	Co. H, 32nd North Carolina	1838	7/1/1863	Killed in action	Unknown
Teague, John Morgan	Capt., Co. K, 44th Alabama	1828	7/2/1863	Killed in action	Unknown
Tedder, Newton J.	Co. D, 17th Mississippi	1837	Jul. 1863	Hollywood Cemetery, Richmond, Va., reburial lists	Richmond, VA
Teel, Josiah W.	Co. B, 24th Virginia		7/3/1863	Missing in action and presumed dead	Unknown
Telly, William	Co. G, 53rd Virginia		8/9/1863	Mortally wounded and died at Camp Letterman	Unknown
Temple, George G.	Co. C, 11th Mississippi	1830	7/3/1863	Killed in action	Unknown
Tenney, Nathaniel B.	Lt., Co. G, 11th North Carolina	1836	7/1/1863	Killed in action	Unknown
Terrell, Henry	1st Co., Richmond Howitzers		8/4/1863	Hollywood Cemetery, Richmond, Va., reburial lists	Richmond, VA
Terrell, James Macon	Co. F, 12th North Carolina	7/22/1842	Jul. 1863	Killed in action, July 1-3	Unknown
Terrell, John Warren	Cpl., Co. F, 12th North Carolina	1/11/1840	Jul. 1863	Missing in action and presumed dead; brother of James M. Terrell	Unknown
Terrell, Joseph R.	Woolfolk's Battery (Va.)		7/3/1863	Killed in action	Unknown
Terrell, William P.	Co. H, 45th North Carolina	1836	7/7/1863	Oakwood Cemetery, Raleigh, NC, reburial list	Raleigh, NC
Testament, T.M.	Co. A, 26th North Carolina	1844	7/1/1863	Killed in action	Unknown
Tew, Ashley B.	Co. E, 20th North Carolina	1835	7/3/1863	Oakwood Cemetery, Raleigh, NC, reburial list	Raleigh, NC
Tharington, W.H.	Co. G, 47th North Carolina	1843	7/3/1863	Killed in action	Unknown
Thatcher, Samuel	Capt., Co. I, 11th Georgia		8/13/1863	Mortally wounded, July 2nd, and died at Hagerstwon, Md-buried there	Hagerstown, MD
Thaxton, William E.	Co. K, 14th Virginia	1842	7/3/1863	Killed in action	Unknown
Theus, Simeon B.	Sgt., Co. F, 59th Georgia		7/8/1863	Hollywood Cemetery, Richmond, Va., reburial lists	Richmond, VA
Thibaut, Louis	Louisiana Guard Artillery		7/1/1863	Hollywood Cemetery, Richmond, Va., reburial lists	Richmond, VA
Thomas, Abraham J.	Co. F, 38th Virginia		7/9/1863	Hollywood Cemetery, Richmond, Va., reburial lists	Richmond, VA
Thomas, D.I.	Co. H, 13th Georgia		7/6/1863	Mortally wounded July 1st	Unknown
Thomas, David Woodley	Co. H, 3rd Arkansas		7/2/1863	Killed in action	Unknown
Thomas, Gideon B.	Co. A, 51st Georgia		7/10/1863	Mortally wounded-died at unknown place in Gettysburg	Unknown
Thomas, Henry W.	Co. K, 32nd North Carolina		7/3/1863	Killed in action	Unknown

NAME	REGIMENT	BIRTH	DEATH	COMMENT	BURIAL
Thomas, James Morgan	Co. C, 1st Virginia	10/23/1826	7/3/1863	Killed in action	Unknown
Thomas, James S.	Sgt. Maj., 27th Virginia	1839	7/3/1863	Killed in action	Unknown
Thomas, James S.	Co. A, 28th Virginia	1843	7/3/1863	Missing in action and presumed dead	Unknown
Thomas, John	Co. I, 45th North Carolina	1841	7/1/1863	Killed in action	Unknown
Thomas, John William	Co. K, 3rd Virginia		7/3/1863	Killed in action	Unknown
Thomas, L. Jackson	Co. H, 5th Florida		7/2/1863	Killed in action	Unknown
Thomas, Lewis	Cpl., Co. A, 38th North Carolina	1837	7/1/1863	Killed in action	Unknown
Thomas, Lewis Pinckny	Co. K, 3rd South Carolina	10/11/1845	7/2/1863	Killed in action	Unknown
Thomas, Robert	Co. E, 52nd North Carolina	1832	7/3/1863	Killed in action	Unknown
Thomas, Robert E.	Co. M, 8th South Carolina		7/2/1863	Killed in action per the Charleston Courier, July 1863	Unknown
Thomas, Samuel W.	Co. E, 1st South Carolina		7/16/1863	Mortally wounded-died at unknown place in Gettysburg	Unknown
Thomas, William Marion	Co. E, 11th Georgia	1837	7/2/1863	Killed in action	Unknown
Thomas, William Robert	Lt., Co. K, 3rd South Carolina	11/8/1835	7/4/1863	Magnolia Cemetery, Charleston, SC, reburial list	Charleston, SC
Thomason, George L.F.	Sgt., Co. H, 37th North Carolina	1836	8/16/1863	Mortally wounded and died at Chester, PA	Phil. National Cem.
Thomason, James H.	Co. F, 53rd Virginia		7/3/1863	Killed in action	Unknown
Thompson, A.L.	21st North Carolina		7/24/1863	Mortally wounded and died at Chester, PA	Hagerstown, MD
Thompson, A.L.	Co. H, 48th Georgia		7/2/1863	Killed in action	Unknown
Thompson, George	Co. H, 20th North Carolina	1841	7/19/1863	Mortally wounded-died at unknown place in Gettysburg	Unknown
Thompson, George W.	Co. F, 14th Virginia	1836	7/3/1863	Killed in action	Unknown
Thompson, Hugh	Co. K, 51st Georgia	1817	7/2/1863	Killed in action	Unknown
Thompson, James E.	Co. B, 10th Georgia		7/2/1863	Killed in action	Unknown
Thompson, James E.	Co. I, 48th Georgia		7/2/1863	Killed in action	Unknown
Thompson, John Templeton	Co. K, 23rd North Carolina	3/6/1831	7/1/1863	Killed in action	Unknown
Thompson, John W.	Co. G, 10th Alabama	1824	9/19/1863	Hollywood Cemetery, Richmond, Va., reburial lists	Richmond, VA
Thompson, Joseph Hunter	Sgt., Co. F, 6th North Carolina	1831	7/20/1863	Mortally wounded, July 2nd, and died at Mt. Jackson, VA	Mt. Jackson, VA
Thompson, Pleasant Hossey	Lt., Co. G, 3rd Arkansas	1838	7/2/1863	Killed in action	Unknown
Thompson, Risden N.	Co. I, 52nd North Carolina	1843	9/24/1863	Oakwood Cemetery, Raleigh, NC, reburial list	Raleigh, NC
Thompson, Samuel T.	Dement's Battery (Md.)	7/12/1835	7/2/1863	Killed in action	Baltimore, MD
Thompson, Thomas B.	Sgt., Co. G, 52nd North Carolina	1833	8/10/1863	Oakwood Cemetery, Raleigh, NC, reburial list	Raleigh, NC
Thompson, W.M.	Co. F, 26th North Carolina	1845	7/1/1863	Killed in action	Unknown
Thompson, William	Co. E, 13th North Carolina	1845	7/30/1863	Mortally wounded-died at unknown place in Gettysburg	Unknown
Thompson, William D.	Sgt., Co. G, 52nd North Carolina	7/31/1829	7/3/1863	Killed in action	Unknown
Thompson, William R.	Co. A, 7th Louisiana	1838	7/21/1863	Died at Jordan Springs Hopital, Winchester, VA; interred Stonewall Cemetery	Winchester, VA

NAME	REGIMENT	BIRTH	DEATH	COMMENT	BURIAL
Thorn, Thomas J.	Lt., Co. D, 16th North Carolina	1838	7/30/1863	Mortally wounded and died at Chester, PA	Phil. National Cem.
Thornell, J. Amos	Co. D, 11th Mississippi	1839	7/3/1863	Killed in action	Unknown
Thornton Joseph A.	Co. B, 57th Virginia		Jul. 1863	Killed in action, July 1-3	Unknown
Thorpe, Thomas	Sgt., Co. G, 7th Louisiana		7/2/1863	Killed in action as color bearer	Unknown
Thrasher, William N.	Co. A, 13th Mississippi	1832	7/2/1863	Killed in action	Unknown
Thrower, William H.	Co. E, 52nd North Carolina	1841	7/3/1863	Killed in action	Unknown
Thurman, William H.	Sgt., Co. G, 53rd Virginia		7/3/1863	Killed in action	Unknown
Tice, James R.	Co. B, 42nd Virginia	1842	7/6/1863	Hollywood Cemetery, Richmond, Va., reburial lists	Richmond, VA
Tickle, Abasalom B.	Co. K, 47th North Carolina	1831	Jul. 1863	Hollywood Cemetery, Richmond, Va., reburial lists	Richmond, VA
Tickle, Andrew F.	Co. K, 47th North Carolina	1840	Jul. 1863	Mortally wounded-died on unknown date in Gettysburg	Unknown
Tickle, George R.	Co. K, 47th North Carolina	1841	7/3/1863	Missing in action and presumed dead	Unknown
Tickle, George Sanford	Co. A, 53rd North Carolina		7/1/1863	Killed in action	Unknown
Tiffany, John	Lt., Co. D, 27th Virginia	6/29/1842	7/10/1863	Mortally wounded-died at unknown place in Gettysburg	Unknown
Tillery, Hugh Taylor	Co. F, 3rd Arkansas	1843	7/2/1863	Killed in action	Unknown
Tilley, Robert P.	Sgt., Co. G, 53rd North Carolina	1843	7/4/1863	Oakwood Cemetery, Raleigh, NC, reburial list	Raleigh, NC
Tilley, William M.	Co. G, 53rd North Carolina	1832	Jul. 1863	Mortally wounded-died on unknown date in Gettysburg	Unknown
Tilman, James P.	Co. F, 49th Virginia		Jul. 1863	Mortally wounded-died on unknown date in Gettysburg	Unknown
Timberlake, Benjamin H.	Co. B, 53rd Virginia	1833	7/13/1863	Mortally wounded-died at unknown place in Gettysburg	Unknown
Timberlake, George W.	Sgt., Co. A, 3rd North Carolina	1838	8/8/1863	Died as POW at David's Island, NY	Cypress Hills, NY
Tinsley, David W.	Cpl., Co. I, 48th Georgia	1840	7/2/1863	Killed in action	Unknown
Tison, William L.	Co. H, 9th Georgia		8/8/1863	Died as POW at David's Island, NY	Cypress Hills, NY
Todd, R. Henry	Cpl., Co. B, 53rd North Carolina	1832	7/1/1863	Killed in action	Unknown
Todd, R.L.	Co. D, 11th North Carolina	1844	7/26/1863	Hollywood Cemetery, Richmond, Va., reburial lists	Richmond, VA
Todd, William R.	Co. C, 48th Georgia	1839	7/2/1863	Killed in action	Unknown
Tomlinson, William J.	Co. I, 57th Virginia	1825	Jul. 1863	Killed in action, July 1-3	Unknown
Tompkins, John	Co. C, 1st Virginia		Jul. 1863	Missing in action and presumed dead	Unknown
Tompkins, Thomas B.	Lt., Co. A, 45th Georgia		7/3/1863	Mortally wounded, July 3rd, and died the same day	Unknown
Toney, William Washington	Co. B, 4th Alabama	1831	Jul. 1863	Killed in action, July 1-3	Unknown
Torgee, George W.	Blount's Battery (Va.)		7/3/1863	Killed in action	Unknown
Torrence, Leonidas	Cpl., Co. H, 23rd North Carolina		7/7/1863	Mortally wounded-died at unknown place in Gettysburg	Unknown
Totten, John C.	Co. A, 13th North Carolina	1835	7/19/1863	Mortally wounded and died at Farmville, VA	Farmville, VA
Totten, William R.	Lt., Co. K, 13th North Carolina	1838	7/10/1863	Mortally wounded-died at unknown place in Gettysburg	Unknown

NAME	REGIMENT	BIRTH	DEATH	COMMENT	BURIAL
Townes, Daniel C.	Capt., Co. A, 38th Virginia		7/3/1863	Killed in action per the Richmond Sentinel, August 1, 1863	Unknown
Townsell, M.L.	Co. F, 26th North Carolina	1841	7/1/1863	Killed in action	Unknown
Trammell, Montreville P.	Co. H, 2nd North Carolina Battalion.	1840	10/1/1863	Mortally wounded-died at unknown place in Gettysburg	Unknown
Traylor, Albert Thomas	Lt., Co. C, 7th South Carolina	8/2/1838	7/8/1863	Hollywood Cemetery, Richmond, Va., reburial lists	Richmond, VA
Traynham, William B.	Sgt., Co. B, 20th North Carolina	1839	7/9/1863	Oakwood Cemetery, Raleigh, NC, reburial list	Raleigh, NC
Traytor, William	Co. I, 20th Georgia		11/21/1863	Died as POW at David's Island, NY	Cypress Hills, NY
Traywick, William H.	Co. A, 8th Alabama	1817	9/4/1863	Hollywood Cemetery, Richmond, Va., reburial lists	Richmond, VA
Treadaway, James Alexander	Co. H, 43rd North Carolina	1844	10/19/1863	Mortally wounded and died in Richmond, VA-buried in Hollywood Cemetery	Richmond, VA
Tredway, Thomas Booker	Sgt., Co. I, 53rd Virginia	8/13/1844	7/3/1863	Hollywood Cemetery, Richmond, Va., reburial lists	Richmond, VA
Trent, Andrew C.	Co. E, 48th Virginia		7/2/1863	Killed in action	Unknown
Trice, Thomas C.	Co. D, 13th Georgia	3/29/1840	7/22/1863	Mortally wounded-died at unknown place in Gettysburg	Unknown
Trimmer, William	Co. G, 15th Alabama	1842	7/3/1863	Killed in action	Unknown
Triplett, James H.	Sgt., Co. K, 11th North Carolina	1843	7/1/1863	Killed in action	Unknown
Triplett, Jesse F.	Sgt., Co. C, 26th North Carolina	1834	7/3/1863	Killed in action	Unknown
Triplett, John W.	Sgt., Co. K, 53rd North Carolina	1839	7/3/1863	Killed in action	Unknown
Trout, William R.	Co. C, 16th Georgia		7/2/1863	Killed in action	Unknown
Trucks, John David	Co. F, 44th Alabama	1830	7/8/1863	Mortally wounded-died at unknown place in Gettysburg	Unknown
Truitt, John D.	Co. A, 14th South Carolina	1842	7/1/1863	Killed in action	Unknown
Tucker, -	Co. F, 6th Alabama		7/14/1863	Mortally wounded-died at unknown place in Gettysburg	Unknown
Tucker, David	Cpl., Co. A, 8th Alabama		7/3/1863	Killed in action	Unknown
Tucker, James G.	Sgt., Co. F, 53rd Virginia		8/12/1863	Mortally wounded and died at Camp Letterman	Unknown
Turnbow, James M.	Lt., Co. G, 4th Alabama	1839	7/2/1863	Killed in action	Unknown
Turner, George W.	Co. D, 20th Georgia	1841	7/2/1863	Killed in action	Unknown
Turner, J.T.	Co. G, 22nd South Carolina		8/9/1863	Magnolia Cemetery, Charleston, SC, reburial list	Charleston, SC
Turner, Lycurgus	Sgt., Co. C, 6th South Carolina	1841	7/1/1863	Killed in action	Unknown
Turner, T.J.	2nd North Carolina		8/1/1863	Oakwood Cemetery, Raleigh, NC, reburial list	Raleigh, NC
Turner, William	Co. D, 5th Texas		7/6/1863	Mortally wounded, July 2nd, and died four days later	Unknown
Turquais, Pierre	Co. F, 10th Louisiana		8/18/1863	Mortally wounded and died in Louisiana Hospital, Richmond, VA-interred Hollywood Cem.	Richmond, VA
Tweedy, George Dabney	Co. C, 11th Virginia	4/6/1842	7/3/1863	Hollywood Cemetery, Richmond, Va., reburial lists	Richmond, VA

NAME	REGIMENT	BIRTH	DEATH	COMMENT	BURIAL
Tyler, William M.	Co. A, 42nd Mississippi	8/8/1828	7/3/1863	Killed in action	Unknown
Tyson, William Thomas	Cpl., Co. E, 38th North Carolina	1840	7/26/1863	Mortally wounded-died at unknown place in Gettysburg	Unknown
Udurley, Moses	Richmond Fayette Artillery (Va.)		7/3/1863	Killed in action	Unknown
Underdown, William Josiah	Co. F, 26th North Carolina	5/16/1845	7/3/1863	Mortally wounded, July 1st, died two days later	Unknown
Underwood, Thomas J.	Co. K, 47th North Carolina	1838	7/1/1863	Killed in action	Unknown
Upchurch, Jubal	Co. E, 47th North Carolina	1829	7/1/1863	Missing in action and presumed dead	Unknown
Ussery, S.W.	Co. A, 1st South Carolina		7/1/1863	Killed in action	Unknown
Utley, Gaston	Cpl., Co. C, 47th North Carolina	1815	Jul. 1863	Mortally wounded July 3rd, and died on unknown date	Unknown
Utley, Henry	Co. D, 48th Georgia		Jul. 1863	Mortally wounded, July 2nd, and died on unknown date	Unknown
Valentine, Alexander H.	Co. F, 17th Mississippi	1829	7/2/1863	Killed in action	Unknown
Valentine, Edward W.	Co. G, 11th Virginia	1844	7/3/1863	Killed in action	Unknown
Van Dyke, Charles R.	Co. F, 4th Georgia		7/2/1863	Killed in action	Unknown
Van Dyke, William L.	Co. F, 4th Georgia		7/2/1863	Killed in action	Unknown
Van Lantz, Joseph T.	Cpl., Taylor's Battery (Va.)		1863	Mortally wounded per the Richmond Sentinel, July 27, 1863; died on unknown date	Unknown
Vandegriff, Joseph	Co. C, 10th Louisiana	1833	7/31/1863	Died as POW at David's Island, NY	Cypress Hills, NY
Vanderford, Wade Hampton	Co. H, 15th South Carolina	1830	7/12/1863	Magnolia Cemetery, Charleston, SC, reburial list	Charleston, SC
Vannoy, Elijah Ross	Sgt., Co. F, 52nd North Carolina	1842	7/3/1863	Killed in action	Unknown
Varner, McKenzie C.	Co. L, 22nd North Carolina	1836	1863	Mortally wounded-died on unknown date in Gettysburg	Unknown
Vaugh, William Thomas	Co. B, 5th Alabama		8/6/1863	Mortally wounded and died at Harrisonburg, VA	Harrisonburg, VA
Vaughan, Alexander Wilkes	Co. H, 38th Georgia	12/22/1826	7/17/1863	Mortally wounded-died at unknown place in Gettysburg	Unknown
Vaughan, George W.	Co. L, 48th Mississippi	1831	7/2/1863	Killed in action per the Richmond Enquirer, July 16, 1863	Unknown
Vaughan, John L.	Co. B, 56th Virginia		7/29/1863	Hollywood Cemetery, Richmond, Va., reburial lists	Richmond, VA
Vaughan, T.Y.	Co. E, 23rd North Carolina	1840	7/1/1863	Killed in action	Unknown
Vaughan, W.J.	Co. H, 1st Virginia		7/3/1863	Killed in action	Unknown
Vaughn, James T.	Co. H, 13th North Carolina	1842	7/1/1863	Killed in action	Unknown
Vaughn, Joshua	Co. B, 15th Georgia	1835	7/2/1863	Killed in action	Unknown
Vaughn, W.W.	Co. H, 53rd Georgia		7/2/1863	Mortally wounded, July 2nd, and died the same day	Unknown
Vaughn, William	Co. F, 4th Georgia		7/2/1863	Killed in action	Unknown
Vaughn, William	Co. K, 55th North Carolina		7/7/1863	Mortally wounded-died at unknown place in Gettysburg	Unknown
Vay, James Septime	Lt., Co. A, 8th Louisiana	8/8/1842	7/2/1863	Killed in action	Unknown
Vehorn, Elias	Co. F, 13th South Carolina	1837	10/13/1863	Mortally wounded-died at unknown place in Gettysburg	Unknown

NAME	REGIMENT	BIRTH	DEATH	COMMENT	BURIAL
Vellines, John A.	Co. I, 3rd Virginia	1840	7/26/1863	Mortally wounded-died at unknown place in Gettysburg	Unknown
Vermillion, John Matlock	Capt., Co. A, 48th Virginia	7/21/1831	7/2/1863	Killed in action	Unknown
Vermillion, John Smith	Co. C, 37th Virginia	1832	7/4/1863	Obituary Abingdon Virginian, August 14, 1863	Unknown
Vermillion, Levi H.	Co. G, 24th Virginia	2/21/1843	7/9/1863	Hollywood Cemetery, Richmond, Va., reburial lists	Richmond, VA
Vest, Willis M.	Co. C, 57th Virginia	1842	8/19/1863	Mortally wounded and died at Baltimore, MD-buried there	Baltimore, MD
Vick, Nathan W.	Co. E, 33rd North Carolina		7/2/1863	Killed in action	Unknown
Vick, William H.	Co. D, 32nd North Carolina	1840	Jul. 1863	Oakwood Cemetery, Raleigh, NC, reburial list	Raleigh, NC
Victory, John, Jr.	Sgt., Co. B, 1st Texas	1834	7/8/1863	Hollywood Cemetery, Richmond, Va., reburial lists	Richmond, VA
Vinagum, Thomas V.	Co. F, 13th North Carolina	1839	8/24/1863	Mortally wounded and died at Staunton, VA-buried there	Staunton, VA
Vines, George	Co. F, 50th Virginia		Jul. 1863	Killed in action on either July 2nd or 3rd	Unknown
Vinson, Leven	Sgt., Co. L, 15th Alabama	1836	7/2/1863	Killed in action	Unknown
Waddell, George Washington	Pee Dee Artillery (S.C.)		7/2/1863	Killed in action	Unknown
Waddell, William D.	Co. H, 1st Virginia	1830	8/12/1863	Mortally wounded and died at Chester, PA	Phil. National Cem.
Waddle, W.T.	Co. B, 13th Georgia		7/1/1863	Killed in action	Unknown
Waddy, George R.	Co. D, 55th Virginia	1822	7/9/1863	Mortally wounded in action-died at unknown place in Gettysburg	Unknown
Wade, Benjamin H.	Lt. Col., 57th Virginia	1830	7/5/1863	Mortally wounded, July 3rd, and died two days later	Unknown
Wade, Littleton R.	Co. E, 32nd North Carolina	1844	7/7/1863	Oakwood Cemetery, Raleigh, NC, reburial list	Raleigh, NC
Wade, Thaddeus M.	Co. D, 28th Virginia	1836	9/16/1863	Mortally wounded and died at Chester, PA	Phil. National Cem.
Waesner, Solomon E.	Co. E, 28th North Carolina	1837	8/18/1863	Oakwood Cemetery, Raleigh, NC, reburial list	Raleigh, NC
Wagg, Samuel P.	Capt., Co. A, 26th North Carolina	1840	7/3/1863	Killed in action	Unknown
Waggy, Henry	Co. F, 25th Virginia	1841	7/2/1863	Hollywood Cemetery, Richmond, Va., reburial lists	Richmond, VA
Wagoner, Daniel	Cpl., Co. M, 21st North Carolina	1839	7/2/1863	Killed in action	Unknown
Wakefield, John Williams	Co. I, 14th South Carolina	2/26/1845	7/5/1863	Mortally wounded per the Charleston Courier, July 1863	Unknown
Walden, Franklin	Co. A, 48th Georgia	1837	7/2/1863	Killed in action	Unknown
Walden, Isaac	Co. B, 22nd Georgia		7/2/1863	Killed in action	Unknown
Walden, William	Co. C, 3rd Arkansas		7/2/1863	Missing in action and presumed dead	Unknown
Waldron, William L.	Lt., Co. I, 42nd Mississippi	1829	7/1/1863	Killed in action	Unknown
Walker, Anderson W.	Co. D, 4th Alabama	1835	9/20/1863	Hollywood Cemetery, Richmond, Va., reburial lists	Richmond, VA
Walker, Benjamin F.	Co. I, 30th North Carolina		8/12/1863	Oakwood Cemetery, Raleigh, NC, reburial list	Raleigh, NC

NAME	REGIMENT	BIRTH	DEATH	COMMENT	BURIAL
Walker, Charles L.	Lt., Co. F, 26th Georgia	1820	9/3/1863	Laurel Grove Cemetery, Savannah, Ga., reburial list	Savannah, GA
Walker, George H.	Lt., Co. C, 24th Virginia		7/3/1863	Killed in action	Unknown
Walker, George M.	Co. D, 2nd Mississippi	1842	7/1/1863	Killed in action	Unknown
Walker, George Raysor	Lt., Co. G, 5th Florida	7/26/1828	7/2/1863	Mortally wounded, July 2nd, and died the same day	Unknown
Walker, J.D.	Co. F, 32nd North Carolina	1845	7/1/1863	Killed in action	Unknown
Walker, James H.	Cpl., Co. H, 57th North Carolina	1830	Jul. 1863	Killed on July 2nd or 3rd; reinterred in Cabarrus Co.,NC after the war	Cabarrus Co., NC
Walker, James W.	Co. K, 13th North Carolina	1830	7/1/1863	Killed in action	Unknown
Walker, John B.	Cpl., Co. F, 7th Virginia	1842	7/3/1863	Killed in action	Unknown
Walker, John Blount	Co. I, 30th North Carolina	1838	8/13/1863	Mortally wounded-died at unknown place in Gettysburg	Unknown
Walker, John Chisum	Co. I, 4th Texas	1841	9/1/1863	Mortally wounded-died at unknown place in Gettysburg	Unknown
Walker, John H.	Co. G, 14th South Carolina	1833	7/1/1863	Killed in action per the Charleston Courier, July 1863	Unknown
Walker, John Henry	Lt., Co. D, 3rd South Carolina	1839	7/2/1863	Killed in action	Unknown
Walker, John M.	Co. E, 12th Alabama		Jul. 1863	Missing in action and presumed dead	Unknown
Walker, Marshall H.	Cpl., Co. H, 6th North Carolina	1842	7/1/1863	Oakwood Cemetery, Raleigh, NC, reburial list	Raleigh, NC
Walker, Morgan A.	Cpl., Co. F, 57th North Carolina	1834	7/30/1863	Mortally wounded-died at unknown place in Gettysburg	Unknown
Walker, Nathan W.	Co. I, 18th Virginia	1828	8/8/1863	Hollywood Cemetery, Richmond, Va., reburial lists	Richmond, VA
Walker, P.E.	Lt., Co. A, 7th South Carolina	1836	7/20/1863	Mortally wounded and died at Hagerstown, MD-buried there	Hagerstown, MD
Walker, Robert R.	Co. G, 8th Georgia		7/2/1863	Hollywood Cemetery, Richmond, Va., reburial lists	Richmond, VA
Walker, William P.	Sgt., Co. D, 3rd Georgia		7/15/1863	Mortally wounded-died at unknown place in Gettysburg	Unknown
Wall, John	Sgt., Co. E, 14th Tennessee		7/3/1863	Killed in action	Unknown
Wall, William D.	Co. F, 21st North Carolina		Jul. 1863	Mortally wounded, July 1st, and died on unknown date at Gettysburg	Unknown
Wallace, Daniel C.	Co. F, 13th North Carolina		7/7/1863	Mortally wounded, July 3rd, and died on July 7th or 8th	Unknown
Wallace, H.M.	Co. H, 23rd North Carolina	1833	7/1/1863	Killed in action per the Edgefield Advertiser, September 30, 1863	Unknown
Wallace, John Beauford	Sgt., Co. D, 14th South Carolina	1838	7/2/1863	Killed in action per the Charleston Courier, July 1863	Unknown
Wallace, R.R.	Co. G, 8th Georgia		7/3/1863	Killed in action	Unknown
Wallace, Stephen A.	Co. B, 3rd Arkansas	1836	8/22/1863	Hollywood Cemetery, Richmond, Va., reburial lists	Richmond, VA
Wallace, William P.	Co. C, 23rd North Carolina	1838	7/1/1863	Killed in action	Unknown
Wallace, William P.	Co. H, 4th Virginia		7/3/1863	Killed in action	Unknown
Wallace, William T.	Sgt., Co. D, 2nd North Carolina Battalion		7/2/1863	Killed in action	Unknown

NAME	REGIMENT	BIRTH	DEATH	COMMENT	BURIAL
Waller, George	Co. E, 5th North Carolina	1841	7/1/1863	Hollywood Cemetery, Richmond, Va., reburial lists	Richmond, VA
Waller, John D.	Co. A, 13th Georgia		7/1/1863	Killed in action	Unknown
Waller, John R.	Co. I, 52nd North Carolina	1833	7/23/1863	Hollywood Cemetery, Richmond, Va., reburial lists	Richmond, VA
Waller, William W.	Co. F, 2nd South Carolina	1828	7/2/1863	Killed in action	Charleston, SC
Walrond, John P.	Lt., Co. D, 28th Virginia	1839	7/31/1863	Hollywood Cemetery, Richmond, Va., reburial lists	Richmond, VA
Walters, Charles W.	Lt., Co. C, 38th Virginia		7/3/1863	Killed in action	Unknown
Walters, Henry T.	Cpl., Co. A, 13th North Carolina	1837	7/3/1863	Mortally wounded, July 2nd, and died the next day	Unknown
Walters, James F.	Co. I, 3rd Georgia		7/22/1863	Mortally wounded and died at Chester, PA	Phil. National Cem.
Walthall, J.J.	Sgt., Co. E, 5th Texas	1828	7/5/1863	Hollywood Cemetery, Richmond, Va., reburial lists	Richmond, VA
Wamsley, Louis W.	Co. K, 8th Florida	1838	12/20/1863	Mortally wounded-died at unknown place in Gettysburg	Unknown
Ward, Eliza Alonzo	Co. C, 60th Georgia		10/5/1863	Laurel Grove Cemetery, Savannah, Ga., reburial list	Savannah, GA
Ward, James	Co. E, 26th North Carolina	1833	7/1/1863	Killed in action	Unknown
Ward, Jesse James	Co. D, 20th North Carolina	1840	7/1/1863	Killed in action	Unknown
Ward, Julius	Co. I, 61st Virginia		7/2/1863	Killed in action	Unknown
Ward, Robert Adams	Co. I, 53rd Virginia	1/6/1840	7/3/1863	Killed in action	Unknown
Ward, William Alfred	Co. G, 57th Virginia	1829	7/3/1863	Killed in action	Unknown
Ware, George W.	Co. K, 13th North Carolina		7/12/1863	Hollywood Cemetery, Richmond, Va., reburial lists	Richmond, VA
Ware, James S.	Co. B, 12th South Carolina	1841	7/1/1863	Killed in action	Unknown
Ware, Robert A.	Cpl., Co. I, 19th Virginia	1834	8/21/1863	Died of wounds at home in Virginia	Unknown
Ware, Thomas Lewis	Co. G, 15th Georgia	1838	7/2/1863	Laurel Grove Cemetery, Savannah, Ga., reburial list	Savannah, GA
Warner, M.	Co. K, 13th Mississippi	1822	7/11/1863	Mortally wounded-died at unknown place in Gettysburg	Unknown
Warren, Bartlett Y.	Co. D, 13th North Carolina	1834	7/1/1863	Killed in action	Unknown
Warren, Thomas Jefferson	Capt., Co. D, 15th South Carolina	1824	7/2/1863	Killed in action	Charleston, SC
Warwick, Robert W.	Co. F, 47th Virginia		7/1/1863	Killed in action	Unknown
Wasden, Joseph	Col., 22nd Georgia	9/21/1829	7/2/1863	Laurel Grove Cemetery, Savannah, Ga., reburial list	Savannah, GA
Washburn, Jacob	Co. B, 22nd North Carolina	1844	Jul. 1863	Missing in action and presumed dead	Unknown
Wate, Charles H.	Co. G, 1st South Carolina	1845	7/1/1863	Killed in action	Unknown
Waters, John D.	Co. L, 1st Texas	1844	7/2/1863	Killed in action	Unknown
Waters, Pembrook S.	Lt., Co. A, 14th Tennessee		10/11/1863	Mortally wounded-died at unknown place in Gettysburg	Unknown
Watkins, Alsey	Co. E, 47th North Carolina	1828	7/3/1863	Killed in action	Unknown
Watkins, Aurelius Augustus	Lt., Co. C, 18th Virginia	1839	7/3/1863	Killed in action per the Richmond Sentinel, July 15, 1863	Unknown
Watkins, Charles A.	Sgt., Co. H, 45th North Carolina	1844	7/23/1863	Died as POW at David's Island, NY	Cypress Hills, NY

NAME	REGIMENT	BIRTH	DEATH	COMMENT	BURIAL
Watkins, Charles N.	Co. A, 23rd Virginia		7/2/1863	Killed in action	Unknown
Watkins, David J.	Co. I, 3rd Georgia		7/2/1863	Killed in action	Unknown
Watkins, Greenwood Leflore	Co. G, 18th Mississipi	1847	7/2/1863	Killed in action	Unknown
Watkins, W.B.	Co. C, 59th Georgia		8/13/1863	Mortally wounded and died in Maryland	Maryland
Watson, A.A.	Co. K, 11th Georgia		7/2/1863	Laurel Grove Cemetery, Savannah, Ga., reburial list	Savannah, GA
Watson, George W.	Co. E, 53rd North Carolina	1843	7/23/1863	Mortally wounded and died at Chester, PA	Phil. National Cem.
Watson, James F.	Cpl., Co. B, 11th Georgia	1842	7/14/1863	Hollywood Cemetery, Richmond, Va., reburial lists	Richmond, VA
Watson, Rufus	Co. G, 5th North Carolina	1843	7/12/1863	Mortally wounded-died at unknown place in Gettysburg	Unknown
Watson, Samuel C.	Lt., Co. F, 33rd North Carolina		7/6/1863	Mortally wounded-died at unknown place in Gettysburg	Unknown
Watson, Samuel H.	Co. E, 5th Texas	1842	9/13/1863	Hollywood Cemetery, Richmond, Va., reburial lists	Richmond, VA
Watson, William	Co. A, 61st Georgia	1836	8/3/1863	Mortally wounded and died at Hagerstown, MD-buried there	Hagerstown, MD
Watts, Francis M.	Co. D, 15th South Carolina		7/2/1863	Killed in action per the Charleston Courier, July 1863	Unknown
Watts, William B.	Co. C, 1st South Carolina		8/8/1863	Mortally wounded and died at Frederick, MD; interred in Mt. Olivet Cemetery	Frederick, MD
Watts, William T.	Co. G, 4th Virginia		8/27/1863	Hollywood Cemetery, Richmond, Va., reburial lists	Richmond, VA
Way, Anderson M.	Co. G, 26th North Carolina	1840	7/1/1863	Killed in action	Unknown
Wearherby, J.M.	Co. A, 1st South Carolina		7/22/1863	Died as POW at David's Island, NY	Cypress Hills, NY
Weatherington, George W.	Co. H, 2nd Mississippi	1839	7/1/1863	Killed in action	Unknown
Weathers, John Jabez	Co. H, 5th Texas	1831	7/2/1863	Killed in action	Unknown
Weathersbee, J.B.	Co. A, 1st South Carolina		8/11/1863	Died as POW at David's Island, NY	Cypress Hills, NY
Weathersby, Thomas C.	Co. E, 5th Texas	11/9/1830	7/2/1863	Killed in action	Unknown
Weaver, James J.	Cpl., Co. I, 53rd Georgia		7/3/1863	Killed in action	Unknown
Weaver, John	Co. D, 2nd Virginia		Jul. 1863	Mortally wounded and died on unknown date at Martinsburg, VA-buried there	Martinsburg, WV
Weaver, John A.	Purcell Battery (Va.)		7/3/1863	Hollywood Cemetery, Richmond, Va., reburial lists	Richmond, VA
Weaver, S.D.	Co. G, 47th North Carolina	1836	7/1/1863	Killed in action	Unknown
Webb, Alphonso [Elfarzo] F.	Co. H, 44th Alabama	1844	7/2/1863	Killed in action	Unknown
Webb, Edmund T.	Co. A, 10th Louisiana	1838	7/3/1863	Killed in action on Culp's Hill	Unknown
Webb, Emmett M.	Cpl., Co. D, 1st Maryland Battalion		Jul. 1863	Killed in action, July 1-3	Unknown
Webb, Ferdinand H.	Co. D, 28th Virginia	1842	7/25/1863	Mortally wounded and died at Chester, PA	Phil. National Cem.
Webb, J.W.	Co. G, 5th Texas	1838	8/7/1863	Mortally wounded, July 2, and died in Texas Hospital, Richmond, VA	Richmond, VA

NAME	REGIMENT	BIRTH	DEATH	COMMENT	BURIAL
Webb, James R.	Brooke's Battery (Va.)		1863	Mortally wounded per the Richmond Dispatch, August 26, 1863	Unknown
Webb, John	Co. E, 13th South Carolina		7/1/1863	Killed in action	Unknown
Webb, John Askew	Co. G, 13th Georgia	1/20/1835	7/27/1863	Mortally wounded-died at unknown place in Gettysburg	Unknown
Webb, John L.	Co. E, 45th North Carolina		7/1/1863	Killed in action	Unknown
Webb, Jordan C.	Cpl., Co. G, 18th Virginia		10/11/1863	Died of wounds at Ft. Delaware, DE	Finn's Point, NJ
Webb, Robert L.	Co. D, 23rd North Carolina	1836	7/1/1863	Killed in action	Unknown
Webb, William Henry Graham	Sgt., Co. K, 55th North Carolina	11/8/1842	9/21/1863	Mortally wounded and died at Chester, PA	Phil. National Cem.
Webber, Frank	Sgt., Co. H, 10th Louisiana		7/10/1863	Mortally wounded-died at unknown place in Gettysburg	Unknown
Webster, Henry L.	Co. A, 5th North Carolina		8/3/1863	Mortally wounded-died at unknown place in Gettysburg	Unknown
Weed, J.W.	Co. G, 26th Alabama		7/31/1863	Mortally wounded and died at Winchester, VA	Winchester, VA
Weeden, Robert A.	Cpl., Co. K, 47th North Carolina	1839	7/23/1863	Oakwood Cemetery, Raleigh, NC, reburial list	Raleigh, NC
Weekly, John T.	Co. I, 50th Georgia		7/2/1863	Laurel Grove Cemetery, Savannah, Ga., reburial list	Savannah, GA
Weeks, Andrew Jackson	Co. I, 13th Mississippi	1843	7/2/1863	Killed in action	Unknown
Weeks, Sampson	Co. K, 15th South Carolina	1833	7/2/1863	Killed in action	Unknown
Welch, James	Co. A, 1st North Carolina	1832	Jul.1863	Killed in action, July 1-3	Unknown
Welch, Jonathan	Co. G, 2nd North Carolina Battalion	7/5/1832	7/12/1863	Mortally wounded-died at unknown place in Gettysburg	Unknown
Weldon, Eli	Co. I, 57th North Carolina	1842	7/2/1863	Hollywood Cemetery, Richmond, Va., reburial lists	Richmond, VA
Weldon, J.W.	Co. G, 53rd Georgia		7/2/1863	Laurel Grove Cemetery, Savannah, Ga., reburial list	Savannah, GA
Wells, David H.	Co. F, 17th Mississippi	1845	7/3/1863	Killed in action	Unknown
Wells, John Logan	Co. E, 18th North Carolina	1831	7/3/1863	Killed in action	Unknown
Wells, Ludy Young	Co. I, 2nd Mississippi	1840	7/5/1863	Mortally wounded, July 1st, and died four days later	Unknown
Wells, M. Lafayette	Co. D, 11th North Carolina	1829	7/1/1863	Killed in action	Unknown
Welsh, John Payne	Capt., Co. B, 27th Virginia	1831	7/15/1863	Mortally wounded and died at Williamsport, MD-buried there	Williamsport, MD
Welsh, Shepherd	Co. G, 20th Georgia		7/10/1863	Mortally wounded-died at unknown place in Gettysburg	Unknown
Welsh, Willis W.	Co. E, 7th Virginia		7/3/1863	Hollywood Cemetery, Richmond, Va., reburial lists	Richmond, VA
Werthiem, Hyman	Lt., Co. E, 8th South Carolina		7/2/1863	Hollywood Cemetery, Richmond, Va., reburial lists	Richmond, VA
Wessinger, Wesley Francis	Co. I, 15th South Carolina	1839	7/4/1863	Magnolia Cemetery, Charleston, SC, reburial list	Charleston, SC
West, Henry G.	Co. G, 3rd Virginia	1837	7/16/1863	Mortally wounded-died at unknown place in Gettysburg	Unknown

NAME	REGIMENT	BIRTH	DEATH	COMMENT	BURIAL
West, Henry H.	Co. A, 3rd North Carolina	1843	7/6/1863	Mortally wounded and died at Frederick, MD; interred in Mt. Olivet Cemetery	Frederick, MD
West, Joseph	Co. A, 3rd South Carolina	1844	7/5/1863	Mortally wounded-died at unknown place in Gettysburg	Unknown
West, Lloyd	Co. H, 20th North Carolina	1839	7/1/1863	Killed in action; reinterred at West Cemetery, Sampson Co., NC	Sampson Co., NC
West, Thomas H.	Co. I, 47th Virginia		Jul. 1863	Missing in action and presumed dead	Unknown
West, William J.	Co. B, 13th Mississippi	1838	7/13/1863	Hollywood Cemetery, Richmond, Va., reburial lists	Richmond, VA
West, William M.	Co. G, 2nd South Carolina		7/28/1863	Mortally wounded per the Charleston Mercury, August 28, 1863	Unknown
West, Winborn	Co. A, 3rd North Carolina	1835	7/2/1863	Killed in action	Unknown
Westmoreland, David	Co. K, 52nd North Carolina	1840	7/3/1863	Killed in action	Unknown
Westmoreland, Elijah M.	Co. E, 14th South Carolina	5/7/1840	7/2/1863	Killed in action	Unknown
Weston, Samuel W.C.	Co. M, 6th Alabama		7/1/1863	Killed in action	Unknown
Whaley, William	Co. A, 43rd North Carolina	1817	7/5/1863	Mortally wounded, July 1st, and died four days later	Unknown
Wham, Benjamin F.	Lt., Co. B, 42nd Mississippi	1830	9/3/1863	Hollywood Cemetery, Richmond, Va., reburial lists	Richmond, VA
Wham, John G.	Sgt., Co. B, 42nd Mississippi	1833	7/1/1863	Killed in action	Unknown
Wheeler, Artemus H.	Co. K, 5th Florida	1832	7/17/1863	Mortally wounded and buried on Jacob Schwartz Farm	Unknown
Wheeler, Council	Co. A, 3rd Georgia		7/2/1863	Laurel Grove Cemetery, Savannah, Ga., reburial list	Savannah, GA
Wheeler, Peter Carr	Co. C, 13th South Carolina	1/15/1839	7/1/1863	Killed in action	Unknown
Wheless, Spier Coffield	Co. D, 43rd North Carolina		8/16/1863	Mortally wounded and died at Staunton, VA-buried there	Staunton, VA
Wherry, James A.	Co. H, 12th South Carolina	1843	7/21/1863	Died as POW at David's Island, NY	Cypress Hills, NY
Whetsell, Charles H.	Co. C, 37th Virginia		7/8/1863	Mortally wounded-died at unknown place in Gettysburg	Unknown
Whitaker, H.A.	Co. A, 1st NC Cavalry	1827	7/3/1863	Killed in action	Unknown
Whitaker, William T.	Co. H, 26th Georgia		Jul. 1863	Killed in action, July 1-3	Unknown
White, Amos A.	Co. B, 23rd North Carolina	1841	7/1/1863	Killed in action	Unknown
White, Clinton	Co. H, 1st North Carolina	1843	7/26/1863	Mortally wounded-died on unknown date in Gettysburg	Unknown
White, Daniel M.	Cpl., Co. L, 2nd Mississippi	1840	7/1/1863	Killed in action	Unknown
White, Elihu	Sgt., Co. E,13th South Carolina	1838	7/20/1863	Died as POW at David's Island, NY	Cypress Hills, NY
White, George W.	2nd Rockbridge Arty. (Va.)		7/3/1863	Hollywood Cemetery, Richmond, Va., reburial lists	Richmond, VA
White, Henry	Co. C, 55th North Carolina	1838	8/8/1863	Oakwood Cemetery, Raleigh, NC, reburial list	Raleigh, NC
White, Henry P.	Co. G, 57th Virginia		7/27/1863	Hollywood Cemetery, Richmond, Va., reburial lists	Richmond, VA
White, James	Co. F, 11th North Carolina	1842	7/16/1863	Mortally wounded and died at Baltimore, MD-buried there	Baltimore, MD

NAME	REGIMENT	BIRTH	DEATH	COMMENT	BURIAL
White, James Francis	Co. C, 47th Virginia	9/21/1842	8/21/1863	Mortally wounded, July 3rd, and died at Staunton, VA	Staunton, VA
White, James L.	Co. C, 55th North Carolina		7/1/1863	Killed in action	Unknown
White, James O.	Co. D, 24th Virginia		7/3/1863	Killed in action	Unknown
White, John E.	Co. H, 2nd North Carolina Battalion.		7/1/1863	Killed in action	Unknown
White, Joseph H.	Co. F, 49th Virginia		7/3/1863	Killed in action	Unknown
White, Martin Van Buren	Co. E, 3rd Arkansas	1838	7/5/1863	Mortally wounded, July 2nd, and died three days later	Unknown
White, Perry S.	Co. K, 8th Alabama	12/17/1844	11/11/1863	Died of wounds at Pt. Lookout, MD	Pt. Lookout, MD
White, Solomon H.	Capt., Co. D, 32nd North Carolina		7/15/1863	Mortally wounded-died at unknown place in Gettysburg	Unknown
White, Stephen H.	Co. C, 5th Florida		7/3/1863	Killed in action	Unknown
White, Thomas Allen	Co. K, 22nd Georgia	4/23/1830	7/3/1863	Laurel Grove Cemetery, Savannah, Ga., reburial list	Savannah, GA
White, William	Co. H, 22nd North Carolina	1841	Jul. 1863	Killed in action, July 1-3	Unknown
White, William	Co. B, 60th Georgia		Jul. 1863	Killed in action, July 1-3	Unknown
White, William	Co. K, 56th Virginia		10/30/1863	Mortally wounded-died at unknown place in Gettysburg	Unknown
White, William P.	Sgt., Co. E, 13th Georgia		7/1/1863	Killed in action	Unknown
Whitehead, Willis Simmons	Co. D, 43rd North Carolina	1838	7/15/1863	Mortally wounded-died at unknown place in Gettysburg	Unknown
Whitfield, George Booker	Co. K, 4th Alabama	1841	7/2/1863	Hollywood Cemetery, Richmond, Va., reburial lists	Richmond, VA
Whitley, G.D.	Co. F, 5th North Carolina	1836	7/23/1863	Mortally wounded-died at unknown place in Gettysburg	Unknown
Whitley, Henry	Co. F, 1st North Carolina	1843	1863	Mortally wounded, July 3rd, died on July 17th or August 3rd	Hagerstown, MD
Whitley, John J.	Co. E, 2nd Mississippi		7/16/1863	Hollywood Cemetery, Richmond, Va., reburial lists	Richmond, VA
Whitley, Jolley B.	Co. I, 30th North Carolina	1837	7/3/1863	Killed in action	Unknown
Whitten, Craven Jenkins	Co. H, 17th Georgia	3/8/1833	7/2/1863	Killed in action per the Augusta Chronicle & Sentinel, July 30, 1863	Unknown
Whitten, John J.	Co. B, 2nd Mississippi	1829	7/1/1863	Killed in action	Unknown
Whitten, Thomas L.	Sgt., Co. E, 28th Virginia		7/3/1863	Killed in action per the Richmond Sentinel, July 30, 1863	Unknown
Whittington, John A.	Co. I, 21st North Carolina	1842	7/1/1863	Killed in action	Unknown
Whittle, Joel Millege	Co. B, 14th South Carolina	1845	8/19/1863	Mortally wounded and died at Chester, PA	Charleston, SC
Whitton, Austin	Co. G, 14th South Carolina	1841	7/6/1863	Mortally wounded, July 3rd, and died three days later	Unknown
Whorley, William	Co. F 28th Virginia		7/3/1863	Missing in action and presumed dead	Unknown
Whyte, Solomon H.	Capt., Co. G, 32nd North Carolina	1839	7/13/1863	Hollywood Cemetery, Richmond, Va., reburial lists	Richmond, VA
Wick, N.W.	Co. E, 33rd North Carolina		7/2/1863	Killed in action	Unknown
Wicker, Lewis	Co. G, 26th North Carolina	1828	7/1/1863	Killed in action	Unknown
Wicker, Louis M.	Sgt., Co. H, 30th North Carolina	1831	7/1/1863	Hollywood Cemetery, Richmond, Va., reburial lists	Richmond, VA

NAME	REGIMENT	BIRTH	DEATH	COMMENT	BURIAL
Wicker, Thomas Jefferson	Co. C, 21st North Carolina		7/23/1863	Mortally wounded-died on unknown date in Gettysburg	Unknown
Wier, John A.	Co. K, 3rd Virginia		7/8/1863	Hollywood Cemetery, Richmond, Va., reburial lists	Richmond, VA
Wiggins, John J.	Co. K, 26th North Carolina	1843	7/1/1863	Killed in action	Unknown
Wiggins, Lewis H.	Co. G, 3rd North Carolina		7/2/1863	Killed in action	Unknown
Wiggonton, Green H.	Co. I, 48th Alabama		7/2/1863	Killed in action	Unknown
Wilborn, Joseph H.	Sgt., Fraser's Battery (Ga.)		7/3/1863	Killed in action	Unknown
Wilborne, John A.	Co. I, 23rd North Carolina	1840	7/1/1863	Killed in action	Unknown
Wilcher, William J.	Co. K, 57th Virginia		7/3/1863	Killed in action	Unknown
Wilcox, Albert J.	Lt., Co. F, 5th Alabama		7/1/1863	Hollywood Cemetery, Richmond, Va., reburial lists	Richmond, VA
Wilcox, Harmon Husband	Co. H, 26th North Carolina	2/25/1845	7/2/1863	Oakwood Cemetery, Raleigh, NC, reburial list	Raleigh, NC
Wilder, John	Co. G, 10th Louisiana	1829	7/3/1863	Killed in action on Culp's Hill	Unknown
Wilder, Samuel C.	Lt., Co. B, 38th North Carolina	1830	7/3/1863	Killed in action	Unknown
Wiles, Hugh L.	Co. E, 45th North Carolina	1843	7/3/1863	Killed in action	Unknown
Wiles, Thomas A.	Co. E, 45th North Carolina	1840	7/3/1863	Killed in action	Unknown
Wiley, Eli R.	Cpl., Co. M, 21st North Carolina	1841	Jul. 1863	Killed in action	Unknown
Wilkerson, Elbert	Co. B, 11th Georgia		7/22/1863	Mortally wounded-died on unknown date in Gettysburg	Unknown
Wilkerson, Henry W.	Co. H, 2nd South Carolina	1836	7/2/1863	Killed in action	Charleston, SC
Wilkerson, James T.	Co. D, 18th Virginia		Jul. 1863	Missing in action and presumed dead	Unknown
Wilkerson, Madison	Sgt., Co. C, 6th North Carolina	1826	1863	Mortally wounded, July 2nd, and died on unknown date	Unknown
Wilkerson, Thomas J.	Co. D, 13th Georgia		7/13/1863	Mortally wounded and died at Howard's Grove Hospital, Richmond, VA; interred in Oakwood Cem.	Richmond, VA
Wilkerson, W.D.	Cpl., Co. I, 23rd North Carolina	1829	7/4/1863	Mortally wounded, July 1-3	Unknown
Wilkerson, William G.	Co. I, 23rd North Carolina	1838	7/1/1863	Killed in action	Unknown
Wilkes, James P.	Co. A, 2nd North Carolina Battalion.	1845	7/1/1863	Killed in action	Unknown
Wilkins, David Crockett	Co. E, 11th Mississippi	1842	7/3/1863	Killed in action	Unknown
Wilkins, Henry Martin	Co. E, 11th Mississippi	1840	7/3/1863	Killed in action	Unknown
Wilkins, Newton Reece	Sgt., Co. G, 11th Mississippi	1838	8/16/1863	Mortally wounded and died at Richmond, VA-interred in Hollywood Cemetery	Richmond, VA
Wilkins, Samuel J.	Lt., Co. A, 44th Georgia		7/7/1863	Mortally wounded, July 3rd, and died four days later	Unknown
Wilkinson, Neill	Co. B, 53rd North Carolina	1829	7/3/1863	Killed in action	Unknown
Willard, Benjamin B.	Sgt., Co. G, 38th Virginia		7/3/1863	Killed in action	Unknown
Willey, Frederick Edward	Carpenter's Battery (Va.)	1842	7/2/1863	Hollywood Cemetery, Richmond, Va., reburial lists	Richmond, VA
Williams, Abram	Sgt., Co. M, 2nd Florida		7/3/1863	Killed in action	Unknown
Williams, Beverly W.	Sgt., Co. B, 53rd Virginia		7/3/1863	Killed in action	Unknown
Williams, Charles W.	Co. E, 56th Virginia	1833	7/8/1863	Hollywood Cemetery, Richmond, Va., reburial lists	Richmond, VA

NAME	REGIMENT	BIRTH	DEATH	COMMENT	BURIAL
Williams, D. Taylor	Brooks Arty. (S.C) Rhett's		7/2/1863	Killed in action	Unknown
Williams, David	Cpl., Co. D, 20th North Carolina	8/1/1835	7/1/1863	Killed in action; interred in National Cemetery as 20th Connecticut	Gettysburg Nat. Cem.
Williams, David L.	Co. G, 5th North Carolina	1839	7/1/1863	Hollywood Cemetery, Richmond, Va., reburial lists	Richmond, VA
Williams, George R.	Co. B, 5th North Carolina	1835	7/1/1863	Hollywood Cemetery, Richmond, Va., reburial lists	Richmond, VA
Williams, George W.	Sgt., Co. D, 48th Mississippi		7/2/1863	Killed in action per the Richmond Enquirer, July 16, 1863	Unknown
Williams, Gresham G.	Co. A, 3rd Georgia		7/2/1863	Killed in action	Unknown
Williams, Harden H.	Co. G, 9th Georgia		7/2/1863	Killed in action	Unknown
Williams, Henry L.N.	Maj., 9th Louisiana	1836	7/5/1863	Hollywood Cemetery, Richmond, Va., reburial lists	Richmond, VA
Williams, James	Co. A, 35th Georgia		Jul. 1863	Killed in action on July 2nd or 3rd	Unknown
Williams, James A.	Co. E, 56th Virginia		7/19/1863	Hollywood Cemetery, Richmond, Va., reburial lists	Richmond, VA
Williams, James H.	Co. C, 11th North Carolina	1844	1863	Mortally wounded-died on unknown date in Gettysburg	Unknown
Williams, James M.	Sgt., Co. B, 22nd Georgia		10/25/1863	Mortally wounded, July 2nd, and died at Harrisburg, PA; interred in Soldiers' Lot	Harrisburg, PA
Williams, James M.	Co. I, 6th North Carolina	1842	7/2/1863	Oakwood Cemetery, Raleigh, NC, reburial list	Raleigh, NC
Williams, James W.	Lt., Co. G, 11th North Carolina	1839	7/1/1863	Oakwood Cemetery, Raleigh, NC, reburial list	Raleigh, NC
Williams, Jesse M.	Cpl., Co. G, 13th Georgia		7/1/1863	Killed in action	Unknown
Williams, John	Co. F, 52nd North Carolina	1842	7/3/1863	Killed in action	Unknown
Williams, John Bennett	Sgt., Co. A, 40th Virginia	1831	7/1/1863	Hollywood Cemetery, Richmond, Va., reburial lists	Richmond, VA
Williams, John T.	Co. H, 3rd North Carolina	1838	7/2/1863	Hollywood Cemetery, Richmond, Va., reburial lists	Richmond, VA
Williams, John W.	Co. A, 7th Tennessee	1836	9/7/1863	Hollywood Cemetery, Richmond, Va., reburial lists	Richmond, VA
Williams, John W.	Sgt., Co. F, 21st North Carolina	1841	7/1/1863	Killed in action	Unknown
Williams, John W.	Co. A, 6th Alabama		Jul. 1863	Killed in action, July 1-3	Unknown
Williams, Joseph	Co. A, 22nd North Carolina	1836	7/1/1863	Killed in action	Unknown
Williams, Killis F.	Co. K, 37th North Carolina	1843	8/19/1863	Died as POW at David's Island, NY	Cypress Hills, NY
Williams, Lawson P.	Co. I, 38th North Carolina	1825	7/15/1863	Mortally wounded-died at unknown place in Gettysburg	Unknown
Williams, Lemuel H.	Co. G, 9th Virginia		7/3/1863	Killed in action while carrying the colors	Unknown
Williams, Leonidas Fenton	Co. H, 53rd Virginia	1839	7/3/1863	Killed in action	Unknown
Williams, Lewis	Sgt., Co. A, 47th Virginia	1844	Jul. 1863	Killed in action, July 1-3	Unknown
Williams, Lewis Burwell	Col., 1st Virginia	9/13/1833	7/3/1863	Killed in action	Richmond, VA
Williams, Simon A.	Co. I, 9th Louisiana	1842	8/13/1863	Mortally wounded, July 1st, and died at Mt. Jackson, VA	Mt. Jackson, VA
Williams, Simon P.	Co. E, 23rd North Carolina		7/1/1863	Killed in action	Unknown

NAME	REGIMENT	BIRTH	DEATH	COMMENT	BURIAL
Williams, Thomas A.	Co. E, 56th Virginia	1845	Jul. 1863	Missing in action and presumed dead	Unknown
Williams, W.H.	Co. B, 5th Louisiana	1837	7/4/1863	Mortally wounded, July 2nd, and died two days later	Unknown
Williams, W.R.	Co. C, 53rd Virginia	1838	8/4/1863	Hollywood Cemetery, Richmond, Va., reburial lists	Richmond, VA
Williams, W.W	Co. F, 3rd Georgia		7/1/1863	Killed in action	Unknown
Williams, William	Co. B, 60th Georgia		7/3/1863	Laurel Grove Cemetery, Savannah, Ga., reburial list	Savannah, GA
Williams, William A.	Sgt., Co. I, 45th North Carolina	1839	7/6/1863	Oakwood Cemetery, Raleigh, NC, reburial list	Raleigh, NC
Williams, William C.G.	Co. A, 38th Virginia	1832	7/3/1863	Killed in action per the Richmond Sentinel, August 1, 1863	Unknown
Williams, William H.	Sgt., Co. D, 13th Mississippi	1842	1863	Mortally wounded-died on unknown date in Gettysburg	Unknown
Williams, William Ovid	Co. G, 18th Virginia		7/3/1863	Killed in action	Unknown
Williamson, James	Co. F, 11th Virginia	1840	7/4/1863	Hollywood Cemetery, Richmond, Va., reburial lists	Richmond, VA
Williamson, James Colon	Co. C, 20th North Carolina	1838	7/1/1863	Killed in action	Unknown
Williamson, Marmadine D.	Sgt., Co. C, 20th North Carolina	1836	7/1/1863	Killed in action	Unknown
Williamson, Peter Ballantine	Co. D, 5th Texas	6/19/1839	9/5/1863	Hollywood Cemetery, Richmond, Va., reburial lists	Richmond, VA
Williford, Hardy	Co. B, 48th Georgia	1840	1863	Mortally wounded, July 3rd, and died at Staunton, VA in 1863	Staunton, VA
Williford, Thomas	Co. G, 2nd North Carolina	1844	8/5/1863	Oakwood Cemetery, Raleigh, NC, reburial list	Raleigh, NC
Willis, Count D.A.	Co. E, 57th Virginia		Jul. 1863	Missing in action and presumed dead	Unknown
Willis, Thomas	Co. I, 13th South Carolina	1842	7/2/1863	Killed in action	Unknown
Willis, Thomas	Co. F, 55th North Carolina		7/1/1863	Killed in action	Unknown
Willis, Thomas W.	Cpl., Co. C, 7th South Carolina	1839	7/2/1863	Killed in action	Unknown
Willoughby, Isaac	Co. G, 25th Virginia		7/13/1863	Mortally wounded-died at unknown place in Gettysburg	Unknown
Willoughby, John B.	Co. C, 38th Georgia	1843	8/3/1863	Laurel Grove Cemetery, Savannah, Ga., reburial list	Savannah, GA
Wills, William D.	Co. K, 13th Georgia		7/1/1863	Killed in action	Unknown
Wilmoth, Ezekiel	Co. C, 21st North Carolina	1832	7/1/1863	Killed in action	Unknown
Wilson, Allen T.	Co. G, 17th Mississippi	1840	7/2/1863	Killed in action	Unknown
Wilson, David	Co. D, 11th Georgia		8/30/1863	Died as POW at David's Island, NY	Cypress Hills, NY
Wilson, E.J.	Sgt., Co. C, 8th Alabama	1842	Jul. 1863	Killed in action, July 1-3	Unknown
Wilson, Francis C.	Lt., Co. F, 20th North Carolina	1841	7/1/1863	Death notice Fayetteville Observer, March 28, 1864	Sampson Co., NC
Wilson, George A.	Co. E, 2nd Mississippi	1838	7/1/1863	Killed in action	Unknown
Wilson, George D.	Co. I, 38th North Carolina	1837	7/1/1863	Killed in action	Unknown
Wilson, George W.	Co. C, 3rd North Carolina	1838	7/23/1863	Mortally wounded-died at unknown place in Gettysburg	Unknown
Wilson, H. Lee	Co. E, Phillips Legion (Ga.)		7/2/1863	Killed in action	Unknown
Wilson, J.B.	Co. A, 59th Georgia		7/3/1863	Killed in action	Unknown

NAME	REGIMENT	BIRTH	DEATH	COMMENT	BURIAL
Wilson, J.H.	Co. K, 38th Georgia		7/2/1863	Killed in action	Unknown
Wilson, J.W.	Cpl., Co. B, 13th South Carolina		7/1/1863	Killed in action	Unknown
Wilson, James T.	Co. L, 2nd Florida	1834	7/2/1863	Killed in action	Unknown
Wilson, John	Co. B, 12th North Carolina	1835	7/12/1863	Mortally wounded-died at unknown place in Gettysburg	Unknown
Wilson, John A.	Co. D, 5th Virginia	1826	7/18/1863	Hollywood Cemetery, Richmond, Va., reburial lists	Richmond, VA
Wilson, John J.	Lt., Co. F, 20th North Carolina	1843	7/1/1863	Killed in action	Unknown
Wilson, Joseph	Co. I, 26th North Carolina	1831	7/1/1863	Killed in action	Unknown
Wilson, Nathaniel Claiborne	Maj., 28th Virginia	9/12/1839	7/3/1863	Killed in action; reinterred in Old Family Burial Ground, Fincastle, VA	Fincastle, VA
Wilson, Newton	Co. E, 32nd North Carolina	3/12/1840	7/3/1863	Mortally wounded, July 3rd, and died the same day	Unknown
Wilson, Robert R.	Co. G, 2nd Florida	1841	Jul. 1863	Mortally wounded, July 2nd, and died on unknown date	Unknown
Wilson, Robert W.	Sgt., Co. F, 5th Louisiana	1840	7/2/1863	Killed in action while carrying the colors	Unknown
Wilson, Thomas	Co. L, 2nd Florida	1830	7/2/1863	Killed in action	Unknown
Wilson, W.B.	Co. B, 5th Texas		1863	Mortally wounded, July 2nd, and died on unknown date	Unknown
Wilson, William	Capt., Co. B, 26th North Carolina	1841	7/1/1863	Oakwood Cemetery, Raleigh, NC, reburial list	Raleigh, NC
Wilson, William M.	Co. E, 47th North Carolina	1838	7/1/1863	Killed in action	Unknown
Wilson, William R.	Co. D, 2nd Georgia Battalion.		7/2/1863	Killed in action	Unknown
Winburn, Jesse	Co. B, 2nd Mississippi	1832	7/1/1863	Killed in action	Unknown
Winchel, William H.	Co. G, 12th Georgia		7/8/1863	Mortally wounded-died on unknown date in Gettysburg	Unknown
Winchester, William H.	Lt., Co. I, 13th North Carolina	1840	8/1/1863	Mortally wounded and died at Chester, PA	Phil. National Cem.
Windolph, John H.	Co. A, 1st Maryland Battalion		Jul. 1863	Killed in action, July 1-3	Unknown
Winecoff, Joseph C.	Cpl., Co. B, 20th North Carolina	1838	7/1/1863	Killed in action	Unknown
Winfield, Marcellus J.	Co. D, 1st Virginia		7/3/1863	Killed in action	Unknown
Winfrey, James A.	Sgt., Co. A, 7th Tennessee		7/3/1863	Killed in action	Unknown
Wingate, Angus	Co. A, 11th North Carolina	3/3/1839	7/3/1863	Killed in action	Unknown
Wingate, John A.	Sgt., Co. F, 8th Florida	1845	8/1/1863	Hollywood Cemetery, Richmond, Va., reburial lists	Richmond, VA
Winger, Christopher Columbus	Co. K, 57th Virginia	7/18/1841	7/3/1863	Killed in action	Unknown
Winger, Martin Van Buren	Co. K, 57th Virginia	5/10/1843	7/3/1863	Killed in action	Unknown
Wingfield, M.J.	Co. D, 1st Virginia		7/3/1863	Killed in action	Unknown
Wingler, Reinheart	Co. D, 26th North Carolina	1840	7/1/1863	Killed in action	Unknown
Winn, David Read Evans	Lt. Col., 4th Georgia	7/5/1831	7/1/1863	Laurel Grove Cemetery, Savannah, Ga., reburial list	Savannah, GA
Winston, Henry M.	Cpl., Co. F, 45th North Carolina	1845	8/14/1863	Died as POW at David's Island, NY	Cypress Hills, NY
Winters, Leonard	Co. K, 50th Georgia		9/30/1863	Mortally wounded and died at Chester, PA	Phil. National Cem.
Winters, Moulton	Cpl., Co. D, 11th North Carolina	1842	7/1/1863	Killed in action	Unknown

NAME	REGIMENT	BIRTH	DEATH	COMMENT	BURIAL
Wise, Ambrose	Cpl., Co. G, 57th North Carolina	1834	7/2/1863	Missing in action and presumed dead	Unknown
Wise, James W.	Co. K, 47th Alabama		7/2/1863	Killed in action	Unknown
Witherington, Matthew	Co. D, 50th Georgia		10/17/1863	Mortally wounded and died at Harrisburg, PA; interred Soldiers' Lot, City Cemetery	Harrisburg, PA
Wofford, Charles W.	Co. D, 14th Tennessee	1836	7/1/1863	Killed in action	Unknown
Wofford, John	Co. F, 13th South Carolina		7/1/1863	Killed in action	Unknown
Wolcott, Walter W.	Lt., Co. A, 21st Mississippi		7/2/1863	Killed in action	Unknown
Wolf, Henry F.	Co. B, 13th North Carolina	1838	7/19/1863	Died as POW at David's Island, NY	Cypress Hills, NY
Wolfe, R.J.	Cpl., Co. D, 2nd Florida		7/8/1863	Mortally wounded-died at unknown place in Gettysburg	Unknown
Wolff, Milton Y.	Sgt., Co. D, 3rd South Carolina Battalion	1830	7/2/1863	Killed in action per the Charleston Courier, July 1863	Charleston, SC
Womack, Charles Henry	Co. H, 14th Virginia	1834	8/16/1863	Hollywood Cemetery, Richmond, Va., reburial lists	Richmond, VA
Womack, James H.	Co. I, 28th Virginia		7/3/1863	Killed in action per the Richmond Sentinel, July 30, 1863	Unknown
Womack, John Parker	Cpl., Co. C, 55th North Carolina	1840	7/2/1863	Mortally wounded, July 1st, and died the next day	Unknown
Womack, John W.	Co. I, 18th Virginia	1841	7/3/1863	Killed in action per the Richmond Sentinel, July 29, 1863	Unknown
Womack, William Edward	Co. H, 42nd Mississippi	8/27/1841	7/15/1863	Mortally wounded-died at unknown place in Gettysburg	Unknown
Womble, William W.	Cpl., Co. D, 20th North Carolina	1832	7/9/1863	Mortally wounded-died at unknown place in Gettysburg	Unknown
Wombles, James T.	Co. A, 5th North Carolina		7/1/1863	Hollywood Cemetery, Richmond, Va., reburial lists	Richmond, VA
Wood, Ashley Brice	Co. K, 3rd Arkansas	1825	7/15/1863	Mortally wounded, July 2nd, and died at Harrisonburg, VA-buried there	Harrisonburg, VA
Wood, David	Co. H, 33rd Virginia		7/17/1863	Hollywood Cemetery, Richmond, Va., reburial lists	Richmond, VA
Wood, George Washington	Lt., Co. B, 60th Georgia		7/23/1863	Laurel Grove Cemetery, Savannah, Ga., reburial list	Savannah, GA
Wood, Henry William	Co. D, 53rd Virginia		7/3/1863	Killed in action	Unknown
Wood, John W.	Co. K, 50th Virginia		Jul. 1863	Killed in action on either July 2nd or 3rd	Unknown
Wood, Penuel H.	Co. I, 5th North Carolina	1846	7/12/1863	Mortally wounded-died at unknown place in Gettysburg	Unknown
Wood, Richard B.	Lt., Co. B, 19th Virginia	1842	7/3/1863	Killed in action	Unknown
Wood, William	Co. D, 11th North Carolina		9/5/1863	Died as POW at David's Island, NY	Cypress Hills, NY
Wood, William T.	Co. I, 7th Virginia	1838	7/3/1863	Killed in action	Unknown
Woodall, Marion J.	Lt., Co. D, 26th North Carolina		9/8/1863	Died as POW at David's Island, NY	Cypress Hills, NY
Woodard, Gray Wilson	Co. A, 55th North Carolina	12/24/1827	7/1/1863	Killed in action	Unknown
Woodard, Thomas	Co. E, 52nd North Carolina		8/22/1863	Mortally wounded, July 3rd, and died at Petersburg, VA	Petersburg, VA
Woodburn, D.P.	Cpl., Co. H, 38th North Carolina	1837	Jul. 1863	Killed in action	Unknown
Woodburn, Theodore B.	Co. F, 2nd North Carolina Battalion	1833	7/1/1863	Killed in action	Unknown

NAME	REGIMENT	BIRTH	DEATH	COMMENT	BURIAL
Woodel, Richard	Co. H, 18th North Carolina	1840	7/3/1863	Killed in action	Unknown
Woodruff, Clifford Hartsfield	Co. H, 11th Georgia	8/20/1838	7/2/1863	Killed in action	Unknown
Woodruff, James Earl	Co. A, 13th Mississippi	6/11/1845	7/2/1863	Killed in action	Unknown
Woods, A. Jack	Sgt., Co. H, 59th Georgia		7/2/1863	Killed in action	Unknown
Woods, John B.	Sgt., Co. F, 25th Virginia		8/9/1863	Died as POW at David's Island, NY	Cypress Hills, NY
Woods, John J.	Sgt., Co. K, 19th Virginia	1843	7/30/1863	Mortally wounded-died at unknown place in Gettysburg	Unknown
Woodward, George O.	Co. I, 1st North Carolina	1843	1863	Missing in action and presumed dead	Unknown
Woodward, John R.	Maj., 1st Texas	1832	8/26/1863	Mortally wounded-died at unknown place in Gettysburg	Unknown
Woodward, Joseph	Co. C, 47th North Carolina		7/3/1863	Killed in action	Unknown
Woody, Moses M.	Co. I, 45th North Carolina	1835	7/1/1863	Killed in action	Unknown
Woody, Thomas F.	Page's Battery (Va.)		7/2/1863	Killed in action	Unknown
Wooley, Andrew	Co. A, 1st South Carolina		7/2/1863	Mortally wounded, July 2nd, and died the same day	Unknown
Wooley, Ely	Co. A, 1st South Carolina		7/2/1863	Killed in action	Unknown
Wooten, Oscar	Co. E, 55th North Carolina	4/30/1843	9/22/1863	Mortally wounded and died at Chester, PA	Phil. National Cem.
Worcester, Louis	Lt., Co. B, 7th Louisiana	1827	7/2/1863	Killed in action	Unknown
Workman, George W.	Co. I, 32nd North Carolina	1842	7/3/1863	Killed in action	Raleigh, NC
Worley, James M.	Co. F, 21st Mississippi	1840	7/3/1863	Hollywood Cemetery, Richmond, Va., reburial lists	Richmond, VA
Worrell, Levi	Co. B, 5th North Carolina	1843	7/1/1863	Hollywood Cemetery, Richmond, Va., reburial lists	Richmond, VA
Worsham, Thomas Lafayette	Cpl., Co. C, 37th North Carolina	1830	7/3/1863	Killed in action	Unknown
Worsham, William T.	Co. F, 18th Virginia	1838	7/3/1863	Killed in action per the Richmond Sentinel, July 30, 1863	Unknown
Worth, D.M.	Co. H, 12th South Carolina	1840	7/1/1863	Killed in action	Unknown
Worthington, Lewis H.	Co. E, 5th Florida	1832	7/3/1863	Killed in action	Unknown
Worwick, William W.	Co. C, 24th Georgia	1847	Jul. 1863	Killed in action per the Southern Christian Advocate	Unknown
Wrenn, Fenton Eley	Lt., Co. I, 3rd Virginia	Oct. 1839	7/3/1863	Killed in action	Unknown
Wright, H.C.	Co. A, 1st Texas		8/18/1863	Died as POW at David's Island, NY	Cypress Hills, NY
Wright, Harvey A.	Co. H, 37th North Carolina	1841	7/3/1863	Killed in action	Unknown
Wright, Henry	Co. C, 8th Alabama	1842	Jul. 1863	Killed in action, July 1-3	Unknown
Wright, Henry Clay	Co. A, 1st Texas		8/19/1863	Mortally wounded-died at unknown place in Gettysburg	Unknown
Wright, Jesse M.	Co. K, 44th Georgia		1863	Mortally wounded, July 1st, and died on July 8th or September 1st in Gettysburg	Savannah, GA
Wright, John	Co. B, 13th South Carolina	1843	7/2/1863	Killed in action	Unknown
Wright, John H.	Cpl., Co. I, 35th Georgia		7/6/1863	Laurel Grove Cemetery, Savannah, Ga., reburial list	Savannah, GA
Wright, Minton Augustus	Lt., Co. K, 57th North Carolina		7/2/1863	Missing in action and presumed dead	Unknown
Wright, Thomas Jefferson	Cpl., Co. B, 16th Virginia	7/29/1843	7/3/1863	Hollywood Cemetery, Richmond, Va., reburial lists	Richmond, VA

NAME	REGIMENT	BIRTH	DEATH	COMMENT	BURIAL
Wright, William	Co. H, 2nd South Carolina		7/2/1863	Killed in action	Unknown
Wrightson, William C.	Lt., Co. G, 1st Maryland Battalion		7/3/1863	Killed in action	Unknown
Wyant, James C.	Capt., Co. H, 56th Virginia	1829	7/31/1863	Mortally wounded and died at Chester, PA	Phil. National Cem.
Wyatt, Adam	Co. B, 26th North Carolina		7/1/1863	Killed in action	Unknown
Wyatt, Andrew	Sgt., Co. B, 26th North Carolina		7/1/1863	Killed in action	Unknown
Wyatt, David H.	Co. K, 7th Georgia		7/10/1863	Mortally wounded-died at unknown place in Gettysburg	Unknown
Wyatt, Frederick	Co. K, 6th North Carolina	1830	7/1/1863	Killed in action	Unknown
Wyatt, W.W.	Co. H, 23rd North Carolina		7/20/1863	Mortally wounded-died at unknown place in Gettysburg	Unknown
Wyche, James	Co. G, 47th North Carolina		8/12/1863	Mortally wounded and died at Chester, PA	Phil. National Cem.
Wyndham, John A.	Co. F,11th Mississippi	1845	7/3/1863	Killed in action	Unknown
Wyrick, W.P.	Co. C, 12th South Carolina		7/26/1863	Died as POW at David's Island, NY	Cypress Hills, NY
Yancey, Armenious C.	Sgt., Co. G, 14th Virginia	1842	7/2/1863	Killed in action	Unknown
Yancey, Joseph S.	Lt., Co. G, 14th Virginia	1840	7/4/1863	Mortally wounded, July 3rd, and died the next day	Unknown
Yancey, S. Peter	Co. D, 12th North Carolina		7/26/1863	Oakwood Cemetery, Raleigh, NC, reburial list	Raleigh, NC
Yancey, William Hilary	Lt., Co. E, 14th Virginia	1838	7/4/1863	Mortally wounded, July 3rd, and died the next day	Unknown
Yarborough, Joseph T.	Co. I, 45th North Carolina	1838	7/1/1863	Killed in action	Unknown
Yarbrough, George N.	Capt., Co. H, 8th Georgia	1834	7/2/1863	Killed in action	Unknown
Yarbrough, John Ripley	Co. B, 8th Alabama		7/2/1863	Killed in action	Unknown
Yates, John Terry	Co. I, 18th Virginia	1842	7/3/1863	Missing in action and presumed dead	Unknown
Yates, William H., Jr.	Co. E, 42nd Mississippi	1835	7/3/1863	Killed in action	Unknown
Yaunts, Reubin C.	Co. E, 11th North Carolina	1834	7/1/1863	Killed in action	Unknown
Yawn, George W.	Co. B, 11th Georgia	1837	7/15/1863	Hollywood Cemetery, Richmond, Va., reburial lists	Richmond, VA
Yeager, Monroe	Co. I, 2nd Mississippi	1843	7/3/1863	Killed in action	Unknown
Yeaman, William Hall	Co. A, 38th Virginia		7/3/1863	Killed in action per the Richmond Sentinel, August 1, 1863	Unknown
Yearger, William P.	Co. E, 22nd Georgia		8/11/1863	Mortally wounded and died at Chester, PA	Phil. National Cem.
Yeatman, Thomas J.	Co. D, 40th Virginia		7/3/1863	Mortally wounded, July 1st, and died two days later	Unknown
Yeatts, Jennings T.	Sgt., Co. H, 21st Virginia	1841	7/2/1863	Killed in action	Unknown
Yerby, D. Newton	Co. A, 26th Alabama		Jul. 1863	Killed in action	Unknown
Youell, Robert	Co. C, 1st Virginia		7/3/1863	Killed in action	Unknown
Young, Beverly Daniel	Co. I, 11th Mississippi	1830	8/29/1863	Died as POW at David's Island, NY	Cypress Hills, NY
Young, Franklin J.	Co. C, 6th Alabama		Jul. 1863	Hollywood Cemetery, Richmond, Va., reburial lists	Richmond, VA
Young, George P.	Sgt., Co. K, 48th Georgia	1839	7/13/1863	Hollywood Cemetery, Richmond, Va., reburial lists	Richmond, VA
Young, Henry H.	Co. C, 2nd Georgia Battalion		7/2/1863	Killed in action	Unknown

NAME	REGIMENT	BIRTH	DEATH	COMMENT	BURIAL
Young, John A.	Capt., Co. G, 8th Georgia		7/10/1863	Hollywood Cemetery, Richmond, Va., reburial lists	Richmond, VA
Young, John R.	Cpl., Co. G, 3rd North Carolina	1823	7/25/1863	Mortally wounded and buried at Presbyterian Church Cemetery, Gettysburg, PA	Gettysburg, PA
Young, Lawson George	Lt., Co. F, 49th Georgia	1832	7/22/1863	Killed in action	Unknown
Young, Peter	Co. E, 16th North Carolina		7/8/1863	Mortally wounded-died at unknown place in Gettysburg	Unknown
Young, Samuel M.	Lt., Co. K, 11th North Carolina	3/14/1838	7/7/1863	Hollywood Cemetery, Richmond, Va., reburial lists	Richmond, VA
Young, William	Cpl., Co. A, 61st Georgia		7/1/1863	Laurel Grove Cemetery, Savannah, Ga., reburial list	Savannah, GA
Young, William H.	Capt., Co. K, 3rd South Carolina	1833	7/2/1863	Killed in action	Unknown
Yount, Miles Logan	Co. F, 38th North Carolina	1824	7/1/1863	Killed in action	Unknown
Zehring, Jacob	Sgt., Co. K, 7th Virginia Cavalry	2/1/1838	7/3/1863	Killed in action; reinterred in Solomons Lutheran Church Cemetery, Forestville, VA	Forestville, VA
Zeigler, Thomas F.	Co. D, 24th Virginia	5/24/1844	7/16/1863	Hollywood Cemetery, Richmond, Va., reburial lists	Richmond, VA
Zimmerman, Israel	Co. F, 26th North Carolina	1828	7/24/1863	Mortally wounded and died at Hagerstown, MD-buried there	Hagerstown, MD
Zinn, Henry Lewis	Co. B, 48th Georgia	9/29/1842	7/2/1863	Missing in action and presumed dead	Unknown
Zweigler, George	Co. E, 10th Louisiana	1832	8/12/1863	Died as POW at David's Island, NY	Cypress Hills, NY
Zweigler, William F.	Co. D, 24th Virginia	3/8/1843	7/16/1863	Mortally wounded-died at unknown place in Gettysburg	Unknown

Confederate dead near center of the battlefield of Gettysburg
by Alexander Gardner, Library of Congress

Lieutenant Colonel David R. E. Winn,
4th Georgia. *History of Doles-Cook
Brigade* by Henry W. Thomas. Killed in
action July 1, 1863. For more information
see pages viii–ix in Preface.

Colonel Waller Tazwell Patton, 7th
Virginia. Virginia Military Institute
(VMI) Archives Collection. Mortally
wounded July 3, 1863. Buried at Stonewall
Cemetery, Winchester, Virginia.

ABOUT THE AUTHORS

Robert K. Krick is renowned as the expert on the Army of Northern Virginia. He is the author of numerous articles and 14 books including *Civil War Weather in Virginia* [2007], *The Smoothbore Volley That Doomed the Confederacy* [2002] and *Conquering the Valley* [1996]. He served the National Park Service for over thirty years, most recently as the chief historian at Fredericksburg & Spotsylvania National Military Park.

Chris L. Ferguson is an expert on Confederate military records. He is the author of *Hollywood Cemetery, Her Forgotten Soldiers* [2001] and *Southerners at Rest: Confederate Dead at Hollywood Cemetery* [2008].

CPSIA information can be obtained at www.ICGtesting.com
Printed in the USA
BVOW06s1623230914

367965BV00006B/32/P

9 780971 195080